'Gothic For Ever'
A.W.N. Pugin,
Lord Shrewsbury, and the
Rebuilding of Catholic England

'I will not let anything pass for Cheadle that is not the true thing. It must be perfection' (A.W.N. Pugin). St Giles', Cheadle: view through screen towards the Blessed Sacrament Chapel. (Mark Titterton)

'Gothic For Ever'
A.W.N. Pugin,
Lord Shrewsbury, and the
Rebuilding of Catholic England

Michael Fisher

Spire Books Ltd

PO Box 2336, Reading RG4 5WJ

www.spirebooks.com

To Isobel
for whom I have saved the best till last.

Spire Books Ltd
PO Box 2336, Reading RG4 5WJ
www.spirebooks.com

CIP data: a catalogue record for this book is available from the British Library.

Designed by John Elliott.

Printed by Information Press Ltd, Eynsham, Oxford.

ISBN 978-1-904965-36-7

Contents

Pugin's letters – editorial note

In his prolific correspondence, Pugin wrote quickly and often passionately. He developed a kind of shorthand, and he was not always grammatical. Words in mid-sentence sometimes start with a capital letter and opening words with lower case, punctuation is erratic, and his Cockney background comes out in such mis-spellings as 'wery', 'warious', and 'sewere'. In the extracts and quotations used in this book, no attempt has been made to correct Pugin's spelling or punctuation. For the most part the extracts have been taken from the three published volumes of Pugin's letters: M. Belcher (ed.), *The Collected Letters of A. W.N. Pugin,* with acknowledgements to Oxford University Press.

Preface by the Most Reverend Bernard Longley, M.A., S.T.L., Archbishop of Birmingham

When Pope Benedict XVI visited St Mary's College, Oscott on the last day of his Official Visit to England and Wales in 2010 he commented on the beauty of the Chapel where he addressed the bishops. The chapel is an important shrine for the Catholic community of the Archdiocese of Birmingham and indeed for the whole country. It was opened in 1838 at a turning point in the life of the Church in our land, the beginning of the 'Second Spring' following the long twilight years of recusancy. Referring to the consecration Dom William Bernard Ullathorne OSB, later to become the first Bishop of Birmingham, commented, 'Pugin, with his dark, flashing eyes and tears on his cheeks, superintended the procession of the clergy; he was in raptures and declared that it was the greatest day for the Church in England since the Reformation'.

Augustus Welby Pugin had been introduced to Oscott by John, 16th Earl of Shrewsbury, and had caught the attention and admiration of Bishop Thomas Walsh. As a result Pugin was given the task of decorating and furnishing the chapel and making it the dwelling-place of the 'beauty of holiness' which it has remained to the present day. With the financial and moral support of Lord Shrewsbury and Bishop Walsh, Pugin designed and furnished churches, convents and schools across the Midlands, including tiny rural gems at Radford in Oxfordshire and Stone in Staffordshire alongside the magnificence of St Chad's Cathedral in Birmingham. North Staffordshire has long been a heartland of Catholic life and, with Lord Shrewsbury living at Alton Towers, it was here that Pugin was able to undertake a number of major and important works. The area has become known as 'Pugin-land' and it is a major part of our national as well as Catholic heritage.

Michael Fisher has brought energy, enthusiasm and scholarship to his passion for Pugin and all of this is reflected in this remarkable and significant book. It is a major contribution to Pugin studies and a fitting contribution to the commemoration of the bicentenary of Pugin's birth in 2012. The book is based on detailed and thorough research and provides a fascinating study of a remarkable architect and designer whose influence has been so wide-ranging.

But this is no mere dry work of architectural history. Pugin was a passionate and committed Catholic whose faith was the heart of his life and work. Michael Fisher has ensured that this flows through the whole book and informs and illuminates every aspect of his analysis of Pugin's work. I am most grateful to Michael for giving us this timely book which will give renewed enjoyment and will deepen our appreciation of Pugin and his work in an important part of our Archdiocese.

✠ Bernard Longley
Archbishop of Birmingham

Foreword: Alexandra Wedgwood

Gothic For Ever was an expression used by Pugin in some of his writings to underline his passionate belief in the enduring qualities of the art and architecture of the Middle Ages. According to Pugin, Gothic, and particularly English Gothic of the fourteenth and fifteenth centuries, was the only appropriate style for the building and decoration of an English church. That his churches and patrons were Catholic needs no saying. So the area of north Staffordshire was described by Sir Nikolaus Pevsner as 'Pugin-land'. It is also a Catholic land, and a place in which to ponder the difference between Catholics and Protestants and the whole character of the Gothic Revival in England. A local newspaper correspondent commented on the opening ceremonies of St Giles' Church, Cheadle, in the late summer of 1846: 'We can scarcely imagine anything more calculated to make men forget that they are living in a Protestant country than the scene and circumstances now presented … here was enough sight and sound to affect the dullest imagination, and make one almost fancy it as a vision of past ages.' The essential figure to make possible Pugin's vision was John Talbot, sixteenth earl of Shrewsbury, who was prepared to put some of his great wealth into the creation of this Catholic and Gothic Revival. The story of his friendship with Pugin has always been very one-sided, in large part because the earl kept most of the letters that Pugin wrote to him, whereas few of his to Pugin have survived. The picture emerges of an attractive, gentle and scholarly aristocrat who took his position as the leading catholic layman of his day very seriously. The end of the Catholic branch of the Shrewsburys led to the impoverishment of Catholic projects in north Staffordshire, but the attraction of the Gothic Revival did not die. The style was taken up in the Anglican church, eventually turning into the Arts and Crafts Movement, and had a remarkable flowering in this locality.

Michael Fisher guides his readers through this complicated story with an expert hand. He has indeed the perfect qualifications for doing so, being both a historian with local and ecclesiological interests and an Anglican priest. He is already the author of an innovative book, *Alton Towers: A Gothic Wonderland*, 1999, and here he sets the magnificent seat of the Shrewsburys into its rich background. His detailed knowledge of medieval church fittings demonstrates why the simple little building of St Mary's Catholic Church, Uttoxeter, was in reality such a revolutionary one. It was the first to display 'the true thing', which Pugin was to elaborate to such good effect in St John's, Alton, St Mary's, Brewood, St Wilfrid's, Cotton and above all in the splendid St Giles', Cheadle. As well as Pugin and Lord Shrewsbury, the leading protagonists, Michael Fisher also describes the fascinating lesser characters who move in and out of the story. His wide reading has worked out all the connecting links, both personal and religious, between the people he introduces, such as the university connections between F.W. Faber and Michael Watts Russell, and he shows this with great skill. Nor does he forget to mention the local craftsmen, the Baileys and John Bunn Denny of Alton and Thomas Roddis and Thomas Harris of Cheadle. This would please 'the Good Earl John', who was always concerned that his charitable works should benefit his own estate workers. The illustrations are excellent, the result of much imagination and research, and the colour plates taken by Mark Titterton, with the help of Karl Barton, are superb.

Michael Fisher's enthusiasm and knowledge illuminates this episode, which was dealt a heavy blow one hundred and sixty years ago with the premature deaths in the autumn of 1852 of both the earl and his architect. Since then, though many of their architectural ideals lived on until the end of the nineteenth century, as is shown in this book, there have been long periods when their achievements were neglected or, worse, scorned and destroyed. The end of the twentieth century and the beginning of the twenty-first century, however, have shown a major revival of interest in the ideas, forms and colours of the Gothic Revival – Pugin's 'true principles' – and the architecture and decoration of Alton Towers and St Giles' Church, Cheadle, are now widely known and appreciated. The bicentenary of Pugin's birth, the first of March, 2012, will be marked by great celebrations.

There are many reasons to see the beauties of north Staffordshire, but this book will add significantly to the pleasure and understanding of a visit. I strongly recommend it.

Alexandra Wedgwood
December 2011

Introduction & acknowledgements

In October 1849 A.W.N. Pugin arrived at Alton for the first time by train, along the newly opened branch line of the North Staffordshire Railway. It was by the same route that – as a ten-year-old schoolboy – I was taken on my first excursion into 'Pugin-land' just over a hundred years later, when steam trains still ran along the picturesque Churnet Valley Line, bringing visitors to the famous gardens of Alton Towers. On that summer's day, the destination of our family outing was not Alton Towers, but the village on the opposite side of the valley, and that is when the seeds of my affection for Pugin's work were planted. Setting foot for the first time in the precincts of Alton Castle was to enter a different world: a microcosm of the Catholic England which Pugin and Lord Shrewsbury had sought to rebuild. There was the Castle on the edge of a cliff, the coloured tiles of the Chapel roof shimmering in the sunlight; St John's Church with its glorious altar and screen; the sixteenth earl's coronet and hatchment still hanging above his memorial, and the statue of St Joseph where we lit our votive candles. It thrilled me then, and it thrills me still. To visit this most extraordinary and tranquil place is to probe the minds of Pugin and his noble patron, and the eternal concepts of beauty and truth which they wished to set at the very heart of this village community, accessible to all. Votive candles are still lit in prayerful memory of those who first took me there and kindled my enthusiasm, and I must record my thanks to them here too.

In those childhood days I knew nothing of Pugin: he was a discovery made during my time as a history undergraduate at Leicester University, when I had the chance to see one of the early fruits of the Pugin-Shrewsbury partnership, Mount St Bernard Abbey; and Grace Dieu, the former home of Ambrose Phillipps de Lisle. My principal interest then was medieval England, but I also chose the Victorian age as a special study, which is how I encountered Pugin and Newman and others who shaped the nineteenth-century Catholic and Gothic Revivals: an intoxicating mixture. Among the other converts, I discovered Frederick William Faber, and learned that it was during his time at Cotton, he wrote my grandmother's favourite hymn, *Hark, hark, my soul*.

Returning to Staffordshire, I revisited Pugin's buildings at Alton and Cheadle, viewing them now with a better-informed eye. Eventually the opportunities to research and publish came my way as my understanding of the importance of Staffordshire in the history of the Gothic Revival grew, and made me want to promote the unique architectural heritage of my home county. One such opportunity was a commission from Alton Towers in 1998 to carry out a survey of the Towers buildings, in the course of which I found, through examining the extensive correspondence between Pugin and Lord Shrewsbury, just how deeply involved Pugin was at the Towers, and just how much – despite the architectural idiosyncrasies – he loved its peaceful and overtly Catholic ambience. Pugin's letters also revealed how personal was the relationship between earl and architect. Thus I was brought into ever closer contact with the mind of Pugin through the buildings which I had known since childhood. This meant delving into theology as well as architectural history; and although I was raised an Anglican, my beliefs and outlook have been shaped by the same forces that worked so powerfully upon Pugin: a love of Gothic architecture and an appreciation of the old English Liturgy for which our medieval churches were built. What began as an architectural excursion developed into a spiritual journey which is still in progress.

It is of course quite possible to view church buildings purely as works of art, and from no particular religious standpoint, just as it is possible for an agnostic to enjoy listening to Gregorian chant. To understand the reasons why Pugin – and those who followed him – built and decorated as they did, it is nevertheless important to be aware of the concepts which he sought to express. Whether one happens to agree with them or not is another matter. I have therefore explored the theological significance of these buildings and their contents, and I have also supplied a glossary of ecclesiastical terms, many of which were unfamiliar in Pugin's own day, even to churchmen.

The fruits of my earlier researches appeared in 2002 as a self-published paperback under the title of *Pugin-land*. That book is now long out of print, and the bicentenary of Pugin's birth requires a re-visiting of the theme with a new and much larger publication that takes account of further study and research, and a fresh set of illustrations. I hope it will prove to be a fitting tribute to this most extraordinary man whose vision of a restored Catholic England was expressed so magnificently and so completely in the heart of rural Staffordshire, and that the illustrations will show that – contrary to popular belief – Gothic is not all about darkness and haunted ruins, but about light and colour, beauty and splendour, with the soaring lines of its architecture lifting the human spirit heavenwards.

I have received much valuable assistance and advice in the course of my research and in the preparation of this book, and I would like to record my thanks to all who have helped me in any way. The clergy of the various churches have allowed me free access to the buildings and to archives and other items in their custody, and I am particularly indebted to Fr Sandy Brown, parish priest of St Giles', Cheadle, for his help and friendship over many years. I am grateful to the Squire de Lisle for answering my queries about Pugin and Ambrose Phillipps, and for providing me with a copy of the relevant section of Abbé Vandrival's journal. Pugin kept up a voluminous correspondence, but he did not, alas, keep many of the letters he received once they had been acted upon. A good deal has therefore to be deduced from Pugin's own letters held in various collections. Much of what is known about the relationship between Pugin and Lord

Shrewsbury is contained in the private Franklin collection, copies of which are in the House of Lords Record Office. When I first began my research, very few of Pugin's letters had been transcribed, so there was no alternative but to get to grips with the originals, this in itself being a most valuable learning exercise. Since then, however, Pugin scholarship has benefited enormously from Dr Margaret Belcher's progressive editing of the letters, three volumes of which are now in print. I thank Mr M.R. Darley and Mr B. Astbury, the headmaster and the former bursar of Stafford Grammar School (Burton Manor) for answering my queries and allowing me free access to the Manor and to relevant archive material, and the Sisters of Charity of St Paul for giving access to Aston Hall and its archive. The assistance and encouragement of other Pugin scholars and enthusiasts is greatly appreciated, particularly that of Brian Andrews, Paul Atterbury, Dr Margaret Belcher, Fr Brian Doolan, Dr Rory O'Donnell, Dr Rosemary Hill, Dr Gerard Hyland, Tom Knill, John Scott, Dr Stanley Shepherd, and the Pugin Society's president, Mrs Sarah Houle. Through the generosity of the Pugin Society it has been possible to commission Mark Titterton, of Ceiba Graphics, and Karl Barton, to take new photographs which reveal their skill and imagination. Generous financial support for this publication has also come from Alton Towers Resort, a reflection of their commitment to the conservation of the historic buildings in their care. Geoff Brandwood, of Spire Books, took the pictures for chapter 8 (St Mary's, Brewood), in addition to editing my text, suggesting improvements, and offering valuable advice throughout the production process. John Elliott, also of Spire Books, who is responsible for the design and layout of the book, has patiently endured the author's last-minute alterations and insertions. I am indebted to Neil Phillips, of the firm of Pugin, Hardman & Powell, for access to his collection of drawings and artefacts, and for his enthusiastic support of my work. My wife, Isobel, has accompanied me on very many site visits, helped with the selection of illustrative material, and shown remarkable patience during the long periods when I have been completely absorbed, physically and mentally, in 'Pugin-land'.

Acknowledgements of permission to reproduce archival material, pictures and photographs, are due to Roger Bennett (10.14, 10.15), Michael Blaker (10.13), the Getty Research Library (4.2, 4.3), Ingestre Arts Centre (2.1, 2.3), Neil Phillips (1.4, 1.6, 3.17, 9.7, 9.14), Henry Potts (3.15), Staffordshire Archives Service and Trustees of the William Salt Library (1.1, 1.9, 1.13, 1.15, 3.2, 4.1), and the Tasmanian Museum & Art Gallery (6.29).

I was delighted when Archbishop Bernard Longley – a successor of Bishop Thomas Walsh who shared Pugin's Gothic vision – agreed to write a preface for this new publication. Finally I wish to express my sincere gratitude to Lady Wedgwood, that most eminent of all Pugin scholars, for so kindly consenting to write the foreword, and for her keen interest in the current programmes of conservation and restoration in the buildings at Alton of which Pugin once wrote, 'I am nowhere so happy'.

Michael Fisher,
November 2011

1.1 'Perched on the edge of a rocky precipice like some Rhineland Schloss': lithograph of Alton Castle by Newman & Co., 1860 (Staffordshire County Record Office).

1

Pugin-land

'I have prayed from a child for the restoration of the Long Lost glory of catholic England'

A.W.N. Pugin to J.R. Bloxam, October 1840

Cheadle is *Pugin*-land. Such was Sir Nikolaus Pevsner's introduction to the great church of St Giles in this north Staffordshire market-town. 'What haunts you for miles around', he added, 'is the raised forefinger of Pugin's steeple pointing heavenwards.'[1] Pevsner was echoing A.W.N. Pugin's own belief in the heaven-pointing spire as a beautiful and instructive emblem of a Christian's brightest hopes. Known locally as 'Pugin's Gem', the church, magnificent as it is, is but one of a cluster of buildings in Cheadle designed and built by Pugin between 1841 and 1848: there is also the presbytery, the school, and the convent of St Joseph, but that is not all. 'Pugin-land' extends well beyond the confines of Cheadle into the surrounding countryside with its deep wooded valleys and secluded villages. Four miles away, just outside the village of Cotton, another Pugin spire beckons – that of St Wilfrid's Church which, along with the adjacent college, forms another complex of Catholic buildings. A mile or so further along the Farley road, Alton Towers appears on the horizon; that great Gothic mansion to which Pugin made significant alterations and additions throughout most of his working life. On the opposite side of the Churnet Valley is the most dramatic of all of Pugin's domestic buildings – Alton Castle **(1.1)** perched on the edge of a rocky precipice like some Rhineland *Schloss*, and, behind the castle, the church and hospital of St John which, along with St Giles, Pugin declared to be the only buildings on which he could look with complete satisfaction. The nearby town of Uttoxeter is the place where Pugin's career as practising architect can be said seriously to have begun with the building of the little church of St Marie, Balance Street, in 1838 – a keynote building which Pugin himself described as the first true revival of its kind in England. Add to this list three or four houses and lodges in and around Alton which Pugin built or enlarged, and we have a total of thirteen buildings, both ecclesiastical and domestic, all situated within a few square miles of north-east Staffordshire, and including those which he himself considered to be his most successful. This is Pugin-land indeed; and there is no area of comparable size where the full range of Pugin's work as an architect, designer, and Gothic propagandist can be so readily studied and appreciated. Nor can one think of a more naturally beautiful part of the country as a setting for these fine buildings. This often comes as a surprise to those who are unfamiliar with north Staffordshire, and who imagine the area to be overwhelmingly industrial. Yet it was the dramatic landscape of deep valleys, sandstone cliffs and dense woodlands which attracted the 15th earl of Shrewsbury (d. 1827) to enlarge Alton Lodge into what soon became the family's principal home. It delighted Pugin too, and he enthused about the natural beauties of the landscape and its eminent suitability as a setting for fine buildings constructed from local materials. He firmly believed that buildings should appear to 'grow' naturally from the sites in which they were placed, and he did not miss an opportunity to apply this principle to the Romantic environment of the Churnet Valley.

Augustus Welby Northmore Pugin (1812-52) **(1.2)** was the only son of a French émigré artist, Auguste Charles Pugin (*c.*1768-1832) and his English wife Catherine Welby (*c.*1768-1833). Born in London, he was taught largely by his father, and received little formal education. Yet he grew up to be England's leading exponent of the revived Gothic style – the architect of over 100 buildings, both ecclesiastical and secular, and the author of eight major publications on architecture and design for which he not only wrote the text but drew all the illustrations and designed the bindings. At the age of 25 he became Professor of Ecclesiastical Antiquities at St Mary's College, Oscott, just north of Birmingham, and the co-founder, with John Hardman junior (1811-67) of the Birmingham metalwork and stained glass manufactory for which he was the sole designer. For Herbert Minton (1793-1858), the Stoke-on-Trent potter, Pugin designed a wide range of encaustic floor-tiles, wall-tiles, dinner-services and jardinières, and in conjunction with John Gregory Crace of London (1809-89) he produced designs for wallpaper, textile fabrics, and furniture.

Pugin is probably best-remembered as the creator of the majestic interiors of the New Palace of Westminster. These included carved woodwork, wall-coverings, chairs and benches, light-fittings, inkstands, door-handles, key-plates and stained glass, in which he revealed his multi-faceted genius as a Gothic designer. The Hardman Archive in the Birmingham Museum and Art Gallery contains 2,000 drawings relating to Westminster alone, all from Pugin's hand. Pugin was a prolific letter-writer. His correspondence with John Hardman alone, who was not just a business partner but also a close friend, runs to 1,054 known letters. This huge volume of correspondence, and all of his drawings, were done personally. He employed no clerks, worked almost entirely from home, and apart from his eldest son Edward (1832-75) he had only one pupil in the formal sense, namely Hardman's nephew, John Hardman Powell (1827-95). At the Great Exhibition of 1851 the 'Mediaeval Court', which was principally the creation of Pugin and Hardman, diffused the revived Gothic style widely amongst the rising middle classes, while the house which Pugin designed for himself and his family in Ramsgate – The Grange – became the model for a new style of family home which was given its first full-blown expression in Staffordshire: Burton Manor on the outskirts of Stafford, built by Edward Pugin, 1854-6, It also provided the model for the rebuilding of Aston Hall, near Stone, also by Edward Pugin, and of similar date.

Pugin's personal and private life was no less eventful than his professional one.[2] He found time for three marriages and eight children, plus two or three

1.2 A.W.N. Pugin: the only known photograph of him: from a daguerreotype (private collection).

unsuccessful courtships, and he operated a one-man lifeboat service off the coast at Ramsgate. Personal misfortune and illness dogged him. Bereft of both his parents and his first wife at the age of 21, Pugin remarried within a twelvemonth of his becoming a widower, only to become a widower again at 33. Hyperactive, and subject to bouts of melancholia, Pugin was afflicted with severe eye problems exacerbated by overwork, and other physical ailments, all of which contributed to his tragically early death at the age of 40. When, towards the end of his life, his doctors told him that he had tried to pack a hundred years into fourscore, it was an understatement, for most of Pugin's major works were carried out between 1836 and 1851.

The revival of Gothic began in the eighteenth century, becoming increasingly popular as part of the Picturesque and Romantic Movements. A growing fascination with the Middle Ages, as reflected, for example, in Sir Walter Scott's *Waverley Novels*, was complemented by serious archaeological studies of medieval architecture and art such as John Britton's *Architectural Antiquities of Great Britain,* which appeared in four volumes between 1807 and 1826, and to which Pugin's father contributed a number of architectural drawings. The ground was therefore well prepared before Pugin burst upon the scene. Unlike other architects who designed Gothic buildings – and some of them quite competently – Pugin viewed Gothic not as just another architectural style to be chosen according to individual whim or fancy by the 'trade', with details culled and plucked from the now readily-available source books such as Britton's, or Auguste Pugin's *Specimens of Gothic Architecture* (1821-2), but as a principle in which architecture and the visual arts were fully integrated, and infused with the same spirit that had created the great buildings of the Middle Ages. His preferred appellation, 'Pointed, or Christian, Architecture', says it all. His principles included construction methods, the choice of materials, the design and disposition of ornament: and these could be applied as much to secular buildings as to ecclesiastical ones, but in Pugin's vision of a revived Gothic England, nothing was purely secular. This vision, with its crocketted spires and gilded altars, schools, religious houses, almshouses for the poor, and noble residences for the *grand seigneur,* received its unique expression in north Staffordshire, with one church – St Giles', Cheadle – drawing together the many strands of Pugin's creative genius and showing the world what an English Catholic church should be. 'It will be a textbook for all good people', predicted one observer, and so it was.

But this was Cheadle, not London – a Moorlands market town set in an area of small villages, scattered farmsteads and small-scale mining and metalworking operations; a hilly landscape deeply scoured by the Churnet Valley, and reached by narrow, winding roads which plunge suddenly and precipitously. Only towards the end of Pugin's life was the area linked by railway to the nearest large towns such as Derby and Stoke-on-Trent, and even then it bypassed Cheadle with its population of some 5,000. Given Pugin's acknowledged status as the leading Gothic propagandist who lived most of his life in London and the south of England, it has to be asked why rural and rugged north Staffordshire, rather than the more affluent south, should have so large a number of Pugin buildings of such quality and variety as to make it *par excellence* the place in which to study and understand his ideas as well as his buildings. The answer lies principally in the enthusiastic support and financial backing which Pugin received from John Talbot (1791-1852), the sixteenth earl of Shrewsbury, whose home – Alton Towers – was situated in the heart of the Staffordshire Moorlands, only four miles from Cheadle. Lord Shrewsbury was England's premier earl and most prominent Catholic layman, committed to promoting the Catholic cause wherever he had influence. He saw in the young convert Pugin not only a brilliant designer of Gothic art and architecture, but a man of deep faith and passionate commitment who was prepared to devote his skills to the service of the Church. Without Lord Shrewsbury's patronage, many of Pugin's ideas would almost certainly have remained on paper or would have been considerably reduced as indeed was the case in other places where he was not so fortunate. At Alton and Cheadle, however, buildings actually increased in size and magnificence as the work progressed. The scale of the building activities on and around the Shrewsbury estates at Alton has been likened to the *folie de bâtir* of King Ludwig II of Bavaria (1864-86), for all of the thirteen buildings mentioned above were erected within just fourteen years (1838-52). There was, in fact, a link between the Talbots and the Bavarian royal family: in 1834 Ludwig I (1825-48) elevated the earl's elder daughter, Mary, to the rank of princess; but that was 30 years before the accession of his castle-building grandson.[3] The aims were in any case very different. Whereas Ludwig II built to glorify himself and the Wittelsbach dynasty, Pugin and Lord Shrewsbury sought to restore the former glories of Catholic England in the wake of the 1829 Catholic Emancipation Act.

The impact of these buildings upon the landscape was dramatic enough, and with them came sights and sounds which had not been seen or heard in the area since the sixteenth century – outdoor processions, priests, monks and nuns in full habit, and the sound of the Angelus ringing out across town and countryside from the new towers and bell-cotes, and from the great bell of the Towers chapel itself, morning, noon and evening. When Pugin spoke of the 'Real Thing,' as he was wont to do, he meant not merely the revival of medieval art and architecture, but of the whole panoply of Catholic worship and devotion as it had been known in England before the advent of 'the sacrilegious tyrant Henry and his successors in church plunder.'[4] Meanwhile the ceaseless activity on and around the various sites, in the quarries and associated workshops, provided work for large numbers of men who might otherwise have been unemployed during the 'hungry forties' when industrial unrest and Chartist agitation manifested themselves in north Staffordshire as in other parts of the country. As Pugin saw it, the Gothic-Catholic revival had a vital social dimension which is clearly revealed in the buildings at Alton, Cheadle and Cotton, and in the masons' community which he set up midway between the two at Counslow Hill where sandstone was quarried. Pugin's concern for these people did not end when their lives ended. From the Counslow quarry came stone for the numerous memorials found, for example, in the Catholic burial-ground at Alton; memorials designed in 'true' Christian style. Proper provision for the burial of the dead, with appropriate rites and with fitting monuments, was another matter of principle of which Pugin gave full expression in the churchyards at Alton, Cheadle and Cotton.

'Pugin-land' was, and to a degree still is, a place apart. Defined partly by its geography, and having a distinct history, the Moorlands has a dialect which is quite different from that of the nearby pottery towns of Stoke-on-Trent, as indeed the Potteries dialect is a world apart from that of south Staffordshire and the Black Country. Cheadle is 'Chaydul', Leek is 'Layke', and half a pound is 'ayfa pynde.' It was into this somewhat closed community that Pugin came in 1837 with his Cockney speech tinged no doubt with a slight French accent inherited from his father, his unconventional manner, and clad more like a sailor than an architect. One wonders how they understood him, and he them, but the evidence shows that he found good friends among the workforce at Alton and Cheadle, that he was as comfortable in the stonemasons' shed as he was in the earl's great house, and that he enjoyed the villagers' lively festivities at Alton as much as the grand receptions at the Towers.

Among the various figures who crossed the north Staffordshire landscape and helped Pugin to transform the Churnet Valley into a Gothic paradise, none was more prominent than John Bunn Denny (1810-92) who became clerk of works at Alton Towers in 1839, a position which he held until 1856. Little is known of Denny's background, except that he was born at Swainsthorpe, a few miles south of Norwich, that he was originally a bricklayer by trade, and that, following his appointment, he and his wife Jane took up residence in Alton village. How he came to the attention of Pugin and Lord Shrewsbury is likewise unknown, but his arrival on the scene in 1839 was considered significant enough for Pugin to record it in his diary, where entries rarely run to more than half a dozen words confined to the most important event of the day: 'July 1. At Uttoxeter. Deny arrived.' What is certain is that by this time Denny must have acquired sufficient skill in the building trade, and at least a basic knowledge of architectural practice, in order to take on such a responsible position. Unlike the Uttoxeter-based builder-architect, Thomas Fradgley, whom he supplanted, Denny was a Catholic, a factor which would have weighed heavily with Pugin who strongly disapproved of having protestants superintending the construction of Catholic buildings. Only slightly older than Pugin, he was also of that rising generation of 'Young England' which embraced the Gothic vision. Much more is learned from the correspondence which passed between Pugin and Lord Shrewsbury, in which Denny emerges as the trusted man on the ground with responsibilities for the churches as well as the continuing work at the Towers. He had quickly to immerse himself in Pugin's 'true principles' of architecture and design and instil them into the workforce, learn how to work to Pugin's detailed drawings and instructions, accompany him on site inspections, and keep him and Lord Shrewsbury informed of progress between visits. The letters also reveal that Denny had financial responsibilities too, receiving monies remitted by the earl to Pugin for the payment of workmen and the purchase of materials. Pugin's letters would sometimes include a reprimand – or a 'blowing up' as he sometimes put it – to be passed on to a subordinate. Denny was not himself immune from the occasional 'blowing-up' when Pugin felt he had claimed too much credit, or otherwise overstepped the mark. Nevertheless, Pugin held Denny in very high regard, describing him as 'indefatigable', and a man in whom he had complete confidence.[5] Denny's responsibilities were therefore considerable, for between 1841 and 1846 work was taking place simultaneously on three complex

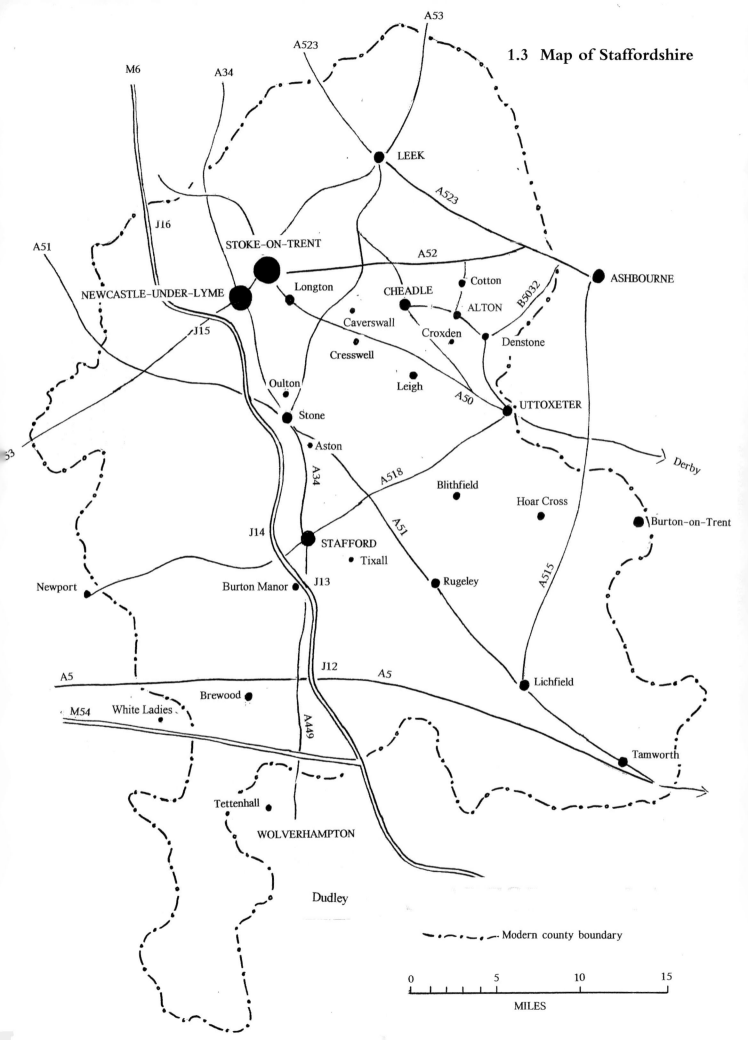

1.3 **Map of Staffordshire**

MILES

- - - Modern county boundary

A53
A523
A34
M6
J16
LEEK
A523
A51
STOKE-ON-TRENT
A52
Cotton
ASHBOURNE
NEWCASTLE-UNDER-LYME
Longton
CHEADLE
ALTON
B5032
J15
Caverswall
Croxden
Denstone
Cresswell
Leigh
A50
Oulton
UTTOXETER
Stone
Derby
Aston
A34
A518
Blithfield
Hoar Cross
Burton-on-Trent
J14
STAFFORD
Tixall
A51
Newport
Burton Manor
J13
Rugeley
A515
A5
J12
A5
Lichfield
Brewood
M54
White Ladies
A449
Tamworth
Tettenhall
WOLVERHAMPTON
Dudley

sites, and at the stone-quarry. The buildings at Alton and Cheadle embraced the full range of Pugin's architectural designs and decorative schemes, both ecclesiastical and secular, and they were the ones in which, on his own admission, he took the greatest pride. Though Pugin did not establish a conventional architectural practice, and – apart from his son, Edward – had only one pupil, namely his future son-on-law, John Hardman Powell, it is true to say that by working with Pugin as closely as he did, and enjoying his confidence and trust, Denny was a true disciple, as thoroughly immersed in Pugin's principles of Gothic design and building as any formal pupil could hope to be, and he later acknowledged his indebtedness for everything he knew, describing Pugin as his 'only friend.'[6] Following the deaths of Pugin and the sixteenth and seventeenth earls of Shrewsbury, Denny left Alton and later emigrated to Australia where eventually he became architect in his own right, designing Gothic churches and furnishings in the Pugin style, and drawing deeply on all that he had learned during his sixteen years in 'Pugin-land'.

'Pugin-land' has its outposts, some still within the current boundaries of Staffordshire (1.3), others no longer so. Among these is St Mary, Brewood, on the Staffordshire-Shropshire border. Here too Lord Shrewsbury had a significant contribution to make, and local materials were used, but it was Pugin's trusted builder, George Myers, rather than Denny and the builders from Alton, who carried out the work. Nearer to Cheadle is the plain little chapel of St Anne in Stone, overshadowed now by the much grander church of St Dominic. Then there are a number of minor works such as Pugin's additions and alterations to the Benedictine convent at Caverswall Castle, to the Cresswell Mission, and to the second church of St Austin in Stafford. Pugin's Anglican commissions are exemplified locally by his restoration of the chancel at Blithfield, important furnishings, tiles and glass at Leigh (near Uttoxeter), and the Masfen memorial window at St Mary, Stafford. The restoration of St Mary, Stafford, by George Gilbert Scott in 1842-4 took place while Pugin was working on St Giles, Cheadle, and it is the outstanding example of Pugin's early influence upon a key Anglican architect. This influence reached its apogee after Pugin's death with G.F. Bodley's Holy Angels' at Hoar Cross (1876). Not only does Staffordshire have the best of Pugin, it has also some of the best work of celebrated architects who were inspired by him. County boundaries may be arbitrary, nor do they circumscribe architectural taste. It is nevertheless true that Staffordshire was the home of several important landed families who were drawn into the Gothic Revival and who were willing to employ the best architects and designers to build churches for them.

County boundaries may not only be arbitrary, they may also change. Until 1911 the parish of Handsworth (now a Birmingham suburb) was a part of south Staffordshire. It contained the small township of Perry Bar, and the larger one of Handsworth itself. In the days when it lay within Staffordshire, Handsworth was important for Pugin for several reasons. In the first place it was the location of Perry Hall (demolished in 1928), the home of John and Elizabeth Gough who inherited it in 1828. Following extensive alterations to the house, Mrs Gough ordered a large quantity of furniture from Pugin who, at the age of eighteen, had set up a carving and joinery business in Hart Street, London. The furniture he produced was generally in the chunky Jacobean style, heavily carved (1.4),

1.4 Early furniture design by Pugin (Hardman private collection).

and larger items such as sideboards, were flat-packed for ease of transport. Pugin told Mrs Gough: 'The back of your sideboard is in 5 pieces but I send you a sketch of it so that any of your people can fix it in five minutes.'[7] Pugin may therefore be credited with the invention of flat-pack, self-assembly furniture. The Perry Hall commission not only gives a Staffordshire dimension to Pugin's early, pre-architectural career; it is the most important source of information about the Hart Street business, and it was probably his most significant private commission at this time. Although this particular enterprise ended in financial disaster, Pugin was to return to furniture design as a part of his revival of 'The Real Thing'. Handsworth was also the home of Pugin's best friend and business associate, John Hardman junior, and his father, also John (1767-1844). In 1842 the Hardman family home in Hunter's Road was altered and enlarged by Pugin who also suggested a change of name from Woodlands House to St John's as better befitting the residence of a Christian gentleman. Just across the road from the house, Pugin built the first Mercy Convent to be established in the Midlands, on land donated by John Hardman who also contributed over £5,000 towards the cost of the buildings and furnishings. Lord Shrewsbury gave £2,000 to this project which was an early expression of Pugin's conviction that the revival of the religious Orders was an essential part of the restoration of Catholic England.

Until the creation of the West Midlands Metropolitan County in 1974 the Black Country town of Dudley (a metropolitan borough from 1986) was geographically within south Staffordshire, and it was here that Pugin built one of his first churches, Our Lady and St Thomas of Canterbury (1839-40), on a site given by another recent convert to Catholicism, the Hon. and Revd George Spencer (1799-1864). Pevsner was not always kind to Pugin. Of the Dudley church he wrote, 'Like most Pugin churches, a disappointment.'[8] Yet it is a large church, with a five-bay nave and aisles, though minus the tower which Pugin intended, and it was much-altered in the 1960s. At the time, however, it was described by Pugin as 'a compleat facsimile of one of the old English parish churches'[9] and it was illustrated in his *Present State of Ecclesiastical Architecture in England* (1843) where it is shown as having all the furnishings he considered to be necessary, including a roodscreen, and parcloses at the ends of the aisles **(1.5)**. It was on account of such details that Pugin came into conflict with those who, although they may have welcomed Gothic architecture as a more dignified setting for Catholic worship than the styles they had been used to, did not necessarily want a wholesale return to the Middle Ages in terms of furnishings and fittings, vessels and vesture. Bishop Nicholas Wiseman (1802-65), the newly appointed coadjutor to Bishop Walsh of the Catholic Midland District, was one who took some convincing. He contemplated the removal of the screen at Dudley, and he actually upset some of the other arrangements that Pugin had introduced into the church at his own expense. Pugin was moved to write, 'our New Bishop has no feeling for old English Antiquities. All his ideas are drawn from Modern Rome & nothing is left but to submit till some change takes place.'[10] By the time of the consecration in March 1842, however, Wiseman had, apparently, become reconciled to screens and medieval-style vestments, so that 'it was quite like an old English consecration … Dr. Wiseman is now completely *ad usum Sarum* which is a great blessing.'[11] At Dudley, Pugin was able to demonstrate another important point, namely that churches built in the 'true' Gothic style, inclusive of all the necessary fittings and ornaments, were actually less expensive than neo-Classical ones, or indeed Georgian-Gothic ones in which large sums were expended on such things as sham plaster-vaulting to cover up internal roof-structures, or cast-iron pillars as substitutes for stone ones. The total cost of his church at Dudley, Pugin proudly asserted, which could accommodate 600 people, and with all its furnishings, vessels, vestments and stained glass, amounted to £3,160, 'which fully proves for how moderate a sum a real Catholic church may be erected, if the funds are judiciously employed.'[12]

The controversies, however, were far from over, and Pugin had many more battles to fight. By *ad usum Sarum,* Pugin meant the Sarum (i.e. Salisbury) Rite which had been the most widely used liturgy in pre-Reformation England. A new generation of clergy needed to be taught it, and also how to use the new Gothic churches and their furnishings as its proper setting. This was to be the function of the seminaries, and a big step forward was made with the opening in 1838 of St Mary's College, New Oscott, only just out of Staffordshire on its south-eastern border with Warwickshire, to replace an existing seminary, Old Oscott (later renamed Maryvale) in Handsworth parish.[13] The re-founding of Oscott brought together the four people who were principally responsible for advancing the Gothic and

1.5 St Mary & St Thomas of Canterbury, Dudley, from *True Principles,* 1843.

Catholic revival in Staffordshire, and indeed throughout the whole of the Catholic Midlands: Pugin, Hardman, Lord Shrewsbury, and Bishop Thomas Walsh (1776-1849), Vicar Apostolic of the Midland District, who was one of Pugin's most enthusiastic supporters and the driving force behind the establishment of New Oscott and the building of St Chad's Cathedral, Birmingham.

Until the restoration of the Catholic Hierarchy in 1850, England was organised into four districts, each served by a bishop under the title of Vicar

1.6 The brass made for the Great Exhibition to Pugin's design, and adapted as a memorial to Bishop Milner. Drawing by J.H. Powell (Hardman private collection).

Apostolic. Staffordshire formed part of the Midland District (reorganised as the Central District in 1840). All but one of its successive Vicars Apostolic resided in the county, and from 1756 at Longbirch, a house in Brewood belonging to the Catholic Giffard family. Bishop Walsh's immediate predecessor was Dr John Milner (1752-1826) who, soon after his arrival in 1802, moved to the Great House (later renamed Giffard House) in Wolverhampton, a town known in the mid-seventeenth century as 'Little Rome' on account of the large number of Catholics who lived there.[14] In this present context, Bishop Milner is important because of the deep and lasting impression he made on Pugin through his writings on Gothic architecture published between 1798 and 1809. Not only did Milner advance a definite chronology for Gothic, classifying it into three clear divisions, he also believed that Gothic had a powerful moral and spiritual dimension, an idea which was to become the touchstone of Pugin's own work. In his second lecture at Oscott (1838) Pugin cited Milner as a model for the students to follow, asking them to remember that the restoration of ancient art was not just a matter of taste, but 'most closely connected with the revival of faith itself.'[15] Milner had been deeply involved with the development of Old Oscott as a seminary, and Pugin designed a large chantry chapel for him at New Oscott. Although the plan never materialised, Pugin saw to it that a fitting memorial brass was placed elsewhere in the college chapel. In Wolverhampton, Milner is commemorated in the church that was built with his legacy of £1,000 next to Giffard House – St Peter and St Paul (1828). The brass designed by Pugin for the 1851 Great Exhibition, showing a priest in full vestments under an elaborate canopy, was adapted in 1865 as a memorial to Milner, a placed on the south wall of the nave **(1.6)**. In 1841 Milner's successor, Thomas Walsh, ended the long association of the Vicars Apostolic with Staffordshire by moving his church and his residence to Birmingham, into buildings newly designed by Pugin: St Chad's Cathedral and the Bishop's House.

Pugin's first recorded excursion into Staffordshire was in the autumn of 1833, when he visited Lichfield as part of an extensive architectural tour of the West Country and the Midlands 'in search of the picturesque and beautiful.'[16] His stay in Lichfield was memorable for two reasons. First of all he arrived at his lodgings late at night, and in the dark he unwittingly crept into the wrong bedroom. Aware of the presence of something soft and warm in the bed, he found it to be 'the thigh of a female occupant already turned in.' There were loud screams and shouts, chambermaids came rushing in with lighted candles, and Pugin had some difficulty in persuading all concerned that it had been a genuine mistake.[17] He was also in for another unpleasant surprise when he visited Lichfield Cathedral on the following day. He found that the fabric of the building had been repaired, and its interior refitted, by 'the Wretch' James Wyatt (1746-1813), whose attempts at Gothic were considered by Pugin to be execrable, assisted by local builder-architect Joseph Potter (c.1756-1842). It made him very angry,[18] and as for the town of Lichfield, Pugin dismissed it as 'a dull place – without anything remarkable.'

By the time of Pugin's next visit to Staffordshire four years later, some significant developments had taken place in his life and work. In 1835 he became a Roman Catholic, having become convinced, through his studies of medieval architecture and history, that 'the roman Catholick church is the only true one – and the only one in which the grand & sublime style of church architecture can ever be restored.'[19] From that moment onwards Pugin's whole career was directed towards the advancement of the Catholic cause. In 1836 he published his seminal book, *Contrasts*, which established his reputation and also marked a turning-point in the Gothic Revival.[20] A satirical and controversial book, illustrated with visual jokes, *Contrasts* was an attack on what he saw as the wretched state of early nineteenth-century architecture compared with the 'noble edifices' of the Middle Ages **(1.7)**. There was a powerful religious element too: as the decay and spoliation of medieval architecture had been consequent upon the rise of Protestantism, so its revival would be a part of a general recovery of a true Catholic spirit. It was Pugin who invested the Gothic Revival with the high moral and theological dimensions that

1.7 'Contrasted episcopal residences', from *Contrasts*, 1836.

it had previously lacked: Gothic architecture was primarily *Christian* architecture. Though not everyone necessarily shared his Catholic vision, *Contrasts* caught the mood of late-Georgian England in which Gothic architecture was already becoming popular as part of a growing fascination with the Middle Ages. The book ran to a second edition in 1841. It was through *Contrasts* that Pugin first encountered the antiquary and scholar Dr Daniel Rock (1799-1871), domestic chaplain to the Earl of Shrewsbury, and it may have been through Rock that Pugin was first introduced to the earl himself.[21]

In March 1837 Pugin visited New Oscott for the first time, and saw the college buildings which had been designed in the Tudor-Gothic style by none other than James Wyatt's former associate, Joseph Potter, and which were now nearing completion. The choice of Potter as architect was almost certainly influenced by Dr John Kirk, priest of the Lichfield Mission, a scholar and a substantial benefactor of Oscott. Potter, a Catholic architect, carried out additions and improvements to Kirk's mission-church, to which Pugin added a rood-screen in 1841. He had also designed a Tudor-Gothic church for Lord Shrewsbury at Newport, Shropshire (1832). Pugin's visit to Oscott in 1837 was to have momentous consequences. Within a few months, he had supplanted Potter as architect, joined the college staff as Professor of Ecclesiastical Antiquities, and, having met members of the Hardman family at Oscott, sent detailed plans for the future Cathedral of St Chad, Birmingham, to John Hardman senior, and persuaded his son to venture into the production of ecclesiastical metalwork. This was no mean achievement for a young man in his mid-twenties who had been a Catholic for barely two years.[22]

It was the President of Oscott, Dr Henry Weedall (1788-1859) who took Pugin on a three-day visit to north Staffordshire at the beginning of August 1837. They took in some notable Catholic sites of which there were a surprising number in this part of the county: historic houses where the Catholic faith had been nurtured during Penal times, others which had more recently become homes to religious communities, and missions which were set to expand in the wake of Catholic emancipation. Pugin was no doubt introduced to members of local Catholic families whom Weedall already knew. They visited Stafford Castle, which was in the process of being rebuilt on its medieval foundations by the Jerningham family, who were also the principal benefactors of the second Catholic church of St Austin, on the outskirts of the town. Built in 1791 in the Georgian-Gothic style, St Austin's was designed by Edward Jerningham (1774-1822), an amateur architect responsible for the rebuilding of the castle to strengthen his brother George's claim to the barony of Stafford. Here was another piece of historical romanticism that would have appealed to Pugin. He may also have learned about William Howard, Viscount Stafford, who had suffered martyrdom in 1680.[23] Pugin's diary records a visit to 'Priory Stafford' on 19 August. This may well refer to the ruins of the Augustinian Priory of St Thomas on the east side of Stafford. Following the Dissolution, the Fowler family acquired the site. Remaining loyal to the Catholic faith until the 1730s, the Fowlers had maintained a well-furnished private chapel with its own resident chaplain, so it had both medieval and recusant associations which would have interested Pugin.[24] After leaving Stafford, Pugin and Weedall went on to Caverswall, a seventeenth-century house built into a thirteenth-century castle which still retained its moat, and was home to a community of Benedictine nuns who had escaped from Ghent during the French Revolution. Caverswall, and its offshoots, were later to be of some importance to Pugin and to his eldest son, Edward.[25] Finally they visited Aston Hall – another moated site – on the outskirts of Stone, where the Simeon family had maintained a Jesuit chaplain and which was now a Catholic Mission served by Franciscans. Edward was to carry out important work here too, in the 1850s. Unbeknown to Pugin and Weedall, the bones of St Chad of Lichfield lay hidden under the altar of the chapel, having been brought there in the 1790s by a member of the Fitzherbert family and then forgotten.[26] After their rediscovery two years later by the new chaplain, the Revd Benjamin Hulme, Pugin designed a splendid reliquary for them, and this was enshrined above the high altar of St Chad's Cathedral in Birmingham in readiness for its opening in June 1841. Pugin had a great devotion to St Chad as one of the foremost saints of the English Church, and just before the reliquary was removed from its temporary resting place at Oscott, he wrote to his Oxford friend, J.R. Bloxam, 'tomorrow evening will be a solemn procession for the translation of the relicks of St Chad. I am sure you would feel great devotion on the solemn occasion. I feel great veneration for the relicks of this saxon Bishop which have been I may almost say miraculously restored to us.'[27]

Towards the end of August 1837 Pugin returned to Staffordshire, staying briefly at Wolseley Hall between Stafford and Rugeley; the home of Sir Charles Wolseley who was also a recent convert to Catholicism. His conversion had been brought about by their mutual friend, the Leicestershire squire Ambrose Phillipps. Finally, on 31 August, Pugin arrived for the first time at Alton Towers, where he stayed as a guest of Lord Shrewsbury for the next four days.

Pugin's subsequent visits to Alton Towers were many and frequent, sometimes extending over a week or two. This was especially true while the buildings at Cheadle and Alton were in progress, but it was a convenient base from which to visit a growing number of other commissions in the north of England, while being not a great distance away from Birmingham and Oscott. Quite clearly he loved the area: 'I look forward with delight to get into such a haven', he wrote to Lord Shrewsbury, announcing an impending visit in July 1843.[28] The survival of Catholicism in this area through the penal years also impressed him, and there were local resources and skills at hand to assist its expansion through the creation of new buildings in the 'true' Catholic style. Lord Shrewsbury's huge new chapel at the Towers, already built by the time Pugin arrived, may not structurally have been to his liking, but it was redecorated and re-furnished by him, and it was extremely important in the liturgical revivals which Pugin – in association with the earl's domestic chaplain, Dr Daniel Rock – saw as an essential part of the restoration of pre-Reformation English Catholicism. Eyebrows were raised at the prominent role taken in the sanctuary by Pugin – a married layman and, until recently, a Protestant – at the opening of the chapel at New Oscott in 1838, and not long afterwards senior clergymen began to voice complaints. At Alton, however, he could have full rein, and so Lord Shrewsbury's chapel became the setting for a full-blown revival of the Sarum Rite which, to Pugin's great delight, drew many observers, both Catholic and Anglican.

Not only that: Pugin, with his flair for the dramatic acquired during teenage years when he worked in West End theatres as a fly-man and set-designer, found himself drawn into the Talbots' attempts to re-create their illustrious medieval past in the new Gothic mansion, parts of which were clearly designed for display rather than habitation. The importance of those years at the Covent Garden theatre has sometimes been overlooked, but, as John Hardman Powell later reflected,

> It was the very romance of his artistic career, and, after the fire at Covent Garden Theatre had destroyed the last of his fairy world, he would speak of this period of scene

painting as one of great artistic enjoyment and of considerable advantage to him in his profession; for he would say: 'Striving to make things appear real made me study the true effects of shadow, and laying on colour in bucketfuls gave me vigour.'[29]

Alton Towers provided Pugin with the biggest stage-set of his career, built by a family whose exploits in the French wars had been dramatized by Shakespeare. It is against this theatrical background that one can understand how he was drawn into the creation of an equestrian figure of the first earl of Shrewsbury to lord it over the other armoured figures and battle-flags in the grand entrance, the casting of replica Talbot tomb-effigies to lie in the plaster-vaulted Octagon made to resemble the chapter-house of a great cathedral, and the pyrotechnic illumination of the north front of the Towers as the backdrop for the arrival of the Pretender to the throne of France.

Staffordshire was well-endowed with a variety of suitable building stones which Pugin was able to use to great advantage, notably the sandstones and gritstones of the Moorlands. The Counslow quarry, between Cheadle and Alton, yielded different colours of sandstone, from white to deep red, and a hard grey sandstone was quarried at Alton Park. To the south-east, near Tutbury, alabaster was being mined only to be crushed to make plaster, until Pugin pioneered the revival of carving in this fine material for altars and statues. A revival of another kind took place in Stoke-on-Trent where the pottery manufacturer Herbert Minton began to produce encaustic and printed tiles to Pugin's designs, followed by tableware and decorative ceramics also designed by Pugin. This alone would give Staffordshire a prominent place in the revival of Gothic art, since these items found their way into churches, public buildings and private homes all over the country, and overseas too.

The association with Minton was particularly important to Pugin. He believed that, after stained glass, encaustic tiles were amongst the most important forms of decorative art, and there were some significant medieval survivals, for example at Winchester Cathedral and Westminster Abbey. The recovery of this lost art was an important part of the Gothic Revival. Pugin and Minton were not the only designers and manufacturers who attempted it but their partnership was the most successful and productive, and this stemmed partly from their personal friendship and also from Minton's own determination to succeed in perfecting the production methods and also extend the range of what was possible using modern methods. Pugin was himself driven by technology, believing that once a design had been worked out in accordance with ancient authorities, there was no reason why the actual production should not be carried out with the aid of machinery.

The process of encaustic tile production involved pouring liquid clay, or 'slip', of a contrasting colour into indented patterns on a prepared base tile. Samuel Wright (1783-1849) of Shelton, Stoke-on-Trent, had developed a process in the 1830s, and Minton used and developed it under licence. A recently discovered letter shows that Pugin was in contact with Minton in the summer of 1840 in connection with the production of tiles for the Convent of Mercy at Handsworth.[30] This pre-dates what is generally believed to have been Minton's first commission for an encaustic pavement, at the Temple Church in London (1841). The floors for the Hospital of St John at Alton were also early (1841), which makes the removal of the bulk of these tiles in the 1960s all the more regrettable. The Talbot iconography on the surviving ones is identical to that at Handsworth. From 1841 onwards Pugin travelled frequently to Stoke in connection with his work for Lord Shrewsbury, and the Minton Archive includes a large number of watercolour designs – some signed by Pugin – for tablewares, door-plates and majolica ware, as well as encaustic tiles. The most important commission of all was for the encaustic pavements of the New Palace of Westminster. A set of full-colour patterns for these survives, made up from Pugin's original drawings.

The raw materials for much of Pugin's metalwork was also sourced within north Staffordshire. Two miles along the Churnet Valley north-west of Alton is the village of Oakamoor which by the 1830s had become the centre of a thriving copper and brass industry, using ores mined locally at Ecton and Mixon. The Cheadle Copper and Brass Company, as it was called, produced high-quality metal in various forms. Invoices in the archives of John Hardman & Company show that by the 1840s Hardman was a regular customer, ordering rolled brass, or 'latten', in sheet form, also 'gilding metal' which had a higher copper content, and tubes, rods and wires. Much of this would have been turned into the wide range of ecclesiastical metalwork that Hardman was now making to Pugin's designs, and which was being sought after for churches all over Britain, and overseas. Some of it came back to Staffordshire in the form, for example, of the magnificent brass gates at the entrance to the Blessed Sacrament Chapel in St Giles', Cheadle, the gilt-brass chandeliers in the state rooms at Alton Towers, and the fine memorial brasses to members of the Talbot family in St John's, Alton.

Another major industry in north Staffordshire was silk, centred upon the Moorland town of Leek, about ten miles north-west of Cheadle. By 1840 the spinning, dyeing and weaving of silk had become concentrated in seven mills, employing about 750 people. The design of textile fabrics was a significant part of Pugin's *oeuvre*: a wide range of patterned fabrics in woven wool, cotton and silk, and also woven braids and motifs which could be appliquéd on to vestments and altar-frontals.[31] As with everything else, these were carefully researched with reference to surviving medieval examples. Pugin did not, however, avail himself of the products of the Leek silk mills which were geared to the domestic market. Instead he turned to the London firm of John Gregory Crace to whom he supplied designs for wallpaper and textiles. Thomas Brown of Manchester, and Lonsdale and Tyler of London, were amongst those who supplied Pugin with woven braids, while John Hardman's sister, Lucy Powell, set up a workshop in Birmingham for the making and embroidering of vestments. Machine-woven braids and appliqués were much less expensive than hand-embroidery. Nevertheless Pugin firmly advocated the revival of the ancient art of embroidery for which England had been renowned throughout medieval Europe, but confessed that the full recovery of these skills would take time. He did not live to see it, but the success of the Leek School of Needlework in the 1880s in the revival of hand-embroidery techniques, using locally produced silks and metallic threads, would have pleased him greatly (see p. 304-5).

Given the importance of Leek as a developing industrial centre as well as a market town – 'The Capital of the Moorlands' – with a population greater than that of Cheadle, it has to be asked why it seems to have escaped the attention of

1.8 The ruins of Croxden Abbey which formed Pugin's inspiration for Nottingham Cathedral (Michael Fisher).

Pugin and Lord Shrewsbury, and why it did not acquire a large new Catholic church until 1887. Lord Shrewsbury was indeed involved in Leek, first as the donor of £130 towards the £700 needed for a Catholic chapel in Fountain Street, on the north side of the town. The chapel was built in 1828 by James Jeffries, the priest from Cheadle who had taken a room in the town as a Mass centre. He then built a presbytery adjoining the chapel, and the first resident priest was appointed in about 1832.[32] It is clear that by 1841 a new and larger church was being planned by Lord Shrewsbury and Bishop Walsh. Pugin, naturally, would be the architect. Other considerations intervened: by the end of that year Cheadle had been started, and Pugin's scheme for St Barnabas' Cathedral, Nottingham (1841-4), was proving more costly than the earl had anticipated. 'I fear we shall have to defer Leek', he wrote to Walsh in November,[33] and that appears to have been the end of the matter.

Pugin was adept at observing and sketching medieval buildings, and details of them, which he could later use as 'authorities' when it came to designing his own buildings. Surviving collections of his drawings include very few of Staffordshire, but there was a good deal to attract his interest, and it is known from other sources that he visited medieval sites on and around the Shrewsbury estates. The most obvious of these is Alton Castle for which a number of sketches survive in the V&A, but in the rebuilding of it Pugin and Lord Shrewsbury made little attempt to replicate what was known to have been there prior to 1840. Not far away were the ruins of the twelfth-century Cistercian abbey of Croxden **(1.8)**, founded by one of Lord Shrewsbury's ancestors, Bertram de Verdun of Alton Castle. Certain features of Croxden – including the south transept and west front – were utilised by Pugin in his design for St Barnabas' Cathedral in Nottingham to which Lord Shrewsbury was the principal contributor, so Pugin must have made sketches of these. The earl himself influenced the design of St Barnabas, and said that he envisaged it as a revival of Croxden, as Pugin reminded him when he began to show concern about the cost: 'Did not your Lordship say often how much you wanted to see Croxton revived & is not the west end a compleat revival of that simple old church with the high and narrow Lancet windows.'[34] Thus, in contrast to most of Pugin's other large churches, Nottingham is in the First Pointed or 'lancet' style. It is cruciform in plan with a central tower, it has a large retro-choir furnished with three chapels, and as originally built it had an enclosed choir and presbytery; i.e. it is basically monastic in concept.

A few miles east of Alton, and just inside Derbyshire, is the fine medieval church of St Barlok at Norbury, the ancestral home of the Fitzherbert family who were noted for their adherence to the Catholic faith, at great personal cost, during the Penal years. The chancel retains its full complement of medieval glass, which would have delighted Pugin, as would the alabaster monuments to the Fitzherberts. He arranged for a plaster replica of one of these to be made for Alton Towers.[35] Pugin also visited some medieval sites near the Shrewsbury estates on the Staffordshire-Shropshire border, including the church at Albrighton where he noted the alabaster tomb of Sir John Talbot, and he was particularly moved by the ruins of White Ladies Priory and its Catholic burial-ground. The survival of Catholicism in these areas was remarkable, and owed much to the tenacity of local landed families who, in the Penal times, maintained clandestine chapels and private chaplains, and encouraged their tenants in the faith of their fathers. To see the old hiding-places and secret chapels at Boscobel House and Moseley Hall brings home the totalitarian nature of the governments of the sixteenth and seventeenth centuries, and the fortitude of those who suffered imprisonment, barbaric torture, and cruel death for the 'crime' of practising the faith which had for over 1,000 years been the faith of the entire nation. In no other European country – with the exception of France during the Revolution – were Catholics subjected to the sustained levels of state-sponsored persecution as applied in England for the three centuries prior to the 1829 Catholic Emancipation Act. This helps to account for the triumphalism and euphoria which accompanied emancipation; and yet, because of anti-Catholic sentiment ingrained into the English mind by earlier propaganda and popular myth, there were many who still regarded Catholicism as foreign, and Catholics as a race apart. The work of Pugin, Lord Shrewsbury and Ambrose Phillipps needs to be viewed against that landscape; buildings of what Bl. John Henry Newman called the Second Spring of English Catholicism.

Yet the signs of spring were there before 1829, for example in the Catholic Relief Acts of 1778 and 1791, and in the widespread sympathy felt for those who sought refuge in England from anti-Catholic persecution during the French Revolution. Under the 1791 legislation Catholics were allowed to worship openly, and, subject to certain conditions, Catholic chapels could be built, provided that they were registered, and thirteen were immediately registered in Staffordshire. Significantly, perhaps, they had to be called chapels rather than churches, no crosses or other obvious iconography were to be placed on the outsides of such buildings, and worshippers would cling to old habits such as talking euphemistically about going to 'Prayers' rather than to 'Mass.'[36] Old prejudices died hard too. On a railway journey, Pugin inadvertently upset another passenger by crossing himself while saying private prayers. 'You are a Catholic, sir,' the lady declared. 'Guard, guard, let me out – I must get into another carriage.'[37]

Apart from the Shrewsbury's chapel at Alton, the finest Catholic chapel in the area was the one attached to Tixall Hall, four miles west of Stafford, the home of the Clifford family. It was built in 1827-8 to the design of the Catholic architect Joseph Ireland (c.1780-1841) in the Tudor-Gothic style, and in 1845 it was removed stone by stone to Great Haywood, about two miles distant, following the purchase of the Tixall estate by the Anglican Earl Talbot of Ingestre (**1.9**). Built entirely of

1.9 Tixall Hall Chapel. Drawing by J. Buckler, 1841 (Staffordshire Views, William Salt Library, Stafford).

1.10 St Mary's, Cresswell: Stourton memorial window (Michael Fisher).

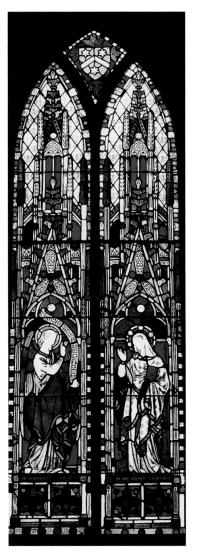

stone, it has square-headed mullioned windows, battlements, an octagonal south-west turret, and an ornate west front with a statue of St John the Baptist in a niche over the entrance. Originally it had a polygonal apse at the east end, with rich tracery in the windows, but sadly this is no longer extant. Pugin's diary records a visit to Tixall in July 1844 when the plans for the removal of the chapel were already in hand, but it is not known whether he had any part in the operation, or indeed by whom it was undertaken. Though on a smaller scale than the new Alton Towers chapel of 1832, there are similarities in detail – for example the apse, the tribune carried on three arches at the west end, and the ornamentation of the stonework – which raise the question as to whether Joseph Ireland, who is known to have worked for Lord Shrewsbury, was involved in the design of the Towers chapel along with its known architects, Joseph Potter and Thomas Fradgley.

Barely two miles from Tixall is Mount Pavilion, Colwich, a Georgian Gothic house begun in about 1824 by the little-known Leicestershire architect, Robert Chaplin for Viscount Tamworth, who died before it was finished. It was then sold to a community of Benedictine nuns who occupied it from 1834, having adapted the entrance hall and an adjoining boudoir into a chapel. It was known thereafter as St Mary's Abbey. Local tradition has it that Pugin designed the three windows over the altar and the reredos but there is no direct evidence for this in Pugin's diary or correspondence. It is possible, however, that he may have called at the abbey on one of his visits to Staffordshire, for example in August 1837 when he stayed with Sir Charles Wolseley whose home was within sight of Colwich.

In north Staffordshire, private chapels in the homes of Catholic nobility and gentry were supplemented by a number of missions established after the second Relief Act. Chief among these was the Cresswell Mission which replaced the private chapel at Painsley Hall, the home of the Draycott family and their descendants, the Langdales and Stourtons. The Cresswell Mission became the mother church of the whole of north Staffordshire, and by 1835 eight chapels had been built within its circuit.[38] These included a new chapel – St Filumena's – at Caverswall (1813), built so that the growing congregation no longer had to use the nuns' chapel at the castle; and the Lane End Chapel on the outskirts of Longton (1819). A small chapel at Cobridge (Stoke-on-Trent) dating from 1781 was considerably enlarged in the 1830s. The enlargement of Alton Lodge into Alton Abbey (later Alton Towers) included the building of a chapel on the north front of the house which was from the beginning intended for the local Catholic population as well as for the Shrewsbury family. It was complete by 1819, and the baptism register dates from 1820. A chapel was built in Cheadle in the 1820s, and its first resident priest, Fr James Jeffries, also looked after the mission in Leek to which Lord Shrewsbury contributed £130 and which opened in 1829. A mission room was opened at Uttoxeter in 1830. With the exception of the Towers chapel, all of these buildings were quite plain, and were later replaced in grander style, and the Towers gained a new and larger chapel in 1832. Only the 'mother church', the Cresswell Mission itself, has survived intact, and this is in many ways fortunate. Now known as St Mary's and refurnished at different times since it was built in 1816, its basic structure is typical of Catholic chapels generally at the beginning of the nineteenth century. Built of brick, with pointed windows and buttresses, it has neither aisles, nor chancel, nor an east window, and at the west end there is a large gallery supported on cast-iron columns. In other words, it is little different structurally from the nonconformist chapels of the period. Pugin added a few refinements, including a stained glass window on the north side of the sanctuary. Made by Hardmans, it is of two lights, and depicts the Annunciation (1.10): it was given in 1848 in memory of Mary, Dowager Lady Stourton (d. 1841), the principal benefactor of the mission. Pugin suggested that a second window might be put in on the opposite side of the church, in memory of the late Sir Edward Vavasour (d. 1847), Lady Mary's brother-in-law, with figures of St Edward and St George, but nothing seems to have come of it.[39] Pugin is also credited with the design of the elegant churchyard cross, and although there is no documentary evidence for this, some of the gravestones of the early 1840s have the unmistakable air of Pugin about them – floriated crosses with simple inscriptions in a lettering style identical to those in St John's churchyard at Alton. Also at Cresswell was a rare collection of late medieval vestments, namely four chasubles which had been in use at Painsley Hall during the Penal years, and which may have come originally from the nearby

1.11 St Mary's Cresswell:
detail of medieval
embroidery (Michael Fisher).

parish church of St Margaret, Draycott-le-Moors. The embroidered orphreys
included figures of saints and of the Virgin and Child **(1.11)**.[40]

The significance of Cresswell lies not in its architecture or furnishings, but in
its function as the hub of the north Staffordshire missions. Adjoining the east end
of the chapel are the domestic buildings which housed not just the priest, but also
a small seminary established in about 1816 by the Revd Thomas Baddeley who
was assisted there from 1819 by William Wareing, later Bishop of Northampton.
Among the priests trained at Cresswell were Fr James Jeffries and Fr Francis Fairfax,
the first priests to reside at Cheadle.

A similar story of dogged survival and revival could be told of the district
around the Shrewsbury estates on the Staffordshire-Shropshire border, where the

Catholic faith was flourishing in the missions at Longbirch and Black Ladies close to Brewood, and where families such as the Giffards and the Whitgreaves had maintained private chapels and priests. Thus the Staffordshire landscape was well-prepared for the arrival, in 1837, of Pugin, with his high hopes of converting England through Gothic art and architecture, of demonstrating to the nation that, far from being foreign, Catholicism was a part of the English climate, and of proving that, far from being a paradox, to be English *and* Catholic was the most natural thing in the world.

If, as Dr Wiseman hoped, Catholicism was to expand, rather than merely survive as in pre-Emancipation days, a more vigorous approach was needed towards the conversion of England than was within the capabilities of the average secular priest such as those brought up in the homespun manner of rural seminaries like Cresswell. Oscott would provide a part of the answer, but Wiseman, fresh from Rome in 1840, looked also towards the Italian missionary Orders such as the Rosminians and the Passionists. Lord Shrewsbury's friend, Ambrose Phillipps (1809-79), brought Fr Aloysius Gentili and the Rosminians to work in the rural communities near his Leicestershire home of Grace Dieu, and in 1842 Pugin built a small church and school for them at Shepshed. With Phillipps' encouragement, Bl. Dominic Barberi (1792-1849) and the Passionists came to England and they settled at Aston Hall, Stone, in 1842, replacing the secular chaplain, Benjamin Hulme. In spite of some initial opposition, and even ridicule, they achieved remarkable success through their regular visits to Stone, where Barberi said Mass in a room in the Crown Hotel. By December 1843 he had 86 converts, and it

1.12 St Anne's, Stone
(Michael Fisher).

was proposed to build a chapel in Newcastle Street. Pugin prepared a design for it costing a modest £1,000, but Wiseman advised economy, and so the scheme as scaled down to a school-cum-chapel which eventually cost £600 (of which Wiseman contributed £150).[41] The builder was Pugin's trusted friend, George Myers. Dedicated to St Anne, the building consists of a buttressed nave, and a chancel, of brick with stone dressings **(1.12)**. The chancel could be closed off from the nave by means of large doors when the nave was used as the schoolroom, a similar arrangement to the one Pugin made at St John's, Alton. The doors are long gone, but the hinge-pins remain. There are few refinements apart from the three-light east window depicting St Anne holding Our Lady as a child, the gable-crosses (now missing), the statue of St Anne over the west door, and some Minton tiles. 'Poor Pugin', commented Pevsner, 'nearly always what he dreamt to be rich, dignified, elevating, turned out to be mean – for lack of money';[42] but – as with Pugin's church at Dudley – Pevsner misjudged. Like the church at Shepshed, St Anne's was a new mission rather than the aggrandisement of an existing one, and it was built to fulfil an immediate need. Richness was not a consideration. In terms of its structure, however, St Anne's is no less a 'true principles' church than St Giles, Cheadle. It has a clearly defined nave and chancel, there is nothing flimsy about it, and it could not possibly be taken for anything other than a church.

Thanks to the endeavours of the Passionists, St Anne's was soon outgrown. By the autumn of 1850 the need for a larger church coincided with the wish of William Ullathorne (1806-89) to secure premises within the diocese for Mother Margaret Hallahan and the Third Order of Dominicans. Ullathorne had been Vicar Apostolic of the Western District from 1846, had succeeded Thomas Walsh in the Central District in 1848, and became first Bishop of Birmingham at the restoration of the Hierarchy. The first attempt at settling the Dominicans in north Staffordshire was made at Longton, near to the Lane End mission, in the autumn of 1850. Told by local people that Longton was 'the fag end of the Potteries', Mother Margaret soon concluded that it was 'the fag end of the world.'[43] The problem was solved when one of the community's Staffordshire patrons made a gift of land adjacent to St Anne's. Given that Pugin had built St Anne's, it might have been thought that he was the natural choice as architect of the new church, but Ullathorne favoured another Catholic architect, Charles Hansom (1817-88) whom he had earlier employed in building St Osmund's, Coventry. Hansom, indeed, had already made his mark in the area in 1847 as the architect of the Passionists' new church at Aston-by-Stone, and the church of St Joseph and St Etheldreda at Rugeley (1849-50) with its tall spire. Bishop Ullathorne favoured Gothic, and at his consecration as bishop in 1846 had made a statement by ordering the use of the ample Gothic chasubles which had been the cause of much controversy only a few years previously. Nevertheless, Ullathorne considered Pugin's buildings – and Hardman's metalwork – to be somewhat expensive, and he famously remarked that 'anything Pugin can do, Mr Hansom can do better.'[44] Hansom was a conscious imitator of the Pugin style, and one of those of whom Pugin wrote, 'these men can afford to sell cheap, for they steal their brooms ready made.'[45] In any event, by the time St Dominic's was planned, Pugin was ill, and in the last months of his life, but it underlines the fact that in his latter years he was overtaken by 'broom-stealers' who were quite willing to deck their churches with stained glass and metalwork designed by Pugin and made by Hardman, as Hansom did at Rugeley, and more spectacularly at Erdington Abbey on the edge of Birmingham. Looking to the continuation of his 'true principles' amongst the rising generation, and more fearful of 'pagan' neo-classicists than Gothic plagiarists, Pugin took a philosophical view: 'Any man who possesses the true spirit of Christian art, so far from desiring to occupy an unrivalled position, is delighted when he is equalled, and overjoyed when he is surpassed.'[46] Begun in 1852, St Dominic's, is in the late thirteenth-century style, with additions by Gilbert Blount (1819-76), an architect much-favoured by the Dominicans, and metalwork and glass by Hardmans.[46] Ullathorne had a particular fondness for St Dominic's, and he was buried there in 1889, with a 'Puginesque' sarcophagus by J.S. Hansom.

Caverswall Castle, four miles from Cheadle, was one of the places Pugin first visited with Dr Weedall in 1837 **(1.13)**. It was occupied by a community of Benedictine nuns for whom Pugin later carried out improvements in the chapel, but Caverswall was important for personal reasons too. The nuns ran a boarding-school, and it was there that Agnes – Pugin's eldest daughter by his second wife, Louisa – was sent in the autumn of 1848 at the age of twelve. It may seem curious that Pugin, whose home was in Ramsgate, should have sent his daughter so far away to school, but there was good reason. Although Pugin's third wife, Jane Knill (1827-1909) was his 'first-rate Gothic woman'[48] who fully shared his vision of Catholic England, Agnes did not take to her new stepmother and so, in October 1848, just a few weeks after the marriage, she was sent to Caverswall, which placed her far enough away from Jane, but which also enabled her father to visit while he

1.13 Caverswall Castle, 1817: aquatint by J. Sutherland (Staffordshire Views, William Salt Library, Stafford).

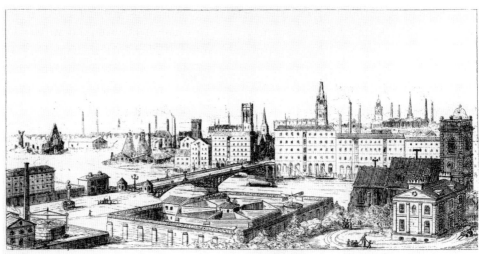

THE SAME TOWN IN 1840

1. St Michaels Tower, rebuilt in 1750. 2. New Parsonage House & Pleasure Grounds. 3. The New Jail. 4. Gas Works. 5. Lunatic Asylum. 6. Iron Works & Ruins of St Maries Abbey. 7. Mr Evans Chapel. 8. Baptist Chapel. 9. Unitarian Chapel. 10. New Church. 11. New Town Hall & Concert Room. 12. Wesleyan Centenary Chapel. 13. New Christian Society. 14. Quakers Meeting. 15. Socialist Hall of Science.

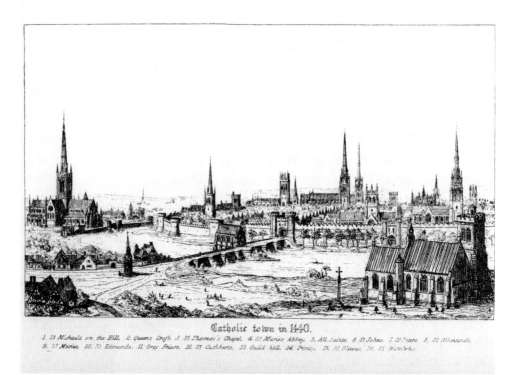

Catholic town in 1440.

1. St Michaels on the Hill. 2. Queens Cross. 3. St Thomas's Chapel. 4. St Maries Abbey. 5. All Saints. 6. St Johns. 7. St Peters. 8. St Alkmunds. 9. St Maries. 10. St Edmunds. 11. Grey Friars. 12. St Cuthberts. 13. Guild hall. 14. Trinity. 15. St Olaves. 16. St Botolphs.

1.14 A.W.N. Pugin: 'Contrasted Towns', from *Contrasts* (1841 edition).

was staying at Alton. Discipline appears to have been strict:

> The pupils wear an uniform of buff-coloured cotton; they are not suffered to ramble beyond the bounds of the gravel walk which surrounds the moat. … they walk two and two, like other boarding-school girls, and in their half-hour's exercise along the walk in the garden, are required, as a religious duty, to utter their ave-marias and pater-nosters in a low voice.[49]

Agnes was no more happy at Caverswall than she had been at home. Pugin, who was at Alton Towers for a few days in mid-October, went over to see her, and was quite concerned. Yet it was to his friend John Hardman, rather than to Jane, that he expressed his concern: 'I have just been over to Caverswall. poor Agnes is very ill. she looks quite pulled down. it is sad to see her. she will now appreciate the comforts of home.'[50] For her part, Jane expressed the hope that Agnes would 'alter very much before she leaves for good, otherwise I do not know what I shall do.'[51]

Pugin visited Caverswall for what was almost certainly the last time on 28 November 1851, again while staying at Alton Towers. A few days later he was home in Ramsgate, and the brief entries in his diary tell their own story: 'Taken ill', 'Very ill', 'Very unwell'. He may have begun a diary for 1852, but it does not survive, and although he and Jane kept in touch with Lord and Lady Shrewsbury, Pugin never saw Alton, or the Shrewsburys, again. Both earl and architect died within eight weeks of each other in the autumn of 1852.

The premature deaths of Pugin and Lord Shrewsbury left much unfinished work to be completed by the young Edward Pugin (1834-75) and by the seventeenth earl, but it was to be a brief association. The death of Earl Bertram in 1856 marked the end of the senior, Catholic, line of the Talbot family, with serious consequences for the churches of the Pugin-Shrewsbury partnership. Some noteworthy buildings do, however, date from this later period including the little-known Burton Manor, Stafford (1854), St Mary's Abbey at Oulton, near Stone (1854), the new St Austin's Church, Stafford (1862), and St Gregory's, Longton, built in 1869 to replace the Lane End chapel.[52] Significantly, the architect of all of these was Edward Welby Pugin who was also responsible for the completion of unfinished structural work at Alton Towers. The discovery in 2011 that Edward Pugin was also the architect of Aston Hall (Aston-by-Stone) – a large house very similar in style to Burton Manor, and of 1855-6 – adds significantly to his catalogue of works in north Staffordshire.

Among the criticisms levelled at A.W.N. Pugin were that much of his work was left unfinished, that some of his buildings were starved, and that many looked far better on the drawing board than they did in reality. If this was the case, then it was due to circumstances beyond his control, such as shortage of money on the part of those who commissioned him. In self-critical mood, Pugin himself confessed that he had spent his life in 'thinking of fine things, studying fine things, designing fine things, and realising very poor ones.'[53] He could not say that of his work for Lord Shrewsbury. If Alton Castle was left unfinished, it was only because death intervened; and Cheadle, as completed in 1846, far exceeded the expectations of 1841. St Giles' was, if anything over-done. Pugin's church at Brewood is no less a 'true principles' church than St Giles', and in terms of seating capacity it is just as commodious. It has aisles, a properly furnished chancel, a porch and a spire, and all for just over £2,000. Twenty such churches could have been built for the sum that Lord Shrewsbury expended on Cheadle. St Giles', however, was built for a different purpose. Here Pugin set out to give practical expression to all of his ideas on architecture and ornament as propounded in publications such as *The True Principles, The Present State,* and *The Glossary;* and he drew together the widest possible range of 'authorities', both English and continental, that it was possible to do in one place. Everything that he wrote and spoke about – passionately – is here translated into three-dimensional reality. St Giles' is above all the full expression of the theological basis of what Pugin believed a parish church should be. St Giles', Cheadle, St John's, Alton, St Marie's, Uttoxeter, the Towers Chapel – all of these attracted unprecedented attention from English and foreign visitors, and from the Press, even while in the course of construction. They were studied, sketched and imitated by both Catholic and Anglican architects and designers. 'It will be a text Book for all good people,' Lord Shrewsbury said of St Giles'. 'It will surely do good, and improve the taste of young England,[54] and so it did. For this alone, north Staffordshire deserves to be called 'Pugin-land'.

Lord Shrewsbury's expression, 'Young England', carries other connotations, and the name was applied to a political movement which gained ground in the Tory party under the influence of Disraeli. Those who spearheaded the Gothic/Catholic revival of the 1830s and '40s were not elderly gentlemen looking back wistfully to a bygone age that was dead and buried, but young men with passion and a vision for the present and future of England as the accession in 1837 of an eighteen-year-old queen seemed to mark the dawn of a new age. Pugin was 24 when *Contrasts* was published, just as the Hanoverian age was drawing to a close. His friend Hardman was just a year older, Ambrose Phillipps was 27, and the nascent architect, George Gilbert Scott, who was soon to be awakened by the 'thunder' of Pugin's writings, and who drooled over the decorations at St Giles', was 25. It was the junior common rooms of Oxford and Cambridge which kindled the theological fires of Tractarians and Camdenians, and the Middle Ages provided a source of inspiration for the renewal of England that was different from the radicalism and socialism that were gaining ground as a consequence of the squalor of the new industrial towns and the lack of proper provision for the underprivileged. The second edition of Pugin's *Contrasts* contained a new pair of engravings which tell of this more eloquently than pages of print. A 'Catholic Town' of 1440, full of graceful spires, noble buildings and well-ordered cottages is contrasted with a view of the same town in 1840, now full of smoking chimneys and bleak factories, decaying churches, a jail, and a 'Socialist Hall of Science' (**1.14**). Pugin's notion that Gothic had a profound moral content that affected all aspects of life was novel indeed, and it inspired an Irishman named McCann to write some verses which one can easily imagine being sung by Oxbridge undergraduates – and even Oscott seminarians – to the tune, maybe, of *The Vicar of Bray*:

> Oh! Have you seen the work just out
> By Pugin the great builder?
> Architectr'al Contrasts' he's made out
> Poor Protestants to bewilder.
> The Catholic Church, she never knew –
> Till Mr Pugin taught her,
> That orthodoxy had to do
> At all with bricks and mortar.
>
> But now its clear to one and all,
> Since he's published his lecture,
> No church is Catholic at all

1.15 Gothic in the Steam Age: Alton Castle with the railway in the foreground, *c*.1852 (William Salt Library, Stafford).

> Without Gothic architecture.
> In fact, he quite turns up his nose
> At any style that's racent,
> The Gracian, too, he plainly shows
> Is wicked and ondacent.[55]

Yet 'Young England' did not despise modern technology, nor did it revolt completely against machine-industry in the way that the later Arts and Crafts Movement did. Pugin stated that 'in matters purely mechanical, the Christian architect should gladly avail himself of those improvements and increased facilities that are suggested from time to time' on the grounds that money saved on the more mechanical parts of the building could be used for enrichment and variety of detail. '... if I were engaged in the erection of a vast church, I should certainly set up an engine that would saw blocks, turn detached shafts, and raise the various materials to the required height'[56]. The use of iron reinforcements at the centre of stone columns and cavity walls did not trouble him unduly, nor did the selective use of machined components in the production of church metalwork as Hardman was doing it in Birmingham. Pugin welcomed the railway age; steam trains facilitated his many cross-country journeys and speeded up the delivery of mail. He began to dabble in railway architecture, and compared his own frenetic activity to a 'Locomotive ... always flyin about.'[57] He took a keen interest in the progress of the North Staffordshire Railway, and when the Churnet Valley branch-line opened in 1849, he looked forward to travelling all the way to Alton by train for the first time, and even dreamed of building a station there. A watercolour of the early 1850s captures this strange blend of neo-medievalism and Victorian technology. A steam train is shown pulling out of Alton station, yet the scene is dominated by Pugin's Romantic castle, and the 'venerable almshouse' of St John, on the hill beyond the River Churnet **(1.15)**.

The station – so different from the one Pugin had in mind for Alton, and manifestly not by him – still stands, but the railway line closed in the 1960s. Yet the faithful still go to Mass in St John's, where 'good Earl John' lies buried, while the castle, with its turrets and coloured roof repaired and refurbished on behalf of the Catholic Youth Association, provides for spiritual and educational needs of rising generations of a different 'young England' in an idyllic setting. The Talbots' great house, which gave shelter as well as employment to Pugin, lies empty and part-ruined at the centre of a theme-park, but on the opposite side of the valley, beyond Counslow Hill, the raised forefinger of St Giles' spire beckons both worshipper and visitor to experience the perfect expression of what this 'Mediaeval Victorian' believed an English parish church should be.[58]

2

Prest d'accomplir:
the earl and the architect

The redie minde regardeth never toyle,
But still is Prest t'accomplish heartes intent
Abrode, at home, in every coste or soyle
The dede is done, that inwardly is mente,
Which makes me saye to every virtuous dede
I am still prest t'accomplish whats decreed.[1]

Prest d'Accomplir – 'ready to accomplish' – is the Talbot family motto which, along with the rampant lion, was repeated time and again in the wall-coverings, cornices, ceilings, windows, metalwork, and other items designed by Pugin for Alton Towers. It also expresses something of that enterprising spirit of earl and architect through whose efforts so much was accomplished on and around the Alton estate between 1837 and 1852. '*Prest d'Accomplir*' though he may have been, it was Pugin's own battle cry, *En Avant!* which impelled the sixteenth earl to undertake far more than he sometimes considered desirable or affordable, and not all of it was accomplished without controversy between Pugin and his most illustrious and enthusiastic patron.

Although much has been said and written about Pugin's extraordinary career and achievements, the sixteenth earl of Shrewsbury **(2.1)** has remained a shadowy figure. A biography planned shortly after his death never materialised,[2] the first edition of the *Dictionary of National Biography* ignored him altogether, while Denis Gwynn's examination of the earl's role in promoting the Catholic cause – *Lord Shrewsbury, Pugin and the Catholic Revival* (1946) – has been out of print for many years.

Where facts are lacking, myths and legends often abound, and not a few have attached themselves to Lord Shrewsbury. On the one hand, the extent of his benefactions was subject to popular exaggeration even in the 1850s, and one of Denis Gwynn's objectives was to set that particular record straight. More recent and local myths of a somewhat sinister kind have included the monstrous suggestion that the earl had built Alton Towers as a residence for his mistress, and that the building of St Giles', Cheadle, had been undertaken as a penance. There was, of course, no mistress.[3] The earl inherited the Towers from his uncle when it was to all intents and purposes finished: he practised a near-ascetic lifestyle, and the building of St Giles' was a part of his widespread promotion of the Catholic cause in which he passionately believed. If there was an unseen

2.1 John Talbot, sixteenth earl of Shrewsbury, by John Julius Hamburger, at Ingestre Hall (Mark Titterton).

hand at work, it was that of A.W.N. Pugin, impelling him to undertake more than he had originally intended, and leaving behind a lasting memorial in the fine Catholic buildings of Alton and Cheadle. Then there is the legend of the oak tree in the woods below the Towers, bound with chains lest a falling branch should signal the untimely death of a member of the earl's family. The chained oak is there for sure: the sole survivor of a number of 'spar-oaks' anciently used as anchor-points in a haulage system for bringing heavy goods up the steep side of the Churnet Valley. When its original function was quite forgotten, folklore supplied a new one to satisfy those for whom natural causes did not adequately explain the early demise of several of the earl's relatives. It is time that the real John Talbot – 'The Good Earl' - emerged from the shadows.

John Talbot was born on 18 March 1791, the second son of John Joseph Talbot, younger brother of Charles, the fifteenth earl. His mother was Catherine, daughter of Thomas Clifton of Lytham Hall. John Joseph was heir presumptive to the Shrewsbury titles and estates, in the event of the fifteenth earl dying without male issue. The Talbots were indeed notoriously bad at producing male heirs who survived infancy. Not since 1667 had the titles passed directly from father to son. All, however, could trace descent from John, the 'Grand Talbot'

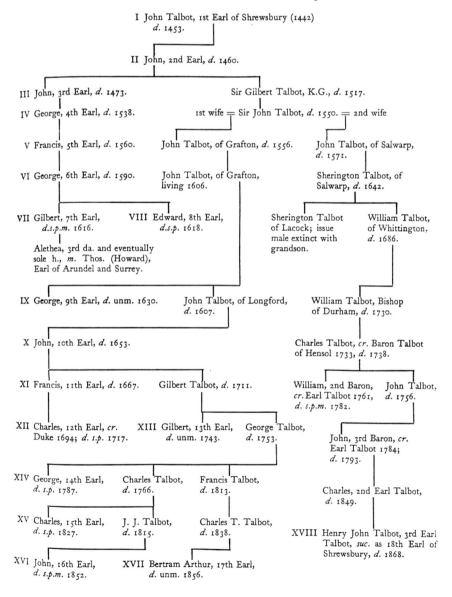

2.2 The lineage of the Talbot earls of Shrewsbury

(d. 1453), who had won fame – and his earldom – on the battlefields of the Hundred Years' War **(2.2)**.

The home of this particular branch of the Talbot family was Grafton Manor, on the outskirts of Bromsgrove, Worcestershire. The house had been in Talbot hands at least since the early sixteenth century, and had been the home of John Talbot of Grafton (d. 1556) who was effectively the founder of the second line of the Talbots who succeeded to the Shrewsbury titles and estates on the death of the seventh earl in 1616 and who remained in possession until the death of the seventeenth earl in 1856. The early sixteenth-century manor house was given a new Renaissance-style entrance in 1567, and further additions were made by the architect David Brandon in the 1860s. To the west of the house, and connected to it, is a late-medieval chapel for which Pugin designed a reredos in 1850.[4] The chapel served as the local Catholic Mission until the opening of St Peter's, Bromsgrove, in 1862.

At the Reformation the Talbots remained firmly Catholic, and with few exceptions continued so in the first and second lines of succession. Gilbert Talbot, who became the thirteenth earl (1717-43) on the death of his cousin, was also a Jesuit priest. On account of their religion the Talbots were effectively barred from public life, from the universities, the armed services, and from parliament, until the repeal of most of the Penal Laws in the 1820s. Young John Talbot was therefore educated in various Catholic institutions, and by private tutors. His early life was plagued by misfortune. His mother died when he was only a few weeks old, and in 1797 John Joseph took a second wife, Harriet Ann Bedingfield, who bore him a son, George Henry, and a daughter, Mary. Following this second marriage, John, and his elder brother Charles, seem to have become progressively distanced from their father. First of all they were placed in the care of the dowager Countess of Shrewsbury, who lived at Lacock Abbey, Wiltshire, and as soon as they were old enough they were sent to the preparatory school attached to the Benedictine College at Vernon Hall, Lancashire. In 1802 Charles died tragically while at the school, and John was removed almost immediately to Stonyhurst. From 1806 to 1810 he was at St Edmund's College, Ware.[5] During his time here he displayed his emerging talent as a creative writer by publishing an ode entitled *A Farewell to the Muses,*[6] which was the winning entry in a poetry competition. John excelled at Greek, and he won a medal for rhetoric. In 1810 he was placed under the care of the Revd Dr John Kirk (1760-1851) of Lichfield, an author and scholar who was later to have a prominent role in the founding of Oscott College. Then, to complete his education, he was sent to the Revd John Chetwode Eustace, whose fame as a classical tourist was established in 1813 with the publication of his two-volume *Tour through Italy.*[7]

It was no doubt through Fr Eustace that John Talbot initially acquired the love of Italy that was to stay with him for the rest of his life. The Napoleonic Wars raging across Europe made it impracticable for him to undertake the Grand Tour which had once formed an essential part of many a young English gentleman's education. Foreign travel was not, however, impossible, and in 1812 John made an extensive tour through Spain, Portugal, and many parts of the

2.3 Maria Theresa, Countess of Shrewsbury, by John Julius Hamburger, at Ingestre Hall (Mark Titterton).

Mediterranean coast including North Africa. In Spain he even entered the war-zone itself, and was so sickened by the carnage of the Peninsular War that he determined to return to England as soon as possible. He embarked in a small brig, which, after a stiff engagement, was captured by a Yankee privateer. John Talbot himself took an active part in the fight, was taken prisoner, but later released minus all his belongings, so he made his way back to England as best he could.[8]

2.4 Alton Towers: entrance/Dining Room with paintings of the Talbot family. Drawing by Samuel Rayner, *c.*1840 (Potteries Museum, Stoke-on-Trent).

On the 27 June 1814 he married 19-year-old Maria Theresa **(2.3)**, eldest daughter of William and Anne Talbot of Castle Talbot, Co. Wexford; a distant relative, and strikingly beautiful. For the next 38 years they were hardly ever apart, and their devotion to each other is movingly expressed in the simple inscription on Maria's memorial in St John's Church, Alton.[9] They had two daughters: Mary Alethea Beatrix, born in 1815, and Gwendaline Catherine, born two years later. Between the two daughters was born a son, John, who died in 1817 aged only four months. For a time they lived at Hampton-on-the Hill, near Warwick, in a house made available to them by their friend, Lord Dormer; and later at Littleover Hall. They were not at this time particularly wealthy, and from 1821 they spent a good deal of time abroad, mainly in Italy, where the cost of living and of raising children was less than in England. In the 1820s they became absorbed into the social and artistic life of Rome, and this was reflected in the future earl's tastes as a student and collector of fine art. As one might expect, they made friends amongst the Catholic hierarchy, and even became acquainted with Pope Pius VII. In 1824 the painter J.P. Davis (1784-1862) painted a very large canvas showing Pius VII giving a blessing to the kneeling figures of John and Maria Talbot and their two daughters. Shown standing close to the Pope were Cardinal Gonsalvi and the sculptor Antonio Canova. The painting was later hung in the Dining Room at Alton Towers. It can clearly be seen in the fine drawing of the room made in about 1840 by Samuel Rayner **(2.4)**, and it earned the artist the nickname of 'Pope' Davis.

On 6 April 1827 Charles, fifteenth earl of Shrewsbury, died at his London residence in Stanhope Street, after a long illness. The funeral took place on 18 April at what was then the Bavarian Embassy Chapel in Warwick Street, 'in a style of extraordinary pomp and splendour.'[10] From being plain Mr and Mrs Talbot, John and Maria Theresa now became the Earl and Countess of Shrewsbury in England, and of Wexford and Waterford in Ireland. After the various legacies, annuities and charitable bequests had been settled under the terms of his uncle's will, John received a residual legacy of approximately £400,000 along with all the estates, furniture and other personal property. The Shrewsbury estates were spread over several counties including Derbyshire, Shropshire, Staffordshire, Nottinghamshire and Yorkshire. The principal houses were Heythrop, Oxfordshire, a Baroque palace of around 1706 by Thomas Archer for the twelfth earl; and the Gothic Alton Abbey which had been developed and extended by the fifteenth earl as a summer residence, and where building work was still in progress.[11]

In 1831 Heythrop was gutted by a disastrous fire which destroyed most of the furniture, paintings and other items accumulated by the family over the previous century or more. Such as survived were taken to Alton Abbey which – now renamed Alton Towers – became the principal Talbot residence. Though Earl John may have intended originally to do no more than complete the structural work in the house and gardens which his uncle had left unfinished, he soon embarked upon a building programme of his own to accommodate vast new collections of art, armour and furniture. This included the great galleries on the south side of the house, and a big west wing extension containing a State Drawing Room, libraries, and state bedrooms and boudoirs for the exclusive use of visiting royalty. In October 1832 the Princess Victoria, then aged thirteen, visited Alton with her mother, the Duchess of Kent, and she recorded her impressions in her diary. The dowager Queen Adelaide stayed at the Towers in August 1840 when a hundred beds were made up for the accommodation of distinguished guests.[12]

Earl John's education, and his travels on the continent, had given him a taste for fine art and antiquities; and now that he had considerable resources at his disposal, he was in a position to make extensive additions to the collections which his uncle had started to accumulate at Alton from about 1810 onwards. The most conspicuous of these was the collection of pictures, which by the time of the 1857 sale numbered just over 700. They were hung throughout the house, but the biggest displays were in the linked galleries which formed a part of the grand entrance. The Picture Gallery appears to have been purpose-built to accommodate an entire collection of paintings once belonging to Laetitia Bonaparte – the mother of the deposed Emperor – which the earl had acquired on one of his visits to Rome. It included works by Canaletto, Guercino, Poussin, Titian, Tiepolo, Tintoretto, Velasquez and Van Eyck; and the celebrated *Belisarius*, painted in 1780 by Jacques-Louis David (1748-1824).[13]

Earl John also commissioned new work from leading painters and sculptors. The focal point of the Talbot Gallery, added to the gallery range in 1840, was a full-size statue in marble of Raphael by Caccarini, a pupil of Canova. Pietro Tenerani (1789-1870), the sculptor who also became General Director of the museums and galleries of Rome, executed busts of Gwendaline, the earl's younger daughter, and of Henri, Duke of Bordeaux, who visited Alton in 1844. Among the painters from whom the earl commissioned work was Durantini who copied Domenichino's *Communion of S. Jerome* and Raphael's *The Transfiguration* to hang in the new Chapel.[14] The earl seems especially to have admired the work of the Riepenhausen brothers, Franz (1786-1830) and Johann (1788-1860), who lived and worked as members of the German artistic community in Rome. They had close links with the 'Nazarene' movement, and were much influenced by Italian art of the late medieval and Renaissance period, notably that of Raphael in whom Lord Shrewsbury had a particular interest. Amongst the works which Lord Shrewsbury bought from them was a portrait of St Elizabeth of Hungary[15] for the music room, also pictures of St Thomas Becket and Archbishop Lawrence O'Toole (of Dublin) for the Chapel, and an immense canvas – said to have been the largest ever framed in England[16] – showing an insurrection which took place in Rome after the coronation of the Emperor Frederick Barbarossa (1123-90). As well as the emperor himself, the picture included King Henry 'the Lion' of Saxony, and Pope Adrian IV. The picture occupied almost the whole of the east wall of the state dining room at Alton. In 1832 Johann Riepenhausen presented the earl with an album of twelve watercolour drawings representing scenes from the life of Raphael.[17] Another member of the German community in Rome was Eduard Hauser (1807-64), whom the earl commissioned to paint the Last Judgment for the chancel arch of St Giles', Cheadle.

The Armoury at Alton Towers contained one of the largest private collections of armour in the country,[18] while elsewhere in the house were large quantities of fine china and porcelain, including a Dresden chandelier valued in 1851 at 1,000 guineas,[19] and of course some costly furniture. Far from being hidden away for the enjoyment of a privileged few, the treasures of Alton Towers were seen by many. Not only did the earl allow free access to the park and gardens for people of the locality and further afield, he also opened the galleries and state rooms, and 'though hundreds daily wandered through its beautiful saloons, a shilling's worth of loss or damage was never sustained.'[20] Meanwhile, when in residence at Alton, the family lived in the secluded eastern part of the house, in the smaller rooms surviving from the old Alveton Lodge, the original building to occupy the site. When, at the time of the great sale in 1857, these areas were finally open to view, Earl John's bedroom attracted attention and comment not on account of its splendour, but because it was the plainest room in the house, and the simplest in its furniture.[21]

The opening of the gardens and the house to the public was perceived as a part of the general philanthropic attitude of Earl John towards the local community. Though he slipped easily into the role of grand seigneur, he was well aware of his duties and responsibilities. He was generous in his support of schools and hospitals, and was a founder-governor of the Staffordshire Infirmary. When it was suggested that he should build a monastery close to Alton, he chose instead to build the Hospital of St John in Alton village, along with the school and Guildhall for the local people, because it was of more practical value both for its own sake and as a part of the Catholic mission. He set up a fund for the insurance of cottagers' cows, and on hearing that a Cheadle resident had been attacked and robbed on the road to Ashbourne, he sent him a gift of money.[22] A foreign observer noted that in cases of illness or hardship among the tenantry the earl would freely provide whatever was needed, including medicines and the services of a doctor.[23] In the 'Hungry Forties' anyone out of work could apply to Lord Shrewsbury's agent and be given a job on road-building or other construction work. During this time, some 66 miles of roads and carriage drives were laid in and around the Alton estate. Yet the 'Good Earl' as he was locally known, had an almost puritanical side to his character. Whenever he entertained 'the county' to some great ball, and the grand entrance was banked up with flowers and plants, he insisted that as soon as the last carriage had departed in the early hours of the morning, the gardeners must be up and ready to start removing everything so that no trace of the previous evening's event would remain by the time he came down to breakfast. Though the destitute and unemployed were given work and wages with no questions asked, an estate worker who dared to dig his garden on a Sunday was evicted from his cottage.[24]

The Shrewsburys' family Chapel at Alton Abbey had, from its opening in 1820, been attended by Catholics from the villages of Alton and Farley as well as by domestic servants and estate-workers. The earl was particularly devout. It was his custom to rise punctually at six in the morning, spend over an hour in prayer, hear Mass daily in the Chapel, and set aside time each day for meditation and spiritual reading.[25] In 1832-3 a large new chapel was built on to the east end of the house to accommodate a growing number of worshippers. In these pre-Pugin days the earl continued to employ Thomas Fradgley of Uttoxeter, the builder/architect he had inherited from his uncle, and also Joseph Potter of Lichfield whom he commissioned in 1832 to build a substantial church and presbytery at Newport, Shropshire, where there had been a Talbot mission since the seventeenth century. He also subscribed to the church in Leek which opened in 1829 as an offshoot of the Cheadle Mission.

In 1828-9 most of the remaining Penal Laws discriminating against Catholics were repealed. The first to go was the Test Act, which had effectively barred Catholics from public office by requiring office-holders under the Crown to make a declaration against the doctrine of Transubstantiation.[26] Lord Shrewsbury himself published a weighty volume running to 432 pages explaining why Catholics could not conform, under the title of *Reasons for Not Taking the Test*, in the very year that the Act was repealed. Then in 1829 came the Catholic Emancipation Act, which meant, among other things, that Lord Shrewsbury and the other Catholic peers were able to take their seats in the House of Lords and to assume an active role in public affairs. Lord Shrewsbury was admitted to the House on 13 April 1831. In 1837 he attended the funeral of William IV not just as the premier earl, but also as hereditary High Steward of Ireland, and he carried the banner of Ireland in the procession. In politics he confessed that he was by nature a Whig rather than a Tory, because he believed in civil liberties and religious toleration which the Tories had generally opposed: but he acknowledged too that by the early 1840s so many major reforms had been accomplished that the difference between the two parties had become very narrow.[27] He nevertheless opposed the repeal of the protectionist Corn Laws which kept the price of wheat – and hence of bread – artificially high.

Being an earl of Ireland as well as of England, and with an Irish wife, Lord Shrewsbury was deeply involved in Irish affairs. Both the earl and countess were distressed by the tragedy of the Irish famine of the 1840s, and they abhorred the sharp practices of many absentee landlords. Yet the earl was wholly opposed to the movement for the repeal of the 1801 Act of Union spearheaded by Daniel O'Connell (1775-1847) whose election to Westminster had precipitated Catholic Emancipation. He also criticised Irish clergy whose public denunciations of iniquitous landlords allegedly provoked acts of violence and even murder. The earl's letters on this subject in the *Morning Chronicle*, and his criticism of the Irish bishops for not taking a firmer line with their clergy and not doing enough to relieve the plight of the poor, involved him in a bitter controversy with Dr McHale, Archbishop of Tuam, and with Frederick Lucas, the somewhat abrasive editor of the Catholic magazine, *The Tablet*. Both Lord Shrewsbury and his friend, Ambrose Phillipps, believed that the continuing presence at Westminster of Irish peers and members of Parliament was vital to the furtherance of the Catholic cause in England; hence their opposition to O'Connell and the repealers, and their dismay at the apparent indifference of the Irish Catholics – preoccupied as they were with economic and political matters – to the conversion of England. The earl's views on the Irish Question in general were expressed in yet another publication, *Hints Towards the Pacification of Ireland* (1844) which ran to a second edition. In the 1830s family affairs came to the fore. Both of the Shrewsbury daughters had inherited their mother's noted good looks, and, given their cosmopolitan background, it is hardly surprising that they found suitors amongst European royalty and aristocracy. In the summer of 1834 Lady Mary, then aged nineteen, was betrothed to the 33-year-old Prince Frederick of Saxe-Altenburg, a close relative of King Ludwig I of Bavaria. Both Queen Adelaide (herself a German princess) and the Queen of Bavaria were instrumental in arranging the match which was widely applauded around the courts of Europe. The Emperor of Austria proposed to make Mary a princess of the Empire, but King Ludwig insisted on raising her to the rank of princess himself, under the title of Princess Talbot.[28] For reasons which are not clear, the marriage – planned for September 1834 – never took place,[29] but Mary retained the title of Princess in her own right, which doubtless enhanced her eligibility.

A second match was eventually found amongst the aristocracy of Italy. On the 6 April 1839 Princess Mary married Filippo Andrea, Prince Doria Pamphili-Landi, a member of a noted Roman and Neapolitan family whose vast residence – the Palazzo Doria Pamphili – was the repository of art-collections on the scale of the Shrewsburys'. Cardinal Guistiani officiated at the marriage, which took place in the Chapel of the Shrewburys' own residence in the Via del Corso, and this was followed by a service of thanksgiving in St Peter's.[30] This was the second Talbot marriage into a Roman patrician family to have taken place within four years, the younger daughter having already married Prince Borghese in 1835. At the age of 24 Mary found herself mistress of a large household in the magnificent Palazzo Doria on the Via del Corso in the centre of Rome. Mary, Lady Arundell, wrote sarcastically of Lady Shrewsbury, 'If Roman princes make happiness, what a happy woman she must be,' but then she had a low opinion of the countess, possibly formed out of jealousy of the Shrewsburys' high standing in Rome, and she thought that Lady Shrewsbury was overfond of 'diamonds and going out and great dinners and driving with her four horses in the Pincio instead of enjoying the beauties of Rome.'[31]

In the summer of 1839 Prince and Princess Doria joined the earl and countess at Alton, where they were greeted enthusiastically by a large crowd of villagers and tenantry on their arrival on 3 July, the procession from Uttoxeter to the Towers being accompanied by the Alton and Matlock brass bands. On arrival at the Towers, the family proceeded to the Chapel which was profusely decorated with flowers and packed to capacity. A solemn *Te Deum* was sung in thanksgiving for the safe arrival of the prince and princess. The *Orthodox Journal* describes the festivities which followed:

> the Earl and Countess, Prince and Princess, and Miss Talbot, presented themselves to the assembled thousands from the battlements of the terrace, and were again greeted with the most deafening shouts and the roar of cannon. The tenants, mechanics and labourers then sat down to a substantial repast, during which his Lordship, the Countess, and the Prince and Princess visited their guests, and conversed familiarly with all whom they recognised. ...The merry dance on the green succeeded the conclusion of the toasts, and the Prince, with Miss Talbot, sister to the Countess of Shrewsbury, joined with the greatest hilarity in 'tripping the light fantastic toe' for some time … Such a day of grandeur has seldom been witnessed in the county of Stafford. The beautiful gardens were thrown open to all the respectable visitors.[32]

It was the intention of the earl and countess that the prince and princess

2.5 Gwendaline Borghese: engraving from A. Zeloni, *Vie de la princesse Borghese*, 1843.

would return to Alton at regular intervals. A suite of rooms – designed by Pugin – was built as an extension to the family apartments at the north-east corner of the Towers, adding an upper storey to the former Chapel which had been converted into a drawing room.[33] Known as the Doria Suite, it consisted of bedroom, dressing room and boudoir, all lavishly furnished. Mary and Filippo did in fact spend a few more summers at Alton. They were there, for example, in 1842, and in 1846 when St Giles' Church, Cheadle, was opened. They had four children, one of whom was born at Alton in August 1846 and was named

– appropriately – Gwendaline, after Mary's sister who had died in 1840. Mary died in 1857 and was buried behind the high altar in the church of St Agnese in Rome. The Prince commissioned a fine monument by Tenarani, and was himself buried there in 1876.

The younger daughter of the earl and countess, Gwendaline Catherine **(2.5)**, was named after Gwendaline (Gwenllian), daughter of Rhys ap Gruffydd, prince of South Wales, whom Gilbert Talbot married in the thirteenth century. Gwendaline grew up into a young woman of great beauty, charm and intelligence. Her principal biographer, Alexandre Zeloni, treats her with such reverence and adulation that one might think he was recording the life of a saint.[34] When only a few days old she displayed a degree of alertness that was noted and remembered by her mother. The child was apparently fascinated by a garland of white flowers which the countess was wearing in her hair, and this may explain why Gwendaline is shown wearing such a garland in the likeness of her included in Eduard Hauser's painting of the Last Judgment over the chancel arch in the church at Cheadle. In May 1835 she was married, aged eighteen, to Marcantonio Aldobrandi, prince of Salmona, who became Prince Borghese on the death of his father in 1839. The marriage, which took place in the private chapel of the Odescalchi Palace, was conducted by Cardinal Carlo Odescalchi, and Cardinal Thomas Weld, a relative of Lord Shrewsbury.

Gwendaline Borghese, as she now was, undertook a great deal of charitable work in Rome, visiting hospitals, almshouses and orphanages, as well as visiting the poor in their homes. During the cholera epidemic of 1837 she insisted on remaining in the city to nurse the sick and dying, and when the epidemic abated she arranged care for the many orphans whose parents had fallen victim to the epidemic.

Prince and Princess Borghese had a daughter, Agnese, and three sons, Camillo, Gian Battista, and Francesco who was born in England during a family visit in 1840. They spent the summer at Alton Towers, and were there at the time of the grand reception for Queen Adelaide. Following their return to Rome in the autumn, Gwendaline contracted scarlet fever and died on 22 October, just a few weeks short of her 23rd birthday. The three boys also died, within a few weeks of their mother.

The princess was given what amounted to a state funeral. Rome came to a standstill as the cortege progressed to the church of St Mary Major. Pope Gregory XVI, who had a high regard for Gwendaline, and who spoke of her death as a public calamity, appeared at a window along the route and blessed the coffin as it passed by. He also ordered the great central doors of the basilica to be opened to admit the cortege – an honour normally reserved for royalty. After the funeral Mass the coffin was interred in the magnificent Borghese Chapel within the basilica.[35] Almost immediately there were reports of miracles having taken place in Gwendaline's name, and, because of her countless works of charity, she acquired popular saintly status. This is reflected in Zeloni's biography, and also in a collection of around 40 poems and eulogies held in the Vatican Library.

Lord Shrewsbury, to whom Gwendaline had always, according to Zeloni,

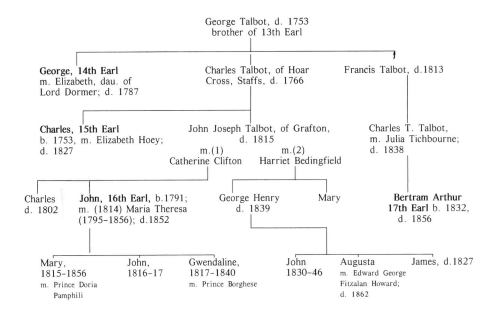

2.6 The family of John Talbot, sixteenth earl of Shrewsbury.

been *l'ange du papa*, was devastated with grief and for a time he seriously considered leaving England altogether to live in Rome so as to be near her burial place. The Shrewsburys were already spending an increasing amount of their time abroad. They had given up their London house in Stanhope Street, and when in the capital they took rooms at Mivart's Hotel (later Claridges) in Brook Street. In addition to their residence in Rome, they had the Villa Belmonte in Palermo.

The death of the Princess Borghese and her sons was not the only set of tragic circumstances to seriously affect the future prospects of the Talbot family. Although the hopes of having a son and heir to succeed to the earldom had all but faded by the 1830s, Lord Shrewsbury had a half-brother, George Henry, from his father's second marriage (2.6). George Henry died in 1839, leaving a nine-year-old son, John. The earl now looked upon this nephew as his heir and successor, and undertook his education, but then John also died, aged sixteen, in 1846. All hopes for the second, Catholic, line of the family now lay with thirteen-year-old Bertram Arthur, son of Lord Shrewsbury's cousin, Charles Talbot.[36] Bertram was brought under the tutelage of the earl and countess who provided him with rooms at Alton Towers, and a private tutor. They also took him on their visits to Italy, which they thought would benefit the boy's delicate health.[37] The French traveller and writer, Abbé Vandrival, who visited Alton in May 1847, was shown around the Towers by Bertram himself, and he was greatly impressed by the boy's knowledge, his fluency in four languages, and his general demeanour.[38] The earl's half-sister, Mary – known simply as 'Miss Talbot' – was also living at the Towers at this time. 'This lady is wonderfully kind and very pious', Vandrival observed: 'she has refused several advantageous marriage proposals and prefers to stay as she is'.

At the time of his visit to Alton, Vandrival was staying with Ambrose Phillipps de Lisle (1809-75) of Grace Dieu, Leicestershire, one of the group of Romantic Catholics who gathered around Lord Shrewsbury. He and his wife, Laura Clifford, were particularly close to the earl. Brought up in the Church of England, Phillips had converted to the Catholic faith at the age of sixteen, much to the annoyance of his father, and he was responsible for the conversion of a good many others including a near neighbour of Lord Shrewsbury's, Sir Charles Wolseley, and George Spencer, the younger brother of Earl Spencer of Althorp.[39] He had some important Staffordshire connections. Henry Ryder, bishop of Lichfield from 1824 to 1836, was an uncle by marriage, and the bishop himself was a younger son of Lord Harrowby of Sandon Hall. Phillipps was recklessly generous in his promotion of the Catholic cause in the rural communities around Grace Dieu, and he encouraged Lord Shrewsbury to show similar generosity on a grander scale around Alton.[40] Several of the earl's publications were written as letters to Ambrose Phillipps. In reality they are erudite works running, in some cases, to over 300 pages, and with copious footnotes. His *Letter Descriptive of the Estatica of Caldaro and the Addolorata of Capriana* (1841) went into a revised and enlarged second edition. It concerns Lord Shrewsbury's visits to the celebrated holy women of South Tyrol – Maria von Morl of Caldaro who was a visionary, and Domenica Lazzari of Capriana who had received the stigmata.[41] The earl's *Letters on the Present Posture of Affairs* (1841 and 1842) were concerned, amongst other things, with Irish affairs and the disputes with Daniel O'Connell. These letters reveal his quite remarkable political perspectives and breadth of scholarship, and his intellectual and spiritual relationship with Ambrose Phillipps who clearly regarded Lord Shrewsbury – eighteen years his senior – as his principal guide and mentor. It was, however, the earl's encounter with A.W.N. Pugin which did more than anything else to change the direction of his life and the scale of his benefactions to the church. Pugin found in Phillipps also a man after his own heart who shared his enthusiasm for Christian architecture and the revival of the English Catholic Church, and they became lifelong friends.[42] Within a few weeks of Pugin's first visit to Alton Towers, Lord Shrewsbury declared to Phillipps that Pugin was, 'decidedly the Catholic architect of the day with more zeal, talent, Judgment and experience than perhaps any man so young has hitherto acquired in any profession whatsoever. I look upon Pugin as the greatest acquisition for our body (i.e. the Catholic Church) for an immense time past. ... He is the man to encourage.'[43]

The precise date and exact circumstances of Lord Shrewsbury's first encounter with Pugin are somewhat uncertain. Pugin's biographer, Benjamin Ferrey, gives the date as 1832 and the location as Edward Hull's furniture shop in Wardour Street, London,[44] where the earl allegedly saw some of Pugin's drawings and requested an introduction. Lord Shrewsbury was indeed furnishing the new west wing at Alton Towers at this time, and it is known that Pugin designed some Gothic furniture for it,[45] but Hull did not set up in Wardour Street until 1834. A similar story was told by Sir Thomas Wyse, M.P. (1791-1862) who had been a friend of Lord Shrewsbury's since their schooldays at Stonyhurst.[46]

Pugin's diary, however, makes no mention of Lord Shrewsbury until 3 October 1836 when he noted his reply to some earlier communication from the earl.

By the summer of 1836 Dr Daniel Rock, domestic chaplain to Lord Shrewsbury from 1827 to 1840, had read some of Pugin's published works. He wrote to congratulate him specifically on his designs for church silverware, and offered to show him a medieval chalice and processional cross in his collection.[47] It is therefore quite possible that it was Rock who brought about Pugin's introduction to Lord Shrewsbury. Like Pugin, he was keen to revive the old English liturgy and the ornaments and vestments which went with it. In 1833 he published *Hierurgia,* a two-volume study of the Mass written mainly for the benefit of Protestants, with commentary on the text, and detailed explanations of the various Catholic doctrines connected with it. *Hierurgia* carries a dedication to Lord Shrewsbury dated 18 March – the earl's birthday. Rock's zeal for the Gothic Revival, and for the Sarum Rite were later expressed in his three-volume work, *The Church of Our Fathers* (1849-54).[48] To have found such a man already installed at Alton Towers as chaplain must have been a source of great delight to Pugin, and there is no doubt that they furthered each other's research. Pugin publicly acknowledged his indebtedness to Rock for correcting him when, early on in his career, he was on the point of violating the principles of English Christian architecture by introducing foreign elements: 'I once stood on the very edge of a precipice in this respect, from which I was rescued by the advice and arguments of my respected and reverend friend Dr. Rock, to whose learned researches and observations on Christian antiquities I am highly indebted.'[49]

The correspondence between Pugin and Rock continued long after Rock left Alton to become chaplain to Sir Robert Throckmorton at Buckland in Berkshire. His departure from Alton came about as the result of disagreements with Lord Shrewsbury who concluded that, whatever his abilities as a scholar, Rock was not the effective missionary needed to further the Catholic cause in the neighbouring villages, which had now become a priority. 'He has some good qualities, but a very weak mind which study and seclusion seem to have altogether overpowered ... I can assure you that it will be a great relief to us all to be quit of him, for he has long made himself very disagreeable.'[50] Like Pugin, however, the earl continued to correspond with Rock, who was invited back to Alton as a guest from time to time, and shortly before his death the earl invited him to stay at the Villa Belmonte in Palermo.[51] His successor as the earl's chaplain was Dr Henry Winter who stayed until 1866. He took up residence in the new buildings at St John's in Alton village, for Lord Shrewsbury had declared that after his experiences with Dr Rock he would have no more chaplains in residence at the Towers because 'they are almost sure to be spoilt.'[52]

Meanwhile, following his first visits to Alton in the summer of 1837, Pugin had begun to work for Lord Shrewsbury as architect at the Towers and as the designer of the many churches which – encouraged by Ambrose Phillipps – the earl financed wholly or in part. Though the extent of Lord Shrewsbury's benefactions has sometimes been exaggerated,[53] his financial support for the Catholic Revival was greater than that of any other individual. The three

2.7 St Alban's, Macclesfield: woodcut from *The Present State,* 1843.

buildings – or groups of buildings – which he financed entirely were Alton Castle and St John's Hospital (1840-51), and St Giles' Church, Cheadle, with its associated school, convent and presbytery. Elsewhere in Staffordshire he made very substantial contributions to St Mary's, Uttoxeter (1838-9) and St Wilfrid's, Cotton (1846-8), and a much more modest ones to the Mercy Convent at Handsworth (1840-1: then within Staffordshire), and St Mary's, Brewood (1844). Outside the county he was the principal benefactor of Mount Saint Bernard Abbey, Leicestershire (1840-4) and St Barnabas, Nottingham (1841-4), and he made large donations to St Mary's, Derby (1837-9) and St George's, Southwark (1838-48). As Pugin's first buildings began to take shape, the earl's confidence in him as a designer and architect was confirmed, so that, as early as September 1839, he wrote to Bishop John Briggs, Vicar Apostolic of the Northern District, that 'in consequence of the lamentable failure of most of our modern chapels, I have come to the resolution to subscribe to no buildings which are not erected under the designs and superintendence of Mr Pugin.'[54]

The church which Pugin and Lord Shrewsbury planned for the silk-manufacturing town of Leek never materialised, but over in Cheshire, some ten miles north-west of Leek, there was another silk town with a growing Catholic population, namely Macclesfield. Here the Pugin-Shrewsbury partnership led to the building of the large church of St Alban's (1839-41), a project which illustrates the importance to Pugin of Lord Shrewsbury's patronage outside north Staffordshire **(2.7)**. The original designs for the church had been obtained from the Catholic architect, Matthew Hadfield (1812-85), but when the earl

2.8 Hood of cope from the Shrewsbury vestments at St Chad's Cathedral, Birmingham (Jane Dew).

offered to increase his subscription by £50 a year 'should the committee agree to avail themselves of Mr. Pugin's talents,'[55] Hadfield was dismissed, and Pugin produced new designs for the first church into which he introduced a rood screen, an item which for him was to become a *sine qua non* in the design of an English parish church, and the subject of a good deal of controversy. Dr Rock laid the foundation stone on 2 April 1839 with a silver trowel handed to him by Pugin.

In addition to his financial support for the churches which Pugin designed, Lord Shrewsbury made gifts of vestments, furniture, statues, metalwork and stained glass. At Macclesfield, his gift of £1,000 towards the building costs was complemented by further contributions for the east window and the organ. Some items were specially commissioned, but others were medieval antiquities which formed part of the earl's collection or which Pugin encouraged him to buy. He gave a splendid fifteenth-century brass eagle lectern to St Chad's Cathedral,[56] and a parcel-gilt altar-cross of similar date to St John's, Alton.[57] His private collection included items formerly belonging to the Bridgettine convent of Syon, near Brentford. Among them was the Syon cope, a rare and beautiful example of English medieval needlework which had survived the final dissolution of the convent in 1558 and had been taken by the nuns to continental Europe.[58] Other medieval vestments in his collection were given to Oscott, including a fifteenth-century set from Wexford cathedral. He also owned rare copies of the Sarum Missal and Antiphonal of fifteenth- and sixteenth-century dates,[59] and a number of altarpieces. The earl's generosity extended to new items too, notably the so-called 'Shrewsbury vestments', a complete High Mass set and matching cope, made in figured red and gold fabric richly ornamented with woven braids **(2.8)**. They were commissioned for the consecration of St Chad's cathedral, Birmingham, in 1841 and are still in use there.

For his part, Pugin freely expressed his gratitude to Lord Shrewsbury, not only for the patronage which came directly from him, but also for the introductions which he was able to arrange – often at gatherings at Alton Towers – to other potential clients and to leading churchmen. When, in 1843, he published his *Apology for the Revival of Christian Architecture in England*, he prefaced it with a dedication to Lord Shrewsbury ornamented with an illuminated initial letter encapsulating the figure of the architect keeling before his noble patron and presenting a copy of his work **(2.9)**. The text, printed in black-letter pays tribute to the earl's encouragement of the Revival, and praying that he might 'continue to increase the spiritual welfare of these realms by reviving the ancient glories of the English Church'. Nor were these activities confined to England. Among the people whom Pugin met at Alton Towers was John Hyacinth Talbot (1794-1868), an uncle of the countess, and an Irish M.P. and landowner. It was largely through him that Pugin secured a number of important Irish contracts, including St Peter's College, Wexford, to which Lord Shrewsbury also contributed.[60]

The extensive correspondence which passed between Pugin and Shrewsbury amounts to over two hundred known letters. Pugin's habit of destroying most incoming letters once they had been dealt with means that very few of Lord Shrewsbury's have survived, but the ones that still exist reveal a relationship that ran much deeper than the purely professional one of architect and patron, and this was reinforced by their mutual devotion to the Catholic faith and their commitment to the revival of the English Catholic Church. Shrewsbury's letters almost invariably begin, 'My dear Pugin', the use of the surname alone indicating, in those days, a degree of familiarity close enough as to allow the more formal style of address – 'Mr Pugin' – to be dispensed with, as was then common amongst friends. Pugin, however, following standard etiquette, always began his letters with 'My dear Lord Shrewsbury,' signing off with, 'your Lordship's devoted servant ...' Many of Pugin's letters were concerned with work in progress at Alton and Cheadle, sometimes in considerable detail if the Shrewsburys were away from home for any length of time, as was often the case, but the letters also included such subjects as the Irish Question, Chartism, the restoration of the Catholic hierarchy, foreign travel, and family matters too. Earl and architect consoled each other in bereavement, as for example when the earl's younger daughter and her children died in 1840, and after Pugin's

My very good Lord,

It would be most unnatural and ungrateful in me, when putting forth a Treatise relating to the Revival of Christian Architecture in England, were I not to dedicate the same in an especial manner to your Lordship, who has been the main support in the furtherance of that good work, and to whom I am so greatly bounden.

2.9 The earl and the architect: allegorical representation of Pugin and Lord Shrewsbury: Detail from the Preface to Pugin's *Apology*, 1843.

second wife, Louisa, died quite suddenly in 1844. Lord Shrewsbury attended Louisa's funeral at St Chad's Cathedral, Birmingham, which touched Pugin deeply. When he plunged himself into a pit of black despair following the frustration of his plan to marry Mary Amherst – a relative of the earl whom he had met at Alton Towers – as his third wife, it was to Lord Shrewsbury as well as his friend John Hardman that Pugin poured out his grief in a series of heart-rending letters:

> I suffer all the agony of despair. sleep has quite forsaken me. I cannot tire myself out. I cant rest. I cannot work – as soon as I can Settle all the works I have in hand I propose quitting England & giving up my profession....I am a broken man & it is no use trying to go on – I have endeavoured to conceal what I feel, but I cannot bear the internal agony. ... I feel myself abandoned without a kind word after all I have done, & sacrificed Thousands for her sake. My dear Lord Shrewsbury is this just? Is it Christian? [61]

Quite clearly Pugin expected the earl to act as some kind of intermediary in this passionate affair. One would dearly love to know how Lord Shrewsbury responded to such a delicate situation in which social status very probably played a part, and which involved a relative on the one hand and a valued friend on the other. Pugin saw it as a match made in heaven, but Mary's mother viewed things very differently. Though Pugin claimed descent from a noble Swiss family (the Corbières of Fribourg), adopted a coat-of-arms, and for a time styled himself 'de Pugin', he was not what Mrs Amherst considered a gentleman. He was twelve years older than Mary, and already had six children from his previous marriages. Although Bishop Wiseman approved of the marriage, as did Mary's brother, Francis, who was a friend of Pugin, Mrs Amherst put about an unfounded story that Lord and Lady Shrewsbury disapproved, and concluded that she would rather see her daughter dead than married to Pugin. The affair ended when Mary, influenced by the Italian mission priest, Luigi Gentili, became a nun.

Happier times in Pugin's life were shared with Lord Shrewsbury too. When, after yet another unsuccessful courtship, he finally met and married Jane Knill – his 'first-rate Gothic woman' – the earl wrote a warm letter of congratulation: 'Providence has now rewarded you for all your past sufferings & given you a happy home for the rest of your days.'[62] A little later Lady Shrewsbury sent Jane a rosary which had been blessed for her by the Pope.[63]

Earl and architect were as different in temperament as they were in background and upbringing: the gentle, eirenic and self-effacing Lord Shrewsbury, and the ebullient, passionate Pugin. In spite of their friendship there were disagreements and misunderstandings – for example over the design of the new dining room at Alton Towers, and the plan and furnishing of St Giles', Cheadle – with Pugin pushing his ideas to the limit with an alarming degree of forthrightness and candour. Yet through all of Pugin's bluff and bluster the relationship held firm, and the factor which outweighed all others in Lord Shrewsbury's estimation of him was that Pugin viewed his whole career as a designer and architect as subservient to the Catholic cause. Their friendship extended to an invitation to Pugin to take some rest from his work and join the earl and countess on holiday at the Belgian resort of Spa in August 1841. The invitation was accepted, but, to the earl's disappointment, Pugin made an excuse to cut his visit short, and on the return journey he was attacked on board his coach and robbed in broad daylight at knifepoint by 'a ferocious looking rascal in a conical hat, moustache and beard; a compound of both infidel and republican'. The incident was described in graphic detail in Pugin's next letter to Lord Shrewsbury which included a diagram of the vehicle in which the incident took place, and the salutary lesson which Pugin had learned: 'whenever I see a man with a conical hat, a beard, and a pipe I shall avoid him most Carefully.'[64] Pugin longed to show the earl his new family home in Ramsgate, and the church of St. Augustine he was building next door to it. The earl did indeed make a visit in March 1847, and Pugin hoped he would return. During the hot summer he wrote, 'Cannot you take refuge from the London Heat by running down to St. Augustines. The Sea Breeze constantly blowing is delicious. the garden is all Roses and Honeysucles. A delightful perfume, brass beadstead with a Mattrass – every possible inducement.'[65]

Lord Shrewsbury's broad knowledge of art and sculpture, and his renown as a collector, were no doubt significant factors in his appointment in December 1841 to the Royal Fine Arts Commission set up under the presidency of Prince Albert to superintend the decoration of the New Palace of Westminster. It seems that he may not actually have taken up this appointment,[66] but nevertheless Pugin later expected him to take action over 'the monstrous selection of statues for the Palace … there are the names of Wiclif, John Knox, Bunyan – John Westley!!'[67] The earl's tastes in matters of art and architecture were broader than Pugin's, and, on account of his education and subsequent career, he had cultivated a deep love of Italy and all things Italian. How then he coped with Pugin's wholesale denigration of 'pagan' Rome – 'the Vatican is a hideous mass, and St. Peter's is the greatest failure of all'[68] – is something of a puzzle, for it became well-known. Pugin's daring outbursts most certainly provoked indignation in Rome. It was even predicted that Italian customs officers would soon be adding to their list of questions, 'Are you a Gothic Man?'[69] Meanwhile, in England, the fashionable Warwick Street Chapel, where the Talbots worshipped when in London, was for Pugin the epitome of everything that was loathsome in the Catholic architecture and furnishing of the Hanoverian period. Built almost like a theatre, with galleries on cast-iron columns painted to resemble wood, and a moulded plaster ceiling, it was nicknamed the 'Shilling Opera' where operatic settings turned the Mass into popular entertainment for which tickets could be bought in advance. The new Chapel at Alton Towers – though generally Gothic in form – was little better internally when Pugin arrived in 1837, and as part of his attempt to improve things he set about disposing of pictures and cast-iron statues which he considered inappropriate.[70]

Many of Lord Shrewsbury's gifts and benefactions in the Midlands were in support of projects initiated by Bishop Thomas Walsh (1779-1849), vicar apostolic of the Central District from 1840 to 1847 **(2.10)**. In Pugin's view, Walsh was the only bishop in England to have advanced the dignity of the Catholic Faith through his encouragement of the revival of 'true' art and architecture: 'Dr Walsh found the churches in his district worse than barns; he will leave them sumptuous erections. ... The greater part of the vestments were filthy rags, and he has replaced them with silk and gold.'[71] A project dear to the heart of Walsh, Pugin and Lord Shrewsbury was the establishment of the new College of St Mary at Oscott for the training of a new breed of English missionary priests, distinct from the homespun variety trained in small local seminaries such as the Cresswell mission, bookish clerics like Dr Rock, and different also from the Italian Passionists and Rosminians favoured by Ambrose Phillipps. Much as he himself loved Italy, Lord Shrewsbury knew that importing Italian priests who had little knowledge of English might serve only to reinforce the prejudices of those who were wont to refer to the Catholic Church as 'the Italian Mission'. 'We must,' he wrote to Phillipps, 'have a new race of zealous English missionaries such as are now bringing up at Oscott under the good Bishop and Pugin.'[72] They would learn all they needed to know about the true English liturgy and church furnishings from 'Professor' Pugin whose lectures to Oscott students were both scholarly and witty. It is not difficult to imagine the hilarity of young seminarians as they listened to Pugin's denunciation of Warwick-street styles of worship, performed by 'a set of dissipated musicians taken from the theatre and the ball-room – drowsy from their last night's orgies.'[73] Not everyone would find it so amusing, however, and before the lecture was printed in the *Catholic Magazine* Pugin was advised by the editor to tone it down. He refused.

It was Bishop Walsh who undertook the building of St Chad's Cathedral in Birmingham (1839-41), designed by Pugin with a full complement of appropriate furnishings including a controversial rood screen. The project drew together the four key figures in the Catholic Revival in the Midlands – Lord Shrewsbury, Walsh, Pugin and Hardman, all with their respective roles. Pugin viewed Walsh almost as a reincarnation of the great fourteenth-century church-building Bishop of Winchester, William Wykeham (1324-1404), with Lord Shrewsbury as the bountiful grand seigneur, and Hardman as the manufacturer of medieval art in all its richness. This quasi-medieval arrangement was one which Pugin vastly preferred to the squabbling church-building committees which generally held sway at this time, and whose members had little understanding of Christian architecture as Pugin saw it. 'Churches should not be built on the same principles as barrack contracts' he wrote in 1844, and as for church-building committees, they treated him not as a Catholic architect but just like any other businessman, ordering him in and out 'like a Pork contractor in a workhouse.'[74]

Not everybody within the Catholic Church shared Pugin's Gothic passion as enthusiastically as Bishop Walsh and Lord Shrewsbury, and his incisive wit attracted censure as well as admiration. There was hostility from some who were attached to the old styles of building and furnishing, and who thought that Pugin's influence was totally out of proportion to his standing. He was, after all only a layman, and a relatively recent (1835) convert. Bishop Peter Baines, Vicar Apostolic of the Western District, was totally opposed to Pugin and attempted to have his new-style vestments officially banned. Pugin therefore branded

2.10 Bishop Thomas Walsh, wearing the full Gothic chasuble and mitre designed by Pugin (from a painting by J. R. Herbert at St. Mary's College, Oscott).

him as a 'pagan: 'the only really pagan' Bishop we had. many others have bad taste but he was a confirmed Pagan.'[75] Among the old Catholic families of the Midlands, few were more loyal to the Church than the Throckmortons of Coughton Court (Warwickshire), yet, as Pugin reminded Lord Shrewsbury, Sir Charles Throckmorton had vowed that 'nothing I make should ever enter his house,' and as for St Chad's Cathedral, 'the only subscription he would make would be a barrel of powder to blow it up.'[76] In this case Pugin had the last word, for when Sir Charles died in 1840 his widow commissioned a memorial brass from Hardman's, and it was made, inevitably, to a design by Pugin.

In contrast to the hostility shown by Catholics such as Baines and Throckmorton, Pugin found that his thoughts on church architecture and design were being welcomed enthusiastically by members of the Anglican Church – notably those of the Cambridge Camden Society and the Oxford Architectural Society. At times he felt that Anglicans were doing more than many '*soi-disant*' Catholics to promote the Revival, thus causing even more annoyance within his own Church by expressing sympathy with 'the Oxford men' and applauding their achievements. Ambrose Phillipps went even further and dreamed of a re-union of the two Churches. Bishop Wiseman, President of Oscott from 1840 to 1847, was also sympathetic for a time, but Lord Shrewsbury was more cautious. Though knowledgeable of Anglican history and of the Catholic Revival in the Church of England,[77] he doubted the sincerity of some of the 'Oxford men' because they did not take what to him seemed to be the obvious course by converting individually. While he too hoped for reconciliation, he concluded that 'there is only one ground upon which we can meet – the authority of the Church, the doctrines of primitive antiquity as defined by (the Council of Trent), and promulgated and received as such.'[78]

Lord Shrewsbury's confidence even in clergymen of other churches who did submit to Rome must have been severely shaken by the scandalous conduct of one in whom he showed a particular interest, and to whom he showed exceptional kindness – the Revd Pierce Connelly (1804-83). A minister of the American Episcopal Church, and of Irish ancestry, Connelly resigned his parish in Natchez, Mississippi, and, along with his wife, Cornelia, travelled to Rome in the winter of 1835-6 with the intention of being received into the Catholic Church.[79] Among those whom they met soon after their arrival in Rome were Lord and Lady Shrewsbury who were wintering there, and the earl stood sponsor for them when they were eventually received in Holy Week 1836. Later in the year they visited England at Lord Shrewsbury's invitation and stayed at Alton Towers as a house guest while the family were in residence during the summer. By 1841 Connelly had become convinced that he had a vocation to the Catholic priesthood. Cornelia concurred with the view, even though she realised that this would involve separation from herself and their children, and that she herself would have to enter a religious order. Connelly took their eldest son, Mercer, to England, where he was sent to school at Stonyhurst, at Lord Shrewsbury's expense. The earl also found Connelly an appointment – pending a final decision from Rome about possible ordination –as travelling companion to a young Catholic gentleman, Robert Berkeley.[80] Both Pierce and Cornelia were together at Alton in the summer of 1843, before setting off for Rome to lay their petition for separation before the authorities.

It was no doubt on one of their visits to Alton that the Connellys first encountered Pugin, and they were also introduced to George Spencer, Ambrose Phillipps and Bishop Walsh, thus being drawn into the coterie of Romantic Catholics who frequented the Towers. They had suffered the tragic loss of two of their children: Elizabeth who died in 1839 aged only seven weeks, and two-year-old Henry who in 1840 met an horrific death by falling into a vat of boiling maple syrup. Pugin designed a beautiful headstone to be placed on the children's grave in New Orleans. Carved by George Myers, it included a crucifix and the kneeling figures of the children with their patron saints, St Henry, and St Elizabeth of Hungary.[81]

One of the most remarkable facts of this bizarre story is the ease with which the Connellys were rapidly absorbed into the society of the rich and famous, both in England and in Europe. In addition to the gatherings at Alton, they attended half a dozen aristocratic dinner-parties in Paris in the autumn of 1843 while *en route* to the Vatican. On arrival in Rome they were welcomed by Lord Shrewsbury's son-in-law, the Prince Borghese, who agreed to provide for the education of the Connellys' youngest son, Frank. They had at least two audiences with Pope Gregory XVI who appeared to take a personal interest in them.

In April 1844 the Holy See issued a deed of separation. Cornelia became a postulant at the convent of Trinità dei Monti, and just over a year later Connelly was ordained priest in the Chapel of the Trinità, where he also said his first Mass while Cornelia sang in the choir. In spite of his earlier resolve never to have another chaplain living in the house, Lord Shrewsbury installed Fr Connolly as chaplain at Alton Towers in May 1846 and gave him special responsibility for the education of his cousin, Bertram Arthur Talbot, who had now become his heir following the death of his nephew, John. It was Connelly who welcomed the Abbé Vandrival to the Towers in May 1847 and introduced him to young Bertram. Having heard Connelly's own account of his conversion, Vandrival, concluded that here was 'a great soul, strong and devout' and an admirable example of those who 'pass each day from Anglicanism to Catholicism.'[82]

Meanwhile, with the encouragement of the Pope and Bishop Wiseman, Cornelia too had come to England as foundress of the Society of the Holy Child Jesus, established first in Derby and then at St Leonard's-on-Sea. Connelly intervened, first to try to establish some control over the (Anglican) Court of Arches to reclaim Cornelia and have conjugal rights restored, with Cornelia, of course, contesting this. In May 1849 the Court of Arches ruled against him, likewise the Judicial Committee of the Privy Council to which Connelly appealed in 1851. His fury at this outcome knew no bounds. He renounced his priestly orders and the Catholic faith, then published a series of scurrilous pamphlets on the 'detestable enormities' of Rome. These culminated in an open letter addressed to Lord Shrewsbury under the title, *Reasons for abjuring allegiance to the See of Rome* (1852). In the same year he made a final appeal to the House of Commons in terms so slanderous that a debate was held over whether or not it should appear in print. Nothing came of the appeal, and Connelly eventually left England for Italy where he acted as rector of the American Episcopal Church in Florence until his death in 1883.

Possibly because of the exalted circles in which he had moved, in Rome, Paris, at Alton Towers and elsewhere, and because of his spectacular rise in the estimation of Lord Shrewsbury and some of the cardinals, including Fransoni, the Prefect of Propaganda, Pierce Connelly seems to have entertained false hopes of rapid preferment in the Church. The disappointment of these hopes, and the failure of his subsequent attempts to regain control over Cornelia, exposed a sinister side to his character. Wiseman, who had been on Lord Shrewsbury:

> But, my dear Lord, I do feel myself called to say that if on action, or otherwise, Mr. Connelly's letters are published, he will appear to Your Lordship and to others in a very different light from what he has been till now. His shallowness, vanity, wild fanaticism. … his presumption, and his ingratitude to the noble house that his give him its confidence, will I think make Your Lordship not regret that Providence has removed a baleful influence from the heir of your line.[83]

Quite apart from the anguish and embarrassment caused personally to Lord Shrewsbury by the actions of one in whom he had placed such great trust, the Connelly affair came at a most inopportune moment for the Catholic

2.11 John Talbot, sixteenth earl: engraving, 1851, from a portrait by Joseph Lynch (Alton Towers Resort Ltd).

cause in general. Plans were afoot to end the missionary status of the Catholic Church in England and to institute a regular hierarchy with English territorial titles, and with an Archbishop of Westminster at its head. Bishop Wiseman was in Rome to conduct the negotiations, and at Michaelmas 1850 Pope Pius IX issued a brief establishing thirteen dioceses to replace the old apostolic districts. Monsignor George Talbot, a relative of Lord Shrewsbury's who was a confidant of the Pope, claimed to have influenced him to send Wiseman back to England as cardinal and first Archbishop of Westminster.[84] Prior to his return to England, Wiseman issued a pastoral letter, 'From out of the Flaminian Gate', announcing the establishment of the hierarchy and his own appointment. It provoked allegations of 'Papal Aggression' and the last serious outbreak of 'no popery' violence to be seen in England. The Pierce Connelly affair served only to reinforce the prejudices of those who wished to beat the anti-Catholic – and anti-Tractarian – drum.[85]

Lord Shrewsbury was in Rome when the storm broke, and he was horrified by what he heard of the disturbances. 'All Europe is astounded at the folly and tragedy of England', he wrote to Pugin, 'and no-one can comprehend how to reconcile such absurdity with the wisdom of so great a nation'.[86] Though he supported the restoration of the hierarchy, he strongly disapproved of the insensitive way in which it had been introduced by Wiseman without any reference to the leading Catholic laity of England. He would also have liked to have seen the restoration of the Convocations, and a regular system of Catholic parishes, as a way of safeguarding the interests of the lower clergy. The earl also objected to the clumsy way in which the Prime Minister, Lord John Russell, reacted to Wiseman's pastoral letter by introducing the Ecclesiastical Titles Bill of 1851. The Bill sought to make all territorial titles illegal for Catholic bishops. He voiced his opposition to it through an open letter addressed to the Prime Minister, and in a portrait painted at this time **(2.11)**, the earl is shown holding this letter in his right hand. Although the Bill became law, it was never enforced, and it was repealed 20 years later. Pugin played his own part in the furore of 1851. First he published *An Earnest Address on the Establishment of the English Catholic Hierarchy* in which he set out the contentious thesis that in the sixteenth century the English Catholic Church had been betrayed by bishops who had concurred with the policies of Henry VIII rather than lose their wealth and influence. At the time of his death Pugin was working on *An Apology for the Separated Church of England* in which he carried his earlier argument further to the extent that it came to be believed in some quarters that Pugin – disappointed by the hostility of many of the hierarchy to his views on church architecture, and alarmed by the growth of Ultramontanism – may even have considered becoming an Anglican.

Following the death of the Princess Borghese in 1840, Lord and Lady Shrewsbury had been spending an increasing amount of time in Italy. The earl had come to the conclusion that the most practical and lasting way in which he could further the Catholic cause was by putting money into church-building, and he calculated that by staying away from Alton during the summer months he could save at least £2,000 a year which was enough for half a small church or a whole monastery; 'and a church, or chapel, or monastery will endure (it is to be hoped) for many a long day, and be infinitely more instrumental in the conversion of the people than any personal exertions we can make at home.'[87] Though the Shrewsbury estates were vast, they were strictly entailed, which meant that there were definite limits to the resources which the earl could allocate to church-building, and the earl was conscious more than anyone else of the contrast between the enormous private expenditure that were required to fulfill his social obligations at Alton Towers, and the relatively small sums of money which he was able to give to the Church.[88] The virtual closure of Alton Towers as a residence for long periods was a sacrifice he was pleased to make; the census returns for 1851 reveal that the number of domestic staff had been pared to a minimum, and the earl also sold off all but a very few of his fine horses and closed down the stud farm for which Alton had once been famous. He dressed simply, ate frugally, abstained almost totally from alcohol, and accounted very strictly for every penny of expenditure. This latter point is made very clear in his correspondence with Pugin. He considered postal envelopes to be a complete waste of money, and continued instead simply to fold his letters and seal them with wax in the old-fashioned way. 'You should write on a single sheet', he told Pugin, 'and not put it into an envelope – if it weighs ever so little it pays double and that is a heavy charge in these sad times.'[89] Such economies were born not of miserliness, but of the earl's overwhelming desire to divert as much of his disposable income as possible into the furtherance of the Catholic cause. In addition to donations and gifts of furnishings and vestments to individual churches, he was able to make regular

2.12 Funeral of Lord
Shrewsbury in the Towers
Chapel (*Illustrated London
News*, 25 December 1852).

contributions to Bishop Walsh's general fund for the support of the Catholic
missions. Lord Shrewsbury was the first President of the Catholic Institute
established in 1838 to circulate Catholic tracts, organise lectures, and support
schools; and also lay President of the *Oeuvre* set up in the following year to
organise nation-wide collections in aid of the propagation of the Faith.[90] In
1846 he was honoured by the Pope, who appointed him Knight Grand Cross
of the Order of St Gregory, an award which he doubtless valued more than all
his territorial lordships.

Among those who were in regular contact with the earl and countess
during their absences in Italy were Pugin and Ambrose Phillipps. Pugin kept
them informed of the continuing work at Alton Towers, St John's Hospital and
the Castle, and in January 1851 Lord Shrewsbury asked him to send sketches
of the north and south fronts of the Towers to show how the great dining hall
and other new rooms were progressing.[91] When Pugin became very seriously
ill at the beginning of 1852, the earl wrote twice offering to accommodate him
at the Villa Belmonte in Palermo, and sending details of trains and steamers.
'I know of no place where he could pass the Spring and summer with such
advantage', he wrote to Jane Pugin. 'If he would make up his mind to remain
a whole twelve month with us, so much the better.'[92] Pugin had never been
convinced that Sicily was a healthy place in which to live. He had heard that
the gardens of the villa were infested with snakes and lizards, he wondered how

Lord Shrewsbury could stand the summer heat in Palermo, and feared for his health in such a climate. 'There should be a law made as for the Queen, that you should not go above a certain distance from your dominions. I assure your Lordship that I am always in a most anxious state when you go so far away.'[93]

On Pugin's fortieth birthday – 1 March 1852 – Lord Shrewsbury wrote to him from Palermo to say how delighted he and the countess had been to receive news of his quite sudden recovery. He also expressed his hopes for the proposed new cathedral at Shrewsbury of which he was to be the principal benefactor with Pugin, of course, as architect:

> [The Bishop] wrote me an account of you the other day & spoke of you with great affection & in the highest terms. He is delighted with is conference with you upon his little Cathedral. I am anxious to see the plans &c. Give as much decoration inside as the money will admit, but as little outside as possible. … Please God we shall be laying the foundation stone about this time next year. I hope it stands upon a rock & will stand firm till the last day. I am sure you will make a neat little job of it.[94]

Pugin had already made preliminary sketches for the cathedral of Our Lady, Help of Christians, and St Peter of Alcantara, which was to be built for the newly-created Catholic diocese of Shrewsbury. It was to prove to be the very last of their church-building projects. Neither of them lived to see it take shape, and the earl and his architect never met again. Pugin's recovery proved only temporary; he soon relapsed into serious illness, and died at Ramsgate on 14 September 1852.[95] Lord Shrewsbury's reaction to the news is contained in a letter to Dr Rock, sent from Geneva on 25 September: 'Poor Pugin's very sudden departure really makes me sad; tho' I fancy we shall miss him more on our return than now. It is most fortunate, however, that he lived long enough to found and leave a complete school behind him in every branch of his art, his son will prove the most effective as well as the brightest ornament.'[96]

The fears which Pugin had earlier expressed for Lord Shrewsbury's health were not unjustified. In October 1852 the earl and countess left Rome for the Villa Belmonte, but the heat in Palermo was too excessive for Lady Shrewsbury, and they decided to return to Rome. Before they could start back the earl fell ill with malaria. His local physician advised that he be taken to Naples, where he was attended by Mr Roskelly, the surgeon to the British Embassy, but he died on 9 November, aged 61. The grief-stricken countess was herself taken ill with malaria, but recovered; meanwhile the Prince and Princess Doria made the preliminary arrangements for the funeral. The earl's body was placed in a copper coffin which was then filled with sprits of wine, and sealed, before being brought back to England where it first lay in state in St George's Cathedral in Southwark, the last of Pugin's great churches to have been opened, and where a magnificent east window and other gifts testified to Lord Shrewsbury's generosity.

Meanwhile, plans were set in motion for the funeral at Alton. So much needed to be provided and arranged that the date had to be set as late as 14 December, over a month after the earl's death. The arrangements were overseen by Edward Pugin, still fresh from superintending his father's funeral at Ramsgate

2.13 Detail of cope made for Lord Shrewsbury's funeral, now at St Chad's Cathedral, Birmingham (Jane Dew).

only seven weeks earlier, in close collaboration with his brother-in-law, John Hardman Powell, and John Hardman himself, and with Lord Shrewsbury's painter and decorator, Thomas Kearns, supervising the work on site. Hardman's provided all the necessary furnishings and materials, down to the last details. The earl's coffin was of Spanish mahogany covered in crimson velvet. There was a large floriated cross on the lid, and other brass fittings including the famous Talbot hounds. While the Towers Chapel was reordered, the earl's body lay in state in the Talbot Gallery at the west end of the house, where a temporary altar was set up for the daily offering of Requiem Mass.

An engraving made at the time **(2.12)** shows how the Chapel was rearranged for the funeral. The windows were covered with black drapery, also the most decorative parts of the screenwork on the east wall. The sanctuary with its glorious altarpiece was screened off, and an altar vested appropriately for a funeral Mass was set up in front of it. In complete contrast to these sombre surroundings, a large and richly-decorated *chapelle ardente* was constructed in front of the altar. Supported on twelve pillars of carved and gilded wood, it consisted of a great gabled canopy ornamented with the emblems of the earldoms of Shrewsbury, Waterford and Wexford. On the tops of eight of the pillars stood Talbot hounds supporting branched candlesticks, and branched candlesticks also stood on the ground, making a total of between three and four hundred candles, hence the term *chapelle ardente*. Although the textile components were specially made for the occasion, it is almost certain that the hearse itself was the one designed by Pugin for the funeral of his wife, Louisa, and subsequently donated by him to St Chad's Cathedral.[97] Beneath the hearse stood a black-draped catafalque on which the coffin was placed.

In the Hardman metalwork daybook, four large folios are filled with entries relating to the earl's funeral.[98] These include the coffin, the candlesticks and branches for the *chapelle ardente*. Textile items included over 2,000 yards of black drapes, fringes and trimmings for the Towers Chapel and for St John's, Alton, where the interment was to take place, and the great pall to cover the coffin. This must have been one of the most time-consuming items, and was made by John Hardman's sister, Lucy Powell, of Frederick Street, Birmingham, and her associates Lucy and Winefred Brown. Made of black velvet, the pall was ornamented with a large embroidered cross, the *prest d'accomplir* motto of the Talbots, the earl's monogram and the Shrewsbury lion. In addition four black copes were made for the officiating clergy, and a richer one with embroidery for the Bishop of Birmingham, Dr Ullathorne, who was to preside (**2.13**). This, along with the pall and a few elements from the *chapelle ardente*, survive at St Chad's Cathedral.

At the funeral, Dr Ullathorne was assisted by the Bishops of Clifton, Northampton and Shrewsbury. 150 secular priests were present, along with representatives of the various religious orders, and the choir of St Chad's Cathedral were suitably vested in surplices and black caps.[99] The eulogy was given by Dr Henry Weedall, who had been President of Oscott in the 1830s, and who paid tribute to the earl's role as benefactor and as the recognised leader of the Catholic laity. He also quoted from a tribute written by Ambrose Phillipps testifying to the simplicity and gentleness of the earl's character: 'God had placed him amongst the princes of his people, but he walked through the gorgeous Halls of his glorious Palace as few poor men would pace the lowliest cabin. No one ever saw a haughty look or a disdainful smile on his placid face. No one ever heard a discourteous word from his lips.'

Weedall's eulogy was subsequently printed as a pamphlet,[100] and other tributes followed. Wiseman praised the earl's social work as much as his generosity to the Church,[101] while the *Catholic Directory* for 1854 carried a 20-page memoir written by the Revd Edward Price. This was quite exceptional, and not only on account of its length, for, as it was pointed out, it was the policy of the Directory to print tributes only to clergy of the highest rank. The most telling testimonial of all, however, was the silent one paid by the ordinary people of Alton and Farley on the day of the funeral itself. After the requiem in the Towers Chapel the coffin was taken for burial on the Gospel side of the altar in St John's church in Alton. Crowds of people joined in the funeral procession, and it was remembered that when the head of the procession reached the doors of the church, the carriage bearing the coffin could be seen emerging from the archway of Pugin's gatehouse nearly a mile away in the valley below.[102] Whatever else Lord Shrewsbury may have been – England's premier earl, the leading Catholic layman of his day, the wealthy patron of Pugin, and the father-in-law of princes – to the people of the locality he was known by that grandly simple title 'the Good Earl'. The 'gorgeous Halls of his glorious Palace' were stripped of their fabulous treasures within a few years of his death; but on the opposite side of the valley the cluster of buildings in Alton village, along with the great church at Cheadle, continue to serve the purposes for which they were conceived and built, and these are his enduring memorial.

3.1 The east front of the old 'Alveton Lodge' and old round tower incorporated into the new buildings at Alton Towers (Michael Fisher).

3

Living the medieval dream:
Pugin at Alton Towers

'the mansions erected by our ancestors were not the passing whim of a moment, or mere show places raised at such an extravagant cost as impoverished some generations of heirs to the estates, but solid, dignified, and Christian structures'
A.W.N. Pugin, True Principles

Pugin's domestic architecture included schemes for noblemen's houses which were very different in concept and design from both the neo-Classical and the Gothic-style houses that had sprung up across England in the eighteenth and early nineteenth centuries. In Pugin's view, Classical, with its 'pagan' origins in pre-Christian Greece and Rome, was no more appropriate for an English gentleman's house than it was for a church, but there were other considerations too. Neo-Classical buildings were generally rectangular in plan and elevation – box-like structures planned from the outside inwards, with all the various rooms having to be fitted within pre-determined spaces. As against this, Pugin argued his 'true principles' of allowing the plan of a building to govern its elevation, and fitness for purpose. An old English house was planned from the inside out, each part of the building clearly defined according to its function, thus producing an irregular composition with differing roof-levels, cross-gabling, tall chimneys, and windows which varied in size and form, depending on the function of each room, rather than being disposed in uniformly regular rows.

If Pugin despised the neo-Classical, he was no less critical of neo-medieval castles and the 'abbey style' of country house, both of which had become fashionable in the earlier stages of the Gothic Revival Both, he argued, purported to be what they were manifestly not, and neither was really suitable for its purpose. Castles were places of defence garrisoned by soldiers, and abbeys were for communities of monks and nuns. Pugin's ideal of a Catholic mansion, based no doubt on his knowledge of surviving examples such as Penshurst Place (Sussex), was illustrated and described in his *True Principles of Christian or Pointed Architecture* of 1843: 'substantial appropriate edifices, suited by their scale and arrangement for the purposes of habitation.' Unfortunately, he never had the opportunity of realising this vision in its entirety. The houses which he built for himself – St Marie's Grange at Salisbury, and The Grange at Ramsgate – reflected admirably Pugin's principles of design and construction, but they were not on the scale of a nobleman's country residence. In practice, he had to content himself with additions and improvements to existing houses, such as Scarisbrick Hall (Lancashire) and Bilton Grange (Warwickshire).[1] Moreover, some of these commissions obliged him to work on buildings created by other architects in the much-reviled 'castellated' style, such as Taymouth Castle (Perthshire), and the equally-despised 'abbey style' such as Alton Towers, the Staffordshire seat of the Talbot earls of Shrewsbury.

The history of Alton Towers is about the expansion, between 1810 and 1852 of a small hunting-lodge known as Alveton Lodge (Alveton being the ancient form of Alton), into what was allegedly the largest privately owned house in Europe.[2] Located on Bunbury Hill, on the opposite side of the Churnet Valley to Alton village, and within a medieval deer-park, Alveton Lodge was used by the Talbots on rare visits to their Staffordshire estates , their principal residence being Heythrop in Oxfordshire. The lodge consisted of a small Georgian building reserved for the use of the Talbots, and, at the rear of it, a farm-house which was leased to a local family. At the junction of the two there was an old round tower, possibly of medieval origin, and most certainly of some antiquity when the expansion of the house began in about 1810 **(3.1)**. This tower was carefully preserved through all the subsequent alterations, and is still standing today as the only round tower amongst the many after which the mansion was ultimately named.

It was Charles Talbot, fifteenth earl of Shrewsbury, who began the work of extending Alton Lodge into a substantial summer residence for the family. Several architects were employed: Thomas Hopper (1776-1856), William Hollins (1763-1843), and Thomas Allason (1790-1852), the latter being the most significant. The fifteenth earl, a Fellow of the Society of Antiquaries, was aware of his family's medieval roots in north Staffordshire, and this may have influenced his decision. The incorporation of the east front of the old lodge and the round tower into the new buildings seems to have been a deliberate attempt to preserve a part of his heritage when practical considerations might have required their demolition. The 'abbey style' was chosen, partly because it was fashionable, but also on account of the Talbots' staunch Catholicism, and their ancestors' connections with the former Cistercian abbey of Croxden, the ruins of which lay in the neighbourhood. As completed by Thomas Allason in about 1820, Alton Abbey had an imposing north front, the dominant features of which were a lofty entrance hall with a large ecclesiastical-looking window over the doorway and a cross on the gable, a long gallery, and a chapel with a polygonal apse and traceried windows, these three elements being set transversely to the rest of the building **(3.2)**. The house was set in extensive grounds which included the famous valley gardens created out of a waterless rocky wilderness by the fifteenth earl and completed by the sixteenth who succeeded to the titles and estates in 1827. Following a fire which gutted their house at Heythrop in 1831, Alton became the principal residence. A great west wing was added by a local builder-architect, Thomas Fradgley of Uttoxeter (1801-1883) who was clerk of works at the Abbey, and Fradgley, along with Joseph Potter of Lichfield, built the new chapel on the east side of the house in 1832. It was at this time that the house was renamed Alton Towers, reflecting the gradual change in

3.2 North front of Alton Abbey as completed in around 1820. Aquatint by Thomas Allason (William Salt Library, Stafford).

character from 'abbey' to a place in which the Talbots' illustrious medieval past was recreated and celebrated, and the addition of towers and battlements in the 'castellated style'. On first arriving at the Towers in 1837 Pugin was therefore confronted by something of an architectural hybrid which contained many features that would have annoyed him, such as the extensive use of window tracery made of cast iron and timber instead of stone, cast-iron tracery panels attached to doors and painted to look like wood, and vaulting made of *papier-maché* and plaster; precisely the kind of 'sham' he scathingly denounced in his writings.

That Pugin should have carried out alterations and additions at the home of his wealthiest and most influential patron is hardly surprising. It was not until the 1990s, however, that the extent of his contributions to this vast Gothic mansion was fully perceived, surveyed and recorded,[3] and they were considerably more extensive and significant than was formerly thought **(3.3)**. It is now known that they comprised the Talbot Gallery and the Talbot Passage linking the gallery to the West Wing (1839-40), the remodelling of the Octagon (1839-42), substantial fortifications on the north and east sides of the house (1842), new kitchens and servants' accommodation (1841-9), the Doria Rooms (1843), new rooms over the Great Drawing Room and on the north front (1850-2), conservatories on the south side of the house, and other garden buildings (1846-48), the Counslow and Station Lodges (1841 and 1849), and the Great Dining Room (1849-52). Pugin completely altered the internal appearance of the Chapel (1840 and 1851); and he redecorated the Great Drawing Room, Long Gallery,

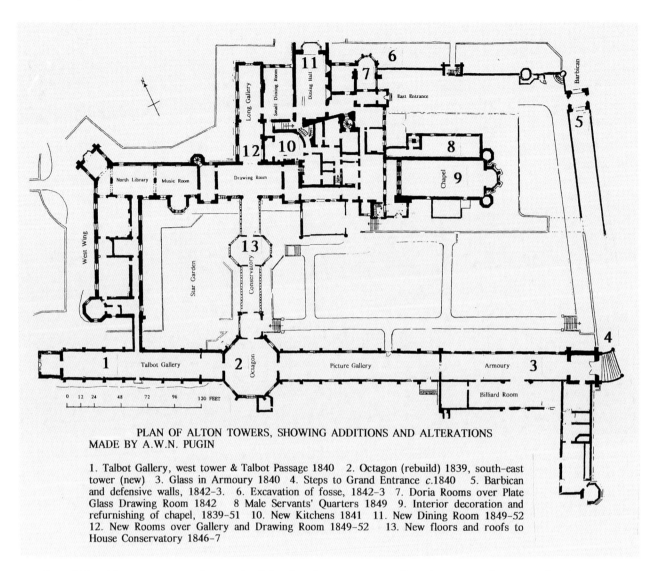

PLAN OF ALTON TOWERS, SHOWING ADDITIONS AND ALTERATIONS
MADE BY A.W.N. PUGIN

1. Talbot Gallery, west tower & Talbot Passage 1840   2. Octagon (rebuild) 1839, south-east tower (new)   3. Glass in Armoury 1840   4. Steps to Grand Entrance c.1840   5. Barbican and defensive walls, 1842-3.   6. Excavation of fosse, 1842-3   7. Doria Rooms over Plate Glass Drawing Room 1842   8 Male Servants' Quarters 1849   9. Interior decoration and refurnishing of chapel, 1839-51   10. New Kitchens 1841   11. New Dining Room 1849-52   12. New Rooms over Gallery and Drawing Room 1849-52   13. New floors and roofs to House Conservatory 1846-7

3.3 Plan of Alton Towers showing Pugin's additions. (Michael Fisher).

and several of the family rooms, as well as designing furniture for the new West Wing, and stained glass, metalwork and woodwork for other rooms.

This catalogue of structural and decorative work reveals Pugin as the Romantic in his completion of the dramatic galleries, the ecclesiastical designer in his transformation of the Chapel, the military engineer in his construction of the barbican and other defences, and the man of *The True Principles* in his masterly creation of the great dining room. 'You will be greatly pleased with the works at Alton', he wrote to Ambrose Phillipps in 1851, 'which have improved the house amazingly.'[4] In the fifteen years following Pugin's arrival at the Towers in 1837 there seems to have been no time at which some major work was not in progress or in prospect, and much remained unfinished at the time of his death in 1852.

When Pugin began work he discovered an invaluable asset in the seasoned band of builders and craftsmen who had been busy there for many years and who therefore possessed all the skills that he needed. Their names appear in the Alton estate accounts along with their trades, most of them being members of local families employed at the Towers through several generations. Pugin would have come to know them well, instilling into them his own ideas and methods of Gothic construction and decoration. Some are mentioned from time to time in his correspondence with Lord Shrewsbury. The most important were the Bailey brothers, John and Peter, who were stonemasons. Their father, Thomas Bailey, had figured prominently in the building of Alton Abbey thirty years earlier, and Bailey descendants still live in the village. The names of Peter and John are carved on the tower of the new Towers Chapel (1832) as the masons responsible for the construction of this most elaborately decorated external feature of the entire building, and also on one of the cascades in the gardens. Such projects demonstrated what they could do, and the later stonework of the Towers tells its own story of how Pugin educated these men in the 'Real Thing'. Nowhere is this seen more clearly than in the construction of windows. The earlier ones generally have stone frames, constructed after the fashion of timber frames, with one stone set vertically to form a jamb, and arched pieces let in above, whereas Pugin, following medieval precedent, built the jambs in horizontal courses, with the moulded stones tailing into the wall. The Baileys' skill and expertise, and Pugin's evident confidence in them, helps to explain why George Myers (1803-75), the trusted builder who worked so extensively for Pugin elsewhere, was used only for the more specialised stone-carving at Alton and Cheadle.[5]

In addition to the stonemasons there was a plasterer named Samuel Firth. Already in his seventies when Pugin arrived, Firth had executed the deeply moulded plaster ceilings in the State Drawing Room and Libraries, and Pugin used him for work in the Octagon. Then there was Thomas Harris, a skilled joiner, who carried out much of Pugin's woodwork at the Towers and in the churches, and Thomas Kearns (c.1799-1858) who was Lord Shrewsbury's plumber, glazier and ornamental painter. Kearns was a key figure in the decoration of rooms at the Towers, and he also worked in the churches at Cheadle and Alton. Pugin used him further afield too, for example at St Barnabas' Cathedral, Nottingham, and St Wilfrid's, Warwick Bridge (Cumbria). These, and many more, worked under the direction of John Bunn Denny (1810-90), who supplanted Thomas Fradgley as clerk of works, and who had responsibilities for the churches as well as the work at the Towers. It was a part of Denny's brief to keep Pugin informed, in between his visits to Alton, of progress on the Towers and the other buildings, and to receive his instructions.[6] Pugin in turn wrote reports for Lord Shrewsbury who spent considerable periods abroad at his villa near Naples. Their concern was by no means confined to the house itself. Pugin and Denny were also involved with the design and construction of ornamental features in the famous Towers gardens.

One of the many extraordinary features of Alton Towers was the series of linked galleries on the south side of the house through which visitors would be conducted before entering the house itself, the former entrance on the north front having been superseded by a new and imposing grand entrance on the east side. Passing under a formidable barbican, and along a gently rising driveway between two huge curtain-walls, they would arrive at the steps of

3.4 St Michael's Gallery, Fonthill Abbey, was the possible inspiration for the galleries at Alton (John Rutter, *The Delineations of Fonthill* [1823]).

a lofty entrance tower flanked by a pair of stone talbots – the dogs associated with the family coat-of-arms at least since the days of the first earl, 'the Great Dogge Talbot' himself (*c.*1384–1453). At the top of the steps visitors would enter through a pair of immense doors, nailed on the outside, and emblazoned on the inside with the full armorial bearings of the Earl of Shrewsbury. A second pair, similarly embellished, led into the 120-foot-long Armoury filled with over 300 items of arms and armour. Beyond was the Picture Gallery, its walls lined with paintings by celebrated artists of the Italian, French, Flemish and German schools. Another change of scene awaited in the Octagon hall, reminiscent of the chapter house of Wells Cathedral, with a central column and vaulted ceiling. Ahead lay the Talbot Gallery, the most splendid of all the galleries, the view into which was filtered by a glazed timber screen. Having caught a tantalizing glimpse of what lay beyond, visitors would be directed by a 90-degree turn out of the Octagon into the House Conservatory filled with the colour and scent of exotic plants, and the songs of birds in gilded cages, before entering the house itself by way of the Great Drawing Room. Thus the Entrance Tower, Armoury, Picture Gallery, Octagon, Conservatory – over 150 yards of them – were no more than a prelude to the sumptuous enfilades of state rooms which lay ahead, crammed with costly furniture and works of art.

The scale and richness of these Romantic interiors exceeded even those of Fonthill Abbey (1796-1812) built on the outskirts of Salisbury by James Wyatt (1746-1813) for millionaire-eccentric William Beckford. No documentary evidence survives to prove that Wyatt had ever worked at Alton, and in any case these buildings date from a decade and more after his death. Yet the Fonthill galleries, linked by a central octagon, were undoubtedly the inspiration for the Alton galleries; so much becomes clear by comparison with John Rutter's illustrations to *The Delineations of Fonthill* (1823) **(3.4)**, while his account of how the glories of Fonthill were revealed little by little to the eye of the visitor could apply equally to Alton which, when the galleries were begun, was still known as 'The Abbey'.

The similarities extended to small Romantic details. Beckford kept a liveried dwarf in his entrance-hall to emphasise the height of the building; at Alton the Talbots had a blind Welsh harper, named in the 1841 census as Edward Jervis, who lived in the Harper's Cottage (subsequently called the Swiss Cottage) at the head of the valley gardens. A drawing of the Armoury from this time by Samuel

3.5 A Romantic interior: the Armoury at Alton Towers, with Lord Shrewsbury's harper, Edward Jarvis. Drawing by Samuel Rayner, *c.*1840 (Potteries Museum, Stoke-on-Trent).

3.6 Pugin's Talbot Gallery: 'The last and noblest of the halls in Alton Towers' (William Adam, 1851). Drawing by Samuel Rayner, *c.*1840 (Potteries Museum, Stoke-on-Trent).

Rayner shows him sitting at the entrance, from where his gentle playing and singing would carry down the galleries and also out into the grounds, much to the delight of visitors **(3.5)**.

Given his distaste for shams, and his clear detestation of Wyatt as 'the monster of architectural depravity', it is somewhat ironic that soon after his arrival at Alton Pugin should have been given the task of completing a set of rooms so reminiscent of Fonthill, which had in any case become a modern ruin by this time, and a byword for architectural folly on a grand scale, following its collapse in 1825. Yet Pugin's work on the Alton galleries effected an even closer resemblance, principally through the addition, in 1839-40, of the Talbot Gallery **(3.6)** to the west side of the Octagon which thus became – as at Fonthill and as it was to be at the New Palace of Westminster – the central element of an axial system of linked chambers.

The combined east-west length of the Alton Galleries and Octagon (480 feet) far exceeded that of the principal axis at Fonthill (280 feet). Every device of lighting, space, and rising levels was exploited to the full, and the view from the new Gallery through the entire range was breathtaking:

> When the reader recollects that the whole of this vista is filled with works of art of the noblest character, or with the remains of antiquity of the most interesting kind, he may have some idea of the magnificent coup d'oeil which presents itself, and of the difficulty we find in giving anything like an adequate description of it.[7]

The construction of the Talbot Gallery – on a level higher than that of the existing buildings – involved raising the walls of the adjoining Octagon by several feet (3.7). The central column had also to be raised. Since the walls were not strong enough to support a stone vault, Pugin had to agree to the reinstatement of sham vaulting made of plaster, and to the retention of cast-iron screenwork at the Picture Gallery entrance. The new Gallery was furnished with two massive chimneypieces similar to the one in the Great Hall at Scarisbrick, and likewise surmounted by suits of armour. Thomas Willement (1786-1871)

Octagon
Alton Towers
August 11th

3.7 The Octagon, Alton Towers. Pugin's screen to the Talbot Gallery lies ahead, and on the right is the entrance to the house conservatory. Watercolour, 1870, attributed to Lavinia Littleton (private collection).

painted over a hundred shields for the heraldic frieze, and Hardman supplied a set of eight sixteen-light coronae bearing the Talbot motto *Prest d'accomplir*. It was the *pièce de résistance* of the entire house. Visitors arriving by the Grand Entrance would catch glimpses of it through Pugin's openwork screen as they passed through the Octagon to the House Conservatory. Only when they had completed the tour of the house would they return, via the West Wing, to enter, as the climax of their visit, what was described as 'the last and noblest of the halls in Alton Towers.'[8]

Even in the Talbot Gallery Pugin had to agree to cast-iron skylights with Gothic tracery to match those of the 1820s Picture Gallery, along with cast-iron roof trusses and corbels cast in the shape of talbot hounds. He also oversaw the copying of two medieval tombs, with recumbent effigies cast in plaster, to stand in the Octagon in place of inappropriate Classical statuary which was removed to other parts of the house. Casts were taken from the tomb of the first earl of Shrewsbury ('The Grand Talbot') in St Alkmund's, Whitchurch, and that of Nicholas Fitzherbert at Norbury Church (Derbyshire), by the plasterer Samuel Firth, now aged 76, under Pugin's instructions. In March 1841 Pugin wrote to Lord Shrewsbury: 'Old Firth the plasterer will be sent off by the middle of the month to Whitchurch to cast the Grand Talbot. He has done the Fitzherbert's beautifully.'[10] The taking of casts had a scholarly purpose too. A second cast of the Fitzherbert tomb was taken, and this was presented by Lord Shrewsbury, along with other casts, to the Oxford Society for Promoting the Study of Gothic Architecture, again under Pugin's supervision.[10] Pugin also had to spend a good deal of time and energy in creating an equestrian figure of the first earl in full armour, mantle and coronet, to stand on a high plinth at the upper end of the Armoury. Much correspondence passed between Pugin and Lord Shrewsbury over the making of the figure and the horse, details of the armour, sword, mantle, and much else.[11] A facsimile of the famous 'sword of the Talbot' was made by Hardman, along with a bejewelled coronet.[12] The project took over two years to complete, and it drew Pugin into dealings with armourers in both England and France, antique-dealers, *papier-mâché* and tailors, along with visits to the Tower of London to study equestrian armour on show there. No doubt Pugin's earlier career in the London theatres helped in the creation of these stage-set pieces and their dramatic surroundings, designed to recreate the Talbots' illustrious medieval past. These were, after all, the years of the spectacular but rain-sodden Eglinton Tournament[13] and a Gothic ball hosted by the Prince Consort and Queen Victoria at which they appeared in the guise of Edward III and Queen Philippa. The compromises, and the constraints under which Pugin had to work in his earlier years at Alton, help to account for the all-or-nothing stance he adopted a decade later over the design of the new dining room. Yet the Great Dining Room – or Banqueting Hall – was also an ingredient in the 'romance of facts' in which Pugin surrounded Lord Shrewsbury with every possible reminder of all that his medieval ancestors had been, including a stained glass image of the Grand Talbot which would face the earl every time he took his place on the dais to preside, as Pugin believed he would, over gatherings of family and tenantry in true medieval fashion.

Meanwhile, on the other side of the south wall, Pugin built vast new kitchens equipped with the most up-to-date ovens, ranges and stoves that Birmingham ironmongers could produce.

Whereas most architects of country houses sited the kitchens as far away from the dining room as possible, on account of fire hazards and the risk of cooking smells pervading the state rooms, Pugin placed the new kitchens at Alton as close as possible, and provided the cooking apparatus with efficient ventilators and flues. Ahead of his time in many aspects of his domestic architecture, he was able to fuse modern technology with medieval dream.

Pugin's additions to the Armoury and entrance included a set of windows executed by William Warrington depicting William I and various Talbot ancestors, and the exterior steps with their attendant stone talbots. It was in the Octagon and Talbot Gallery that Pugin was able to make some of his boldest statements. At the Gallery entrance he set a glazed Perpendicular-style wooden screen, and in the south wall of the Octagon a five-light window with glass by Willement depicting Talbot bishops, which further emphasised the ecclesiastical character of this room. On the south side he built a square tower with pyramid-capped bartizans at the corners, much in the Scottish baronial style. This was probably intended as a look-out associated with the defences constructed in 1842.

It is possible that Pugin's satirical critique of 'castellated architecture' in *The True Principles* (1841) was inspired by one of the many irritating features he found at Alton, where the fortified grand entrance tower with its great studded doors led eventually to the state rooms via the House Conservatory which was completely unprotected.

> On one side of the house machicolated parapets, embrasures, bastions, and all the show of strong defence, and round the corner a conservatory leading to the principal apartments through which a whole company of horsemen might penetrate at one smash into the very heart of the mansion! – for who would hammer against nailed portals when he could kick his way through the greenhouse?[14]

It was not, however, considerations of style, nor the correcting of the errors of his unenlightened predecessors, that were uppermost in Pugin's mind when he undertook extensive fortification of this side of the house in 1842. This was the year of widespread Chartist agitation, with mass meetings, demonstrations and riots in the Potteries towns, and in July striking miners caused disturbances and damage in the Cheadle area. Pugin's diary for 1842 shows that he was at Alton for several days in June-July, and that Lord Shrewsbury was also in residence at this time. While at Alton Pugin noted in his diary under 18 July, 'Home fortified against the colliers,' which has been taken by some to refer to Pugin's own house, but this is unlikely since at this time his family home was in Cheyne Walk, Chelsea. It is much more probable that he was referring to some provisional arrangements at the Towers. As a committed Catholic, Pugin was acutely sympathetic to the needs of the poor and underprivileged, but at the same time he detested socialism and feared revolution, and said that he would 'shoot any Chartist as I would a rat or a mad dog.'[15] On 22 July he travelled through Stoke-on-Trent, calling on Herbert Minton whose workers, like those in other potteries, had struck in sympathy with the miners who were then marching towards Macclesfield. He wrote back anxiously to Lord Shrewsbury: 'I do not perceive any immediate danger, but your Lordship should not by any means relax in vigilance and have all made fast at night till things are really settled. I have not yet got the brass guns as I have heard of a better market for them.'[16]

Other sources make it clear that very substantial fortifications were being constructed at Alton in 1842 and into the following year. In the first place there is the Barbican gateway at the north-east corner of the house, which bears the date 1842, and is a serious piece of defensive architecture (3.8). Associated with it are the high walls which run southwards either side of the carriage drive, giving protection to the hitherto vulnerable east side of the mansion, and the east terrace wall which communicates with the Barbican at its upper levels. These were in themselves considerable feats of civil engineering carried out at some speed; added to which was the excavation of a deep fosse, or ditch, along the whole of the north front, under the very walls of the house itself. The house was built on solid sandstone bedrock which was exposed as the work progressed, and then concealed by the addition of weatherings. The work caused Pugin some anxiety, and it was commented on by at least one foreign observer.[17] The Chartists never came, but the fortifications marked an important stage in Pugin's attempt to transform a Georgian mansion of the romantic 'abbey style' into something more serious.

Amongst the more recently completed buildings at Alton Towers at the time of Pugin's arrival, none was more significant than the new Chapel which had been built on to the east end of the house in 1832-3. It replaced the original private Chapel on the north front, which now became the Plate Glass Drawing Room, with its Gothic windows altered to allow views across the parkland. Lord Shrewsbury and Dr Daniel Rock, his chaplain from 1827 to 1840 and a noted liturgical scholar, had a hand in designing the new building in the 'royal chapel' style with tall ogee-capped turrets flanking the east gable. Built on a grand scale, it measures 90 feet long, 30 feet wide, and 60 feet high, the proportions, with their multiples of three, being in all probability symbolic of the Holy Trinity. At the south-east corner is the bell-tower, adorned with carved panels and friezes, traceried bell-openings and tall pinnacles, making it the most outstanding of the mansion's many towers, as indeed it was clearly intended to be. The inside of the Chapel consists of a single large space with a shallow apse, while at the west end is a tribune, carried on four stone arches and originally linked by corridors to the (now demolished) family rooms and to the state rooms immediately to the west. In the gallery above was a large three-manual organ built by Parsons of Duke Street, London. Narrow side-galleries, fronted by traceried iron railings, ran eastwards along the north and south sides. Payments made in 1832-3 to Thomas Fradgley and to Lichfield architect Joseph Potter indicate their involvement with the design and building of the Chapel, while the decorative stone-carving on the exterior, and on

3.8 Alton Towers: the barbican, ramparts, and east end of the Chapel. Watercolour, 1870, attributed to Lavinia Littleton (private collection).

the tribune, is reminiscent of Joseph Ireland's work in the Catholic chapel at Tixall (1828). Lined throughout with oak wainscot, and with an undecorated panelled ceiling the interior was somewhat sombre, relieved only by framed copies of noted religious paintings by artists such as Raphael and Titian. The abundant use of cast iron painted to resemble wood was precisely the kind of sham which Pugin abhorred, but these are of considerable interest, revealing the skills of the Britannia Ironworks in Derby where most of the structural and decorative ironwork for the Towers was made. The elegant superstructures of the tribune and gallery are of cast iron, likewise the massive corbels supporting the roof, which are in the form of kneeling angels holding open books, and

3.9 The altar and reredos from the Towers Chapel, now at St Peter's, Bromsgrove (Michael Fisher).

which were originally painted brown to match the ceiling. The altar rail was of gilded cast iron, there were cast-iron statues on the wall either side of the apse, and, flanking the altar, a pair of cast-iron angels. Colour was introduced in the form of stained-glass windows in and above the apse, the artist being Thomas Willement.

Shortly after the opening of the new Chapel, the *Catholic Magazine* concluded that, 'as a domestic chapel [it] is not surpassed in beauty and richness, we believe, by any other in England, perhaps not in Europe.'[18] Then, in 1837, Pugin arrived, full of his own ideas of what an earl's domestic chapel should be, and already at work furnishing and decorating Joseph Potter's new chapel at Oscott which, with its open internal space, shallow apse and western gallery, was not unlike the Towers Chapel. The consecration of Oscott in 1838 was a triumph for Pugin who supervised the liturgy as well as designing the furnishings, vessels and vestments, and with Lord Shrewsbury as both observer and benefactor. It is not surprising, therefore, to find that only a few months later he was carrying out similar improvements in the Towers Chapel. His first major work was to add an elaborate triptych reredos to the existing gilt-bronze altar **(3.9)**. Very similar in style to his altarpiece at Oscott, the frame is made of carved and gilded wood incorporating canopied niches containing figures of angels and saints. The narrow hinged side panels have painted figures of St Augustine of Canterbury and St Thomas Becket. A large central niche houses a jewelled crucifix. On either side are panels painted with somewhat fanciful representations of the Earl and Countess of Shrewsbury in fifteenth-century attire, with the earl in armour, reflecting more of the spirit of the Eglinton Tournament than a conventional piece of devotional art: another example of

3.10 The Syon Reliquary from Alton Towers chapel, designed by Pugin and made by Hardman (University of Exeter Heritage Collections).

3.11 'Certainly the Chapel is a wonderful improvement and altogether the work gives great satisfaction' (Pugin): the Towers Chapel after phase 2 of Pugin's alterations. Watercolour by Joseph Lynch, 1854 (private collection).

the 'romance of facts'. Yet their patrons, St John the Baptist and the Blessed Virgin Mary, stand behind them, and local allusions – the east gable of the Towers Chapel and the flag-tower overlooking the Churnet Valley – appear through windows in the background. The artist was almost certainly John Rogers Herbert (1810-1890) who had painted the side-panels on the Oscott reredos. The seven panels on the gradine below were painted by a different artist, perhaps of the Nazarene School. They depict scenes from the Life of Christ, from the Annunciation to the Ascension, with the Last Supper in the middle. In the central space normally reserved for the tabernacle there was a reliquary containing relics once belonging to the Bridgettine convent of Syon before its final dissolution in 1558. Oblong in shape, and with a hipped roof, it was decorated with jewels and enamels, and inlaid with fourteenth-century ivory panels carved with scenes from the lives of Christ and the Blessed Virgin Mary **(3.10)**. Made by Hardman of Birmingham, it is entered to Lord Shrewsbury on 25 July 1840 at a cost of £85 10s.[19]

On the east wall either side of the apse, and continuing into the sanctuary, there was a dado made up of medieval traceried panelling which came from the chapel of Magdalen College, Oxford, following its recent restoration, probably by way of John Rouse Bloxam (1807-91), a fellow of Magdalen and a friend of Pugin.[20] Above the dado, Pugin constructed an elaborate timber screen of tabernacle work rising almost to ceiling level on either side of the apse, and continuing over the arch. Designed to complement the carved woodwork of the reredos, it was made up of tiers of niches decorated with colour and gilt, and containing figures of angels and saints. The largest figures were those of St Augustine, St Chad, St Edward Confessor and St George, principal saints of England, a choice which reflected Pugin's passionate belief in an English Catholic Church. 'Our ancestors were not Roman Catholics,' he wrote to a friend, 'our liturgy was not Roman but peculiar to England … we are of the old school of our Edwards Anselms Thomases Englishmen to the backbone.'[21] The niches over the arch contained figures of angels holding scrolls inscribed with the *Gloria in excelsis*. The screen appears to have been completed in the summer of 1840.[22] It was one of the largest and most elaborate pieces of carved and gilded woodwork ever designed by Pugin, and he never repeated it elsewhere **(3.11)**.

Among Pugin's additions to the sanctuary area was the extension of the medieval panelling with copies of the originals made by Thomas Harris, the earl's joiner and woodcarver; also the installation of a large crucifix on the north wall of the sanctuary in lieu, perhaps, of a rood placed in the more conventional way on a screen, for which there was no space. Pugin had made a similar arrangement at Oscott, where a large crucifix was placed on the south wall of the Chapel. Since both Pugin and Lord Shrewsbury were collectors of medieval church furnishings, the Alton crucifix may have been of some antiquity. Pugin ordered a rich velvet dossal for it, enriched with embroideries, and with a canopy: 'This fills up the vacant space beyond the communion rail in a very satisfactory manner,' he told Lord Shrewsbury. 'It is altogether a very glorious thing, and a great improvement.'[23] More colour was introduced by the application of stencilling to the dado in the main part of the Chapel.

The final phase of Pugin's work in the Chapel was done in 1850. The hitherto plain ceiling was decorated with a pattern of stars and sunbursts on a blue ground. The cast-iron corbels in the form of kneeling angels, originally painted brown to resemble wood, were now coloured and gilded, and the ceiling was given a rich frieze painted on canvas panels, and carrying the Latin text of Psalm 113. A series of tall, narrow panels topped with crockets and pinnacles was placed along the walls below each of the angel corbels, and some of the pictures were given new Gothic frames. Everything appears to have been completed by 1 May 1850 when Pugin wrote home to his wife from Alton, 'I arrived here this morning & am very glad to tell you that both Lord and Lady Shrewsbury seemed delighted with what had been done. Certainly the Chapel is a wonderful improvement'.[24] The effects of Pugin's work were quite stunning, as is shown by a painting of the interior of 1854 by Joseph Lynch, and by contemporary descriptions.[25] Although the Chapel was, most regrettably, gutted in the 1950s, fragments of the screenwork and of the frieze have survived, and the ceiling was restored in 1994 along with one of the frieze-panels. The altar and reredos had been removed to Grafton Manor, Bromsgove, in 1860, to be transferred to the new Catholic church of St Peter in the same town, where it may be seen today.

Until St John's Church in Alton village was opened in 1842, the Towers Chapel served as the parish church for the Catholic population of Alton and Farley as well as being the private chapel of the Talbot family. The *Catholic Magazine and Review* for 1834 states that the number of communicants was then little short of 100. As at Oscott, Pugin equipped the Chapel with all the necessary furnishings, vestments and vessels for the correct performance of the revived medieval English liturgy (the Sarum Rite) as researched and promoted by himself and Dr Rock. Thus the Towers Chapel attracted the attention of both Catholics and Anglicans who were curious to observe how the liturgy should be performed in Pugin's revived Gothic settings. Being a private chapel, it was free from the restrictions and censures which hampered and frustrated Pugin elsewhere in his attempts to re-introduce the Old English vestments and ceremonial. Pugin wrote enthusiastically about the growing number of worshippers and observers including some 'Oxford Men', i.e. members of the Oxford Architectural Society, and Tractarians, both groups with a scholarly interest in the revived old English liturgy. Among those who came in 1839 was Pugin's friend, J.R. Bloxam, who was also curate to John Henry Newman at Littlemore, Newman then being still an Anglican. Bloxam was seen to be in the chapel while Mass was being celebrated, and this was reported to Newman who referred the matter to the Bishop of Oxford. Even though Bloxam was observing rather than actively participating, the informant alleged that he had bowed his head at the elevation of the Host – enough, in those pre-ecumenical days, to incur censure. The consequence was Bloxam's resignation from the curacy.[26]

As he had done at the opening of Oscott, Pugin assumed the role of liturgist and master of ceremonies on a number of special occasions at the Towers Chapel. The first of these occasions was important as much for personal reasons as for professional ones. Pugin's second wife, Louisa, had not become a Catholic at the time of his conversion in 1835, but by the spring of 1839 she had agreed to make her profession, and Pugin arranged that this should happen in the Towers Chapel at a ceremony presided over by Dr Rock. 'I am overjoyed at this glorious result to all my prayers and anxieties', he wrote.[27] The 'glorious result' merited a glorious celebration, and nothing could have been more glorious than the High Mass celebrated in the Chapel on Wednesday, 8 May – the feast of the Appearing of St Michael the Archangel, and the eve of the Ascension – all, as one might expect, *ad usum Sarum*. So splendid was the occasion that the following day Pugin suggested to Rock that an account of it should be published in the *Orthodox Journal* or the *Catholic Magazine*. A full report very soon appeared in both, and also the *Staffordshire Examiner*.[28] The Chapel was lavishly decorated with evergreens and sweet-scented flowers 'emblematical of the sweetness and never-fading beauty of the heavenly Zion'. A garland of flowers was hung across the full width of the building, and the centre-piece was a floral crown suspended directly above Louisa's head.

At the appointed hour, the report continues, as the full organ poured forth its majestic note, Dr Rock, as priest, attended by the Revd Drs Morgan (Uttoxeter) and Fairfax (Cheadle) as deacon and subdeacon, walked in solemn procession from the sacristy to the sanctuary, preceded by the thurifers, acolytes and torchbearers. Their vestments were of the richest gold brocade. A grand High Mass was then sung, with all the usual inexpressibly affecting ceremonies of the Catholic Church. Immediately after the Gospel Dr Rock exchanged his superb chasuble for a splendid cope, robed with which he, at the foot of the altar, intoned the first words of the hymn to the Holy Ghost, *Veni Creator Spiritus* in the old Salisbury chaunt which the choir continued with impressive effect.

Only Pugin himself could have designed the ceremonial candle which Rock presented to Louisa as she prepared to make her profession, and which merited a detailed description in the Press:

> a large wax taper ornamented in the style of the fifteenth century, it arose out of a bouquet of rare exotic flowers. Around the lower part of this candle were rolled three labels, written in Gothic characters with the following ejaculations: Jesu filii Dei, Miserere me – O mater filii Dei, miserere me – S. Michael, ora pro me (Jesus, Son of God, have mercy on me - Mother of the Son of God, remember me – St Michael, pray for me). The higher part was ornamented with a wreath of flowers in brilliant colours, above which, attached by a golden string, was suspended a small Gothic label, upon the richly diapered ground of which was emblazoned, in the style of the fifteenth century, the Archangel Michael overcoming Satan.

On the next day Pugin ordered that the wooden stocks of the six candles for the Chapel altar should be painted in similar style. 'You can get this done as soon as the candlesticks arrive', he told Rock, 'for I should like them to be on the altar – before the Earl returns.'[29] The new candlesticks were made to complement the richness of the altar and its surroundings. Still on the altar in its present (2011) location in Bromsgrove, these tall candlesticks have composite quatrefoil bases and elaborate mouldings on the stems, and they are much more akin to those illustrated in Pugin's *Designs for Gold and Silversmiths* (1830) than to anything known to have been made for him by Hardman. Yet the Hardman metalwork daybook for 28 May 1839 enters to Lord Shrewsbury '6 candlesticks at £10. 10s'. The date is about right, but the price seems ridiculously cheap, even if it refers to the price per candlestick.

The floral arrangements at Louisa's reception were the creation of Alexander Forsyth, the new head gardener whom Pugin had been instrumental in introducing to the Towers in April 1839. Forsyth was also responsible for decorating the Chapel, and for building a triumphal arch of flowers, on the occasion of the arrival, in July 1839, of the Shrewsbury's elder daughter, Mary, and their new son-in-law, Prince Doria Pamphili, following their marriage in Rome. Pugin's role at the Towers extended well beyond that of architect and liturgist into that of supervising arrangements for receiving and entertaining distinguished guests where his flair for the dramatic could be used to great advantage.

Since Lord and Lady Shrewsbury spent much of their time in Italy, there were fewer grand occasions at Alton than there might otherwise have been. Indeed, their decision to live abroad for a good part of the year was designed to reduce household expenditures so as to divert a greater part of their disposable income into church-building schemes. 'Of course we must come sometimes', the earl told Pugin in 1841, 'but I hope not often.'[30] There were, however, some notable exceptions, and of these none was more dramatic and spectacular than the nine-day visit of Henry of Bordeaux, the Legitimist pretender to the French throne, in November 1843, at which Pugin came into his own as master of ceremonies and manager of special effects.

The throne of France was at this time occupied by Louis Philippe (r. 1830-48), of the Orleanist branch of the Bourbon family; the 'Citizen King' created by the deposition of Charles X in the revolution of 1830. In the eyes of true royalists, however, the rightful king was not Louis Philippe but the Duke of Bordeaux whom they hailed as Henry V. It would appear that the duke had met the Shrewsburys in Rome. Henry invested them with the courtesy title of *amis du roi*, and a grand reception was planned for the duke at Alton Towers as part of an extended visit to England. There were certain parallels between the story of Henry of Bordeaux and that of the erstwhile Pretender to the English throne, Charles Edward Stuart, which would have appealed to Pugin given his own family's background in pre-revolutionary France and his fascination with the Stuarts as Catholic heirs to the throne of England.

Pugin's correspondence with Lord Shrewsbury in the autumn of 1843 reveals what was happening under his direction at Alton in preparation for the duke's visit. Instructions were sent to John Denny for the construction of an awning to cover the steps up to the entrance-tower, the provision of 'illumination lamps' for the gardens, and 'fire engines' which were pyrotechnic devices for floodlighting the exterior of the house.[31] The duke's arrival on the evening of 4 November was reported a week later in the *Staffordshire Advertiser*, and described in detail by M. le Vicomte Walsh in his *Relation du voyage de Henri de France en Ecosse et en Angleterre* (1844).[32] Walsh records that, as the duke's carriage approached the mansion, Pugin's 'fire-engines' suddenly erupted into a blaze of a thousand lights, illuminating doorways, windows, terraces, walls, battlements, towers and turrets against the background of the night sky. Pugin then took his place in the line-up of nobles and dignitaries who greeted the prince as he alighted at the entrance-tower. On such an occasion he would have exchanged his casual working attire for evening dress – not that which was customarily worn by Victorian gentlemen, but black silk knee-breeches and silver-buckled shoes, and a black velvet gown of his own design which he would have doffed once the party had progressed into the house. Later in the evening the royal company descended the grand staircase into the State Dining Room where Pugin and Bishop Wiseman were among the 35 guests who sat down to dinner while the earl's harpist, Edward Jervis, played and sang a selection of Welsh folk-songs, alternating with an orchestra which provided French and Scottish airs.

The following day being a Sunday, Mass was celebrated in the Towers Chapel, and the duke and his entourage joined the earl and countess on the tribune where Pugin had provided special prayer-desks and soft furnishings. On the Monday a requiem was celebrated for the anniversary of the duke's grandfather, King Charles X (d. 6 November 1836), in preparation for which Pugin reordered the Chapel. This involved the provision of black drapes and the construction of a catafalque decorated with silver tear-drops and fleurs-de-lis. Pugin remained at the Towers for the rest of the of the duke's visit, which included an excursion to Herbert Minton's tile factory in Stoke-on-Trent. 'I cannot leave Alton till the departure of the Duc De Bordeaux who is here with a numerous suite', he wrote to Bloxam, explaining why he was unable to be in Oxford before 13 November.[33] Gatherings such as these were of great importance professionally, bringing Pugin into contact with prospective clients and other influential figures whom he would never have met but for the patronage and friendship of Lord Shrewsbury. In August 1844 he wrote that Lord Shrewsbury was expecting the Duke of Cambridge, Queen Victoria's uncle, to arrive at the Towers with a large party: 'I must be there at the time and I ought to go a few days before hand.'[34] Pugin was indeed there, and he also ensured that the duke visited Cheadle to see his new church in the process of construction.

When the Shrewsburys were in residence at the Towers, and entertaining on a lavish scale, the house was seen at its best, with the state rooms thronged with guests and resounding with music, as is shown on some of Samuel Rayner's drawings. It was a different matter when the family were away, staff reduced to minimum, and the vast rooms and long corridors filled with silence, shadows, and fleeting reflections in mirrors and windows. Pugin had an innate fear of haunted houses and the supernatural. He would carry two candles – one in each hand – when walking a dark corridor in case one of them blew out, and he told Lord Shrewsbury of a ghastly night he had spent in an 'awful room' at Hornby Castle (Yorkshire), scared by his own candlelit reflection in the mirrors, and too frightened to peep over the bed-covers.[35] Although he clearly loved Alton Towers and its tranquil gardens, and told Lord Shrewsbury that he was 'nowhere so happy,'[36] there were occasions when he felt less than comfortable staying there alone at night. 'I think I passed one of the most dreadful nights in my life at Alton,' he told John Hardman in April 1846. 'I was half dead with fatigue but the moment I dropped off to sleep again I was woke up with the most horrible feelings & ideas – I am quite terrified to go to bed. to be sure I could not have gone to a worse place than alton just now.'[37] The Shrewsburys were away in Italy, and Pugin was in a state of mental and emotional turmoil following the ending of his love affair with Mary Amherst. He was also haunted by the memory of a strange premonition he had had while staying at Alton in

August 1844, that his wife, Louisa, had been taken seriously ill back in London. It became nightmarish reality when Louisa died before Pugin was able to reach home. He had another spooky experience when staying alone at the Towers on a dark and windy night in the autumn of 1849, a year after his marriage to Jane Knill, from whom he hated to be saparated. As if the howling gale were not enough to keep him awake, Pugin heard the sound of a bell tolling every few moments, as if for a funeral. So strong was the wind as it blew through the bell-openings in the Chapel tower that it had set the great deep-sounding bell in motion. 'You cannot imagine anything more desolate than this mansion house', Pugin wrote to Jane, back in Ramsgate.[38]

In the accounts of the banquet for the Duke of Bordeaux in 1843, reference is made to the royal party as having 'descended' the grand staircase into the State Dining Room. This highlights a functional problem which had existed ever since the reorganisation of the house in about 1834 when this room was created by converting the former entrance hall on the north front, no longer needed as such since the construction of the new grand entrance on the south-east side. Set transversely to the main block, and rising through all three storeys, it was an elegant room, with a lofty plaster-vaulted ceiling and much ornamental ironwork including a spiral staircase by which those arriving at the house would have ascended to the principal rooms on the first floor (see above, 2.4). Following its conversion – which amounted to little more than removing the entrance-doors and substituting a window – guests had now to descend by the same staircase into what had become the State Dining Room. It was not a particularly convenient arrangement, and in the early 1840s Lord Shrewsbury proposed to alter it by inserting a new floor ten feet above the level of the existing one, thus raising the Dining Room to the same level as the other state rooms, but with few other changes. Pugin on the other hand, spied a chance to create a truly medieval banqueting hall on a grand scale, complete with the appropriate furnishings and fittings.

In all of Pugin's schemes for noble houses, both executed and unexecuted, provision was made for a great hall in which he imagined that lord and tenant would feast together on major festivals as they had done in the Middle Ages.[39] Alton was to have the most splendid of all, as befitted the home of England's premier earl; and, having compromised his principles again and again over various matters, Pugin was determined that this time the 'true principles' would prevail. Almost inevitably the new Dining Room became the subject of a good deal of controversy between earl and architect, with Lord Shrewsbury expressing his preference for a fairly modest alteration of the existing room, and Pugin arguing the case for a complete rebuilding. Although the alteration of the Dining Room had been discussed as early as 1843, it was still in the planning stage four years later, possibly because the masons were still busy at St Giles', Cheadle, and at Alton Castle. In the meantime, many of those who frequented the Towers had become aware of the scheme, and Pugin knew that opinions were divided, with some expressing the view that the room should not be touched at all. Not even Lord and Lady Shrewsbury were of exactly the same mind over what should be done beyond the basic practicality of

3.12 Interior of the new Dining Room at Alton Towers (author's drawing from original sources, 2001).

NEW DINING ROOM at ALTON:1851

raising the floor-level. What Pugin feared most was that he would be forced into carrying out some half-measure that would destroy the proportions and character of the existing room without creating anything better in its place, and so damage his reputation as a designer. One of the points at issue was the large window in the north gable, with its geometrical tracery and early nineteenth-century stained glass by William Eginton, evocative of the 'abbey style' in which the house had originally been built. Pugin argued that, on Lord Shrewsbury's own admission, it was a church window in design, and therefore inappropriate for a dining room, and that Eginton's glass was 'miserable'. Having first agreed to keep the window if the earl would consent to new glass, Pugin issued an ultimatum. Either the earl must accept the architect's scheme in its entirety, and trust to his professional judgment, knowledge and experience, or he would pull out altogether:

> I intended to make a fine thing suitable to the purpose for which it is destined and not a common room fit only for an hotel. This is the very first room at the Towers that I was called upon to design & it was quite natural that I should wish to produce something that would have a striking effect especially when so many persons were loud in condemning the alteration & declaring that the present room was far better than anything that could be done ... I have nailed my colours to the mast: a bay window, high open roof, lantern, 2 grand fireplaces, a great sideboard, screen, minstrel gallery, all or none.'[40]

3.13 Alton Towers: comparative elevations of the north front before and after Pugin's alterations (Michael Fisher).

ALTON TOWERS – THE ENTRANCE HALL/GREAT DINING HALL

as built by Thomas Allason, c.1818   (b) as rebuilt by A.W.N. Pugin, 1851

Accustomed as Lord Shrewsbury was to Pugin's bluff and bluster, and his seeming lack of regard for the social status of those who crossed him, it is clear that this time he had overstepped the mark. The earl's response is unrecorded, but it must have been a severe one, carrying the threat of dismissal, for Pugin's next two letters, written on 3 and 11 August, are apologetic and conciliatory in tone. He assured the earl that his all-or-nothing letter had been written merely to try and persuade him 'to make a good thing'. He would not, however, push the matter further: 'it has proved already a most unfortunate business & I might almost say a fatal one if it leads to the result to which your Lordsip (sic) alludes. I am truly grieved to think your Lordsip can give me up so easily. You used to have confidence in my judgment on these matters & I may truly say I have ever done my best to deserve it.'[41] Pugin left the final decision about the proposed bay window in the earl's hands, merely pointing out that 'it would not be costly as it would be all masons work.'[42] It is not known how or why Lord Shrewsbury changed his mind, but in the end Pugin got everything he wanted – and more – as the earl gave way on every point and agreed to a complete restructuring of the room, with all the requisite furnishings and fittings **(3.12)**. By March 1848 Pugin had all the drawings and estimates ready, and by October he was able to tell Hardman that he had received the earl's written order for both the north and south windows, and that he would prepare the cartoons over the winter,[43] but it was yet another year before building work started. 'I propose going soon after Easter to see the great work begun,' he wrote in February 1849. 'I have just finished my drawing of the interior and it looks exceedingly well.'[44] The drawing was almost certainly the one that he exhibited later in the year at the Royal Academy.[45]

The 'great work' involved much more than the internal reconstruction of an existing building. The east wall of the room was not of sufficient depth or strength to accommodate the two huge chimneypieces worked in Bath stone, so a brick reinforcement had to be provided on the far side of the wall. This meant closing off the rooms immediately to the east, with consequent disruption, including a good deal of mess and noise, in what were the private quarters of the earl and countess. 'I think the good Earl is sick of his own building', Pugin commented, 'it has cost a great deal more than I could have made a new thing for.'[46] Only in the newly created basement area were any significant traces of the old room suffered to remain.

The raising of the walls by ten feet also created an imbalance in the appearance of the north front (3.13), and this could only be redressed by the addition of a fourth storey west of the dining room, involving yet more upheavals. It was not without good reason that the earl had tried to rein in Pugin's ambitions, although it has to be said that he and the countess were able to take refuge in Italy while most of this work was going on. When Lord Shrewsbury suggested, in October 1849, that he might come and see the work in progress, Pugin prudently dissuaded him: 'your Lordship ought not to look at it while it is going on but see it compleat. It is as bad as looking at plants growing.'[47] Pugin promised to spend as much time as possible at Alton while the work was going on: 'I must not absent myself on any account & now there is a railway it is nothing either in time or expense.'[48] The diaries show that he was at the Towers for extended periods in October 1849 and between July and October 1850, with some brief visits in between. Other work was in progress at this time: the second phase of alterations in the Chapel, and the building of the new gatehouse at the station entrance to the Towers.[49] Pugin's Royal Academy drawing of the Dining Room is, unfortunately, missing. There is, however, a large coloured perspective drawing of the north front showing how it would appear after the completion of all the work (3.14). Highly accurate in

3.14 North front of Alton Towers. 1840s aquatint, possibly by J.B. Denny, showing the actual and proposed alterations (Henry Potts).

3.15 Alton Towers:
Banqueting Hall
chimneypiece (Michael
Fisher).

3.15 Alton Towers:
Banqueting Hall
chimneypiece (Michael
Fisher).

its detail, the drawing shows features that were not actually carried out, such as a large new entrance-porch and flight of steps leading up to the Long Gallery west of the Dining Room. Such an entrance on the north front would have made perfect sense. Apart from the east entrance from the terrace, which was the private access into the family rooms, the only other way into the Towers was the circuitous one through the galleries, octagon and house conservatory which had been designed for effect rather than convenience. It would appear not to be the work of Pugin, but of someone who was thoroughly familiar with his work at Alton and who had handled his working drawings. John Denny had both the knowledge and the skill, and so he is a strong possibility. It has the characteristics of a presentation piece designed, perhaps, to convince Lord Shrewsbury of the desirability of proceeding with the scheme in its entirety.[50]

Pugin's known drawings for the furnishings of the Dining Room include the great brass and crystal chandelier of 42 lights, modelled on one in Nuremberg Cathedral, and which is now in the Palace of Westminster; also details of grates and fire-irons.[51] The two massive chimneypieces were very deeply carved with the Talbot coat of arms and supporters **(3.15)**, with specially designed Minton tiles in the reveals. The lower parts of the walls were clad in carved oak panelling, while at the west end the screens passage and minstrels' gallery (also of carved oak) were to be fronted by a great sideboard made by J.G. Crace. This was made to display the fine array of gilt-metal plate specially made by Hardman, including a great dish 30 inches in diameter, and all richly ornamented with Talbot heraldry and mottoes.[52] Finally, Pugin's stained glass designs for the north and south windows were to be executed by Hardman, the great 27-light oriel filled with heraldic devices pertaining to the Talbots and their related families **(3.16)**, and the south window having as its central feature the figure of the first earl of Shrewsbury. The hall was crowned by a high open timber roof, with arch-braces, wind-braces, and a central lantern from which the chandelier was suspended by a (still extant) chain. The roof timbers are decorated in a red, blue and gold pattern incorporating Talbot lions. Pugin estimated the total cost of this work at £2,271.[53]

Neither Pugin nor Lord Shrewsbury lived long enough to see the 'great work' completed, and it is clear from the 1857 Alton Towers sale catalogue, an inventory of 1869, and the Alton Estate accounts, that work continued in the Dining Hall for many years while furnishings intended for it, such as the chandelier, were stored in other parts of the house. Several items intended for the hall – the chandelier, the Great Talbot window, the sideboard and plate – were displayed in the Medieval Court at the Great Exhibition of 1851 where Pugin's wide-ranging genius as a designer were shown in the work of Crace (wallpaper, fabrics and furniture), Hardman (metalwork and glass), Minton (ceramics) and Myers (carved woodwork and stone). It was something of a paradox that within the marvel of modern technology that was the Crystal Palace, one of the most popular and most widely-reported displays was the Medieval Court, crammed with furniture and works of art designed to evoke the pre-industrial spirit of the fourteenth and fifteenth centuries. All of this was

3.16 Watercolour design for the oriel window, Alton Towers Banqueting Hall by A.W.N. Pugin and J.H. Powell (Hardman private collection).

3.17 'All the entrances should be called gate, and gate houses, after the manner of the ancients' (Pugin): the gatehouse known as Station Lodge (Michael Fisher).

reflected locally too. Passengers arriving from the industrial Midlands by way of the revolutionary new steam-train, as Pugin did for the first time in the autumn of 1849, would find themselves transported into a totally different world: a thickly-wooded river valley with a church, almshouse and fairy-tale castle on one side, and a Gothic prospect-tower on the other, then up through the broad archway of the Gatehouse blazoned with Talbot heraldry **(3.17)**, to catch their first sight of the towers and pinnacles of the earl's mansion, dominated by the lantern-crowned gable of the great dining room. This was 'Pugin-land' indeed, the closest he came to realising his full vision of a restored Catholic England in which all classes were united in a common faith celebrated in the same glorious buildings, with the great bell of the Towers Chapel, which had so scared Pugin in the middle of the night, ringing the Angelus thrice daily across the Churnet Valley, so that people in every walk of life – the countess in the small oratory Pugin built for her in the garden, the masons at work at the castle, the farm-labourers on the estate – might stop whatever they were doing, ponder the great mystery of the Incarnation, and say their grateful *Ave*.

Alton Towers itself was a kind of showroom in which the full extent of Pugin's talents were permanently displayed to distinguished visitors such as Sir Robert Peel who came in the autumn of 1848 and who, according to Pugin, 'took a great interest in Everything & spoke so highly of the buildings to Lord Shrewsbury that he is more than contented.'[54] Benjamin Disraeli knew Alton as he also knew the coterie of Young Englanders and Romantic Catholics, such as Lord John Manners, Charles Scott Murray and Ambrose Lisle Phillipps, who gathered around Lord Shrewsbury and Pugin. In Disraeli's *Coningsby*, the Romantic novel that popularised the idea of Young England, Phillipps is thinly disguised as Eustace Lyle, and although St Genevieve, the Lyle family home, was supposedly modelled on the Phillipps's Garendon Hall, the account of it reads more like a description of Alton Towers: 'In a valley, not far from the margin of a beautiful river, raised on a lofty and artificial terrace at the base of a range of wooded heights, was a pile of modern building in the finest style of Christian architecture ... a gathering as it seemed of galleries, halls and chapels, mullioned windows, portals of clustered columns, and groups of airy pinnacles and fretwork spires'**(3.18)**. The words 'Christian architecture' are perhaps the most telling of all, for that expression was originally Pugin's. In Disraeli's later novel, *Lothair* (1870), Alton Towers became 'Muriel Towers', with its armoury, octagon-hall, and 'long libraries with curiously stained windows, and suites of dazzling saloons'.

The architect Charles Barry, with whom Pugin was associated from 1835 onwards, also visited the Towers, and in 1841 he told a Parliamentary Committee that the style of Pugin's decorations in the Chapel and the Talbot Gallery would apply equally well to the New Palace of Westminster.[55] Without doubt this was a key factor in securing Pugin's employment to design the interiors of the Palace, having assisted Barry in the preparation of his winning competition drawings. Recent reappraisal of Pugin's work at Alton leads to the conclusion that his decorative and structural work there should rank equally.[56] This makes the gutting of Alton in 1951-2 by its post-war owners the more regrettable, but even in their reduced state the Chapel and the Dining Room bear eloquent testimony to Pugin's achievements as a domestic architect,

3.18 Alton Towers and gardens. Engraving by H. Warren *c.*1860 (author's collection).

while other structural features such as the oriel windows of the south front and of the Doria Rooms, the servants' quarters, and the barbican gateway, speak as effectively as a page from *Contrasts* against the 'mock' Gothic of his unenlightened predecessors. Though there was much at Alton that would have annoyed him as much as it was to annoy William Morris (who dismissed the Towers as a 'gimcrack palace'), Pugin was clearly at home there. He delighted in the Romantic North Staffordshire landscape, its rich Catholic history and medieval survivals, he relished the opportunities and the freedom it afforded him as an architect and designer; and, as he assured Lord Shrewsbury, 'I am sure I do not need much inducement to stay, for I am nowhere so happy.'[57]

4

St Mary's, Uttoxeter:
the first 'True Principles' church

' I have effected more than any man living for the restoration of old
anglican ecclesiastical architecture'
A.W.N. Pugin, Letter to J.R. Bloxam, 24 October 1840

Ten miles from the heart of 'Pugin-land', the market town of Uttoxeter lies
on the eastern edge of Staffordshire close to where the River Dove marks
its boundary with Derbyshire. Comparable in size to Cheadle, its population
in the mid-1830s was about 5,000. The town is dominated by the fourteenth-
century tower and spire of St Mary's parish church, the only survivals from
the medieval building, for in 1828 the dilapidated nave was considered to
be beyond repair and so was demolished by the Staffordshire architect James
Trubshaw (1777-1853) to make way for a new one. Though Gothic in overall
style, it was built – like many others of its time – in the Georgian 'preaching-
box' fashion, with galleries but without a chancel, the present one being added
in 1877. Tucked away from view in nearby Balance Street is St Mary's Catholic
church, built by Pugin in 1838-9. Pugin's church has also been considerably
altered and extended since its opening, while its location in a side-street, and
the humble dimensions of the church as originally built, belie its profound
significance in the history of the Gothic Revival, and in Pugin's own career as
an ecclesiastical architect and designer. It was the first church of the Shrewsbury-
Pugin partnership to be completed, and, in Pugin's own words, it 'may truly
be described as the first Catholic structure erected in this country in strict
accordance with the rules of ancient ecclesiastical architecture since the days
of the pretended Reformation.'[1] Though situated in a town, St Mary's was the
prototype of Pugin's 'country church', consisting of a simple nave with a bell-
cote on the western gable and (ideally) a chancel, but without aisles or a tower,
such as could be built inexpensively to serve the needs of rural communities.
It was widely imitated by other architects, and in other countries. Though
simple in design, St Mary's did not lack any of the features regarded by Pugin as
essential for the proper celebration of the English Catholic Rite. St Mary's thus
represented a revival of liturgical furnishings and practices not seen or used since
the sixteenth century, and they plunged Pugin straight away into controversy
with members of the Catholic hierarchy who viewed such revivals as archaic
and irrelevant. Even before it was finished, this church received much publicity,

while its opening in August 1839 was hailed in prose and in verse. Of all of Pugin's Staffordshire buildings, it is the one for which the most complete set of detailed plans and drawings has survived. For all of these reasons, St Mary's is an important building, and of more than local significance. Yet the nineteenth-century local historian Francis Redfern in his *History and Antiquities of Uttoxeter* (1865 and 1886) mentions it merely in passing and without any reference to the architect, just as his account of Alton Towers ignores Pugin altogether. On the other hand John Buckler (1770-1851) included a fine drawing of St Mary's in his systematic record of Staffordshire churches, showing the church as it was in 1839 **(4.1)**.

A Catholic mission was first established in Uttoxeter around 1832 at the instigation of the Revd J. Dunne of the Cresswell Mission, who held weekly services and lectures, first in an outbuilding in the yard of the Old Star in Queen Street, and then in a building at the back of the Blue Bell Inn in High Street.[2] In 1835 the Revd George Morgan joined the Cresswell Mission. He was given responsibility for Uttoxeter, and it was he who initiated the scheme to build a proper chapel. Described as 'a man of action who met difficulties merely as something to be overcome', Morgan – who came from an old Catholic yeoman family in Monmouthshire – is said to have sold his paternal estate to help build the chapel, and he also set about raising subscriptions from other sources. His greatest opportunity came about in December 1836 when he temporarily took charge of Alton while Dr Daniel Rock, chaplain to the Earl of Shrewsbury, went to Rome to recuperate from illness.[2] This brought Fr

4.1 St Mary's, Uttoxeter. Drawing by J. Buckler, 1839 (Staffordshire Views, William Salt Library, Stafford).

Morgan into direct contact with Lord Shrewsbury, who became the principal benefactor. By this time the earl was already in contact with Pugin, who began to work for him in the following year. Thus it was that Uttoxeter came to be the location of the first of Pugin's 'True Principles' churches.

'A bicycle shed is a building; Lincoln Cathedral is a piece of architecture' – so Pevsner introduces his classic work, *An Outline of European Architecture* (1960), by drawing a distinction between structures which are purely utilitarian and ones which are expressive, such as a cathedral, or indeed, St Mary's, Uttoxeter. The church buildings of the first Christian centuries were of course largely utilitarian; practical buildings where the faithful could assemble under cover and set up an altar; and their architectural style was essentially no different from that of the secular buildings of the period. But then – and this is one of the major arguments of A.W.N. Pugin – the Christian era produced its own distinctive architecture and art; that which later came to be called Gothic. The 'pointed style', to use one of Pugin's preferred terms for it, came to be regarded as inseparable from the Christian Faith; hence the title of one of his most influential books, *The True Principles of Pointed or Christian Architecture* (1841).

Pugin believed that Christian architecture had reached its high point in the early fourteenth century with the phase of Gothic which is often referred to as 'Decorated'. Thereafter it fell into decline, first with the so-called 'Perpendicular' style (though, to his subsequent regret, Pugin himself used Perpendicular for some of his earlier buildings); then came the Renaissance with its reversion to the Classical styles of ancient Greece and Rome which Pugin regarded as thoroughly pagan and therefore totally unsuitable for places of Christian worship. Finally there was the Reformation which led to the wholesale destruction of church interiors and a 1,000-years' worth of accumulated Christian art: stained glass windows, statuary, metalwork, wood-carving, and embroidery. Yet here and there, in the ancient churches and cathedrals of England, there were vestiges of what once had been: a rood screen here, a complete stained glass window there; a hammer-beam roof, a painted panel, a fourteenth-century vestment or a late-medieval chalice which had somehow escaped the holocausts of the sixteenth and seventeenth centuries, and these provided the models for his revival. What had once been, Pugin believed, could be again. Let the newly liberated Catholic Church in England abandon the pagan art and architecture of Italy and adopt the styles of the High Middle Ages, and Catholicism would cease to be seen as something alien or foreign to England, and would be viewed instead as being as much a part of the English landscape as the ancient towers and spires under whose shadow the Catholic rites had once been performed until the advent of 'that sacrilegious tyrant Henry VIII and his successors in church plunder.'[3] The re-marriage of the Catholic Faith with the architectural and artistic styles which were fundamentally expressive of it would contribute more than anything else, so Pugin believed, to the rebuilding of Catholic England which would come about in and through that fundamental building, the parish church, set at the heart of the community and open every day, properly equipped with the right furnishings and fittings, and served by clergy who knew how to use them correctly:

It is, in fact, by parish churches, that the faith of a nation is to be sustained and nourished; in them souls are engrafted to the Church by the waters of baptism; they are the tribunals of penance, and the seats of mercy and forgiveness. In them the holy Eucharistic sacrifice is continually offered up, and the sacred body of our Lord received by the faithful; there the holy books are read, and the people instructed; they become the seat and centre of every pious thought and deed.[4]

It seemed extraordinary to Pugin that while branding Catholicism as 'foreign', so many English people clung stubbornly to the name of 'protestant'; a term which had originated in Lutheran Germany and Calvinist Switzerland. The revival of Christian (i.e. Gothic) art and architecture might help to change their minds, but it was not just a question of doing battle with Protestants, for within the Catholic Church there were many who had no wish to abandon current Italian and French fashions of architecture and liturgy in order to return to the Middle Ages. Such people were, in Pugin's mind, an obstacle too, for their tastes and practices would tend to reinforce the popular myth that Catholicism was somehow alien to Britain. In his second lecture to students at Oscott, Pugin launched into a ferocious diatribe against both Renaissance and Reformation when,

Whole nations infected with the contagion of heretical novelties, cut themselves off from unity and truth, committed every revolting excess which the human mind, in its worst state, is capable of conceiving ... infidel supplanted Catholic feelings, ... and the deplorable state of morals ... may very reasonably be attributed, in a great degree, to the loss of Catholic and the introduction of Pagan art.[5]

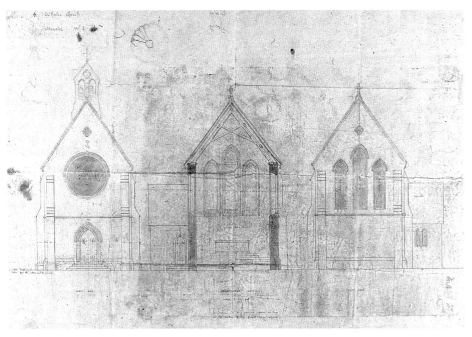

4.2 St Mary's, Uttoxeter: east and west elevations. Drawing by Pugin (Getty Research Library, Los Angeles).

Although the beauties of ancient Catholic architecture were now better understood and appreciated, Pugin maintained that there were still Catholic clergy who made every effort 'to assimilate the true and ancient worship of Almighty God with the degraded service of a Protestant conventicle', with 'tawdry ornaments and pitiable taste'. The revival of ancient art was not, however, simply a matter of taste, so Pugin concluded, but 'most closely connected with the revival of faith itself'.

Having won the admiration of Lord Shrewsbury and Daniel Rock, Pugin was now given an opportunity at Uttoxeter to move beyond satire and polemic, and to demonstrate exactly what he meant by 'the real thing'. The buildings were to consist of a small aisleless church with a presbytery attached, of brick with stone trim, in the lancet style, and with all the correct furnishings. Pugin was most anxious to counter the allegation that Gothic churches were necessarily more expensive to build than the more usual type of Catholic chapel of this period, and to evolve at Uttoxeter a type which could be replicated elsewhere:

> I am willing to prove, beyond all power of contradiction – he wrote in 1839 – that <u>more effect can be produced, and greater space gained</u>, for a given sum, in pointed architecture than in any other style whatsoever, not even excepting the Methodist and Baptist conventicler style, which appears to have been frequently adopted by those who maintain <u>a plain, comfortable chapel to be all that is necessary!!!</u> for the place that is to become <u>the Tabernacle of the Living God</u>, and for the decoration of which the Catholics of ancient days thought they had done little when they had overlaid the sanctuary with gold, and raised its towers to the clouds. ... I may state the present building at Uttoxeter as an instance that a Catholic church, complete in every respect, may be erected for a very moderate sum.[6].

This was the first building in which John Bunn Denny (1810-92) was involved as clerk of works, a post which he held, in respect of the Pugin-Shrewsbury buildings in this area until 1856. Pugin notes in his diary under 1 July 1839, 'At Uttoxeter. Deny (*sic*) arrived'. If this marks the beginning of Denny's work for Lord Shrewsbury, as seems to be the case, then the Uttoxeter church would have been nearing completion when he took it over.[7]

The actual building of St Mary's appears to have been carried out by Peter and John Bailey of Alton, Lord Shrewsbury's builders and stonemasons, whose family had long been involved with building work at Alton Towers. Pugin's detailed working drawings for the church **(4.2, 4.3)** remained in the hands of the Bailey family until 1987.[8] One sheet of drawings shows the west and east elevations, and a transverse section, signed by Pugin and dated 1838. Details of windows, gables and mouldings, are also shown. The plan and elevations show a small sacristy at the south-east corner of the building, and also a west porch, though the latter was never built. Another sheet, dated 1839, contains drawings of the presbytery which was to be linked to the church by a short cloister.

The foundation stone of 'St Marie's'[9] was laid by Fr Morgan on 4 October 1838. As the work progressed, Pugin took up his pen again, and on 20 July 1839 a view of the proposed interior of the church appeared on the front page of the *Orthodox Journal,* with a three-page descriptive article inside **(4.4)**. Both the

4.3 St Mary's, Uttoxeter, presbytery: detail. Drawing by Pugin (Getty Research Library, Los Angeles).

picture and the description made it abundantly clear that this was no ordinary church, but a revival, in every respect, of the ancient ecclesiastical architecture of England which 'is so associated with every recollection that should bind the Catholic of this day with the faith of his fathers, and animate him to exertion, that to oppose its restoration is madness indeed.'[10]

Though externally quite plain, St Mary's had all the essential features which made it clearly recognisable as a church, and a 'true principles' church at that: a buttressed nave with pointed lancet windows, and steeply pitched roofs with crosses on the eastern gables. Though a small west porch appears on the plans, it was dispensed with. Set on the western gable was a double bell-cote, below which was the only major embellishment: a circular window divided into twelve sections, and filled with stained glass. The main entrance was originally under this window, and over the west door on the inside was set the only significant piece of stone-carving: the lion's head from the Shrewsbury coat of arms. Pugin took pains to pay early tribute to the earl, 'whose pious and zealous exertions are effecting wonders in the restoration of Catholic architecture in this country.'[11]

Internally the church consisted of a single open space, without the separately defined chancel that Pugin came to regard as indispensable. It was what Pugin did within this space that makes the church so remarkable in terms of it furnishings and intended use. Though in its basic shape St Mary's may have been little different from the run-of-the mill brick-built chapels of the time, inside the building Pugin proposed his most daring excursions into neo-medievalism, all of which were described in advance in the *Orthodox Journal*. He drew attention to the provision of holy-water stoups just inside the entrance, and of a stone font with a locking cover. He hoped that the latter would signal a general restoration of fonts: 'Old bottles and jugs are but sorry substitutes for fonts. ... It is a most humiliating and shameful consideration, that, in this country, modern Catholic chapels and dissenting meeting-houses can alone be pointed at as wanting this most essential object of church furniture'.

As might be expected, it was in the chancel that Pugin proposed to introduce his most striking innovations. At its entrance there would be an arched rood-beam with a large crucifix and six tapers. Pugin hailed this as the first rood to be set up in a parish church since the sixteenth century, and it paved the way for his general revival of roods and chancel screens. The stone altar would have

VOL. IX.   SATURDAY, JULY 20, 1839.   No. 212.—4*d*.

CHANCEL OF ST. MARIES, UTTOXETER.

THIS small church, which is nearly completed, and which will be solemnly dedicated in the course of a few weeks, may be truly described as the first Catholic structure erected in this country in strict accordance with the rules of ancient ecclesiastical ar-chitecture since the days of the pretended Reformation.

The style is that of the early part of the 13th century: lancet arches, without tracery. Over the entrance doorway is a circular window, divided into twelve compartments, with a

4.4 St Mary's, Uttoxeter: proposed interior. Drawing by Pugin (*Orthodox Journal*, July 1839).

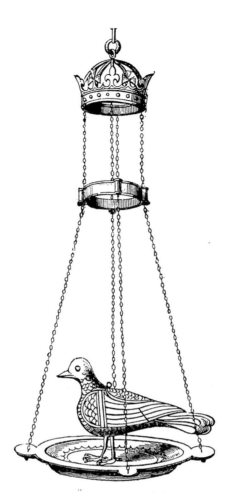

4.5 Pugin's hanging pyx in the form of a dove (*Glossary of Ecclesiastical Ornament*, 1844).

a carved front panel, painted and gilt, and would be equipped with a triptych reredos, with folding side panels which could be closed during the penitential season of Lent. Three gilt lamps would hang in front of the altar, while on the altar itself there would be two large candlesticks – as was the universal custom in pre-Reformation England – as opposed to the now more customary 'big six'. In accordance with the Sarum Rite, two standard candlesticks would be placed in the sanctuary, the candles in them to be lit only at the central part of the Mass, between the *Sanctus* and the communion. The most unusual feature of all was the hanging pyx for the reservation of the Blessed Sacrament. The usual arrangement was to have a tabernacle for this purpose fixed centrally on the altar or on the retable behind it. Instead, Pugin proposed a pyx in the form of a silver dove **(4.5)**, which would be suspended over the altar, and the central panel of the reredos would be decorated accordingly with rays of glory to surround the pyx, and adoring angels on either side. Pugin was careful to cite his 'authorities' for this, stressing that, far from being an innovation, it marked the revival of 'an ancient and formerly general practice.' Other revivals included the provision of stone sedilia, on the south side of the chancel for the priest, deacon and sub-deacon at High Mass, along with a sacrarium for the washing of the sacred vessels and to accommodate the wine and water cruets. In the north wall there was to be an Easter sepulchre for use during the Holy

Week ceremonies which Pugin sought to revive, and which he described in some detail.[12]

To those accustomed to attending Mass in an outbuilding at the back of the Blue Bell Inn, the prospect of having something that actually looked like a church, small though it was, must have been greatly exciting, and a sign too that the Catholic Church was emerging from the shadows into the mainstream of public life in towns like Uttoxeter. The church's more unusual features were, however, bound to excite curiosity and controversy. Pugin was obliged to abandon the proposed hanging pyx in favour of a fixed tabernacle in the form of a battlemented tower, but for this too Pugin was able to cite medieval precedent.[13] The central panel of the reredos was redesigned to depict the Madonna and Child, but otherwise the furnishings of the chancel were carried out exactly as Pugin had described them, and they were thus illustrated in the first of Pugin's *Dublin Review* articles in 1841 **(4.6)**.[14] A quantity of metalwork, all to Pugin's design, was ordered from Hardman's,[15] and Lord Shrewsbury made a special gift of the stained glass for the lancets of the east window. Possibly by Thomas Willement (1786-1871), who was still working for the earl

4.6 St Mary's was the first of Pugin's 'true principles' churches: the interior as built. Woodcut by Pugin (*Dublin Review*, 1841).

4.7 The full medieval form of episcopal vestments as illustrated in Pugin's *Glossary*, 1844.

at Alton Towers in 1839, the glass consisted of geometrical patterns. It was replaced in 1887. Though by no means as rich as the interiors of some of his later churches, the combined effect of all of these furnishings was quite striking as the contemporary illustrations show, and Pugin saw to it that St Mary's lacked nothing that he considered necessary for the correct celebration of the Sarum Rite.

The revival of the English Catholic Rite advocated by Pugin and Dr Rock extended to matters of music – they wished to see the almost exclusive use of Gregorian chant[16] – and to the style of vestments proper to English usage. Regarding the latter, Pugin wanted to revive the very full medieval shape of the surplice, the white robe worn by clerics in choir and by acolytes; and the chasuble, the principal vestment worn by the priest at Mass. Both of these had undergone a process of attenuation in continental Europe over the centuries. The surplice had become much shorter, barely reaching the knees and forearms, and was generally called a cotta. The chasuble was originally a very full vestment, almost circular in shape with a central aperture for putting on over the head, and of calf-length **(4.7)**. This had likewise been cut down, particularly at the sides, to assist the priest's freedom of movement, and was generally shorter. The most extreme examples were the type known, from their shape, as 'fiddle-backs'. Even surviving medieval chasubles had been mutilated to convert them to modern shape, and the left-over remnants used to make smaller items such as stoles.[17] Consequently the original form of these vestments had long been forgotten, so that Pugin's attempted revival of them seemed like innovation, and it was strongly opposed in some quarters. Pugin saw the opening of St Mary's, Uttoxeter, as a prime opportunity to introduce the 'new' chasubles and surplices into a parish church. Dr Rock had already had an ample Gothic chasuble made out of purple material in readiness for use in the Towers Chapel at Advent, and in May 1839 Pugin asked to borrow it to use as a pattern. 'I am fully determined to carry <u>out</u> Uttoxeter,' he wrote, 'I want all the plain chasubles made like your purple one so pray send it to me.'[18]

The use of these vestments at the opening of St Mary's in August brought about an immediate protest from Bishop Baines, the Vicar Apostolic of the Western District, who refused to attend the opening when he discovered that the Pugin vestments were to be used.[19] He was not alone in his view. When the first of Pugin's large churches – St Mary's, Derby – was opened in October 1839, Bishop John Briggs, Vicar Apostolic of the Northern District, complained of '*Pugin* Chasubles, Dalmatics, Albs and Surplices. I could have fancied myself attending a Mass in the Greek church.'[20] Before the end of the year representations had been made to the Propaganda Fidei in Rome which resulted in a reprimand for both Pugin and Bishop Walsh for what were regarded as unauthorised innovations. Pugin pointed out the absurdity of it in a letter to Dr Rock: 'At Uttoxeter Mr Morgan had but *one* wretched vestment of *no colour* for all days, he procured a *compleat set* & they are prohibited as *not canonical*. What a farce.'[21] In a letter written at the same time to Ambrose Phillipps he expressed himself even more forcefully:

> We have a detestable crew to deal with – ignorance, prejudice, timidity, tepidity. All combined … we have a sorry soil to plant in, and that not from protestantism; actually protestants in many cases are far better inclined to Catholicism than half the soi-disant Catholics of our day. Every attempt to restore religion to its antient dignity and glory is met with sneers, insult and opposition from those who ought to be foremost in aiding the great work. … Everything in modern chapels is bad – vestments, music, altars, – and the present Race of Catholics are so used to the miserable expedients which have been resorted to, through necessity, that they will not avail themselves of better things now that they are offered them.[22]

To the modern mind these disputes over clerical vesture may seem purely academic, but to men like Pugin, Ambrose Phillipps and Bishop Walsh the vestments were significant ingredients in a general confection that would set before the eyes of Englishmen the Church of their forefathers in all its splendour; the Latin Mass, of course, but in a form and setting that was unmistakably English. Pugin and Phillipps urged Lord Shrewsbury to make representations to Rome, and his influence may have helped to prevent any formal censure being promulgated, but this was by no means the end of the matter. The underlying issue was one of authority. Bishop Baines regarded the Pugin chasuble as an innovation which needed the sanction of Rome before he could use it. Pugin, Phillipps and Rock believed that it was the post-medieval deviations which lacked proper authority, and that in any event the sanction of the Vicar Apostolic (in this case Bishop Walsh) was sufficient for the reintroduction of a style which had once been universally approved.

St Mary's, Uttoxeter, was opened on 22 August 1839. Dr Walsh presided, wearing the controversial cloth of gold vestments designed by Pugin and paid for by Lord Shrewsbury. Observers noted the censer, processional cross and acolytes' candlesticks, all of silver, which were carried at the head of the procession; the fourteen priests clad in voluminous surplices of the Old English type, and others arrayed in rich copes.[23] Dr Rock sang the Mass, and the address was given by the Revd George Spencer. Lord and Lady Shrewsbury were present, along with their son-in-law and daughter, the Prince and Princess Doria Pamphili; and, of course, Pugin. The choir of Alton Towers Chapel sang, and their repertoire included items by Mozart and Haydn – a small concession to 'modernism'. Later in the year a lengthy poem appeared in the *Orthodox Journal*. Written under the pseudonym 'Britannicus' by someone who had actually attended the opening service, the poem described the ceremonies and – without actually naming them – paid eloquent tribute to bishop, preacher and architect:

> It was a lovely sight to gaze around
> That Gothic fane – while gazing there to feel
> That *he* whose genius framed the sacred pile
> Is one whose noble aim it is to raise
> God's fallen altars thro' the land – to blend
> The holy and the beautiful once more![24]

While extolling the many virtues of Uttoxeter, Pugin could not restrain himself from damning, in the same *Orthodox Journal* article, those who continued to build Catholic churches in the Italian and 'meeting-house' styles. The new church of St Francis Xavier, Hereford, was dismissed as a 'hideous mass of semi-Italian building under the very walls of the venerable pile of Hereford cathedral.'[25] A correspondent to the *Orthodox Journal* who, under the pseudonym 'Catholicus', attempted to defend the meeting-house style as a cheap way of providing new churches, was told by Pugin that 'Methodisticus' would be a more appropriate name for one who dared hold up 'that spawn of the original Protestant faction – the Methodist body – as an example for imitation.'[26] Such intemperate outbursts brought sharp responses even from those who admired Pugin's work; for example:

4.8 St Mary's, Uttoxeter: interior after the alterations of 1913.

I do think Mr Pugin is getting out of his place, and assuming that dictatorial authority that does not belong to him, and using those abusive epithets that ill accord with the gentleman and the Christian. ...We are almost led involuntarily to ask for the Bull appointing him superior of all the Catholics in England. ... Mr Pugin is a diamond, and, we thought, a polished one; but he shews that he is not polished on all sides. He is so fond of antiquity that he cannot avoid mixing the rudeness of a Hector with the valour of a Christian knight.'[27]

Senior clergy treated with varying degrees of good humour and indignation the audacity of a convert of only a few years' standing who dressed like a Bohemian yet dared to lecture them on what they should wear at Mass, and who pushed them around the sanctuary at Oscott like pieces on a chess-board. The friendly Bishop Walsh nicknamed him 'Archbishop Pugens', probably because of his habit of prefacing his signature with a cross, as the bishops did; while the antagonistic Dr Bowden of Sedgley Park, irritated by Pugin's influence over Walsh, emphatically declared, 'If Archbishop Pugens comes here I shall not do anything he advises.'[28] Pugin did not win all his battles, but it is of significance that from 1839 few churches were built in styles other than Puginesque Gothic. The support of Walsh was crucial in effecting the transition from 'chapel' to 'church' architecture, and Pugin said of him that no English bishop since the days of William Wykeham (1324-1404) had 'done so much for the revival of the Glory of the house of God.'[29]

Uttoxeter had an important part in effecting the transition, and it was this church that Pugin had in mind when he wrote in October 1840 that he had done more than anyone living in the restoration of true ecclesiastical architecture: 'I rebuilt the first sedilia, I set up the first Sacrarium, I erected the first Rood & Rood loft. I restored the 2 candlesticks on the altar & the curtains on each side'.[30] It was also in some ways a victim of its own success. By the late

4.9 Among the survivors of subsequent alterations to St Mary's: the front panel of Pugin's high altar (Michael Fisher).

1870s the congregation had outgrown the building, and many had to stand out in the street for Sunday Mass. In 1879 a new chancel was added to the design of Pugin's youngest son, Peter Paul (1851-1904), who also provided a new reredos. The central panel of his father's triptych was taken to a new Catholic chapel at Draycott-in-the-Clay, about five miles distant, where it remained until the closure of that chapel in 1973. St Mary's was enlarged again in 1913 by Henry Sandy of Stafford, who added the aisles, narthex, Lady Chapel and sacristies **(4.8)**.[31] Pugin's Easter sepulchre was moved into the Lady Chapel where is was used for the altar and reredos – with the addition of an Italian mosaic of the Annunciation. Pugin's high altar **(4.9)** with its richly carved and coloured panels is still *in situ* beneath his son's marble reredos of 1879. The last vestiges of his rood-beam were also relocated here: the moulded corbels with figures of angels. For some inexplicable reason the double bell-cote over the western gable was replaced with a single one. If Pugin had not written a description of St Mary's, and illustrated it, his intentions would now be difficult to understand,[32] but in 1839 he was making a bold statement about the service of art to religion, as he had expounded it to the students of Oscott only a few months previously:

> The Mass, whether offered up in a garret, or a cathedral, is essentially the same sacrifice; yet, who will not allow that, when surrounded by all the holy splendour of Catholic worship, these august mysteries appear ten times more overpowering and majestic?'[33]

5

To heaven by Gothic:
St John's, Alton, and Alton Castle

'It will be the most perfect thing in England'
A.W.N. Pugin to Lord Shrewsbury, 24 December 1841

No sooner had the little church of St Mary at Uttoxeter been opened than Pugin was planning his next Staffordshire project – the Hospital of St John the Baptist in Alton village, and the rebuilding of Alton's medieval castle. Nowhere else is it possible to be so completely surrounded by Pugin's buildings – and ones of the highest quality too – than in the precincts of St John's, with the Hospital buildings ranged around three sides of a quadrangle, the adjacent schoolroom/chapel standing on the very edge of a high precipice above the Churnet Valley, with the pyramid-capped towers of the Castle rising from a rocky spur separated from the other buildings by a deep ravine and linked by a timber bridge. Down in the valley, Pugin's gatehouse guards the approach to the Shrewsbury domain, while on the summit the rock-faced Flag Tower hints at the neo-medieval glories of Alton Towers which lie beyond. It was here that Pugin had his best opportunity of moving beyond the mere building and furnishing of a church, important though that was, to the fulfilment of the social ideals of the Catholic Revival which were also set out in his writings as an important part of his vision for the renewal of England. St Giles's, Cheadle, is rightly regarded as Pugin's most perfect revival of an English parish church, but in his own mind the Hospital of St John was of equal importance. 'This job and Cheadle spoils me for all others', he told Lord Shrewsbury. 'They are the only 2 buildings on which I can Look with real satisfaction … I think the hospital is in the most Lovely situation possible … it will be the most perfect thing in England.'[1]

When the second edition of *Contrasts* was published in 1841 it contained two additional sets of illustrations which reveal Pugin's thoughts on what he perceived to have been the social consequences of the English Reformation. The first set contrasts a view of a Catholic town in 1440, bristling with Gothic towers and spires, with a view of the same town in 1840 by which time the forces of materialism and secularisation have swept away most of what was overtly Christian, and ugliness reigns. The second pair of illustrations takes up the theme – topical in the 1840s – of the treatment of paupers under the 1834 Poor Law Amendment Act. 'Contrasted Residences for the Poor' shows

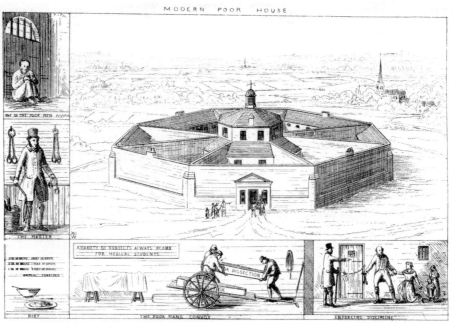

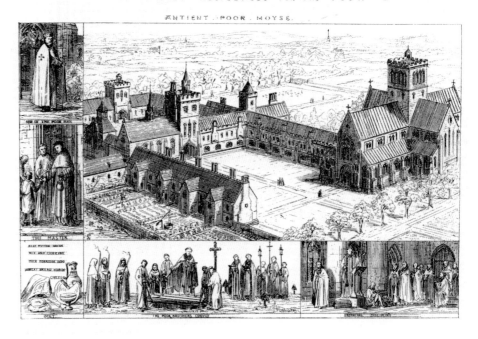

5.1 'Contrasted Residences for the Poor' from *Contrasts*, 2nd edition, 1841.

a spartan utilitarian structure almost identical to the prison building in the 1840 townscape **(5.1)**. Set against this is 'The Ancient Poor House': a splendid range of Gothic buildings which are Pugin's idealised view of the medieval almshouse. Vignettes in the border of each illustration carry the contrast further. The medieval poor are well-dressed and amply fed, and after death they receive a dignified burial will full Catholic rites. On the other hand the modern pauper is threatened with a whip and fetters, is fed on gruel, and when he dies his body is sold for dissection. It is a caricature no doubt, but no more so than Dickens' verbal portrayal of Poor Law institutions in *Oliver Twist*; and unlike the novels of Dickens, Pugin's writings suggested antidotes to the ills he saw around him.

Both sets of etchings made a similar point. In the God-centred Middle Ages, so Pugin believed, there had been social cohesion, and true fellowship. Modern man was by contrast materialistic and unspiritual, and society was deeply divided. *Contrasts* was therefore not merely a book about aesthetics: architecture and art were but the means of reviving the spiritual and social values of the Catholic past. Alton was the place where the vision was to be translated into reality once more, and where Pugin sought to demonstrate how Catholic art and Catholic charity could transform a village into something like the ideal community implied in his view of the medieval town of the mid-1400s. As the new edition of *Contrasts* rolled off the press the buildings were already taking shape: the Hospital of St John the Baptist, and Alton Castle, built entirely at the expense of Lord Shrewsbury, to whom Pugin expressed his highest hopes: 'England is certainly not what it was in 1440, but the thing to be done is to <u>bring it back to that era</u> – & how can this be better Effected than by restoring the Glorious works – of that period, not <u>*mutilated or modernized*</u> but tale quale [exactly] as they existed in the days of England's faith.'[2]

'Hospital' in the medieval sense of the word did not signify a medical institution for the treatment of the sick, but what nowadays might be called sheltered accommodation for the poor and the elderly; that is almshouses with some communal facilities such as a chapel, a hall, and perhaps a library; and a resident warden. Medieval examples include St Cross Hospital in Winchester and Browne's Hospital at Stamford, Lincolnshire. Pugin's diary for 1840 records a visit to Stamford at the beginning of March, at the start of a tour of East Anglian churches, and he was there again in August 1848. Browne's Hospital, founded in 1475, contains many remarkable survivals including fine woodwork and glass, which Pugin undoubtedly saw and noted.

The notion of establishing such an institution at Alton may have been as much Lord Shrewsbury's as Pugin's. After making a grant of land for the founding of a Cistercian monastery in Charnwood Forest (Mount Saint Bernard), Ambrose Phillipps encouraged Lord Shrewsbury to do something similar at Alton. There were medieval antecedents in either case. The Leicestershire seat of the Phillipps family – Garendon Hall – occupied the site of a former Cistercian monastery, while in a valley close to Alton lay the ruins of Croxden Abbey, also Cistercian, founded and endowed in the twelfth century by Lord Shrewsbury's ancestors, the de Verduns of Alton Castle. Initially the earl promised to follow Phillipps' example, and he went some way towards acquiring a site; but in September 1836 he had a change of heart, and wrote to Phillipps from Alton Towers:

> I am apt to think that a society of brothers of Christian Instruction, with almshouses for the poor old people, would be more <u>useful</u> than a regular monkery. What think you? I begin to repent of my promise, not that I do not wish, nay ardently desire, to see a <u>religious</u> establishment on the premises; but I fancy we might have a much more useful one than a Trappist monastery.

125

> The new system of Poor laws makes it once more highly desirable to have almshouses where the poor old forlorn wretches may find a comfortable asylum with the benefits of religion, instead of those horrid haunts the common workhouses.[3]

Whether or not Lord Shrewsbury had by this time actually met Pugin and been influenced by him is a matter for some conjecture. They were most certainly corresponding with each other by the beginning of October 1836. In 1839 Lord Shrewsbury contributed £2,000 towards the building of Mount Saint Bernard's, and Pugin was appointed as architect; but as far as the earl's own estates were concerned there was to be no monastery. Instead the Hospital of St John the Baptist – Lord Shrewsbury's patron saint – was planned as a multi-functional complex of buildings. Pugin began work on the drawings at the beginning of September 1839, completing them on 4 December. His diaries record much travelling about at this time, and attention given to various other schemes, but the fact that Pugin was working on the Hospital plans over a period of several weeks may also be taken as evidence of the great care which he took over a project in which he believed fervently:

> When completed it will present, both in its exterior and internal arrangements, a perfect revival of a Catholic hospital of the old time, of which so many were seized, demolished, and perverted by the sacrilegious tyrant Henry and his successors in church plunder; and in lieu of these most Christian and pious foundations for our poorer brethren, prisons are now substituted for those convicted of poverty.[4]

Here is the man of *Contrasts* rising to the occasion: a 'Gothic passion' indeed!

The site chosen for the Hospital was the area of the Castle, to the south-east of St Peter's parish church in Alton village; a picturesque location high up on the south side of the Churnet Valley, with a sheer drop to the river below. The topography appealed to Pugin, and there is no doubt that the visual impact of a range of buildings in a location such as this influenced their design and deployment: 'The site that has been selected for this hospital', he wrote, 'is one of the most beautiful and suitable for such an edifice that can well be imagined. … When viewed from the opposite hills, its turrets and crosses seem to form but one group with the venerable tower of the parochial church and the varied outline of the castle buildings.'[5]

It is thought that the medieval castle was built by Bertram de Verdun, the founder of Croxden Abbey, in the mid-eleventh century. The Verduns retained possession of Alton until the male line died out in 1316; thereafter it passed by marriage into the hands of the Furnivals. In 1406 John Talbot, later first Earl of Shrewsbury, married Maud Neville, the heiress of the Furnival (and Verdun) properties. Thus the Alton estate, including the Castle, came into the hands of the Talbots, though none of the family seems to have used it as a residence. During the Civil War the Castle was garrisoned for Parliament, and thereafter it fell into decay. An engraving by S. & N. Buck in 1731 shows that considerable portions of the Castle were still standing at this time, but it was an easy quarry for building-stone and rubble for road-mending **(5.2)**. Plundering of the site

5.2 Alton Castle: print by S. and N. Buck, 1731.

continued until the fifteenth Earl put a stop to it,[6] and he took steps to stabilise and preserve what remained.[7] He was after all an antiquarian with a deep interest in his family's Staffordshire roots.

It is difficult to know for certain whether the rebuilding of the Castle formed part of the original scheme or whether it was an after-thought. Pugin's description of work which in 1842 was either in progress or planned mentions only the chapel and Hospital; yet in a footnote he writes that rubbish had been cleared away from the Castle site in 1840, that the location of the Castle chapel was known, and that a twelfth-century thurible had been found buried in the moat.[8] There was a local precedent for castle-building on old foundations. In September 1837 Pugin had visited Stafford Castle, another victim of the Civil War, which had already been partially rebuilt on its medieval foundations by the Catholic Jerningham family who, like the Talbots, were revisiting their Staffordshire roots; but there was more to the rebuilding of Alton Castle than mere antiquarianism.

A deep ravine separates Alton Castle from the Hospital buildings, but they are linked by a bridge, and when viewed either from a distance or from the immediate approach from the village they form a coherent group as Pugin intended they should. Though Lord Shrewsbury resided at the Towers, out of sight on the other side of the valley, the restoration of the Castle had a symbolic value. Castle and almshouse stand together; the architecture is the same noble Gothic; there is no 'contrast' in style, materials, ornament or decoration between mansion and poor-house. In Pugin's vision of England, prince and pauper live cheek-by-jowl in proper dignity and united by a common faith. The church contains no 'squire's pew', and when the time came, the premier earl of England would be laid to rest, not in a grand mausoleum or a lordly family vault, but in a simple grave surrounded by those of his tenantry and bedesmen. Here again is a practical expression of the social ideal portrayed in the 1841 edition of *Contrasts*. Medieval Catholic England was, according to Pugin, 'merry England, at least for the humbler classes; and the architecture was in keeping with the faith and the manners of the times – at once strong and hospitable.'[9]

Pugin's detailed drawings for the Hospital and the Castle do not appear to

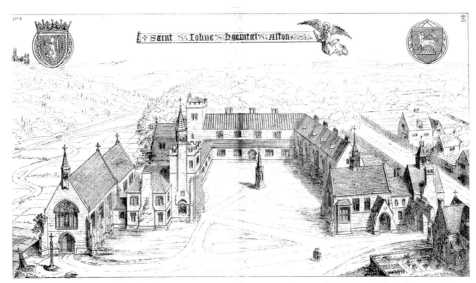

5.3 Hospital of St John: bird's eye view in *The Present State of Ecclesiastical Architecture in England,* 1843.

have survived. What does exist, however, is a bird's-eye view of the Hospital scheme which was used in February 1842 to illustrate an article in the *Dublin Review* **(5.3)**. This was published 1843 as a separate volume entitled *The Present State of Ecclesiastical Architecture in England.* The view shows the buildings arranged around three sides of a quadrangle; the chapel on the north side, the Guildhall buildings on the south, with a residential block connecting them. The northern range had been finished by this time and so the chapel and warden's lodging are shown exactly as built. The remainder of the buildings underwent a degree of modification as the scheme developed, and were the subject of some disagreement between earl and architect. It has to be remembered too that both Pugin and Lord Shrewsbury died before the buildings were entirely finished; and that although some work continued thereafter, it came to an abrupt end with the death of the seventeenth earl in 1856.

Work began in 1840 on the northern range which comprised the chapel, school, and warden's lodging. The chapel would also serve as the parish church for the Catholic residents of Alton and Farley who at this time attended Mass at the Towers Chapel. The earl's newly appointed chaplain, Dr Henry Winter, would take up residence in the warden's lodging, and the school would provide suitable education for local Catholic children. From the very outset the Hospital was seen as much more than a secluded almshouse for the elderly. It was to be rooted in the whole community and to have a role in shaping its future, and that future was avowedly Catholic. The school was particularly important. Apart from a small 'free school' set up in 1682 for the education of twelve children, there was no provision for the education of the poor in Alton, where the population had increased by 46 per cent between 1801 (1,633) and 1831 (2,391). The (Anglican) National Society eventually established a school there in 1845, partly in response to what the Catholic Church was doing.

Outwardly the chapel of St John is of Pugin's 'country church' type, similar to those at Uttoxeter and Warwick Bridge (Carlisle) – a basic nave, chancel, and a simple bellcote on the gable **(5.4)**. Subsequent changes in the way in which the building has been used have, however, obscured the fact that as originally built the nave was designed to function as a schoolroom, while the chapel proper lay east of the chancel arch; but clues are still there. In the first place the statue over the west door is not, as might be expected, that of the church's patron, St John the Baptist, but of St Nicholas, patron saint of children, and at his feet are three small boys in a tub – an allusion to the saint's miraculous restoration to life of three boys who had been murdered in a brine-vat. Secondly, the chancel arch is set with large iron hinge-pins from which were originally hung the doors which could be closed when the nave was being used by the school, and opened when needed to provide additional space

5.4 St John's from the Castle (Mark Titterton).

for worship. For the schoolroom Pugin designed rows of elm benches with hinged flaps which could be raised to form desks, and lowered to turn them into church-seats.[10] Concerned for the comfort of the children, Pugin decided that the seating area should be floored in timber rather than with quarry-tiles which he thought would be too cold for them in winter. Most, if not all of them, would have walked barefoot. The walls were also given a dado of elm 'to prevent the plaster being broken.'[11] A house for the schoolmaster was ready by the winter of 1841,[12] one of a pair of cottages facing the north side of St Peter's churchyard which Pugin adapted and extended for the purpose.

The materials used for the Hospital buildings were local ones, principally Hollington sandstone which takes its name from a village three miles from Alton, and of which there is a great abundance all over the area, in a variety of colours ranging from deep red to off-white. Whereas the church and presbytery at Uttoxeter had, in the interests of economy, been built of brick with a stone trim, the buildings at Alton were to be entirely of stone with much ornamental carving and moulding, thus involving a considerable amount of masons' work. In 1841 Pugin opened a new quarry at Counslow, on a ridge between Cheadle and Alton, and this became the principal source of ready-worked sandstone for St Giles', Cheadle, as well as for the continuing work in Alton village and at the Towers. Pugin wrote enthusiastically about the Counslow quarry and the masons' workshops which were built there:

> The counslow quarry is capitally worked. I think there is as good a masons shed as any in England. they can work in it during the severest frost as it all shuts up & the blocks of stone run into it on a sort of railway from the crane. 2 labourers sleep there to protect the tools and the men have a capital refectory, it is quite a settlement & they turn out a deal of work.[13]

So, in addition to his many other roles in the fields of architecture and design, Pugin appears to have assumed personal responsibility for the quarries, providing facilities for the masons to work together in a self-contained community, and ensuring that the production of worked stone could continue all the year round. The establishment of a masons' community at Counslow seems to have been another of Pugin's revivals, looking back as it did to medieval times when building lodges attached to cathedrals and greater churches served both as workshops and schools where architects and craftsmen would learn together and where skills would be passed on. There is a wider significance too. Having read Pugin's *True Principles,* the central figure of the German Gothic Revival, August Reichensperger (1808-95) took up the notion of the building lodge, or *Bauhütte* as the means whereby the Puginian principles of structural integrity, functional expression, truth to materials and fidelity to medieval precedent, could best be transmitted.[14] Reichensperger was present at the consecration of St Giles', Cheadle, in September 1846.

The quarry-faces at Counslow can still be seen, along with the well from which the masons would have drawn their water. Remains of the buildings mentioned by Pugin still are there too, and portions of the paved wagonways by which stone was transported in one direction to Cheadle, and in the other

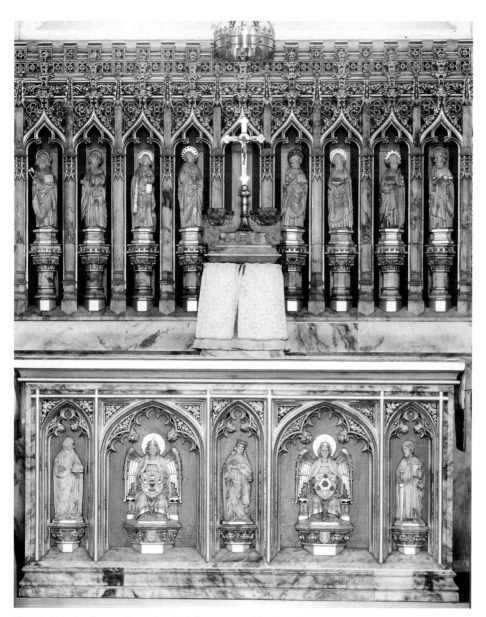

5.5 St John's: altar and reredos by Thomas Roddis (Mark Titterton).

to Alton where construction work was taking place at the Hospital of St John, the Castle, and at Alton Towers. The grooves worn by the passage of many wagons testify to the huge amount of activity which took place at Counslow as these three distinct groups of buildings took shape. The 1841 census figures reveal that in Alton there were 21 men employed in stone-quarrying, and a further 20 stonemasons. Not far from the quarry was a cottage which stood at the entrance to the Earl's Drive, the main entrance to the Alton Towers estate from the Cheadle side. Pugin carried out improvements and additions to this building which was renamed Counslow Lodge. The alterations included the addition of a stone Talbot and various heraldic devices on the gables.

For the altars and for fine carving, Pugin was encouraged by Lord

Shrewsbury to revive the use of alabaster which in medieval times had been used extensively for statues, reredoses and monuments.[15] There were alabaster quarries at Fauld, near Tutbury, which Shrewsbury suggested Pugin might use. At this time, however, the material was being mined only for making gypsum for plaster, and Pugin had to send his own quarrymen:

> I have had a deal of trouble to get it for the people the quarry belongs to are so stupid; they blast it & it all flies into small pieces. We were obliged to send off 2 of our men to quarry the blocks at last, but it is well worth the trouble, it looks exactly like the old thing & when some of the mouldings are gilt it will be rich indeed.[16]

To ensure the success of this revival of a lost art, Pugin needed a skilled sculptor who could learn to use alabaster competently, and he found one in Thomas Roddis of the Sutton Coldfield firm of stonemasons who built Oscott College. He had been trained as a sculptor by Sir Francis Chantrey (1781-1841); Pugin had already used him to carve fittings for St Augustine's church, Solihull (1838), and he moved to Cheadle in 1842. It is known that Pugin provided examples of genuine medieval sculpture for his craftsmen to work from, and there was a collection at Oscott. Fine examples lay close at hand too, for in the church at Norbury, between Alton and Ashbourne, were the alabaster tombs of the Fitzherbert family dating from the fifteenth century. Early in 1841 Pugin sent a plasterer to make casts of one of these to install in the Octagon at Alton Towers.[17] Around the sides of the tomb-chest are figures in rich canopied niches. The reredos which Roddis carved for St John's is so remarkably similar in style that these casts may well have served as models before being assembled at the Towers, figures of saints being substituted for the secular figures portrayed on the sarcophagus. The saints were, in fact, supplied by Pugin ready-made, and they could be of some antiquity.[18] Here Pugin broke one of his own principles, namely that of truth to materials, for although the figures look as though they are made of alabaster they are of carved from wood which has been suitably disguised. The altar itself has alabaster figures of angels and saints under Gothic arches, all richly coloured and gilt (5.5). Pugin was delighted with the result and in February 1842 he wrote from the Towers to Lord Shrewsbury:

> Roddis has produced a glorious altar in the alabaster. It is an exquisite material. I should never have revived it without your Lordship had urged it, and now I am quite delighted with the effort. It has a very rich appearance and the mouldings show through perfectly. Roddis now works in the most exquisite manner & is now indispensable for this sort of work.[19]

Other craftsmen were more local, for example Peter and John Bailey of Alton, stonemasons who had already worked on the buildings at the Towers, Thomas Kearns, Lord Shrewsbury's painter and glazier who carried out the internal decorations at St John's and in other churches of the Pugin-Shrewsbury partnership, and carpenter Thomas Harris. Superintending the entire operation was John Denny who had become clerk of works at the Towers in the summer of 1839. Though Pugin had many other projects in hand, his diaries for 1840–2

5.6 St John's: interior (*Dublin Review*, 1842).

record almost monthly visits to Alton, and some of these were spread over a week or more. This, as well as the regular correspondence which he maintained with the earl and with Denny, reveal Pugin's passionate commitment to this project. Here at any rate his efforts would not be curtailed by lack of funds, and this being the case, he knew that it could make or break his reputation as a working architect. His determination that it should be perfect in every respect is made clear in the lengthy reports which he sent to Lord Shrewsbury during the earl's prolonged stay in Rome during the Autumn and Winter of 1841. The earl was not expected to return to Alton until the Spring of 1842 by which time Pugin hoped that the chapel at the Hospital would be ready for consecration. By the Autumn of 1841 the church at Cheadle was also well under way, and so the Counslow quarrymen and masons would have been extremely busy. Pugin too was active making drawings for several buildings. He was also suffering from bouts of illness, and although Lord Shrewsbury wanted him to join him in Rome so that they could discuss matters face-to-face, he firmly declared that he intended to spend the winter at home. 'I can assure your Lordship', he wrote at the end of September, 'that such a journey as that to Rome would probably cost me my Life at the present time'. In the same letter he gave an account of the buildings, expressing his gratitude to the earl for his encouragement: 'already crowds of people come to see the hospital. ... this and Cheadle are all my hope. Every time I go to these buildings I feel truly grateful to your Lordship for if it had not been for you I never should have had the opportunity of doing a really good thing.'[20]

Crowds more would come in the next few months following the publication of Pugin's enthusiastic description of the work in the *Dublin Review* in February, and the consecration of the altar by Bishop Walsh on 13 July 1842.[21] In addition to the bird's-eye view of the Hospital buildings, Pugin included a woodcut of the interior of the chapel **(5.6)**. In the foreground is the finely carved rood-screen which stood, not under the chancel arch, but to the east of it close to the sacristy door. This was removed in the 1960s to the Birmingham Museum, but the crucifix from it still hangs from the roof. The open timber roof is supported on corbels in the form of angels. The poppy-head benches are particularly fine. 'The benches are precisely similar to those remaining in some ancient parish churches in Norfolk, with low backs filled with perforated tracery of various patterns; the poppy-heads are all carved representing oak and vine leaves, lilies, roses, lions, angels, and other emblems.'[22] The emblems include those of Bishop Walsh and Lord Shrewsbury **(5.7)**. It goes almost without saying that the somewhat crude organ-gallery at the west end is not part of Pugin's original scheme.

The carved benches were far more splendid than those for St Giles', Cheadle, as indeed everything that Pugin did at St John's is splendid. Thus it is easy to forget that this is not a rich man's private chapel, but a place of worship designed principally for the poor people of Alton who, in Pugin's scheme of things, deserved equal consideration at the hands of the Church. How different, therefore, it is from the dingy chapels of the workhouses built by the Protestant State; different too from the arrangements in the nearby parish church of St Peter, where the high-sided box-pews were only for those who could afford to pay 'pew rent' for them, and where the poor were confined to mean benches, if indeed they could find seats at all.

With the exception of the west window, which is by Paul Woodroffe (1875-

5.7 St John's: detail of the bench-end depicting Bishop Thomas Walsh (Mark Titterton).

1954), all the glass for the windows was made by Thomas Willement who had provided glass and other decorations for Alton Towers. The seven windows in the nave have armorial devices of the Verdun, Neville and Furnival families, diagonal bands with the Shrewsbury motto *Prest d'accomplir*, emblems of saints, and the inscription, 'Of your charity pray for the good estate of John the

5.8 St John's: detail of the east window (Mark Titterton).

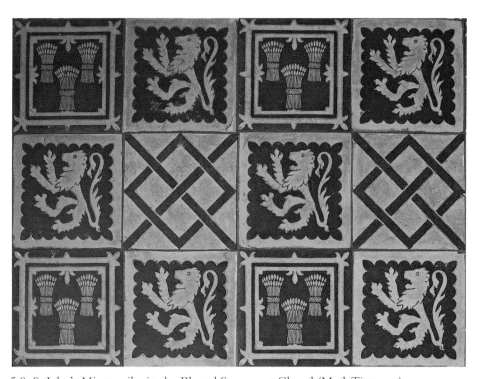

5.9 St John's: Minton tiles in the Blessed Sacrament Chapel (Mark Titterton).

sixteenth Earl of Shrewsbury, who founded this hospital in honour of St John the Baptist, Anno Domini 1840. St. John pray for us. Amen.'

The east window has figures of the Virgin and Child, St John the Baptist and St Nicholas **(5.8)**. All of this glass is listed in Willement's ledger, along with the side windows and the glass in the cloister and Blessed Sacrament Chapel. Drawings by Pugin of details of the east window are also preserved in the Willement collection.[23] Pugin thought he had been overcharged and vowed never to use Willement again,[24] but the quality of the work was never in doubt: 'I feel assured when your Lordship sees the glorious effect of the glass in the schoolroom you will not blame me. It is not for the urchins but the élite who will flock to see the building which should be in all respects a perfect specimen of the style.'[25] Pugin was not here slighting the poor children – such a thing was not in his nature. He was rather indicating the propaganda value of the Hospital which would be of absolutely no concern to the pupils but which he hoped would register with visiting members of the Oxford and Cambridge architectural societies; and after all, where else in England were pauper children taught in such a splendid setting?

As at Uttoxeter the arrangements for the reservation of the Blessed Sacrament were a departure from current practice. No provision was made at the high altar. Instead Pugin added a small chapel on the north side of the sanctuary, citing medieval precedent for such an arrangement. Unlike the main part of the church, this has a stone roof with transverse ribs. Here an alabaster altar carved by Roddis with figures of angels adoring the Blessed Sacrament was furnished with a tabernacle in the form of a gilt tower surmounted by a cross. This tower is no longer extant, and a tabernacle was later placed at the main altar. Another innovation was the Easter sepulchre placed not in a wall-recess as at Uttoxeter, but under the arch separating the side-chapel from the main sanctuary.[26] Pugin was delighted with the result: 'The work is remarkably well done. The small chapel of the sepulchre looks 400 years old.'[27] The Minton tiles which once paved the whole area east of the chancel arch survive only in the side-chapel **(5.9)**. The iconography includes the Talbot lion, the de Verdun fret, and the Chester wheatsheaf signifying the earl's office of Admiral of Chester. Almost identical to those at the Mercy convent at Handsworth, they are amongst the earliest encaustic tiles produced by the Minton–Pugin partnership, which makes the destruction of the bulk of them in the 1960s all the more regrettable.[28]

The stencilled patterns which Thomas Kearns applied to the walls suffered an even worse fate than the tiles, for they were completely destroyed in the 1960s. Though not as intense as those at Cheadle, they were nevertheless quite rich. Pugin himself set out all the patterns in July 1843, and gave Kearns 'the strictest instructions to keep at it with 3 men'[29] before leaving for Antwerp to look for 'authorities' for painted decorations for Cheadle. A few days later he wrote to Lord Shrewsbury, 'I hope the diapering at St. John's is going on well. I left strict injunctions for exertion with Kearns. a building is nothing without diapering and colour.'[30] The mid-twentieth century did not agree with him, and so Kearns' stencilling was completely obliterated. The hanging *coronae* by Hardman were also removed, but old postcard views show what St John's was

5.10 St John's: interior before the removal of the rood-screen (postcard of *c*.1900).

like when everything was still intact, and all the furnishings in their proper place **(5.10)**.

The sacristy, on the south side of the chapel, was fitted out with purpose-

5.11 St John's: medieval cross as restored by Hardman's, and the Pugin candlesticks (Mark Titterton).

built almeries and presses for the vestments and vessels which were provided for the proper performance of the liturgy. Among these items was a medieval altar-cross in silver-gilt which Lord Shrewsbury bought from Samuel Pratt, a London antique dealer (5.11). It was of fifteenth-century date, and an inscription on the base records that it was made by a silversmith named Peter for a German bishop. Pugin congratulated the earl on obtaining such an exquisitely beautiful object at a very reasonable price; 'a glorious acquisition.'[31] Of a most elaborate pattern with much filigree and piercing, it was in need of repair – which may account for its having been sold comparatively cheaply – so it was sent to Hardman's for restoration. Pugin promised to design a pair of candlesticks to complement them, as indeed he did, and Hardman made these too. An annotated drawing for them still exists.[32] The candlesticks have Talbot lions in enamelled shields,

5.12 St John's: the Warden's lodging (Michael Fisher).

and the inscription, taken from St Matthew, chapter 11: *Praecursor Domini venit de quo ipse testatur nullus major inter natos mulierum Joanne Baptista* (the forerunner of the Lord comes, of whom the Lord himself bears witness. Among those born of women there is none greater than John the Baptist). The care lavished on these items reflects Pugin's determination that everything at the Hospital must be perfect. It also illustrates what was quite a common practice of his, namely to put a genuine medieval artefact side-by-side with one of his own designing, as if to challenge the observer to detect the difference.

Pugin was concerned that the sacristy and its contents should be properly looked after by someone who was in sympathy with his principles. He complained often enough about his churches being ruined because the clergy did not know how to use them properly. St Mary's, Derby, was a case in point. Though he had equipped the sacristy with everything, only two years after the opening of the church Pugin found it to be untidy and filthy, and the costly vestments given by Lord Shrewsbury were thrust into a corner instead of being kept in the specially made almeries. Such a thing could not be allowed to happen at Alton:

> What a glorious place the hospital at Alton will be with its Warden, confraternity, brethren, children of the school etc. Why, it could be a little paradise. There is not one Catholic hospital existing at the present time in England. What a revival. But I am certain from the very moment the chapel is completed a person must be appointed to fulfil the regular duties of a sacristan or all will be spoilt and he must be a very responsible person for all in his charge.[33]

To the south of the church is the Warden's lodging with its three-storey tower and with a direct link to the chapel and sacristy **(5.12)**. This was also complete by February 1842. Over the entrance is a statue of St John the Baptist, while the label-stops are carved with likenesses of the Earl and Countess of Shrewsbury. The north side of the cloister was also completed at this time. The windows here are inset with roundels of Willement glass, some incorporating

5.13 St John's: the Calvary, only the second of its kind to be erected since the Reformation (Michael Fisher).

antique glass possibly of Flemish origin. In the cloister there are two memorial brasses made by Hardman to Pugin's designs. One commemorates the 15th earl who died in 1827 and was buried at Heythrop. A brass to the countess's parents, Jane Talbot (d. 1843) and William Talbot (d. 1849) is also located in the cloister. Both of them died at Alton and were buried there. The other family memorials are of course those of the founder and his widow who were eventually buried (1852 and 1856 respectively) on the north side of the sanctuary, and that of the seventeenth earl (d. 1856) on the south side.

Everyone, according to Pugin, should be given a decent burial in consecrated ground with full Catholic rites and an appropriate memorial. The point was made in the almshouse drawing in *Contrasts,* and reinforced in the *Dublin Review* article. After he settled at Ramsgate Pugin provided graves at St Augustine's for the bodies of sailors washed ashore after shipwreck, and designed memorials for them. Such memorials had an important instructional value: 'nothing can be more calculated to awaken the solemn and devout feelings, than passing through this resting-place of the faithful departed. How often is the pious Christian moved to pray for his deceased brother, when he sees graven on his tomb – "Of your charity pray for my soul"'![34]

In the *Apology* (1843), Pugin devoted an entire section to the design of appropriate memorials, condemning the use of 'pagan abominations' such as urns, broken columns, extinguished lamps and inverted torches which in post-Reformation times had replaced the Cross which Pugin viewed as 'the most appropriate emblem on the tombs of those who profess to believe in God

5.14 St John's: memorial to stonemason Thomas Burton (Michael Fisher).

crucified for the redemption of man.'[35] He also showed how the various ranks and professions might be indicated on a memorial, from the nobility in their state robes, to craftsmen and artisans represented by the tools of their trade.

Opened in the same year in which the *Apology* appeared, the churchyard at Alton was planned with infinite care as a model Catholic burial ground. A handsome churchyard cross, carved in stone after the medieval fashion, was placed close to the west door, while in the cemetery east of the church there is a large wooden Calvary under a tiled gable **(5.13)**. According to the Abbé Vandrival, who in 1847 visited St John's in the company of Ambrose Phillipps, this crucifix was only the second of its kind to have been set up in England since the Reformation, the first being that at the Phillipps home at Grace Dieu.[36] It was carefully restored in 2008.

Pugin's concern for the proper care of the dying and the dead is illustrated by a letter written to Lord Shrewsbury on Christmas Eve, 1841, in which he mentions the death of Peter Bailey, of the local family of stonemasons. It also reflects the close relationship which Pugin had with many who worked for him on the buildings at Alton: 'As I arrived at Alton the other day the bell was tolling for poor Peter Bailey. He died very penitent & received all the Sacraments. I designed a stone cross to be placed on his grave. He is buried under the yew tree near the Hospital with a simple inscription cut on the cross.'[37] In the margin of the letter Pugin drew a small sketch of the memorial. Peter Bailey was buried in the nearby parish churchyard of St Peter's, for the cemetery at St John's was not opened until 1843. The burial register gives the date of his funeral as 15 December, and his age as 47. A Mass would no doubt have been said for him at the Towers Chapel, but the actual interment was carried out by the Anglican vicar of Alton, the Revd John Pike Jones, who, in accordance with general practice, would have claimed the right to officiate at all interments in the parish churchyard, whether Anglican or not. This practice was a matter of some dispute between him and the earl's chaplain, Dr Rock. There is a very large yew by the wall closest to the Hospital, but, alas, Peter Bailey's memorial is no longer there. There are, however, many of this type at St John's dating from 1843 onwards: small crosses of varied pattern cut in local stone, but standing no more than two feet tall, and with simple inscriptions in Pugin's characteristic modified Gothic lettering which would have been taught to the local stonemasons. One of these is to Thomas Burton, another stonemason, who died in 1848 aged only eighteen. Appropriately, and in accordance with Pugin's philosophy in such matters, the tools of his trade, the square and compasses, are cut at the centre of the cross **(5.14)**.

There are also memorials of a more elaborate kind, such as the ledger-stone with a floriated cross which Pugin designed personally for the children of Richard Orrell who kept the Shrewsbury Hotel by the Farley entrance to the Towers.[38] Thomas Kearns, the painter who decorated the interior of St John's is also buried here, and although he died some years after Pugin, his memorial is exactly of the coped-slab variety commended in *The Present State*, thus showing that the standards set by Pugin continued at least into the later nineteenth century. As one progresses eastwards into the newer part of the burial ground – and into the twentieth century – the incidence of 'Pray for the soul of' diminishes, even in this most Catholic of surroundings, and gives way to the ubiquitous 'In loving memory', sandblasted into slabs of foreign marble and granite.

The opening of the chapel and school in 1842 marked the completion of the first phase of the Hospital buildings, that is, the northern range as illustrated in Pugin's *Dublin Review* article. The precise shape and function of the remainder of the buildings was still uncertain. As originally conceived the eastern range was intended for the accommodation of twelve 'poor brethren' in more commodious lodgings, no doubt, than those provided in the Middle Ages, for example at Browne's Hospital where the brethren slept dormitory-fashion in cubicles in the Infirmary Hall. It was also envisaged that chaplains serving the north Staffordshire missions might, as they became too old to serve, end their days at St John's in relative comfort. This latter notion was developed out of a conversation which Pugin had with Dr Wiseman in December 1841, and it resulted in a change to the original scheme for the eastern side of the Hospital buildings. Wiseman said that there was an endowment of £40 a year for each priest, but that they were presently lodged individually in farm houses all over the district. Pugin thought that if they could be accommodated at Alton they could live in community as a college of priests, and say the Offices together

5.15 Alton Castle with the surviving medieval remains (Michael Fisher).

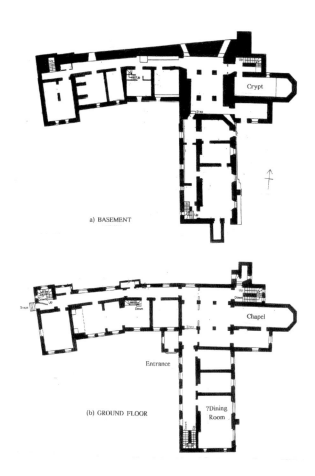

5.16 Alton Castle: plan (Alton Castle Archive, courtesy of Fr Michael White).

in the chapel. He urged Lord Shrewsbury to consider this, and included in one of his letters is a small plan indicating a new scheme for the east range of the Hospital.[39] This would consist of 'a plain convent building … with a common dining room and library for them. … It would be of immense service and become a foundation worthy of the old time'. Under the revised scheme the poor brethren would be housed in the proposed south wing, and a single kitchen would serve both communities.

The organisation of the Hospital was as important to Pugin as the design of its buildings. He made a careful study of the surviving foundation documents for medieval hospitals such as Browne's and St Cross. These convinced him of the need to appoint proper officers, such as the warden and schoolmaster, and to set out firm and precise rules of management:

> unless good and solid rules are established, and the whole placed on a permanent foundation, a few years will render all the labout and expense useless. I think of this night and day … What a glorious place the hospital at Alton will be with its Warden, confraternity, brethren, children of the school etc. Why, it could be a little paradise. There is not one Catholic hospital existing at the present time in England. What a revival.[40]

Although Lord Shrewsbury was a most generous patron, Pugin knew from experience that he was not given to over-spending on any one project, and that he expected the funds to be carefully managed. As if to anticipate any possible objection on the grounds of extra cost, Pugin pointed out that the most expensive part of the Hospital was already complete. The rest would be very simple and could be finished in two years using the existing workforce. Lord Shrewsbury agreed with the idea of accommodating the 'decayed priests', but over the next few months there were yet more changes. The popularity of the new school created a need for more space than could be provided in the existing schoolroom occupying the nave of the chapel. There was also talk of establishing a community of the Sisters of Providence. Meanwhile work had begun on St Giles', Cheadle, a project that was to absorb an increasing amount of Pugin's time, and in the Autumn of 1842 urgent and extensive building operations began at the Towers.[41] Denny's workforce was therefore stretched, and it is not surprising that work at the Hospital slowed down. Discussions between Pugin and Lord Shrewsbury about the next stage of development appear to have resumed in the Spring of 1843, and they proved to be the most controversial: the rebuilding of the Castle.

Alton Castle

With its dramatic location and pyramid-capped towers, Alton Castle is one of the most romantic of Pugin's buildings **(5.15)**, and it is also one of the most

5.17 West wing of Alton Castle during the restoration of 2000 (Michael Fisher).

mysterious in that its purpose is not easy to determine and appears to have changed during the course of construction. The plan of the Castle **(5.16)** is approximately L-shaped, with two wings running west and south of the chapel which stands at the junction. The two wings are different in character, and the more one looks at them the more apparent it becomes that they were built for totally different purposes. Like the chapel, the southern wing is noble in style and ornament. On the first floor are two large rooms with carved stone chimneypieces, and the larger room has a pair of oriel windows. The chimneypieces, the corbelled-out oriels with Pugin's trefoil trademark in the spandrels, and the cornice with its carved bosses, are almost identical with those added by Pugin to the south front of Alton Towers in 1849-51, and this may help to date the south wing of the Castle. As to its purpose, suggestions have been made that it was intended as a residence for the earl's cousin and heir Bertram who, as he approached his 21st birthday (1853), might be expected to set up an establishment of his own. Nearby Cotton Hall, which the earl had purchased in 1843 as a possible future home for Bertram, had been given in 1846 to Frederick Faber and his Brothers of the Will of God.

The Castle might also have been intended ultimately as a dower-house for the countess, should the earl predecease her. Lady Shrewsbury most certainly had a great affection for St John's and attended Mass there frequently when in residence at the Towers.[42] On the building itself there is nothing in the contemporary iconography to identify it specifically with either the countess or with Earl Bertram. The shields on the chimneypieces are blank, and the bosses on the cornice have only general Talbot emblems such as the letters S and T, lion-masks and Talbot dogs. These are, however, enough to indicate that at this stage in the development of the Castle, the southern wing was intended as a residence for a member of that family.

There is no such iconography in the west wing where the cornices are devoid of any ornament, and where there are no grand chimneypieces. The windows are plainer, with fewer cusps in the heads, and the 'Puginian trefoil' is missing. Indeed the whole character of this part of the Castle is gaunt by comparison with the south wing; institutional rather than residential, rising to three storeys with a row of south-facing dormers in the roof, and rows of identical windows **(5.17)**. Built on the very edge of the cliff above the River Churnet, it declines to the south-west part way along its length in order to follow the line of the bedrock. The cellars are partly cut into the rock, and the walls at this level on the north side are enormously thick. The layout of the rooms is institutional too: pairs of identical rooms on the first and second storeys and a row of garrets in the roof. It is not difficult even now to visualise this part of the building as the residence for 'decayed priests' which is what Lord Shrewsbury clearly had in mind for the Castle in 1843.

By the summer of 1843 Lord Shrewsbury had decided to call a halt to the work at the Hospital and to develop the Castle site, using the proposed west wing as the communal residence for aged priests along the lines discussed by Bishop Wiseman and Pugin in 1841. For Pugin, the news that the Hospital was to be left unfinished was bad enough, but the thought of building a Castle for priests was also an affront to his 'true principles'. The design of a building must reflect its function, and priests do not live in castles. Pugin was in Ireland when he received the news, and in response he fired off two letters, one after the other, to the earl. The first, dated 24 June, reveals his anger, his disappointment, and his concern for the way in which the scheme could undermine his credibility as an architect of principle:

> I implore & entreat your Lordship if you do not wish to see me sink with misery to withdraw that dreadful idea about the alteration to the hospital. I would sooner jump off the rocks than build a castelated [*sic*] residence for Priests. I have been really ill since I read the letter. The hospital as designed would be a perfect building. What, no cloister, hall, gatehouse, after it has been engraved and everybody is looking foward to it. I can bear thing as well as anyone, but I would almost as soon cut my throat as to cut that hospital to pieces. For heavens sake, my dear Lord Shrewsbury, abandon this suggestion which must be a device of the Devil to spoil so fair a design. Hence I say no more till I get to Alton, but I know it would spread disappointment on one side and derision on the other.[43]

Of the second letter, written on the very next day, only a fragment has survived, but it reveals Pugin in an even darker mood:

> This Castle at Alton has made me sick at heart after writing a book against mock Castles, a book dedicated to your Lordship,[44] you call on me to violate every principle & build a Castle for Priests!!!! Moses broke the tables of the Law when he saw the Israelites dancing around the golden Calf, & after this. … I could burn everything I ever wrote or drew … & turn fisherman.[45]

The immediate consequence of these letters is not known, except that Pugin did not of course part company with Lord Shrewsbury, or jump off the rocks, or turn fisherman. There was too much to lose, especially Cheadle which, with good reason, he described as 'my consolation in all afflictions.'[46] He had indicated that he would be at Alton by 10 August, and because his diary for 1843 is missing, one can only assume that he was; indeed it would have been a matter of some urgency. The long-term consequence appears to have been a compromise: the Castle scheme would go ahead, and the Hospital would also be completed eventually.

Although a 'castle for priests' was, in Pugin's mind, unthinkable, the idea of adapting Alton Castle into an episcopal residence for Bishop Nicholas Wiseman had much to commend it. The idea appears to have been Lord Shrewsbury's, and it arose from a practical need as well as that of finding a use for the Castle which would earn Pugin's approval. The Catholic Midland District was, geographically, very large; the Irish potato famine of 1845-6 led to mass immigration by Irish Catholics into the Midlands and north where there were opportunities for employment, thus creating the need for new churches and other Catholic institutions. To have the coadjutor bishop resident in the northern part of the district would therefore be advantageous. By the middle of 1847 Lord Shrewsbury had agreed that the central part of the Castle should become an episcopal residence. Pugin's reaction is not known, but *Contrasts*

5.18 The soaring lines of the Castle chapel: the coloured tiles are unique in Pugin's ouevre (Michael Fisher).

(1836) contains a pair of plates entitled 'Contrasted episcopal residences' which expresses his thoughts about what a bishop's house should – and should not – be. A reconstruction of the medieval bishop's palace at Ely (much mutilated in the seventeenth and eighteenth centuries) is contrasted with Ely House, Dover Street, the London residence of the then Bishop of Ely. The palace, with a splendid chapel and great hall, cloister, and crosses on the gables, is quite obviously an ecclesiastical building. Ely House, on the other hand, built in 1772 is Palladian in style, with pedimented windows and nothing, apart from a bishop's mitre set into a medallion, to distinguish it from the houses on either side, or to indicate its function (see 1.7). As with most other things, fitness for purpose was Pugin's guiding principle, and the design of ecclesiastical residences should therefore reveal a Catholic understanding of the office and work of a bishop. Though a castle may be inappropriate as a retirement home for a community of priests, the residence of a bishop should reflect the dignity of his office, with provision for the accommodation of staff, guests and domestic servants, gatherings of clergy, study and prayer. Pugin had already designed and built the bishop's house in Birmingham along these lines, with its fine chapel, hall and library, 'corresponding in style and arrangement with the old ecclesiastical houses,'[47] so the adaptation of Alton Castle as a residence for Bishop Wiseman would have raised few qualms. The soaring chapel, which has been described as a 'Staffordshire Sainte-Chapelle',[48] clearly dominates, thus indicating the essentially religious nature of the building as a whole. It was hoped that the bishop would be able to move in by then end of 1847 but, because of alterations and slow progress in building work, Lord Shrewsbury had to tell him that his residence would not be ready 'before Easter or midsummer next.'[49] By this time Wiseman was in Rome discussing proposals for the restoration of the Catholic hierarchy. While these discussions were in progress the Vicar Apostolic of the London District, Dr Thomas Griffiths, died unexpectedly, and Wiseman was nominated as his successor, so when he returned to England it was to London that he went, as acting Vicar Apostolic, rather than to Birmingham or Alton. Thus ended another attempt to find a practical use for the Castle, and this helps to explain why building operations gradually slowed, and why much interior work remained into the twentieth century and later.

Preparatory work for the buildings at the Castle appears to have begun in September 1843 when a Mr Horden was paid for 'bricks for Alton Castle Chapel.'[50] This also indicates that the chapel was regarded as a priority. It was to be built directly over the crypt of the original medieval chapel, which had been exposed during the clearing of the site, and other basement areas were cut

5.19 The Hôtel Dieu at Beaune, Burgundy (Impressions Combier, Mâcon).

5.20 The Castle: look-out tower: the arches are copied from Browne's Hospital, Stamford, and display the Talbot hounds in the spandrels (Mark Titterton).

into adjacent areas of solid rock. In 1844 Pugin was at Alton from 19 July to the end of the month to supervise, amongst other things, the commencement of work at the Castle, and he notes in his diary that the foundations were started on 27 July.

The earlier controversies were soon forgotten as Pugin became absorbed once more in the work at Alton and Cheadle: 'If I fail in this church may I never come within 20 miles of Alton again which is the severest interdict I could receive,' he had told Lord Shrewsbury.[51] Cheadle was clearly the priority until after the opening in September 1846. Thereafter work at the Castle gathered pace, but not without further disputes. The west wing – the intended residence for the priests – was progressing well in the summer of 1847 and would have been ready for roofing-in before the winter but for a change of plan by the earl himself. Lord Shrewsbury, it seems, wanted to incorporate some features from the derelict palace of Linlithgow, the birthplace of Mary, Queen of Scots,[52] notably the addition of a high roof with dormers to a block which was already intended to be three storeys high. Pugin disagreed:

> There is no comparison between this building and Linlithgow; the latter is an immense pile with a gigantic hall, towers & turrets in every direction, while the castle building if carried up so high with dormers will look like the beginning of a row of houses. Nothing can be more dangerous than looking at points of buildings and trying to imitate bits of them. These architectural books are as bad as the scriptures in the hands of the protestants. If a high roof was to be added the 3rd storey could well have been dispensed with.[53]

In the end Pugin had to concede, and the west wing was built to full three-storey height, complete with high roof, and the dormers on the south side. It is thus taller than the adjacent two-storey south wing, to which it is rather awkwardly joined.

Well might Pugin have compared the picking and choosing of features of different buildings to the protestant habit of ransacking the Bible for handy proof-texts, yet he himself was responsible for other features which make Alton Castle something of a pastiche, albeit a very attractive one. The dramatic location of the medieval ruins, and the deep fosse which separated them from the Hospital buildings, may well have called to mind the French Norman castles which Pugin had seen in his youth, and which were illustrated in Charles Nodier's *Voyages pittoresques et romantiques dans l'ancienne France* (1820).[54] The apsidal chapel is exceedingly high and narrow, with tall windows and a stone-vaulted roof, just like a miniature Sainte-Chapelle, and certainly very different in style from St John's **(5.18)** or indeed from St Giles', Cheadle. Externally the steep roof is covered with coloured tiles, an idea which may have come from the Hotel Dieu, a noted almshouse founded in the fifteenth century at Beaune in Burgundy. The roofs there have brightly coloured tiles arranged in geometrical patterns **(5.19)**. Pugin was travelling in this part of France, between Besançon and Dijon, in June 1847, and Beaune lies only a few miles off this route. It seems unlikely that the architect of a 'perfect revival of a Catholic hospital of old time' would have missed the opportunity of seeing what was one of the best examples. Herbert Minton, the ceramics manufacturer, was asked to experiment with the production of coloured roofing tiles, and by the Autumn of 1848 he had succeeded. 'Minton has perfectly succeeded with the tiles', Pugin told the earl, 'and I have ordered them for the chapel.'[55] This is the only building in which he used coloured tiles to make a patterned roof.

Another hospital, Browne's in Stamford, was the source for the two-light openings set below the pyramid cap of what Pugin called the 'look-out', the tower which stands at the south-west corner of the Castle **(5.20)**. They were copied directly from the cloister arches at Browne's. Having visited Stamford for a second time, in November 1848, Pugin sent the drawings for this tower and gable-end for Lord Shrewsbury's approval.[56] The pyramid caps on the towers may seem like an innovation, but, as Pugin well knew, the towers of medieval churches and castles often had such caps, pyramidal, conical or polygonal, depending on the form of the tower. Their disappearance was generally the result of post-medieval decay. The dramatically tall caps on the twin towers of Southwell Minster (Nottinghamshire) had been removed some 40 years before Pugin's visit there in September 1842, not to be replaced until 1880, but he would doubtless have known of them from earlier drawings.[57] The pyramid caps at Alton Castle, notably the one on the lookout tower, are of the Southwell type. The chapel tower was never finished, and so remains flat-topped.

Actual building work at the Castle seems to have progressed slowly, but Denny and his men were building elsewhere too. No sooner was St Giles' finished (1846) than St Wilfrid's and the other buildings at Cotton were started. After Cotton was finished in 1848 attention turned to the Great Dining Hall and other new rooms at the Towers. That was not, however, the only reason. 'Fine jobs will always be slow', Pugin explained to the earl, who was concerned about the slow progress at the Castle. 'See how the finest trees grow and how long they last in comparison to the quick shooting sorts. Oak versus larch, so it is in building.'[58] 'The work at the castle must be slow. It is impossible to construct so fine and solemn a building very fast.'[59]

The chapel is easily the most fine and solemn part of the Castle, as no doubt it was intended to be. At Alton Towers Pugin inherited a vast barn-like chapel which previous architects had built, and he had to content himself with improving the interior as best he could. At the Castle he had the chance to show what the private chapel of a gentleman's residence ought really to look like when built from scratch by the master himself, and, because the projected rebuilding of Garendon for Ambrose Phillipps never materialised, the chapel at Alton Castle is unique in Pugin's *oeuvre*. In the first place there is a narthex, or ante-chapel, which stands at the junction of the two wings of the building. A pointed doorway at the east end gives access to the chapel itself, although the intended doors were never hung. The narthex extends upwards through both storeys and is crowned with a pyramid-capped lantern. Galleries at first-floor level are carried on stone piers and segmental pointed arches, and there are matching piers and arches in the crypt below. The galleries act as a kind of concourse at this level, with corridors leading from the south and west wings.

In the west gable end of the chapel there is a curious feature of a window in the form of a convex triangle which, because of the form of the roof, is visible only on the outside of the building (**5.21**). It serves as a ventilator, allowing air to circulate in the void between the stone vault of the chapel and the steeply pitched outer roof. It was the subject of a quarrel between Pugin and Denny who, it seems, made some comment to Lord Shrewsbury that because the window did not actually illuminate the chapel it was a sham, and therefore a breach of one of Pugin's basic principles. It appears to have been nothing more than a joke but Pugin, himself the master of cutting satire and abrasive wit, was always extremely sensitive to remarks which impugned his integrity and professional judgement, and in this instance it came from his own clerk of

5.21 Castle Chapel: vaulted roof (Mark Titterton).

5.22 The Castle chapel roof (Mark Titterton).

works, which he counted as disloyalty and ingratitude. Pugin wrote indignantly to Lord Shrewsbury, citing, in characteristic fashion, his medieval 'authorities' for such an arrangement:

> the window in the roof was <u>no sham</u> – any more than the windows in the roofs at Lincoln and Salisbury &c for nothing can contribute more to the preservation of a roof than light & air – & Denny deserves a very sewere reprimand for speaking about matters he does not understand .... I can never permit a man in Denny's position to turn critic – a man who was a bricklayer & whom I have taught everything that he knows.[60]

Denny therefore received a severe 'blowing-up' by letter from Pugin, so severe that he immediately went to the Towers to hand in his notice to Lord Shrewsbury. The earl clearly saw the funny side, and, according to Denny, 'he laughed until I thought he would have rolled off his horse.'[61] Denny was nevertheless mortified by Pugin's reaction, and he wrote a moving apology,

> Your letter cut me to the heart it gave me such a blow that if I had been shot I would not have received a greater shock to find that you the only Friend I have should think that I had betrayed you in such a base and villainous manner. … I would sooner lose my life before I would deceive anyone especially you my only Friend, for I am indebted to you for everything I know.'[62]

The apology was accepted, and Denny was forgiven, but Pugin's subsequent letter to the earl shows how deeply to heart he had taken it:

> I have forgiven Denny & written to him to that effect, as it appears he did not call my gable window a sham one, but I am sure your Lordship will admit that a more horrible charge could not be invented against the author of the <u>true Principles</u> than that of having introduced a sham window especially in such a building as Alton.[63]

The soaring lines of the chapel itself, and the surprising stone-vaulted roof, lift the eye heavenward **(5.22)**. 'It is a room which inspires worship', says Pevsner, but sadly it does so no longer. The stalls have been replaced with refectory tables and the chapel has been turned into a dining area for the use of the young people who now use the Castle as a retreat centre. The corbels from which the vaulting-shafts spring were carved into their present angel-

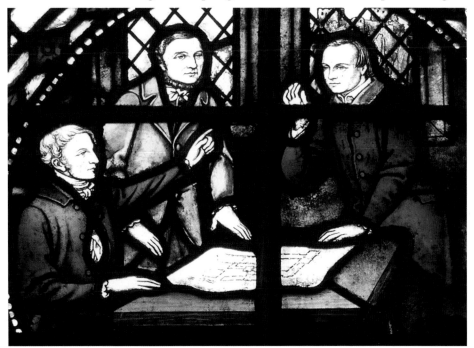

5.23 The Castle chapel: Lord Shrewsbury, Ambrose Phillipps and Pugin, (Mark Titterton).

5.24 St John's Hospital buildings, the main façade (Michael Fisher).

forms only in 1948 in preparation for the Golden Jubilee celebrations of St John's Preparatory School (formerly St Aloysius' School for Little Boys) which occupied the Castle at this time. The capitals of the shafts remain uncarved to this day. These details underline the fact that when the seventeenth earl died in 1856 much internal work was left unfinished. The glass in the windows is likewise of 1948, but it is of interest in that the lower lights form a kind of frieze telling the history of the Castle and Hospital, with reasonable likenesses of Lord Shrewsbury, Pugin, and Ambrose Phillipps **(5.23)**.

With the exception of the cap for the chapel tower, the structural work at the Castle, as distinct from masons' and carpenters' work on the inside, appears to have been completed by the Spring of 1852, when Lord Shrewsbury wrote to Pugin from Palermo:

> I suppose Denny is now at the Hospital having finished the Castle which must be a beautiful object in the summer time – I long to see it again. What a deal will have to be done before our return! … I want to finish the Hospital as a residence <u>before</u> the Castle, that Dr. Winter may get into his new quarters & the Sisters of Providence occupy his old ones, & that the whole yard may be completed & kept neat & trim. Surely the masonry will all be done this summer & autumn, including the gateway & wall – for he has no other job.'[64]

The date of this letter is significant; 1 March 1852 – Pugin's 40th birthday, and his last for he was already in the grip of the final illness which took him to his grave six months later. Aware of Pugin's condition, the earl urged that he should leave immediately for Palermo and take an extended holiday with the Shrewsburys at their Villa Belmonte.[65] It is quite possible that the decision to switch attention from the Castle to the Hospital was taken in the hope that it would aid Pugin's recovery, for the earl knew just how much the project meant to him.

Apart from the gateway and the wall mentioned in the earl's letter, the structural work at the Hospital was already complete by this time, leaving only the interiors to be finished 'as a residence'. The eastern range of buildings intended originally for the 'poor brethren' is shown on a drawing of 1849.[66] The cross-gabled entrance with its corbelled-out oriel, and the dormers **(5.24)**, make it far richer than the 'plain convent building' which Pugin had in mind in 1841 and which is shown in the bird's-eye view of 1842. It was here that the Sisters of Mercy were eventually lodged, but not until 1875, when Dr Winter's successor, Fr Anselm Gurden, moved into what was to have been the schoolmaster's house.

The southern range of buildings consists of the Guildhall **(5.25)**, sturdily-buttressed, and having windows with ogee tracery similar to those in the church at Brewood, with triple lights on the ground floor, and double ones above. The east end of this range is really a separate building, carried, on the south-facing side, by three open arches; and it has a lower roof level. This building forms the junction with the east range, and it was probably intended to accommodate the refectory and the kitchens which, Pugin had said, would serve both the poor brethren and the aged priests.[67] As eventually built, the Guildhall was to house the Upper School. The curious staircase tower at the west end, and the fact that the Guildhall range is different in style from the east range, have led some to doubt of they can be by A.W.N. Pugin at all, and to suggest that they might have been done after 1852 by his son Edward, or even by Fradgley of Uttoxeter.[68] The documentary evidence is, however, clear enough. First of all there is a letter written by Pugin in 1845 to accompany the working drawings:

> I am now enabled to send your Lordship the working drawings of the school and guildhall. I have quite satisfied myself with the staircase tower, and have

5.25 The Guildhall range, intended as the focus of community life (postcard of *c.* 1930).

introduced provision for 3 clock faces which will give it a most picturesque effect. … I think altogether it will make a very substantial and picturesque building.[69]

Only the clock faces are missing from the circular openings set under gables projecting from the saddleback roof **(5.26)**. The top of the tower, with its pyramid-capped bellcote, is similar to those of the school and convent in Cheadle. The Guildhall must have been completed by the Autumn of 1849 because, as stated below, it is known that social functions were taking place there in October of that year. Pugin's consideration of the 'picturesque effect' of his buildings and their environment extended beyond the precincts into the valley below, where any development could impinge upon the prospect of the Castle and Hospital as viewed from the wooded walks below the Towers or from the valley itself. In 1849 the railway arrived in Alton, a branch of the North Staffordshire Railway which linked the towns and villages of the Churnet Valley with the mainline stations at Manchester and Derby. Pugin was enthusiastic about the railways. The great period of railway building coincided exactly with the years when he was most active professionally, giving him a degree of mobility that no previous architect or designer had enjoyed. The railway was thus a key factor in enabling him to undertake so many projects simultaneously in different parts of the country in a working life which spanned little more than fifteen years, and to supervise them personally.

If Alton village was the location of some of Pugin's most spectacular successes, it was also the scene of a sad failure, namely the rejection of his proposals for a railway station that would have complemented his other buildings. The subject of railway architecture interested Pugin, and he included some illustrations in *An Apology for the Revival of Christian Architecture* (1843). It is tempting to think how his ideas might have developed if he had lived longer or had the chance to work with the engineer Isambard Kingdom Brunel (1806-59) with whom he had much in common.[70] The closest Pugin came to being a railway architect, however, was at Alton where he viewed the arrival of the railway as a benefit and as a challenge, thinking that he might have the opportunity to design some bridges and stations. On hearing of the successful launch of the line, he wrote enthusiastically to Lord Shrewsbury, 'This looks well. I hope it will be carried through & then we may get some model stations.'[71] He was most anxious that the earl's estates should be safeguarded against 'vile erections and designs' on the part of the railway company, sending notes about railway bridges for the earl to show to the company, otherwise 'the greatest horrors will be perpetrated under the very walls of the old castle & the whole place ruined. … No engineer ever was a decent architect & if they attempted Gothic it would be frightful.'[72] Clearly, Pugin saw himself as the one to set the standard for railway architecture in this part of Staffordshire.

To begin with, Alton station had just a temporary platform, where Pugin first arrived by train in October 1849, a fact which he noted in a letter to Lord Shrewsbury.[73] He produced some plans and elevations for a permanent station, to be built of brick with a stone trim: 'I have supplied them with everything necessary as far as the exterior is concerned & I think it will make a picturesque building.'[74] When it came to producing detailed specifications of the interior work, however, and putting the designs out to tender – which is what the Company wanted – Pugin admitted that this was not his accustomed way of working, and it was possibly because of this that the Company turned elsewhere. The result was precisely the kind of 'vile erection' that Pugin had most feared: Italianate in style and thus totally at odds with the castle and the station lodge. Perhaps a perverse spirit was at work, a notion that gains credence when it is known that neighbouring stations such as Cheddleton, Oakamoor, Dove Bank and Rocester were all built in Gothic style with high gables, steep roofs, tall chimneys and mullioned windows, of just the kind that Pugin would have built at Alton. As it is, Alton station is the odd one out; moreover it clashes so violently with Pugin's Station Lodge just over the road that they could well have appeared side-by-side in a third edition of *Contrasts* under the title of 'Contrasted Station Buildings.'[75] The architect responsible was almost certainly H.A. Hunt, an engineer-architect who designed other stations for the Churnet Valley Company.

The Station Lodge is a very different building (see 3.18), and it was intended as the entrance to Alton Towers for visitors arriving by train who could then be conveyed by carriage directly up to the house rather than having to take the more circuitous route via the Farley or Quixhill entrances. There was already a building on the site known as Alton Cottage, which was the home of estate worker Joseph Jackson, his wife, and six children. They were to be rehoused in the new building which Lord Shrewsbury wanted to call 'Jackson's Lodge', until Pugin insisted that it be called Gatehouse.[76] Eventually it became known as Station Lodge or Tudor Lodge: a picturesque building, asymmetrical, with fine moulding to the entrance arch, and rich heraldry above it.

It was not just the physical appearance of the village which changed as the buildings took shape. The spiritual and social consequences were far-reaching too, as both earl and architect intended. The free education provided at the new school attracted non-Catholic families, and space for an upper school had eventually to be made in the Guildhall building. The enthusiasm of Dr Winter, who gave evening lectures on aspects of the Catholic Faith, and the charitable work of the Sisters and of the countess too when in residence at the Towers, also played their part. This was indeed the 'Second Spring' of English Catholicism following in the wake of the Emancipation Act. Even before St John's was opened Pugin reported to Lord Shrewsbury,

> It is quite wonderful what Dr Winter has done here. He received <u>whole families</u> into the Church at once. The chapel at the Towers is literally crammed and fresh converts are coming every day.... I expect before many years a regular parish church will have to be constructed to hold the people, but in the meantime the chapel on the hill [i.e. St John's] is indispensable.[77]

By Christmas 1841 he was even more euphoric: 'Nobody now <u>dies</u> a protestant at Alton,' he quipped, 'even if they do not all live catholics.'[78]

The baptism register for St John's (which also records baptisms at the Towers Chapel up to 1842) reflects this trend: a very sharp rise in numbers between

5.26 The Guildhall tower, with circular openings for the intended clock-faces. (Michael Fisher).

1841 and 1846. Dr Winter was a much more effective mission-priest than Daniel Rock had ever been, and was giving regular lectures in the schoolroom on aspects of the Catholic Faith. The social life of the village also found a focus at the Hospital, with the Guildhall functioning as a Mechanics' Institution and as a community centre. In October 1849 Pugin wrote home to his wife, 'There are strange doings here at S. John's. Balls in the Guild Hall, dancing till 2 in the morning, the Rev Dr (Winter) playing the French Horn!!!'[79] Catholic England, as Pugin reminded his readers, was *merry* England.

Not everybody was inclined to be merry, least of all the Revd John Pike Jones, the vicar of St Peter's Anglican church. Jones was not an extreme protestant; indeed, he had been one of the few Anglican clergymen to have argued the case for Catholic Emancipation, and this was no doubt a factor in his appointment to the parish of Alton of which Lord Shrewsbury was the patron.[80] Nevertheless he accused Dr Winter of setting out deliberately to make converts in a much more vigorous way than his predecessor had done, and a war of words ensued. The Abbé Vandrival's statement that in May 1847 Jones had a congregation of only five is almost certainly an understatement,[81] but the parish registers of St Peter's reveal a marked decline in the number of Anglican baptisms in the 1840s, corresponding to the increase at St John's. When it came to the ecclesiastical census of 1851 Jones said, perhaps significantly, that he did not have sufficient data to give the numbers attending St Peter's on census day, 30 March.[82] Attendance at morning Mass at St John's totalled 300, with 104 scholars, while in the evening there were 200 and 104 respectively. The total population of Alton at this time was 2,326.

The death in 1856 of Bertram, the last Catholic Earl of Shrewsbury, and the eventual succession of the Chetwynd-Talbots to the titles (1858) and to the Alton estate (1860) had a profound effect upon the village. The estate accounts show that remaining work on the Castle and Hospital stopped abruptly, and of course the generous financial support hitherto given by the Talbots also ceased. Some villagers considered it prudent to abandon the Catholic Faith so as to identify with their new landlord. It is said that one of them went to work wearing his coat inside-out, to indicate to the new earl that he would quite literally become a turncoat to keep his house and his job.

Thus the scheme which had begun with such optimism in 1840 never came to full fruition. No bedesmen were lodged at the Hospital, no 'decayed priests' came either, and the Castle was home to neither heir nor widow nor bishop. Pugin, in characteristically self-critical mood, once said that he had spent his life thinking fine things and achieving only poor ones. He could not say that of Alton though. It was, along with Cheadle, something that he believed in passionately, and he believed in it right to the end, when he was trying to impress upon a somewhat impatient earl the virtues of progressing slowly with solid and substantial buildings. The quality of the work at Alton speaks for itself; and it speaks too of the skilled craftsmanship of John Denny and those who worked with him – Peter and John Bailey, Thomas Harris, Thomas Kearns, Thomas Roddis, and others whose names are recorded in the estate accounts. The fault, if there is any, lies not with Pugin, but in the failure of the Catholic Talbots to produce a male heir capable of continuing the line and maintaining the level of support for the Church given by Earls John and Bertram. Changes were afoot anyway. The restoration of the hierarchy in 1851, which Earl John supported, diminished the importance of the seigneurial families whose role had been so vital in the years of persecution.

As for the use of the buildings, the schools, which had ever been a part of the scheme of thing, flourished, and the chapel of St John formally became a parish church in 1930. The Hospital became the residence of the Sisters of Mercy who ran the preparatory school established in the Castle in 1921, and when the Sisters left in 1993 the building was for a time used by a community of Benedictine monks. Finally the Castle, which had lain empty since the closure of the preparatory school in 1989, was purchased in 1995 by the Archdiocese of Birmingham on behalf of the Catholic Youth Association, and it has been developed imaginatively as a residential centre for young people. The Hospital now forms part of this complex. Thus the Church has been able gradually to assume responsibility for all of the buildings, and to carry out at least some of the intentions of their architect and founder.

6.1 'a perfect revival of an English parish church' (Photo: Mark Titterton).

6

'Pugin's Gem': St Giles', Cheadle

'I will not let anything pass for Cheadle that is not the true thing. It must be perfection'
A.W.N. *Pugin to Lord Shrewsbury, 23 February 1842*

The opening of the new Catholic church of St Giles, Cheadle, in the late summer of 1846, was accompanied by outdoor processions and neo-medieval splendours which had not been witnessed on the streets of an English town since the sixteenth century, and which would have been almost unthinkable a decade or so earlier. The ceremonies were spread over two days. The formal consecration on Monday, 31 August was essentially a private affair, although the procession of bishops and visiting clergy made a threefold circuit of the church before entering by the west doors, in full view of the crowds who gathered on the street. The celebrations continued into the evening when the Earl of Shrewsbury hosted a banquet for 54 distinguished guests in the State Dining Room at Alton Towers. On the following day – St Giles' Day – the crowds gathered once more in brilliant sunshine to watch the arrival of the eight carriages which brought Lord and Lady Shrewsbury and their guests from the Towers to attend the more public opening service. The reputation of the church had gone before its formal opening, its progress having been widely reported in the Catholic and non-Catholic Press, and through artists and architects who had visited during the five years of its construction. Now, as the long-awaited consecration drew near, 'the whole attention of Catholic Christendom was upon Pugin'[1] who during the course of its design and construction had spared no effort to ensure that his ideal of an English parish church would be perfectly fulfilled **(6.1).** 'I will not let anything pass for Cheadle that is not the true thing', he had promised Lord Shrewsbury: 'It must be perfection.'[2]

Cheadle has two churches dedicated to St Giles: the Anglican parish church built in 1837-8 by James Pigott Pritchett (1789-1868) to replace its decayed medieval predecessor, and Pugin's Catholic St Giles' begun just three years later. Placed side-by-side these two churches might well come from a page of Pugin's *Contrasts*, for they give a striking illustration of the changes which took place over these years, thanks largely to Pugin, in the understanding and application of Gothic church architecture **(6.2).** Based in York, and a nephew of the then

6.2 The two churches of St Giles (postcard of *c.* 1900).

rector of Cheadle, Pritchett designed churches and chapels in the so-called 'Commissioners' style' of Gothic,[3] adapting Perpendicular and Tudor styles to the needs of the Anglican Church at this time. The interior furnishings and decorations of the parish church have been altered drastically since 1838, and it has gained a deep chancel, but at the time of its opening it had all the features which Pugin ridiculed: an embraced west tower, a box-like nave without a proper chancel, 'incorrect' window tracery, galleries on three sides, and a three-decker pulpit obscuring the altar. In other words, it was what Pugin might call a 'government preaching-house' overlaid with a veneer of Gothic ornament. It has to be said, of course, that these arrangements perfectly expressed the state of Anglican worship in the early nineteenth century when the emphasis was on the spoken word, not the performance of a grand liturgy, and when the irreducible minimum of ritual observances required by the 1662 *Book of Common Prayer* had in fact been reduced through decades of neglect. All this was about to change, and had the medieval St Giles' managed to survive just a few years longer, the rebuilding would have been carried out in a very different way under the impact of Pugin's writings, the work of the Oxford and Cambridge architectural societies, and the close proximity of 'the real thing': Pugin's St Giles' to which the 'Oxford Men' (as Pugin was wont to call them) and other Anglican scholars and architects were irresistibly drawn as awestruck devotees and would-be imitators.

It was one of Pugin's frequently voiced complaints that the English Catholic Church of his time was lacking in taste and propriety, that the church buildings were barely distinguishable in design from nonconformist chapels, that their furnishings were foreign and shabby, and that the liturgy was badly performed. The truth of the matter was that the English Catholic Church had only recently emerged, blinking and rubbing its eyes, into the daylight of Emancipation after

250 years of persecution when niceties of architecture, furnishings and ritual were of little concern in comparison with the basic question of the survival of the Catholic Faith. Indeed, some of the dingy chapels and mass-houses were revered as places where the Faith had been nurtured during the Penal times, and on account of their association with some who had actually suffered. As a recent convert, Pugin was not as steeped in recusant history as those who had kept the faith over many generations and at great personal cost. Consequently his passion for the 'real thing' sometimes got the better of him, to the point of alienating those who did not fully share his 'Gothic passion'.

At Uttoxeter in 1839 Pugin had been able to demonstrate that a Catholic church built according to the 'true principles', and properly equipped, need be no more expensive than one which was not; so there was no financial reason for not doing things his way. Though originally conceived as something rather smaller and less ornate than it eventually became, St Giles' was from the beginning intended to be a kind of text-book church in which everything would be done according to the principles set out in Pugin's key writings, with every part of the building designed to instruct, to inform, to have a definite purpose. Unlike the Uttoxeter church, it would have aisles, a tower and spire, and a porch. It was to be the practical expression, in every detail, of the ideal of the medieval parish church as set out in *The True Principles of Pointed or Christian Architecture* (1841):

> An old English parish church, as originally used for ancient worship, was one of the most beautiful and appropriate buildings that the mind of man could conceive; every portion of it answers both a useful and mystical purpose. There stood the tower ... terminated in a heaven-pointing spire surrounded by clusters of pinnacles, and forming a beautiful and instructive emblem of a Christian's brightest hopes. These towers served a double purpose, for in them hung the solemn sounding bells to summon the people to the offices of the church, and by their lofty elevation they served as beacons to direct their footsteps to the sacred spot.
>
> Then the southern porch, destined for the performance of many rites, – the spacious nave and aisles for the faithful ... the impressive doom or judgment pictured over the great chancel arch, – the fretted screen and rood loft, – the mystical separation between the sacrifice and the people, with the emblem of redemption carried on high and surrounded with glory, – the great altar, rich in hangings, placed far from irreverent gaze, and with the brilliant east window terminating this long perspective.

The key phrase here is, 'as originally used for ancient worship'. Pugin intended St Giles' to be the perfect setting for the revival of the Old English liturgy, namely the Sarum Rite which was being researched in depth by Dr Daniel Rock and which, with Pugin's encouragement, had been practised in the chapel at Alton Towers during Rock's time as chaplain to Lord Shrewsbury. Sarum – that is, the liturgy established at Salisbury Cathedral at the time of its building in the thirteenth century – had gradually become the normative rite used in England until the mid-sixteenth century. Although Sarum was little different in form from the Tridentine Mass which had been normative throughout the Western Church since 1570, it was accompanied by a distinctive ceremonial which by the nineteenth century had long been forgotten.[4] It also required a range of medieval-style furnishings, vessels and vestments which had likewise been superseded or abandoned; and in matters of music a return to plainchant which, strictly speaking, was still the only officially sanctioned form of music to be used in the liturgy. Pugin was determined that St Giles' should have everything necessary, even though much of it would be alien to clergy and laity alike, for he believed it was as much a part of the heritage of England as the architecture itself. In the 1830s Pugin had lived close to Salisbury and become thoroughly familiar with every part of the building, knowing that it was the liturgy which had determined the form and layout of the cathedral and the way it had been used throughout the Middle Ages. Both Pugin and Ambrose Phillipps believed that by re-uniting the ancient architecture of England with the liturgy which that architecture expressed, they would put English people back in touch with their rich spiritual heritage and convince them that, far from being 'foreign', 'Roman' or 'popish' Catholic worship was quintessentially English. St Giles' was to be a kind of flagship for *English* Catholicism. It is this which accounts for Pugin's passionate approach to St Giles', his determination that everything should be perfect, and that nothing should be spoiled. This constriction applied as much to Lord Shrewsbury as to anyone else, for notwithstanding the earl's generosity, his devotion to the Catholic Faith and his admiration of Pugin, he sometimes displayed a woeful ignorance of what was, in Pugin's view, the 'real thing'.

The style chosen for St Giles' was the Middle Pointed style of the early fourteenth-century, the period which Pugin had come to regard as the golden age of Christian architecture in England. 'It will be a perfect revival of an English parish church of the time of Edward I,' he told his *Dublin Review* readers in 1841. St Giles' was Pugin's greatest opportunity to show the world what Catholic art could do; and whereas so many of his other buildings were starved because of shortage of money, here he had a wealthy patron who was equally enthusiastic about the role of church buildings in propagating the Catholic Faith. He was determined to make the most of it:

> I am quite willing to stake everything upon the success of Cheadle, and if I fail to produce a glorious effect there then, indeed, it will be time to think of the <u>Roman style.</u> Cheadle will have what none of my other buildings ever got, the means to carry out the work in a solid and finished manner. … When I am annoyed I think of Cheadle and feel happy again.[5]

By the late 1830s there was a practical need for a new Catholic church in Cheadle. A mission had been established in the 1820s by Fr William Wareing (later Bishop of Northampton) as an offshoot of the Cresswell Mission. For a time he used an upstairs room of a private house, no. 4 Charles Street, but it soon proved inadequate. The fifteenth Earl of Shrewsbury (d.1827) regularly attended the mission when he came to Alton without his chaplain, and it was he who commissioned Fr Wareing to look for larger premises. He eventually purchased a building in Charles Street which had been used as an armoury during the Napoleonic Wars, and the adjoining adjutant's house, and these were converted into a chapel and priest's house. The first resident priest was Fr James Jeffries, appointed in 1827 and maintained by the sixteenth Earl of Shrewsbury who in that year succeeded his uncle to the titles and estates. By 1833 the number of communicants had risen to 90, and a school had been established.[6] In the same year Fr Jeffries was succeeded by Fr Francis Fairfax who was to be the first priest of the new St Giles'. The dedication to St Giles, a seventh-century French abbot, was chosen because he had been Cheadle's medieval patron. Indeed, he seems to have been quite popular in north Staffordshire, with other dedications at Newcastle-under-Lyme, Haughton, and the gate-chapel of Croxden Abbey only a few miles from Cheadle. Medieval iconography usually depicted him with a deer, a reference to the story of his being nourished with the milk of a hind while living as a hermit, and of his subsequent rescuing of the animal from the hunters.

Pugin's diary records a visit to Cheadle in October 1839, probably to inspect the site of the new church. In March 1840 he spent several days in Norfolk visiting and sketching medieval churches which he could use as 'authorities' for his own designs. The preliminary drawings for Cheadle were completed by Christmas 1840. 'I have taken great pains with them,' Pugin wrote to Lord Shrewsbury. 'It is the *first really* good thing I have done.'[7] Pugin used three of these drawings, and a ground-plan, to illustrate his first *Dublin Review* article in May 1841 (**6.3**), thus ensuring that St Giles' would attract immediate attention right from the start. The working drawings were complete by early January 1841. 'It would do your heart & eye good to see them,' Pugin wrote to his friend, J.R. Bloxam, 'every detail of an *old English Parish church* is *restored with scrupulous fidelity.*'[8]

'Scrupulous fidelity' involved the close study and drawing of medieval buildings; understanding their form, structure and purpose. In addition to his published works, Pugin's sketch-books, drawings, letters and diaries tell their own stories of wide-ranging study, observation and recording of buildings and details of buildings, both in Britain and in parts of continental Europe. Running through all of them are Pugin's broad theological perspectives which enabled him to interpret and to communicate the principles of Gothic architecture and design in the way one might expect from a man who habitually began his correspondence with the sign of the Cross and the appropriate saint's day in preference to the secular method of dating letters by day and month, and who, in spite of his busy schedule, began and ended each day with a time of prayer. Pugin's correspondence with Lord Shrewsbury and others testifies to the care he exercised over the designs for Cheadle, and there must have been a good many drawings. Few of them have survived. If the working passed into the hands of the clerk of works or the Bailey family of stonemasons – as happened with the Uttoxeter drawings – they subsequently disappeared. Apart from the four preliminary woodcuts he prepared for his 1841 *Dublin Review* article, there are only some details of the Easter sepulchre and sedilia, three sheets of decoration designs done for J.G. Crace, and some metalwork drawings in the John Hardman archive.

6.3 Pugin's drawing of the interior as originally proposed (*Dublin Review,* 1841).

The foundations of St Giles' were laid early in 1841, the year in which
Pugin published *The True Principles.* Pugin promised the earl that he would
stake out the plan himself to avoid there being any mistake in what he then
envisaged as 'a compleat thing in its way as a small parish church.'[9] Existing
structures, such as a beer-shop, were acquired and demolished so as to give the
church the whole of the corner site fronting Bank Street and Chapel Street.
The building was aligned so that the west end would be as close as possible
to the street in order to make the biggest impact when approached from the

Market Square via Cross Street. In respect of St Giles', 'west' and 'east' have always to be understood in the ritual sense, for on account of the narrowness of the site the actual alignment is north-west – south-east. This detail is of some importance when considering the disposition of features such as windows. As at St John's, Alton, the churchyard was planned with scrupulous care, with a large stone cross on the south side as the common memorial to all, as was the medieval custom.

There was no ceremonial stone-laying until 24 February 1842 when Bishop Walsh came to lay a corner-stone, by which time the south side of the church was well-advanced.[10] Most of the stone was quarried locally, at Counslow hill between Cheadle and Alton which yielded excellent sandstones of the 'Hollington' type, and where Pugin set up a masons' community that could work all the year round on dressed stone for Cheadle and for the buildings at Alton.[11]

It appears that Lord Shrewsbury wanted St Giles' to be as far as possible a local product constructed from local materials. Though most of the sandstone came from Counslow, he wanted something stronger for the shafts of the nave pillars because of the weight they would have to carry, and so he requested 'Park stone', a hard grey sandstone from the Alton Park quarry which had been used extensively in the building of Alton Towers. He also obtained some close-grained white Banbury stone for the sedilia and Easter sepulchre because it would take the delicate carving better than Counslow sandstone.[12] Some of the statuary on the outside was carved from ochre-coloured local sandstone, which took fine detail, and was painted red afterwards to match the building stone. Unfortunately some of this has weathered badly, revealing the base colour. The large statues of the four Latin Doctors of the Church which stood under canopied niches at the base of the spire also crumbled, and they had, unfortunately, to be removed for reasons of safety.

Alabaster for the altars came from the Fauld quarry near Tutbury, and it was beautifully carved by Thomas Roddis whose work at St John's, Alton, so delighted Pugin. Roddis also carved the pulpit, out of a single block of stone. It is in the form of an irregular hexagon with one very broad face on the north-west side which incorporates a sacrarium for the adjacent Lady Chapel altar, and it is entered via a doorway from the rood stairs. The statuary includes St John the Baptist (the earl's patron saint), and three noted friar-preachers: St Francis, St Anthony of Padua, and St Bernardine of Siena. Pugin was especially pleased with the quality of Roddis's carving on the capitals of the nave piers, – every one different – which he considered to be equal to those of York Minster.[13] Timber for the roofs and benches in the nave came from the Alton estate, while the encaustic and printed tiles for the floors and walls were made by Wedgwood and Minton of Stoke-on-Trent. Most of Pugin's metalwork – of which St Giles' has one of the finest collections – was made in John Hardman's, Birmingham. To supervise the entire operation Pugin had the services of John Denny who was already in charge of the works at the Towers and St John's. 'Denny is constantly on the ground looking after the men,' Pugin told Lord Shrewsbury. 'His heart is set on the work, and I can thoroughly rely on him'.[14]

In the same letter he promised that all the work would be done by his own men, with the exception of Roddis. This shows that Pugin personally hand-picked the masons, carpenters and others for Cheadle, from amongst those who were already working for him at Alton and at the Towers and whom he had come to know well during his frequent visits. Nothing was to be left to chance. When the earl became concerned at the growing cost of the project, Pugin reminded him that he himself had set the standard:

> now in a recent Letter which I hold your Lordship says it <u>must be a perfect thing</u> & it will be a perfect thing in its way nor do I see any extra heavy expense connected with it. It is your Lordships own stone timber & men with the exception of Roddis the carver & I am sure they will all work well[15]

The use of local materials, local labour, the establishment of the masons' workshops at the Counslow quarry, and Pugin's evident concern for those who worked for him at Cheadle and Alton, and his regular site visits, are evidence of an attitude of mind which differentiate him from architects of the 'trade' variety whose activities were more or less confined to the drawing-board and the office. Pugin firmly believed in the organic culture of the Middle Ages in which architect, artist, craftsman and patron were bound together in the common purpose of affirming the Catholic Faith.

For stained glass, Pugin had to go further afield, to William Wailes of Newcastle upon Tyne, having been disappointed at the quality and the price of work done at the Towers and at St John's by Thomas Willement and William Warrington. 'The Glass painters will shorten my days', he told Lord Shrewsbury, 'they are the greatest plagues I have.'[16] It was not until November 1845 that Pugin's close friend, John Hardman, began making stained glass, by which time the Cheadle windows had been completed. Hardmans were, however, called in to make adjustments to some of the windows, and of course they supplied all of the metalwork for St Giles'. Much of the interior painting was undertaken by the earl's glazier and decorator, Thomas Kearns of Alton, but from 1844 some of the more complex work was done by the London decorating firm of J.G. Crace who worked extensively in many of Pugin's other buildings. Several of the designs which Pugin submitted to Crace for decorations in the chancel still exist.[17] Thus the combined efforts of local and nationally renowned artists, craftsmen and manufacturers, and the generosity of a noble patron, created at St Giles' a stunning interior which brought together the many strands of Pugin's genius as a designer, so much so that some visitors to the church were at a loss as to what to look at first. While the decorating was still in progress, Lord Shrewsbury wrote to Pugin about the visit of the Cheshire ecclesiologist, Rowland Warburton. Entranced by what he saw, he 'pulled out his book to sketch, but as soon as he began one thing, his attention was drawn off to another & a better, & so on till at length he shut up his Book as blank as when he opened it.'[18]

As building progressed, the design was altered; for example the combined height of the tower and spire was increased considerably, the south aisle was extended eastwards by the addition of the Chapel of the Blessed Sacrament,

6.4 The 'heaven-pointing spire' (Mark Titterton).

a north porch was added, and the pillars and walls were completely covered with coloured decoration. So what was to have been a fairly modest parish church grew into something far more grand and ambitious. The cost escalated too, from the £5,000 which Lord Shrewsbury originally agreed to spend, to a final budget of £40,000. Even the original sum was rather more than 'modest' and it needs to be set in the context of other commissions. At Brewood, for example, Pugin was able to build an aisled church with a tower, spire and porch for £2,010. The sudden increase in the funding for St Giles' meant, however, that for once in his life he experienced the exact opposite of what was so often the case. Thus Cheadle – and Alton – provided Pugin with a unique opportunity of realising his vision of a revived Catholic England in all its glory, and this accounts for the infinite care and attention to detail which are reflected in his correspondence with the earl. He also expressed his high hopes and expectations, and what Cheadle meant to him personally: 'it is the <u>first real thing</u> that has been done. It is indeed my great consolation. I pass over all disappointments & mortifications in thankfulness for Cheadle.'[19]

Pugin also referred to St Giles' as 'my consolation in all afflictions,'[20] and there is no doubt that by plunging himself heart and soul into this project he was able to work through the pain and anguish he felt following the death of his second wife, Louisa, in 1844, and the frustration of his plans to marry Mary Amherst as the third Mrs Pugin in 1846. 'I suffer all the agony of despair,' he wrote to Lord Shrewsbury in April 1846, 'The world is cut from under me. How can I design or Study with a broken spirit, without a hope?'[21] To Mary herself he wrote more forcefully, 'you are as much my murderess as if you had stabbed me & indeed less merciful than if you had killed me at once.'[22] In the midst of all this anguish, bitterness, and frustration, St Giles' offered one bright hope. A few days later he wrote to Lord Shrewsbury, 'I was at Alton and Cheadle Thursday and Friday, the sight of that glorious spire somewhat revived me.'[23]

Visible for many miles around, the 'glorious spire' of St Giles' is its most prominent external feature, as indeed it was intended to be (**6.4**). A comparison of the original 1841 design with the tower and spire as they were eventually constructed reveals that several changes took place as the building progressed. The changes amounted to a completely new design for the upper part of the tower and the lower part of the spire. The spiritual and practical necessity of towers with lofty spires, set out in *The True Principles,* was expanded in the first of his *Dublin Review* articles (1841 – reprinted in 1843 as *The Present State*), containing woodcuts of St Giles' and the spire as it was then proposed:

> A church tower is a beacon to direct the faithful to the house of God; it is a badge of ecclesiastical authority, and it is the place from whence the heralds of the solemnities of the church, the bells, send forth the summons. Let no one imagine that a tower is a superfluous expense, it forms an essential part of the building, and should always be provided in the plan of a parochial church.
>
> A tower, to be complete, should be terminated by a spire. ... The vertical principle, emblematic of the resurrection, is a leading characteristic of Christian architecture, and this is nowhere so conspicuous or striking as in the majestic spires of the middle ages.[24]

For Pugin, therefore, spires were as much a *sine qua non* as rood screens were to become, and he had his 'authorities' to hand. In a letter sent in May 1843 to the Oxford Society for Promoting the Study of Gothic Architecture, he asserted that every tower built during the Early English and Decorated periods had, or was intended to have, a spire, and that flat-topped, embattled towers were a product of the fifteenth and sixteenth centuries when Gothic architecture was in decline. This view was challenged by the society's Vice-President, James Ingram, and a good deal of discussion ensued. Having been challenged to prove his claim, Pugin set out his case in some considerable detail in a letter to Ingram which included an exhaustive list of Early and Decorated spires, drawing on his extensive knowledge of English medieval churches, many of which he had visited personally and sketched.[25] This discussion may possibly have influenced Pugin's decision to enlarge and enrich the tower and spire of St Giles', the finest of his executed spires.

Pugin's original plan was for a broach spire with three tiers of lucarnes with gables. At the lower level the lucarnes would be interspersed with small, canopied niches containing figures of saints. By the end of November 1843 he had produced a new design, raising the combined height of the tower and spire to almost 200 feet. Lord Shrewsbury was of course consulted about this, not least because of the considerable additional expenditure involved. Promising that the spire would be 'a most glorious one,' Pugin told the earl that he had 'a rare collection to make it from', indicating that he had a variety of 'authorities' upon which to draw.[26] By the end of March 1844 the approved design had been lithographed, and a copy was sent to J.R. Bloxam: 'I inclose you a lithograph I have just made of the Cheadle spire 190 feet from the ground to the base of cross – which I trust will please you.'[27] He also sent a copy to Dr Daniel Rock, with a similar comment.[28] The fact that such a major alteration could have been carried out at such a late stage in the building process is better understood when it becomes known that the priorities were the construction and roofing-in of the nave, chancel and aisles, so that the fabric could dry out and the interior work could begin. The tower and spire, important though they were, came afterwards, and Pugin even made the point that if sufficient funds were not available for the completion of a church, the tower and spire could be finished at a later date. This is precisely what happened at St Alban's, Macclesfield, where the tower remains only partly built. There were, of course, no financial constraints at Cheadle.

As the height of the tower was increased, the bell-openings were correspondingly elongated. The now taller spire was ornamented with crockets; it had much larger statue niches at the base with elaborately carved gables and pinnacles, and a cluster of four larger pinnacles rising from behind. The main inspiration for it was undoubtedly the spire of Salisbury Cathedral which has a cluster of pinnacles at its base. Under the canopied niches were four large statues of the four Latin Doctors of the Church. While in Paris in May 1844 Pugin wrote to Lord Shrewsbury that he had bought casts 'of the most beautiful character' as models for these statues. 'They are by far the finest I have ever seen'.[29] The four images were completed in October of that year. 'They ought to arrive very shortly,' Pugin told the earl, indicating that the carving had not been done locally, but almost certainly by George Myers at Lambeth. 'they are a fine job. I think very good.'[30] In its final form the spire closely resemblances that for St George's, Southwark, illustrated in Pugin's 1841 *Dublin Review* article but never built. As the design for St Giles' grew, Pugin seized the opportunity to create something rather grander than his spires at St Oswald's, Liverpool, and St John's, Kirkham (Lancashire), which were similar to the one he originally intended for Cheadle. Southwark's loss proved to be Cheadle's great gain, and the spire was later judged to be 'one of the most perfect pieces of C19 Gothic Revival anywhere'.[31]

Pugin's diary notes that the topping-out of the spire took place on 28 March 1844. A floriated cross of gilded wrought iron was fixed at the summit. Just as inside a church the prime function of the rood screen was to display the crucifix – the emblem of redemption – so the spire performed a similar function externally by having a cross fixed to its summit. For this reason, Pugin could not imagine how a fourteenth-century architect could design a tower without a spire, otherwise 'Where would he place the cross? And in those times of mystical architecture, the cross, as surmounting the whole Church, would never have been omitted.'[32] Directly below the spire is the bell-chamber. Pugin says nothing about the acoustic properties of a spire, but he must surely have known that it amplifies the sound of the bells and enhances their resonance. The bells were consecrated on 20 November, and in February 1846 Pugin wrote to Lord Shrewsbury, still wintering in Palermo, that the scaffolding had been removed from the spire and that he had been 'transported with delight' on hearing the bells for the first time: 'the sound of the bells issuing from the tower is ravishing. If everything went on as well as cheadle we should all be in heaven.'[33] The bells were rung again on 2 July when Lord Shrewsbury came to see the church as it neared completion, Pugin, of course, accompanying him.[34] Cast by Thomas Mears of Whitechapel, four of the original six bells are inscribed with invocations to Our Lady, St Francis, St Chad, and St Giles; a reminder that, like much else in Pugin's scheme of things, church bells had a spiritual function as well as a practical one. The others have Biblical texts: *Laudate Dominum de caelis: laudate eum in excelsis* (Praise the Lord of heaven; praise him in the height: Psalm 148), and *Tu es Petrus et super hanc rupem aedificabo ecclesiam meam* (You are Peter, and upon this rock I will build my Church: Matthew 16:18).

St Giles' was not the only project on which Pugin was working. Aged only 29 when the foundations of St Giles' were laid, Pugin already had two major publications to his credit, he was working on a number of other buildings including four cathedrals and two country houses, and while he was occupied with these, more commissions came his way, including the interior designs for the New Palace of Westminster, and more publications flowed from his pen. When Lord Shrewsbury, impatient for results, once joked that he might not have enough to do, Pugin replied with characteristic indignation:

> Your Lordship says I cannot have much to do. Now this is too bad to a man who has hardly time to dine. I never had so much to do. I have several plates to engrave, diverse articles to write, new churches at Newcastle, Birtley, London; finish buildings at Liverpool, London, Loughborough, Downside etc., all sorts of altars, stained windows, screens etc. I have not an instant to spare, nothing to do!!! I am obliged to work without ceasing, why Cheadle

with all its details, tiles, stained windows etc. is almost one man's work. When buildings are carefully finished as mine are with every ornament varied the time they consume is enormous.[35]

The care and energy which the overworked Pugin put into St Giles' are obvious from his writings and from the building itself. His *Dublin Review* article, later included in *The Present State of Ecclesiastical Architecture*, ensured that large numbers of people came to see the church while it was being built and decorated. St Giles' also features prominently in the foreground of the frontispiece to his *Apology* (1843) which shows a bird's eye view of 35 of his churches **(6.5)**. There were those who thought that a market town in the Staffordshire moorlands was an odd location for such an ambitious church, and among them was the earl's former chaplain, Dr Rock, who, despite his admiration of Pugin's work, considered that Cheadle was quite the wrong place, and that few people would

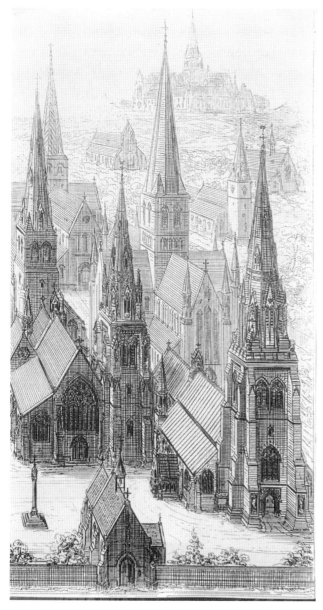

6.5 Frontispiece to Pugin's *Apology*, 1843, showing the proposed spire of St Giles' bottom right.

bother to come and see it.[36] He was soon proved wrong. 'Cheadle … excites immense interest,' Pugin told the earl at the end of August 1841, 'so far from nobody seeing it hundreds come already. It will do immense good.'[37]

At Cheadle, Pugin had the advantage of working for a single patron who shared his enthusiasm for the 'real thing' rather than some squabbling church-building committee such as had dogged some of his earlier enterprises. He had found that, in the interest of economy, such committees were quite prepared to use Protestant craftsmen to produce buildings in any style regardless of the principle of fitness for purpose, and they interfered with the work of the architect. 'Never while I Live will I be shackled or directed by any committee – I regard a catholic committee man a protestant church commissioner much in the same light.'[38] Though he did not have this problem at Cheadle, Pugin sometimes had to argue his case with Lord Shrewsbury when it came to the employment of additional workmen to finish some aspect of the building within a given time, or to increase expenditure. Not everything at Cheadle was plain sailing, and, surprising though it might seem, there were several differences of opinion between Pugin and Lord Shrewsbury over matters of structure, furnishing and decoration, particularly when the earl seems not to have had such a thorough grasp of the 'true principles' as Pugin might have wished. It has sometimes been thought that the expansion of St Giles' into something grander than originally intended was due entirely to Pugin's powers of persuasion over a sometimes hesitant earl, but that was not always the case. In March 1842, when the building was already well advanced, it was Lord Shrewsbury who suggested that the nave be given a clerestory of quatrefoil-shaped windows, and Pugin was obliged to point out that to do so at this stage would mean changing the whole character of the building, raising the level of the nave walls, and altering the tower; so the matter was dropped.[39] It might be argued that, given the subsequent enlargement of the tower and spire, a more lofty nave might have achieved a better balance, but that could not have been foreseen in 1842.

It is a commonly held fallacy that the prime function of the nave of a church is to hold as many people as can possibly be crammed in. The size of a church is often imagined as reflecting its seating capacity; as when visitors marvel at the vastness of some East Anglian church set in a tiny village, and wonder from where on earth the people came to fill it. But there were generally very few seats in medieval churches, and the nave and aisles were not an auditorium filled with a static body of people in fixed seats, but rather liturgical space in which there was movement and drama, for example the festal processions on high days and holy days, and the penitential processions in Lent. Aisles (*aile* = wing) were never intended to be cluttered with seats: they were passageways for processions. The size of the building and the size of the local population were not necessarily related. It was the shape of the liturgy that determined the shape and function of the building, and the Sarum Rite needed space, or, rather, a series of linked spaces in which the different parts of the liturgy could be performed. Fixed seating in the shape of box-pews (which Pugin denounced as 'dozing-pens') came about only after the Reformation when the grand liturgy of previous centuries gave way to the hour-long sermon. Pugin was therefore horrified when Lord Shrewsbury proposed to fill St Giles' with seats running the full width of the nave, without so much as a central passage.

> I have made a church on the effect of which I will stake all I possess ... no-one but your Lordship in this present time could erect such a perfect revival but do not mar it for heavens sake by any modern things. If I was to dispend the benches in one length I might as well pew it from one end to the other. I do not hesitate to say and I speak seriously and advisedly the interior of the church would be ruined spoilt utterly destroyed – now I bear all adversities, miseries, disappointments, bad debts, everything with perfect resignation on the mere hope and delight of Cheadle but I shall sink into utter despondency if your Lordship proposes such dreadful things.[40]

In the end, the seating was arranged as Pugin wished: elm benches in the nave, with a central passage, and in the aisles, following medieval precedent, nothing more than a stone ledge along the walls. The benches presently in the aisles are of a later date; a woodcut of 1847 shows the north aisle as Pugin intended as clear liturgical space **(6.6)**.

Many of Lord Shrewsbury's ideas on church furnishings reflected current taste – or as Pugin would see it, lack of taste – in Catholic church buildings which in certain respects were not unlike nonconformist meeting-houses with their

6.6 The north aisle, published in the *Illustrated London News*, 9 January 1847.

pews and galleries. Large and powerful multi-manual organs were becoming increasingly popular in both Catholic and nonconformist chapels, raised aloft on platforms and galleries. There was one such in the chapel at Oscott, and a huge three-manual one in Lord Shrewsbury's chapel at Alton Towers. Not unnaturally the earl proposed a similar arrangement for Cheadle. To Pugin, however, large organs and galleries were anathema, since both smacked of protestant nonconformity. Moreover, a large organ was totally inappropriate for the type of music he envisaged at Cheadle; strictly Sarum plainchant, with none of the 'fiddling Masses' and quavering operatic sopranos such as had already ruined the opening of some of his other churches. 'Every building I erect is profaned,' he lamented, 'and instead of assisting in conversions only serves to disgust people.'[41.] Pugin was determined that no such thing would happen at 'perfect' St Giles' and so he 'ingeniously got rid of the organ Monstrosity' by proposing an organ chamber to be built over the inner sacristy on the north side of the chancel, big enough to accommodate just a simple single-manual instrument, with a staircase on the outside to that the organist and singers could enter and leave without setting foot in the sanctuary. The provision of a fireplace and flue would ensure that the organ would be kept free from damp. 'Altogether it is an immense improvement at small expense', Pugin argued.[42] Lord Shrewsbury was persuaded, and the 'odious' west gallery was abandoned in favour of Pugin's scheme which forms an interesting multi-gabled group,

6.7 The stone vaulting in the south porch for which Pugin argued powerfully with Lord Shrewsbury (Mark Titterton).

with tall chimneys, on the north side of the church, adding an element of asymmetricality. A large stone lion crouches on the outer sacristy roof. At the west end of the nave, the light from the large window is uninterrupted; there is no stained glass, and the walls are completely unadorned so as to allow the maximum amount of light to be reflected into the nave.

There is no doubt that Pugin's arrangement was a better one. A triple arch with grilles allowed the organist and choir to take their part in the liturgy with a full view into the chancel, but without being seen. Lord Shrewsbury, however, still wanted his western gallery, probably to increase seating capacity since he had lost his argument with Pugin over the proposed seating in the nave, but again Pugin was adamant. A gallery would completely destroy the view down the church from the west doors, and interrupt the lighting of the building from the great west window. This was an important point, because the abundance of stained glass and the absence of a clerestory meant that the principal source of clear light had to be from the west window. Pugin also had an eye to the likely reaction of visiting 'Oxford men' to such an incongruous feature as a gallery, and the consequent damage to his reputation. Thus the idea of a west gallery – and the earl's determination to have it – provoked one of Pugin's most violent outbursts:

> I can only say that when it is erected I shall be almost induced to turn Johnathan (*sic*) Martin and set fire to the building. There are no less than 5 <u>protestant</u> archdeacons pulling down galleries of every kind, all the works of the Camden and Oxford Societies denounce them and now … your Lordship proposes to erect a gallery in the <u>only perfect revival</u> that has been accomplished. What am I to say or do. The gallery would not hold 20 people if crammed full and it would ruin the church. All the learned men will flock to this church as a model and they will see this monstrosity. What a miserable fate awaits every architect of this wretched country. I have lived to see almost every building on which I have set my heart either upset or ruined, and now a gallery at Cheadle, *perfect* Cheadle. Cheadle my consolation in all my afflictions. … Pray my dear Lord Shrewsbury do not mar this great and good work by such a protestantism as a west gallery. All the sublime effect of the tower arch will be lost.[43]

Pugin left the final decision to Lord Shrewsbury once the building work had been completed. In the end the gallery was dispensed with, but high in the south wall of the tower a blocked doorway marks its intended position, and indicates the seriousness of the earl's original proposal.

The south porch was another source of controversy. Porches, as Pugin well understood, were not merely entrances to the church where people might leave their hats and umbrellas, and scrape their shoes. They had a definite liturgical function. Historically the first part of the baptismal rite took place in the porch, so did the reconciliation of penitents. The porch was the correct location of the holy-water stoup from which the faithful would sprinkle themselves before entering the nave, and so prepare themselves for worship and prayer. Following his study of church porches in East Anglia and elsewhere, Pugin was determined to give St Giles' an exceptionally fine south porch, with a groined stone roof.

Lord Shrewsbury thought that a timber roof would suffice, but Pugin argued passionately for a stone one, giving a list of medieval examples. 'I have taken more pains with the south porch at Cheadle than anything I have ever done', he wrote,[44] and one can well believe it **(6.7)**. The porch repays careful study, with its massive angle-buttresses, and the rich carving in the vaulting of the roof and around the stoups which are set under ogee arches. Over the outer door is a statue of Our Lady and the Christ-child, flanked by censing angels, and a floriated cross on the gable. 'The most glorious porch since the old time,' was Pugin's own verdict when he saw it completed in November 1845.[45] The north porch, over which there seems to have been no controversy, is plainer, with a statue of Christ in Majesty giving a blessing. It does not appear on the original plan. The floors of both porches are set with encaustic tiles stamped on the reverse 'Wedgwood Longton', and carrying the text, 'We will go into the house of the Lord with gladness'; while those just inside the inner doors bid those entering to 'pray for the good estate of John the XVI Earl of Shrewsbury of whose goods this church was built'. Wedgwood tiles were also used for the floors of the nave and aisles which have the words *bene fundata est domus domini supram firmam petram* (the house of the Lord is well founded upon a strong rock) worked into the borders. The finer Minton tiles were reserved for the chancel and side-chapels. As one might expect, Talbot iconography is woven into the decoration. The boldest statement is on the west doors **(6.8)** where the gilded ironwork of the hinges is elaborated into rampant lions with engrailed borders, taken directly from the family coat of arms. These represent another diversion from the 1841 drawing in which the doors are shown as quite plain. The lion hinges do not appear in the Hardman metalwork ledgers, and one assumes

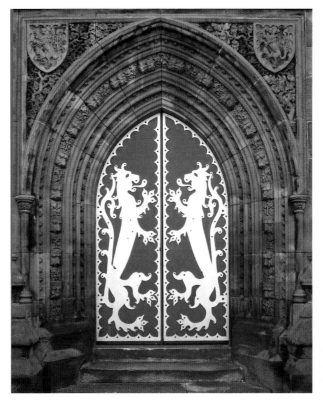

6.8 The Shrewsbury lions on the west doors (Mark Titterton).

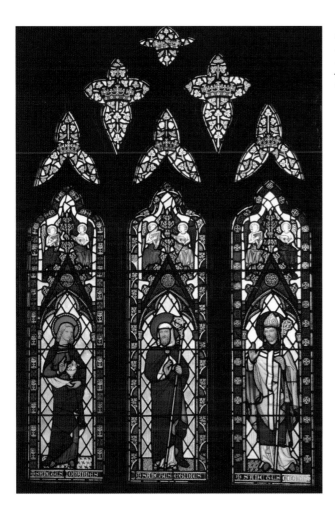

6.9 South aisle window with the figures of St John, St Giles and St Chad (Mark Titterton).

that they were made locally. In the south-west angle of the tower there is the kneeling figure of Lord Shrewsbury, with Christ standing behind him, giving a blessing. Otherwise the allusions are restrained: lion-heads around the west doorway and in the spandrels of the nave arcades, and Talbot hounds on the label stops of the west window.

Naturally, the earl 'of whose goods this church was built' wanted some influence over how it would be used, and although earl and architect were at one in most things, differences of opinion continued to arise over details, with Pugin, almost inevitably, usually winning the argument. There was, for example, a disagreement over the aisle windows. Following ancient precedent, Pugin wanted to make the windows in the south aisle larger than those in the north aisle, and to fill them with stained glass rather than plain. Because the south aisle actually faces south-west, Pugin referred to it in a letter to Lord Shrewsbury as the *west* aisle, and, by reference to the glass in the west-facing state rooms at Alton Towers he reminded the earl that the most beautiful effect of stained glass is produced by light from the setting sun.[46] To reinforce the argument, Pugin protested that he had spent £30 of his own money on an expedition to see and sketch 'the very cream of the Norfolk churches', and that he had then spent weeks on the working drawings for the windows. Once again, the earl gave way. In February 1844 Pugin visited William Wailes' workshop in Newcastle upon

Tyne to see the work in progress, and he was delighted with the richness of the glass and with the standard of draughtsmanship.[47] Furthermore Wailes' glass was up to 60 per cent cheaper than Willement's,[48] which no doubt encouraged Lord Shrewsbury to allow stained glass throughout.

The stained glass was not there simply to look beautiful. It had an instructional value too in its representation of Biblical characters, figures of saints, and the graphic representation and exposition of Christian doctrines. This 'poor man's Bible' as it was sometimes called, was needed no less in the nineteenth century than it had been in the fourteenth, for as Pugin himself observed, 'while the children of this enlightened age are ignorant of the very saint by whom their country was converted to the Christian faith, they are well versed in the legends of Mother Goose and Puss in Boots!'[49] In the south aisle the windows are all of three lights each. The westernmost one has, appropriately for its location in the baptistery, the figure of St John the Baptist in the centre light, flanked by eight personified attributes of the baptised Christian, standing triumphantly on animal forms which represent the opposing vices. Moving eastwards, the next window has in its central light the figure of Our Lady with the moon and stars, and the inscription *pulchra ut luna* (fair as the moon). In the side lights are four seraphim, and titles of Our Lady from the Litany of Loreto in words and symbols (Mystic Rose, Tower of David, Morning Star, House of Gold). The next window has the figures of St John the Evangelist, St Giles and St Chad **(6.9)**; and finally, in the window by the entrance to the Blessed Sacrament Chapel, the Sacred Heart of Jesus in the centre light, with petitions from the Litany of the Holy Name in the side-lights. All of this helps to illustrate the important function of stained glass as a stimulus to prayer and meditation.

In the north aisle, the windows are of two lights each, except for the easternmost, which is of three. The westernmost is set with the heads of six Anglo-Saxon saints: Edmund, Edward the Martyr, Edward Confessor,

6.10 Giving Drink to the Thirsty: detail from the Works of Mercy window (Mark Titterton).

6.11 Pugin's original plan
for St Giles' (A.W.N. Pugin,
Present State, Pl 1).

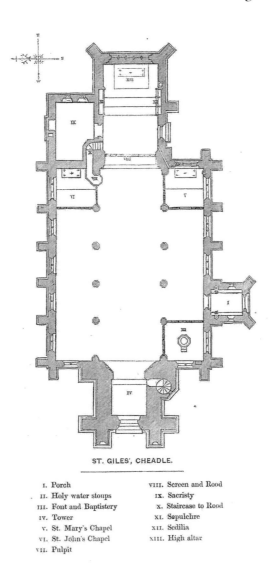

ST. GILES', CHEADLE.

I. Porch	VIII. Screen and Rood
II. Holy water stoups	IX. Sacristy
III. Font and Baptistery	X. Staircase to Rood
IV. Tower	XI. Sepulchre
V. St. Mary's Chapel	XII. Sedilia
VI. St. John's Chapel	XIII. High altar
VII. Pulpit	

Etheldreda, Ethelburga and Mildred. In the middle window there are canopied
figures of St Peter and St Paul. Next to it is one which especially delighted
Pugin when he visited Wailes' factory **(6.10)**. It represents the Holy Spirit
in the form of a dove, and the seven Corporal Acts of Mercy: clothing the
naked, visiting prisoners, giving drink to the thirsty, sheltering the homeless,
feeding the hungry, visiting the sick and burying the dead. Finally, in the Lady
Chapel, a three-light window depicts Our Lady with the Christ-child and the
Annunciation.[50]

The original plan for St Giles' **(6.11)** shows that the nave was to have had
three subdivisions marked off by parcloses: the Baptistery, and the chapels
of St John and of Our Lady at the east end of the north and south aisles
respectively. Of these, only the Baptistery was constructed exactly as planned.
Pugin lamented the fact that proper fonts were seldom to be found in modern
Catholic churches where a jug and basin often sufficed, and in one instance
the sacrament was administered out of an old medicine phial.[51] Its position
just inside the south door, and its enclosure within parcloses emphasises the

importance attached to the sacrament of Holy Baptism as the means of entry into membership of the Church: according to ancient practice only the baptised may be allowed to approach the sanctuary. The Cheadle font, octagonal in shape, was carved from alabaster. At its foot are four demons being crushed by the pedestal, symbolising the destruction of sin. The towering pinnacled canopy was based on the surviving medieval examples which Pugin had seen in East Anglian churches **(6.12)**.

As regards the two chapels originally proposed for the east ends of the aisles, the Lady Chapel was moved over to the north side, while the south aisle was extended to form the Blessed Sacrament Chapel as a distinct structure parallel to the chancel. It appears that Lord Shrewsbury then considered doing away with the chapel in the north aisle altogether, but Pugin protested that it had been provided for in the original estimate, that it would cost barely £100; and that without it the north aisle would look 'like an aisle sacked by the Calvinists'.[52] Pugin finally got his Lady Chapel though minus the parclose screen **(6.13)**. Only the base of this was constructed, forming a very low enclosure in the last bay of the aisle. The chapel was given a superb alabaster altar, carved by

6.12 The font and baptistery (Mark Titterton).

6.13 The finely carved altar and medieval reredos in the Lady Chapel (Mark Titterton).

Thomas Roddis, with figures of angels holding M monograms, and, at the corners, angels with scrolls inscribed *Ave Maria*. Above the altar Pugin placed the fine early sixteenth-century Flemish reredos of carved oak which Lord Shrewsbury had originally earmarked for St John's, Alton, until Pugin objected that it would obscure part of the east window, so to Cheadle it came.[53] The circular window originally intended to terminate the north aisle had to be omitted when it was agreed to relocate the organ loft over the sacristy, so a bold feature was absolutely necessary to fill up what would otherwise have been a blank wall. The aisle walls were appropriately decorated with a tiled dado and rich stencilling above. In the north aisle the predominant colour is blue for Our Lady, while on the south red and gold complement the decor of the Blessed Sacrament Chapel. The Stations of the Cross date from 1864.

At the east end of the nave the great rood, with its attendant figures of Our Lady and St John, was the focus of devotion for the people; while the fretted screen on which it was set was considered by Pugin to be an indispensable feature of an English parish church **(6.14)**. He wrote passionately about screens, and at length, but in *The Present State of Ecclesiastical Architecture* (1843) he expressed most succinctly the prime function of the screen

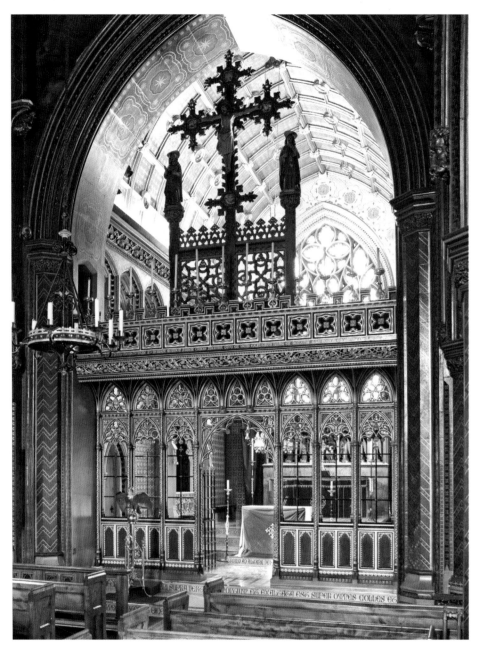

6.14 'To mark the separation between the faithful and the sacrifice': the rood-screen
(Mark Titterton).

> To mark the separation between the faithful and the sacrifice, the nave and
> chancel, emblematic of the Church militant and the Church triumphant,
> into which latter we can alone enter by merits of Christ's passion on the
> cross, whose image, as crucified for our sins, is affixed on high above the
> centre of the screen.[54]

Rood-screens were, of course, another revival, and were unfamiliar to English
Catholics of the nineteenth century. Though Pugin and Ambrose Phillipps
considered the screen to be essential from a liturgical and aesthetic point of
view, others disagreed precisely because it acted as a barrier, conflicting with

the modern 'all-seeing' principle; and the battle for screens dogged Pugin to the end of his life. At Cheadle, however, there was no such argument, and, armed with the sketches of medieval screens made on his East Anglian tours, Pugin set about designing an exceptionally fine one. He was especially delighted with the painted and gilded decorations he saw in East Anglia in April 1844.[55] He made yet another visit there in July 1845, and many of his sketches have survived.[56]

It seems that the timber for the screen was sawn out on site, and by early 1844 the fine carving was well under way. At this point the woodcarver left, and Lord Shrewsbury suggested that the carving could be finished more cheaply by local craftsman Thomas Harris than by engaging a new carver. Harris had already worked for the earl at Alton Towers and, significantly, on the screen at St John's, Alton. In an extraordinary letter, Pugin remonstrated with the earl for running the risk of ruining the screen by practising false economy. The difference in rates of pay amounted to no more than the price of a pound of cheese in Cheadle market, and though an expert carver might charge more per hour, it would be more economical in the long run than 'to have Harris spending time over vile imitations. He is a capital mechanic in tracery and he is excellent, but he has not the least idea of cutting foliage'.[57] To reinforce the point, he illustrated the letter with drawings of a rood screen and a cheese. That a young architect should have been able to address England's premier earl in such a forthright manner, accusing him of penny-pinching, says much about their relationship. Lord Shrewsbury seems to have taken Pugin's rebuff with a dose of good humour, and the quality of the carving on the screen does suggest that another expert carver was called in. The capitals of the shafts, and the cusps of the tracery have very finely carved flowers and leaves; there are angel heads over the doorway, and there is a rich cornice of vine-scroll above the coving. The whole structure is raised on two steps which have Latin texts from the prophet Isaiah cut on the risers in modified Gothic letters: 'The house of the Lord is built on the top of the mountains and exalted above the hills, and all peoples will come to it and say: Come, let us go up to the mountain of the Lord and the house of the God of Jacob' (Isaiah 2: 2-3).

The painting and gilding of the screen was probably done by Thomas Kearns. It is clear that Pugin intended the panels at the base of the screen to be decorated with figures of saints, like the medieval ones he had seen in the church at Castle Acre,[58] but, whether or not through lack of a sufficiently skilled figure-painter, this was never carried out, and the panels remain blank. The main shafts have spiral decorations of the kind that Pugin called 'barber's pole-work', and above the cornice runs the painted text, + *Christus factus est pro nobis obediens usque ad mortem, mortem autem crucis propter quod et Deus exultavit illum et donavit illi nomen quod est super omne nomen* (For us Jesus became obedient to death, even death on the cross, therefore God has exalted him and given him the name which is above all others: Philippians 2: 8-9). Thus the great rood, occupying the central place in the church, draws together the whole of the Redemption history: the atoning death of Christ on the Cross, and his universal sovereignty; while beyond the screen the eye is led onward into the sanctuary to a foretaste of the life of the world to come. How perfectly it is all brought together by

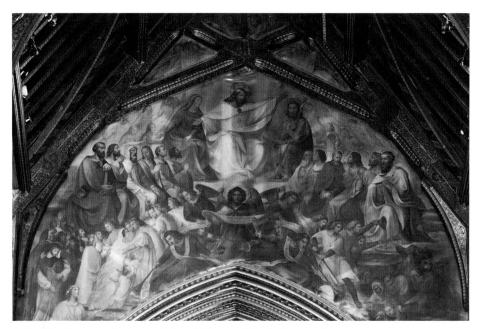

6.15 The Doom painting by Eduard Hauser (Mark Titterton).

Pugin who knew his theology as well as his architecture: no wonder he was so passionate about screens. The rood itself, with its attendant figures of Our Lady and St John, was carved in the Lambeth workshop of Pugin's friend, George Myers, but there was considerable delay in getting it finished in time for the consecration. Myers, it seems, was having problems with some of his workforce, and Pugin was clearly distressed at the apparent lack of Christian spirit and commitment to so sacred a task as the carving of a rood:

> Myers is in great difficulties about the crucifix. His carvers are either drunk or ill or seduced away to work for other people and it is impossible to keep things for a day together. He started the image directly I wrote and it is not yet finished, and the only good carver he had is away. Unless we can get some Christian men we shall never get on.[59]

Above the Rood is the 'Doom' painting; another medieval feature which Pugin sought to revive. These representations of the Last Judgement, with often lurid portayals of the damned being consigned to fires of Hell, need to be seen in conjunction with the rood itself; for it is the sacrifice of Christ on the Cross, and the pleading of that sacrifice in the Mass, which stand between sin and its dire consequences. Pugin would have preferred to have followed medieval precedent by having the painting applied directly to the wall fresco-style, but it was eventually painted on canvas by Eduard Hauser (1807-64), a Swiss pupil of Friedrich Overbeck (1789-1869) who was one of the leaders of the Nazarene school in Rome **(6.15)**. Pugin greatly admired the Nazarenes as 'deserving of the warmest eulogiums and respect for their glorious revival of Christian art and traditions.'[60] and considered Overbeck as 'that Prince of Christian painters.'[61] In fixing the Doom Pugin had to take precautions against damp by allowing air to circulate behind it. Over the years a certain amount of undulation has appeared, confirming Pugin's worst fears that by using canvas for this kind of work the solid 'effect would be lost'.[62] When it came to the painting in the chancel – which the earl also wanted to be done on canvas – Pugin took a much tougher line. A detail worth noticing on the Doom painting is the representation amongst the Blessed of Lady Gwendoline, the younger daughter of the earl and countess, who died in 1840 aged only 23. It is possible, although there is no documentary proof, that Lord Shrewsbury's sudden increase in expenditure on St Giles' may have been intended as a local memorial to Gwendoline (who died and was buried in Rome), and that, like Pugin, he found in the building of this church a source of consolation in times of grief.

Other figure painting in the nave includes the representation of ten Old Testament patriarchs and prophets, copied from Italian frescoes, and painted on thin discs of copper attached to the walls over the arcades. It was Lord Shrewsbury's idea to have them, and for once the earl had his way: 'I think your Lordship's idea of having subjects painted on the spandrils of the arches of Cheadle nave very good and will send the exact size off from Alton,' he wrote.[63] The open roof, also richly painted, has wall-posts, open trusses with pierced tracery at the apex, and wind-braces. The outer roofs are of lead, with elaborate gilded cresting along the ridges.

Lighting in the nave was originally provided by a set of hanging brass *coronae* made by Hardman. 'There was scarcely a church in ancient times which was

6.16 The medieval corona in the chancel which was repaired and restored by Hardman (Mark Titterton).

not provided with a corona, richer or plainer in design, according to the wealth or dignity of the foundation', said Pugin,[64] so St Giles' had a set of five. Each one held 24 tapers, and was inscribed *Domine da nobis lucem* (O Lord, give us light). Sadly, these were removed in the twentieth century and replaced with electric lights suspended from brackets attached to the walls. These were in turn replaced with the present wrought-iron ones made by a local blacksmith. Just to the east of the screen, hanging over the present working altar, is an exceptionally beautiful hexagonal corona with lettering executed in pierced ironwork **(6.16)**. The text links it firmly with the rood: *Tuam crucem / adoramus domine / gloriosam passionem / recolimus etiam / miserere nobis / qui passus es pro nobis* (We adore your cross, O Lord, and we honour your glorious Passion; have mercy upon us for whom you have suffered). It is of fifteenth-century date, and was brought from Flanders, very probably by Pugin, in a badly damaged condition, and was repaired and restored by Hardman. 'The corona for the chancel I shall make out of the old iron one we have got,' Hardman was told, and he charged Lord Shrewsbury £30 for the work.[65] At the time of the consecration of St Giles' in 1846 it was described as 'one of the most beautiful pieces of church furniture in the country.'[66]

At the heart of the Catholic liturgy there lies the breathtaking concept that for a few moments the veil between this world and the next is so very thin that a glimpse may be had of what lies beyond: the worship of the Church on Earth united with that of the Church in Heaven, through Christ who is adored on his throne of heavenly glory and upon earth in his Sacramental Presence upon the altar. Thus the altar is the focal point of the entire building, and its setting is supremely important. So the chancel is differentiated structurally from the nave by its lower roof-level, by the elaborate bell-cote on the east gable of the

6.17 'With angels, archangels, and all the company of heaven': the high altar (Mark Titterton).

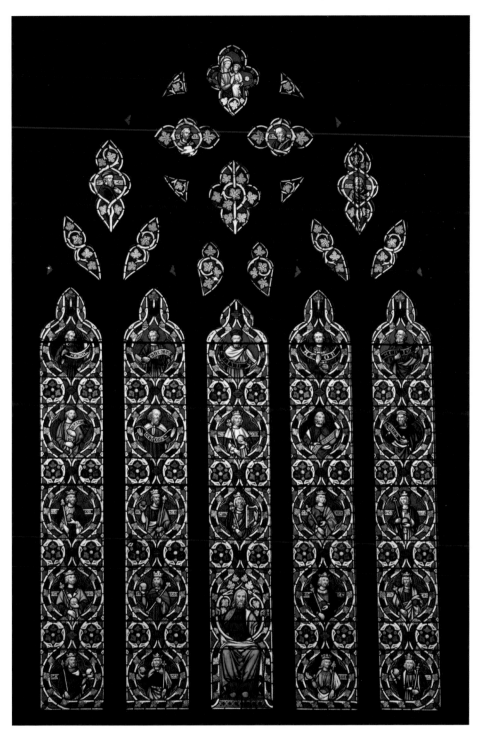

6.18 The east window depicting the genealogy of Christ (Karl Barton).

nave for the Sanctus bell, by the extra mouldings to the windows, and by the statues and other sculptures which adorn the east wall. Internally the dominant theme at St Giles' is the Holy Angels – in the wall-paintings and cornices, on the roof corbels, on the sedilia, and predominantly on the altar and reredos

6.19 'Tiles by Minton in the chancel (Mark Titterton).

(6.17). All of this consciously echoes the words of the Preface to the Canon of the Mass: 'Therefore with angels, and archangels, and with all the company of heaven.' On the altar itself Thomas Roddis carved figures of angels holding musical instruments, ready, as it were, to accompany the singing of the *Sanctus*. Meanwhile, on the reredos, the angels hold censers and torches, ready, just like the thurifer and acolytes at Mass, to honour the Presence of Christ. The central panel depicts the Coronation of Our Lady, the last of the Mysteries of the Rosary and, significantly, the only one which takes place entirely in Heaven. Above the reredos, the east window **(6.18)** links the Old Testament with the New: a Jesse window depicting the ancestry of Christ in accordance with the prophecy of Isaiah – 'And there shall come forth a rod out of the stem of Jesse, and a branch shall grow out of his roots' (Isaiah 11.1). Each of the five lights contains half figures of various ancestors, and at the very top, in the tracery, are the Virgin and Child. Pugin believed the east window of a church to be of considerable importance in terminating the whole west-east perspective of a church, catching the light of the morning sun. On either side of the window, in canopied niches, are the figures of St Giles and St Chad. As the Mass reached its supreme moment, the Sanctus bell high on the gable would ring to signify to passers-by that the Holy Mysteries were being celebrated within; for the absent as well as for those present, and embracing too those whose bodies lay at rest in the churchyard beneath the heaven-pointing spire, the symbol of the Resurrection.

An altar is, by definition, a 'high place', and so it is traditionally raised on a flight of three or more steps to give it prominence, and it is approached with due reverence. The sanctuary at St Giles' rises through four levels, and the risers have appropriate Latin texts incised into them. On the bottom level is part of the invocation *super oblate,* said by the priest at the preparation of the Oblations prior to the Canon of the Mass: *Veni sanctificator omnipotens aeterne Deus* (Come, almighty, eternal God, the sanctifier). The ascent to the altar is then marked by the antiphon *Introibo ad altare Dei + ad Deum qui laetiticat iuventutem meam* (I

6.20 Designed for the celebration of the Sarum Rite: the Easter sepulchre (Mark Titterton).

6.21 The sedilia, arranged in the Old English fashion (Mark Titterton 2011).

will go up to the altar of God, even to the God of my joy and gladness) and the verses of Psalm 43 which form part of the Preparation said by the priest and assistants below the altar steps before Mass, concluding with the *Gloria Patri*.

Each level of the chancel, and the adjoining Chapel of the Blessed Sacrament, is paved with encaustic tiles manufactured by Herbert Minton to Pugin's designs. They are decorated with floriated crosses, *Agnus Dei,* and *Sanctus* motifs **(6.19)**. Some tiles are made up of four colours, and are therefore richer and more expensive than the Wedgwood tiles in the nave. Pugin was greatly excited to know that the Minton floors would be the finest of their kind in Europe.[68] Lord Shrewsbury was concerned about possible damage to these expensive tiles caused through walking on them. Denny suggested that the priest and acolytes should wear cloth overshoes in the sanctuary. The earl agreed, and told Pugin, 'You may then have your tiles, and we shall want no carpet.'[69] The furnishings of the sanctuary were designed for the celebration of Mass according to the Sarum Use, and so, as at Uttoxeter and Alton, there were some significant departures from post-medieval practice. The most prominent feature of the north side of the chancel is the Easter sepulchre, set under a richly carved ogee arch **(6.20)** which appears to have been inspired by the fourteenth-century tomb of Aymer de Valence, Earl of Pembroke, in Westminster Abbey. In the back is a painting of the entombment of Christ executed on a metal panel by Eduard Hauser, and the front of the Sepulchre has five quatrefoils. They are decorated with the emblems of the Passion on shields, exactly as they appear in Pugin's *Glossary of Ecclesiastical Ornament and Costume* (1844). Ornate Easter sepulchres of this kind were still to be seen in many medieval churches, for example at Hawton (Nottinghamshire) and Heckington (Lincolnshire), and Pugin drew on these as his 'authorities'. Historically, the Sepulchre was used in the liturgy of Good Friday and Easter for the symbolic entombment of Christ in the form of the Sacred Host consecrated at the Maundy Thursday Mass. Then, early on Easter morning, came the liturgical drama known as *Quem Quaeritis?* when three clerics, representing the women who went to Jesus' tomb on the first Easter Day, approached the Easter sepulchre to be greeted by a fourth person representing the angel who announced the good news of the Resurrection. These practices had been discontinued in England in the sixteenth century, and were unknown in current Catholic circles.[70] Pugin hoped to revive them, and by providing such a splendid Sepulchre at St Giles' he ensured that there would be no excuse for not doing things properly.

The sedilia set into the wall on the opposite side of the chancel **(6.21)**, are of the medieval prismatory type (i.e with seats and integral piscina) because, in addition to the canopied seats there is also a sacrarium, consisting of a stone basin with a shelf above it, also set under a rich canopy. Pugin was able to cite many surviving medieval examples such as the ones in the cathedrals at Exeter, Lincoln and Salisbury, but again he was attempting to revive long-forgotten practices. The sacrarium was for the *lavabo*, the ritual washing of the priest's hands immediately before the Canon of the Mass, and for the ablution of the sacred vessels at the end, while the shelf above was for the wine and water cruets. Modern practice was to use a small jug and basin for the lavabo, the ablutions were normally consumed by the priest or deacon, while the cruets were generally placed, along with other vessels, on a credence table near the altar. Similarly, instead of fixed sedilia of the architectural kind, modern Catholic churches usually had three movable seats, with the priest occupying the central one. Pugin wished to revert to the medieval custom of the priest occupying the seat closest to the altar, with the deacon and subdeacon sitting to his left, and on lower levels. So the sedilia at St Giles' have their seats set on descending levels, and, as if to make doubly sure that everyone sat in the right place, the seats

6.22 The cloth-of-gold chasuble: one of the few surviving vestments designed by Pugin for St Giles' (Michael Fisher).

are labelled *sacerdos*, *diaconus*, and *subdiaconus,* with the appropriate emblems of each order; chalice and paten for the priest, the Gospel book for the deacon, and wine and water cruets for the subdeacon. There was, it seemed, a need for such instruction. Ambrose Phillipps observed that High Mass with deacon and sub-deacon were in any case a rarity outside London,[71] and Pugin himself was only too painfully aware of the fact that even though better things were now readily available, many clergy clung stubbornly to the customs they had grown up with, and some were bitterly hostile to 'revivals'. Among the objections raised to the revival of sedilia were that costly vestments might get damaged if the clergy were obliged to sit in recesses in the wall. Pugin had an answer for that too:

> I perceive also that <u>Sedilia</u> are denounced, and on the absurd objection of injuring vestments, when the ancient Churchmen have sat in them day by day, week by week, year by year, century after century, robed in vestments of gold of Cyprus, and orphreys of pearl, and gems, and needlework – vestments more costly and beautiful than anything this age has produced ... yet men of new-fangled notions, despising the old paths, do actually sneer at the perpetuation of these appendages of the ancient rites; and on the plea that the buckram flap of a modern chasuble might be crushed, they would remove seats, and arch, and canopy, and priestly emblem, and in their place substitute a <u>stool!!</u>'[72]

At St Giles' at any rate, sedilia and costly vestments were made to mix. Pugin designed a full range of vestments in his own style, with woven braids and orphreys supplied by Lonsdale and Tyler of London, and almost certainly made up by Lucy Powell and her assistants in Frederick Street, Birmingham. The design of the chasuble shows a compromise between the very ample medieval form preferred by Pugin, and the drastically cut-down French and Italian variety. This reflects the earlier disputes over the revival of the full medieval chasuble which had been censured in 1839 by the *Propaganda Fidei* in Rome, and which was actually banned by Bishop Wiseman just before Pugin's death in 1852. Nowadays the Pope himself almost invariably wears one. Most of the St Giles' collection have been quite literally worn out, but some of the embroideries have been worked into newer vestments. The only complete survival is a black chasuble with gold embroidery, used at requiems. A fine cloth-of-gold set, with borders of velvet and appliqués worked with gold and silver wires, was expertly re-mounted on new fabric in time for the sesquicentennial celebrations in 1996 **(6.22)**. At Uttoxeter, Pugin had wanted to revive the medieval English custom of reserving the Blessed Sacrament in a hanging pyx above the altar, but had had to settle for a tower-shaped tabernacle on the altar itself. The original drawing for the chancel of St Giles' makes no such provision **(6.23)**. It shows an aumbry in the north wall just east of the Sepulchre, from which it may be deduced that Pugin planned to use this for reservation, again following medieval precedent. By the time he came to build, however, he had had second thoughts, based on his recent experiment at St John's, Alton, where a tiny chapel on the north side of the chancel was equipped with a Reservation altar. At Cheadle

6.23 Pugin's original design for the chancel (*Dublin Review,* 1841).

6.24 'Porta coeli', as Bl. John Newman described it: the Blessed Sacrament Chapel viewed through the brass gates (Mark Titterton).

he developed this idea into a full-scale Chapel of the Blessed Sacrament, with all the appropriate furnishings and iconography. It appears to have been one of the earliest alterations to the original plan.[73] The chapel forms an extension to the south aisle, and it is denoted externally by its separate gable, an additional weathering, and, at the junction with the aisle, a large buttress with a niche containing a statute of the Risen Christ.

The chapel is divided from the aisle and chancel by metalwork screens and gates, those at the entrance from the aisle being of brass by Hardman **(6.24)**. It is further delineated by having a rib-vaulted roof, richly decorated and picked out in gold. The walls are stencilled with crosses and crowns, and fruiting vines. The alabaster altar, by Roddis, has figures of the six-winged seraphim, the guardians of the Sacred Presence, standing under crocketed canopies, and a cornice with *sanctus* which also runs all around the dado in identical lettering **(6.25)**. The reredos is made up of two panels of richly coloured Minton tiles with the chalice and Host as the dominant motif, and between them, behind the tabernacle, a stencilled panel of fruiting vines. The window above is of three lights. The centre panel shows the Risen Christ, and in the side lights the seraphim hold texts from Jesus' discourse on the Bread of Life (John 6: 54-56). The risers in the steps are lettered *panem coeli dedit eis* (he gave them bread from heaven) and *panem angelorum manducavit homo* (Man has eaten the bread of angels). The entrance arches from the aisle and the chancel are inscribed the antiphon to Psalm 117 as sung at Benediction: *Adoremus in aeternam sacramentum sanctissimum* (Let us adore for ever the most holy Sacrament). The chapel is altogether a perfect expression of Catholic Eucharistic theology, and Bl. John Henry Newman was particularly moved by it. Newman did not fully share Pugin's 'Gothic passion', and he had some harsh words to say about Pugin himself, but when he visited St Giles' for the first time in July 1846 he considered it to be 'the most splendid building I ever saw. ... The Chapel of the Blessed Sacrament is, on entering, a blaze of light – and I could not help saying to myself *Porta Coeli'* (Gate of Heaven).[74]

6.25 Interior of the Blessed Sacrament Chapel: altar by Thomas Roddis, tiles by Minton. (Mark Titterton).

The brass gates at the western entrance to the chapel are worthy of note. Liturgically they serve a similar purpose to that of the rood screen, marking a division between the aisle and the chapel, filtering the view towards the tabernacle and guarding the Blessed Sacrament from 'irreverent gaze'. Pugin produced the drawings in late December 1844 and sent them off to Hardman's in January 1845. The screen is of light and elegant construction, with fleurs-de-lis and crosses and crowns in the cresting, and, in the lower part of the gates, pierced quatrefoils with the Eucharistic symbols of the chalice and host and the *Agnus Dei*. The wax models for these were made by John Hardman Powell (1827-95) who was taken on by Pugin as his only pupil, and they are amongst his early attempts at metalwork design, carried out under the strict supervision of 'the governor' as Powell called him.[75] 'I am already getting Powell into firmness of hand,' Pugin reported to Hardman at the end of December: 'I think I shall make a fine fellow of him.'[76] Powell was paid just £1 for his modelling work on the screen, the overall cost of which began to worry Pugin. Having already vexed Lord Shrewsbury by asking him to advance money to Hardman, Pugin suggested that some other metalwork items, such as the very costly tabernacle, might be pared back. 'If I can cut down the things I will help out the screen or I shall get in great trouble.'[77]. Pugin's original estimate for the screen and for pieces of brasswork for the baptistery and organ loft was £180. In the end they all came out well above Pugin's estimate. The screen alone cost £251, and the other items £24 and £106.[78] Pugin must have prayed hard. 'Next week we fix the Brass screen to the chapel of the Blessed Sacrament which is a most magnificent piece of work,' he wrote to Lord Shrewsbury in May 1846, a few days before Hardman's sent out the invoice, '& will I think delight your Lordship much.'[79] Not only the screen, but most of the other metalwork for St Giles', were drawn out by Pugin over the winter of 1844-5, and there was a considerable quantity of it, as Pugin wanted to ensure that Cheadle was as well-equipped as it could possibly be. Some items could be supplied by Hardman's from stock-in-trade, and when a piece needed to be individually designed, Pugin advised Hardman to make a few others of the same pattern as stock to keep in the new showroom at Great Charles Street, Birmingham, which Pugin had himself planned and furnished for the display and sale of the full range of their goods.[80]

The winter of 1844-5 was a very trying one for Pugin. Living as a widower in his new home at Ramsgate with six children to care for was difficult enough, even with a governess. Memories of Louisa haunted him. He could no longer bear to stay in London because of its associations with her. 'I suffer such depression of spirits that I can hardly work,' he wrote just before Christmas 1844. 'I miss my wife at every turn. I hope time may remove this but at present it is almost insupportable.'[81] Within three months of Louisa's death, and in what some might have considered indecent haste, he had sent a proposal of marriage to Mary Amherst, but having heard nothing from her by 22 December he concluded that 'anything like happiness is mere delusion' and that his work was the only reality[82]. Meanwhile his three-year-old daughter, Katharine, fell down and broke a leg, his private chaplain, Dr Luigi Acquarone, took to heavy

6.26 Rubbing of the memorial to Thomas Roddis: the floriated cross is now missing (Birmingham Museum & Art Gallery).

drinking, and his new pupil, John Powell, was disturbing the household by sleepwalking. 'Between him and the Dr. there is no peace all night & I shall be obliged to go Out to sleep at last!!!'[83] To add to the frustration, a set of metalwork drawings for Cheadle went missing at Hardman's, and Pugin had to do them all over again. On the other hand, Powell's drawing skills were improving, and Pugin was particularly pleased with a jewelled ciborium he drew for St Giles'. 'I think you will understand it,' he told Hardman when posting it to him.' I made Powell draw it out carefully & it is the best thing he has done.'[84]

The date for the opening was set originally for 3 September 1845, but by March of that year it became apparent that this was no longer realistic. Although the building work was virtually complete, most of the interior furnishing and decorating was still to be done, and Lord Shrewsbury had been urging economies with both the workforce and the metalwork. When it was suggested that the consecration could go ahead as planned, leaving any unfinished work to be completed afterwards Pugin disagreed, begging Lord Shrewsbury 'not to spoil Cheadle' for the sake of waiting another year.[85] Pugin had set so much store by this church as the one on which he was prepared to stake his entire reputation, and he could not run the risk that it might not live up to its promise by leaving anything unfinished. The earl consented to a year's delay which, amongst other things, would enable him to spread the cost a little further, and so the consecration was rescheduled for 1 September 1846 – St Giles' Day. A particularly sad blow at this time was the death in October 1845 of the sculptor Thomas Roddis. His contribution to St Giles' was substantial and of superb quality. A few days after his death, Pugin wrote to Lord Shrewsbury, 'I am sure your Lordship will not object to have a small brass plate – with request for prayers for his soul as Carver of the church. It is really due to him for he was a faithful & laborious man – had I known him earlier he would have been a first rate man.'[86] Lord Shrewsbury gave his approval, and Pugin designed the memorial in the form of a floriated cross with masons' tools at the centre, and an inscription below **(6.26)**. It was made by Hardman, and is the only memorial to a private individual to have been placed in St Giles'. The cross, alas, is no longer extant, but the inscription plate may still be seen in the north porch.

In spite of the postponement of the consecration, Pugin became worried in the Spring of 1846 that he still might not be able to finish in time, so he pleaded with the earl for sufficient money to keep the workforce up to strength and to take on extra carpenters, otherwise there might be yet another postponement:

> I have made a careful calculation of the work that has to be done at cheadle & I am quite satisfied that if your Lordsip reduces the pay till June <u>the case is hopeless</u> of compleating the church by September … if the pay is kept to <u>its present amount</u> Several Labourers can be discharged & Joiners & painters taken on who are absolutely wanted at the church – & I am sure that it will be more economical to do this than to allow the church dedication to be put off for another year which must inevitably be the case if the men are reduced. we have not a bench or a door made, no sacristy fittings … We must finish the sacristy fittings or all the vestments and ornaments will be spoilt if there are not places to stow them away.[87]

Pugin even advanced money of his own so that Denny could pay the men until such time as a decision had been reached. Unhappy about the figure of St Giles in the south aisle window, he wrote to Lord Shrewsbury in April to say that he was going to have it improved at his own expense, 'for I cannot bear to see the present S. Giles'.[88]

Pugin's anxiety was fully justified. In January 1846 *The Ecclesiologist,* the journal of the Cambridge Camden Society, published a savage verbal attack on Pugin which both shocked and puzzled him, given that the Society had hitherto been most supportive of his work, and that he had designed their seal. Entitled 'The artistic merit of Mr Pugin', the article alleged that Pugin had failed to live up to the promises set out in his publications, because, compared with the engravings, many of his actual buildings were disappointing, and so had been left in an unfinished state.[89] In his vigorous response, Pugin drew attention to St Giles' which was 'now rapidly advancing towards completion', and which 'far exceeds anything in the way of ecclesiastical decoration that has been attempted in this country'. Young ecclesiologists were invited 'to make a pilgrimage there' in the ensuing summer to see not only the building and its decoration, but also the 'costly ornaments' which reflected the great progress that he and Hardman had made in the design and production of ecclesiastical metalwork, and to judge for themselves.[90] Having thrown down the gauntlet in so public a manner, Pugin could not afford to leave anything at Cheadle unfinished or imperfect. Although he had every confidence in the indefatigable John Denny – 'no man can be more anxious or work harder than Denny'[91] –

6.27 Detail of stencilling on nave pillar (Mark Titterton).

Pugin felt obliged to go to Cheadle more often 'now things are drawing to a close there as so many matters which require attention.'[92]

The intense coloured decoration of the walls and pillars at St Giles' has always excited interest, discussion, and controversy **(6.27)**. In 1849-50 a series of criticisms of Pugin's work appeared in print, this time in the new liberal Catholic magazine, *The Rambler*. In response to comments about church decoration, Pugin replied that as far as Cheadle was concerned, 'it was quite an afterthought of its noble founder to cover it with coloured decorations' thereby creating 'a great anomaly between the simplicity of its walls and moulding and the intricacy of its detail', thus placing the responsibility upon Lord Shrewsbury's shoulders, which he would not have dared to do if there had not been some truth in it.[93] Attention has also been drawn to the illustrations published by Pugin in his 1841 *Dublin Review* article which show the walls and pillars left as plain stonework with almost no decoration apart from the Doom over the chancel arch and some circular patterns over the nave arcades. That some painted decoration was intended from the outset is, however, made clear in a letter from Pugin to Lord Shrewsbury in March 1841 in which he explains that the only reason that it was not shown in the wood-cuts was for fear that the engraver would spoil it.[94] In his lectures to students at Oscott in 1838 Pugin, citing medieval precedent, had stressed the importance of gilding and painting as part of the overall decoration of churches, and he had given practical expression to it in the decoration of the college chapel. Unless supported by coloured decorations on the walls, stained glass windows would suffer by comparison with surrounding plain surfaces, and appear 'spotty.'[95] It was only the iconoclasts of the sixteenth century who had obliterated coloured wall decoration and created the whitewashed surfaces to which most people had become accustomed. There were nevertheless some significant survivals to prove the point. The broad principles having been established, the details of the decoration of St Giles' had to be worked out, and, as ever, Pugin needed to seek out his 'authorities' in the shape of surviving decorative work in English churches. In answering his critics in *The Ecclesiologist,* he referred to nine journeys (eight in England and one abroad) that he had undertaken with the express purpose of studying ancient work, and these are recorded in his diaries, letters and sketch-books. While in Norfolk in April 1844 he wrote excitedly to Lord Shrewsbury about what he had found there. The letter also shows that the decorating of St Giles', although planned, had not yet been started:

> I write a line to say that I am half frantic with delight. I have seen churches with the painting & gilding nearly perfect!!!! Such screens. Exquisite painting. I shall have glorious authorities for Cheadle. I am delighted beyond measure to have seen these before we begin the decoration there – they are far beyond anything I thought we had in England.[96]

Not all of Pugin's sources were English. Two months after his Norfolk tour he was in Paris admiring the recent restoration work at the Sainte-Chapelle, which included diapered patterns painted in bright colours on the pilasters. He was greatly influenced by what he saw at Cologne in 1843, and he took tracings of the original medieval patterns applied to the pillars and the vaulting which were being restored at this time. 'I shall return quite rich in new/old/devices'.[97] Details for some of the windows came from glass which he had seen in Antwerp and Louvain in the summer of 1843, while the brass mounts for the altar missal were copied from the fittings of a medieval hymnal in Mainz Cathedral. In addition to gathering ideas for Cheadle, Pugin was also preparing illustrations for his *Glossary of Ecclesiastical Ornament and Costume.* Published in 1844, the *Glossary* contains 72 superb chromolithographs of a wide range of patterns and designs which could be applied in a variety of ways. Entering St Giles' is almost like walking into a three-dimensional *Glossary,* and both became influential points of reference for artists and designers for decades to come. 'I expect, when finished, it will be a text Book for all good people,' Lord Shrewsbury told Pugin after accompanying two distinguished visitors to see St Giles' while the decoration was in progress. One of these was George Gilbert Scott (1811-78), an avid admirer of Pugin, who was then establishing his reputation as a Gothic architect and church restorer. 'The Stencelling absolutely made the water run down both sides of his mouth'. The other visitor, Rowland Warburton of Arley Hall, Cheshire, described by Lord Shrewsbury as 'a great Puseyite Gentleman,' was a prominent member of the Cambridge Camden Society. Ecstatic at what he saw, he asked the earl if he could borrow some of the stencillers to decorate his new domestic chapel, 'but I told him he could not have 'em till we had done.'[98] It would seem that the sobriquet 'Pugin's Gem', by which St Giles' has long been known, was coined by Lord Shrewsbury himself. In the same letter to Pugin he refers to an imminent visit by George Talbot, a distant relative and former Anglican now in training for the priesthood at Oscott. 'I wait for him to go and see the Gem, which we shall do on the first fine day.'

Although most of the metalwork items for St Giles' were drawn out by Pugin over the winter of 1844–5 and sent off to Hardman's, the actual production was carried out over several months, with most of the pieces arriving singly or in batches between April 1846 and mid-August, i.e. to within a few days of the consecration.[99] This was no doubt intended to spread the total cost to Lord Shrewsbury of around £1,400, which was equivalent to that of building a complete small church,[100] and it was the most extensive collection of metalwork made for any of Pugin's churches. Pugin's original list, as sent to Hardman in December 1844, reveals a comprehensive range of vessels and ornaments, and their estimated cost:

Drawn	Brass screen chapel B Sacrament	}	
Drawn	Brass pillars Baptistry		£180
Drawn	Brass work for organ loft	}	
Drawn	6 standards for Rood		18
Do	2 Candlesticks for altar B Sacrament		15
Do	2 Do Lady chapel		15
Do	4 Do high altar & 2 small		30
Do	2 Elvation Candlesticks with crowns		30
Do	Lamp for high altar	}	
Do	Do Chapel of B Sacrament	}	50
Do	Brass credence table		10
Do	3 sacryng bells Plated		10
	cross for high altar		20
Do	Lady chapel		14
Do	5 Iron coronas for nave		100
	1 Corona for chancel		40
Do	6 plain high candlesticks for funerals		18
	holy water vat		5
Do	Pair of processional Candlicks		6
	Curtain Rods for high Altar		15
Do	small processional cross (the one made)		8
Do	Brass communion rail		12
Do	Ciborium & chalice (feet copper gilt		
	or white metal plated & parcel gilt)		40
Do	2 sets of cruets plated like mine		10
Do	2 brass Thuribles & a boat		
Do	3 cushions for the altars		9
	2 Missall & binding		20
Do	Branches for consecration candles		18
	Pascal candlicks		25
	Lenten herse light		15
	2 offertory basins		6
			739

6.28 Chalice, monstrance and chrismatory made by Hardman for St Giles' (Mark Titterton).

In many cases there was a discrepancy between the estimate and the actual cost of the goods. As previously mentioned, the brasswork for the Blessed Sacrament chapel, baptistery and organ loft, assessed together at £180, came to a total of £381 19s. The cross for the high altar, for which Pugin had allowed £20, was entered into the metalwork daybook on 22 August as 'A Richly Gilt Cross & figure set with Chrystals & Enamels' at £34 10s. The number of standard candlesticks for the rood-screen increased from six to thirteen, at an additional cost of £11 18s. Pugin also submitted a supplementary list which included two extra chalices, holy oil stocks, a pyx for the reservation of the Blessed Sacrament, and a monstrance, and Lord Shrewsbury ordered items for Cheadle on his own behalf. An exquisite blue enamelled cross for the Lady Chapel altar was one of the last pieces to be dispatched from Birmingham, just eight days before the consecration. Originally estimated at £14, it was entered to Lord Shrewsbury at £26.

The letters which passed between Pugin and John Hardman reflect the infinite care that was taken over the design and production of the metalwork for St Giles'. Among the larger items were the paschal candlestick and Lenten hearse. The hearse consisted of a triangular candle stand holding a number of tapers which were symbolically extinguished one by one during the Holy Week office of *Tenebrae*. Paschal candlesticks, used during the Easter vigil ceremonies, received special attention from Pugin in the *Glossary*. The candlestick he designed for Cheadle was similar to the one made for his own church of St Augustine in Ramsgate in 1845. Its stem was of quatrefoil section, and the feet in the shape of crouching lions. For the Cheadle paschal he asked Hardman to make the lion feet 'larger & of greater projection' to prevent it looking top heavy, 'otherwise the Candlestick is magnificent'.[101]

Of the three chalices commissioned for Cheadle, the most important is one of Sienese pattern with a deep conical bowl and a sexfoiled foot set with enamels **(6.28)**. Pugin had seen several examples of medieval originals made by Italian goldsmiths in Siena, and had acquired the base sections of two such chalices. Having had their bowls recreated at Hardman's, one chalice was given to Pugin's new church at Dudley, and the other to St Chad's Cathedral, Birmingham. A new silver-gilt chalice was made to this pattern for Dr Weedall at Oscott, and Pugin had a copy made for Cheadle, but he told Hardman to make only the bowl of silver-gilt, and the rest in copper-gilt. 'Lord Shrewsbury is bound to ask me – & he will be angry if it is all silver.'[102] The Cheadle chalice was entered into the daybook at £25, £12 less than Dr Weedall's, but identical in terms of its design and craftsmanship. With his eye to business, Pugin asked Hardman to make another one for stock. 'I think it would be a good thing to make 3 or 4 of a sort when we have a good pattern.'[103] Another superb piece made specifically for Cheadle but copied later was a 'sunburst' monstrance – the vessel used for the Exposition of the Blessed Sacrament, and Benediction. Made of gilt brass, and set with amethysts, Pugin designed it from medieval examples. His own preference was for Benediction to be given with an enclosed pyx, as it had widely been done in the Middle Ages, to preserve an element of mystery, and also to safeguard the Blessed Sacrament from 'irreverent gaze'. So to complement the 'sunburst' monstrance, he made a standing pyx for the reservation of the Host. It has a tall stem to enable it to be used, if desired, for Benediction and processions of the Blessed Sacrament without Exposition. Appropriately, there is engraved on the front the opening words of St Thomas Aquinas' eucharistic hymn, *Adoro te devote, latens deitas* (O hidden Godhead, I adore thee). To hang before the tabernacle in the Blessed Sacrament Chapel, Pugin designed a beautiful lamp of enamelled silver, inscribed with the attributes ascribed to God: *charitas, benedictio, fortitudo, virtus, honor, sapientia*.

Not all of the metalwork made for Cheadle was elaborately decorated. Beautiful on account of its simplicity, clean lines and restrained ornament, is the chrismatory designed by Pugin to contain the holy oils. Made in plated German silver, it consists of an outer case with a hinged lid in the shape of a pitched roof with pierced cresting along the ridge, looking much like a diminutive reliquary. Inside are two cylindrical oil-stocks with engraved lids. These were for the oil of the catechumens and the holy chrism, both used in the rites of Christian initiation. A matching stock, with a conical lid surmounted by a cross, was made to hold the oil for anointing the sick.

In spite of his stated preference for just two candlesticks on the high altar, with two tall standards on the altar step, Pugin was obliged to provide a 'big six' for Cheadle, just as he had done at St John's, Alton. They are of a very distinctive design, each having a cross within a roundel set into the stem just above the knop, with one of Pugin's favourite mottoes, *Christi crux mea lux* (Christ's cross is my light) engraved on the roundels, and made to match the altar cross. Another unusual set consists of a pair of five-light Benediction candlesticks with an octagonal gallery for the candle sockets, and a splayed octagonal base with lion feet.

The considerable quantities of metalwork and vestments supplied to Cheadle caused Pugin a certain amount of anxiety as regards its proper storage and maintenance. Thus the inner sacristy at St Giles' was fitted out with the necessary 'almeries' – cupboards, drawers and presses – all of sturdy woodwork. In the light of unfortunate experiences elsewhere, Pugin felt that, as at Alton, it was essential to appoint a sacristan who knew how to look after the sacristy and its contents, and who would keep the church clean and tidy. 'Cheadle will be finished most perfectly', he told Lord Shrewsbury, 'but unless there is a responsible person in the shape of a sacristan to look after the church the whole thing will be ruined. Any Catholic church takes the whole time of one man to keep it in a proper state. Such a person is as necessary as the priest.'[104] The sorry state of the sacristy in his new church at Derby, only two years after its opening, convinced Pugin that the clergy left a great deal to be desired when it came to caring for the buildings and their contents. Such a thing could not be allowed to happen at Cheadle. By the end of April 1846 he had found a Mr Wheelwright, 'a most zealous, willing man', to take on the role of sacristan. Wheelwright was also an organist, and thus able to serve St Giles' in a dual capacity.[105] The organ was a small single-manual instrument with about nine stops, built by Parsons of London, the firm who had built a much larger instrument for Alton Towers Chapel in the 1830s. It was quite adequate for accompanying the Gregorian chant which Pugin envisaged as the only music which would be allowed at St Giles'. He wanted none of the florid operatic-style Mass settings that were in vogue elsewhere, but, as in so many of his churches, his hopes were unfulfilled. The organ was later extended, and it has latterly been replaced altogether.

By 26 August all was ready, and Pugin sent Lord Shrewsbury the very last sheet of accounts,[106] a significant act because a Catholic church may not be consecrated until all debts have been paid. The arrangements for the consecration and opening of the church were, as one might expect, quite complicated, with admission by ticket only. Given that the events were to be spread over two days, that invited guests would need transporting to Cheadle from the nearest railway stations at Derby and Stafford, and that some would require overnight accommodation, a good deal of forward planning was required. It seems that Pugin – busy as he then was with glass and metalwork for the House of Lords – had to supervise some of these arrangements. He was certainly responsible for seeing to it that Charles Barry had a carriage laid on from Derby to Alton, and that his artist friends, J.R. Herbert and Clarkson Stanfield, were found accommodation in nearby Ashbourne. Edward Challoner, a timber merchant and a benefactor of Pugin's church of St Oswald, Liverpool, was also invited. 'If it is possible to let him dine', Pugin wrote to Lord Shrewsbury, 'it would be a good thing for he is really a person entitled to respect and attention.'[107] A great cathedral was being planned for Liverpool at this time, and Pugin hoped that Challoner would be a major contributor. Guests arriving via Stafford station were directed to the town's coaching inn, the Swan, from where they would be taken by road to Cheadle, some fifteen miles distant. 'Every horse and carriage has been stopped for the convenience of those going to the function.'[108] Pugin himself arrived at Alton Towers on the evening of Friday, 28 August in order to supervise the final arrangements. Having been ill for much of the summer, and still in a state of emotional turmoil in the wake of the Mary Amherst affair, he must have approached the opening of St Giles' with a mixture of anticipation and anxiety. He had talked about it, written about it, promised great things for it, and staked his entire reputation on its success. He had contacted all the relevant papers and journals, such as the *The Builder, The Tablet,* the *Morning Post,* and the *Staffordshire Advertiser,* sending detailed descriptions of the church and its significance, knowing that they would form their own opinions and pass their own judgements. Back in Ramsgate, John Powell expressed his fears for Pugin in a letter to his uncle:

> The poor Governor wrote yesterday. He says he is very weak and wretched. He dreads meeting anybody he knows and everybody will be at Cheadle opening. The ceremony will cheer him up if all goes on well. If there should be any mull it will be the death of him almost.[109]

The consecration took place on Monday, 31 August. It was essentially a private affair, conducted by Bishop Wiseman, with the newly ordained Revd George Talbot as deacon and Dr Ennis as sub-deacon. First there was a procession around the outside of church during which the bishop aspersed the walls with holy water, using a bunch of hyssop as a sprinkler. Three circuits of the church were made, then, at the singing of Psalm 24, 'Lift up your heads, O ye gates', the west doors were opened, and the procession entered. The altars, completely bare and without ornaments at this stage, were consecrated in turn, the bishop tracing in holy water and holy oil the five crosses incised on each *mensa*, symbolic of the Five Wounds of Christ. The inner walls of the church were aspersed, likewise the floor, and each of the twelve consecration crosses around the walls was anointed in turn with the oil of chrism. Each of these crosses was provided with a candle-bracket incorporating a Shrewsbury lion. The candles were to be lit for the consecration, and on each subsequent anniversary. Bishop Walsh consecrated the altar and tabernacle in the Blessed Sacrament Chapel. All of the altar linen, vessels, vestments and ornaments were dedicated and put in their proper places, and in conclusion a High Mass was sung. It is not difficult to understand why the whole ceremony lasted some four hours; by which time all was ready for the first public service in the newly consecrated church on the following day.

In the evening 54 distinguished guests descended the grand staircase into the State Dining Room at Alton Towers (as yet unaltered by Pugin) and sat down to a sumptuous dinner, while the earl's blind harper, Edward Jervis, played and sang. Some of the company were accommodated at the Towers, while the remainder were lodged at the Shrewsbury Arms at Farley. The list of guests indicates the national and international significance of St Giles' in the history of nineteenth-century church-building. Among them were the Austrian and Sardinian ambassadors.[110] From France came the Comte de Montalembert (1810-70), the Catholic politician and historian who had added a long appendix to Pugin's second edition of *Contrasts* (1841), the stained-glass artist Henri Gérente (1814-49), and the influential Adolphe-Napoléon Didron (*c*.1805-86), editor of the *Annales Archéologiques* the French equivalent of *The Ecclesiologist*. From the German states there was August Reichensperger (1808-95), editor of a similar publication, the *Kölner Domblatt,* and involved with the completion of Cologne Cathedral. Among the leading Catholic laity were Lord and Lady Camoys, Lord and Lady Dormer, Sir Edward Vavasour, and Charles Scott Murray. There was also Charles Barry, and of course Pugin himself. Clerical guests included Bishops Walsh and Wiseman, the Archbishop of Damascus, and John Bede Polding, Archbishop of Sydney, for whom Pugin carried out a number of designs for Australian churches and church furnishings.[111] Lord Shrewsbury's hospitality extended to two recent converts from amongst the 'Oxford Men', Frederick Faber and John Henry Newman. 'All the world there', noted Newman, 'Great dinners.'[112]

On the morning of 1 September, St Giles' Day, Lord and Lady Shrewsbury set out from Alton Towers with members of their family and distinguished guests in a convoy of eight carriages, and in brilliant sunshine. As the bells rang out across Cheadle, spectators from miles around gathered on the streets to see the carriages arrive, and to witness the procession from the schoolroom into the church via the great west doors. At the head of the procession were the thurifer, crucifer and acolytes, one of whom was the earl's thirteen-year-old cousin and heir-presumptive, Bertram Talbot. Meanwhile the choir, borrowed for the occasion from St Chad's Cathedral and led by Pugin's friend, John Hardman, sang the introit psalm (122): 'I was glad when they said unto me: we will go into the house of the Lord', in plainsong. Then came fourteen of the lower clergy wearing long surplices of the old English pattern, the revival of which had involved Pugin in no less controversy than had the revival of the full Gothic chasuble. Next in the procession were 40 priests in full vestments and 13 in copes, followed by 8 deacons in dalmatics, and, finally 10 bishops and the 2 archbishops in white and gold vestments and mitres **(6.29)**. The bishops were Ullathorne (Bath), Riddell (Newcastle upon Tyne), G. Brown and Sharples (Lancashire), J.Brown (Wales), Gillis (Edinburgh), Griffiths and Morris (London), Briggs (Yorkshire) and Wareing (Northampton) who in his days as a mission priest at Cresswell had set up the Cheadle mission in the 1820s. Last of all came Bishops Wiseman and Walsh. Wiseman sang the Mass, and Walsh, as Vicar Apostolic, presided *ex throno*.

The preacher was Bishop Gillis, chosen, no doubt, because of the ancient dedication to St Giles of the cathedral and city of Edinburgh. His sermon was based on Psalm 127: 'Except the Lord build the house, in vain do its builders

6.29 Present at the consecration: Archbishop John Bede Polding. He is wearing a cope given to him by the dowager countess of Shrewsbury c.1855. Oil painting by Eugene Montague Scott (St John's College, University of Sydney. Photo: Tasmanian Museum & Art Gallery).

labour'. Much of what he had to say was in accord with the social concerns of Lord Shrewsbury and Pugin, looking back to the golden age of medieval Catholicism in which the poor were properly cared for, and urging the congregation to support the various works of Christian mercy. Gillis' preaching style, which on his own admission was 'like the aerial steam engine at fifty miles an hour', disgusted Newman, who described it as 'half screaming and bellowing, half whining', but, as he noted with equal disgust, 'ladies of quality were in raptures with it.'[113] Pugin's prominence in the ceremony surprised Didron, who contrasted it with church openings in France at which the architect simply 'hid himself away with his young wife in a corner of the nave.'[114] After the Mass a 'sumptuous collation' was served in the large room above the school, and the celebrations were brought to a close with Vespers and Benediction at four o'clock. On the following morning many of the clergy and other guests who had stayed over another day went to Alton village to see the buildings under construction at the Hospital and the Castle. Pugin did not linger. He went home to Ramsgate suffering from the same kind of physical and emotional exhaustion that had plagued him after the opening of St Chad's, Birmingham, in 1841. 'I returned home immediately after the consecration of Cheadle,' he wrote on 8 September, '& have been confined to the house ever scince. … I am forbidden even to walk about the house.'[115]

Pugin's priming of the Press paid dividends. In addition to the expected coverage in Catholic journals, national and local newspapers carried reports. One of the most detailed of these appeared in the *Staffordshire Advertiser* on 5 September. Though relying heavily on the material sent in by Pugin, it was compiled by a journalist who was evidently familiar with Catholic worship, and who knew St Giles' at first hand. It includes a comprehensive description of the church and its ornaments, as well as an account of the opening ceremony. Likening the scene inside the church to a casket of jewels and gold illuminated by the tapers on the altar and above the screen, it contains the telling words:

> We can scarcely imagine anything more calculated to make men forget that they were living in the heart of a Protestant country than the scene and circumstances now presented … here was enough sight and sound to affect the dullest imagination, and make one almost fancy it a vision of past ages. Certainly there has not been such an ecclesiastical display on the part of English Catholics, nor has their worship been performed with such public splendour, since the Reformation.

Pugin could not have wished for a more glowing testimony to his success in achieving precisely what he had set out to do. On 9 January 1847 the *Illustrated London News* carried a detailed and equally complimentary description of St Giles', including seven illustrations **(6.30)**. 'Probably so perfect a church was never erected in England before, as there is a *completeness* in the building which defies words to express, or representations to give an idea of.' The article also included a tribute to the clerk of works, John Denny, 'to whom great praise is due, for the ability he has displayed in the realisation of the architect's magnificent conceptions.' *The Tablet* was even more fulsome in its praise of

6.30 St Giles' from the south-east, published in the *Illustrated London News*, 9 January 1847.

Denny, 'whose admiration for the Gothic style of architecture and acquaintance with its minutest details has made the erection of this building a labour of love.'[116] This was a step too far for Pugin, who seemed reluctant to share the limelight even with the 'indefatigable' Denny who had, after all, been paid for his services. 'see what I am come to,' he wrote indignantly to Hardman. 'did you see all that humbug in the paper about Dennys love & admiration of gothic architecture &c. – I should like to find out the fellow that got it up.'[117]

Not every observer was carried away. St Giles' was criticised for the over-intensity of its interior decoration, for the overwhelming height of the steeple in comparison with the length and height of the church, for the abundance of stencilled lettering, and for the way in which a church intended to be of the time of Edward I expanded into 'that which prevailed during the reigns of the Edwards which spans from late 13th century to the 15th century.'[118] However, no critic was more forthright than Pugin himself in acknowledging the shortcomings. In his response to *The Ecclesiologist*'s attack on him back in March, in which Cheadle had not even been mentioned, Pugin included the gratuitous remark that there were 'some serious defects'. When asked by Lord Shrewsbury to explain himself, Pugin singled out the shortness of the chancel and the lack of chancel stalls as points which the ecclesiologists might take up, '& it was well to be prepared beforehand.'[119] In answering his critics in *The Rambler,* he pointed out that the building had been altered several times in mid-course as Lord Shrewsbury's funding had increased, and therein lies the fundamental problem, for Pugin believed that the ground plan of a building should govern its elevations, and St Giles' had been planned originally as a 'plain parochial country church.' 'There is a great anomaly between the simplicity of its walls and mouldings and the intricacy of its detail. … Had we commenced on the same scale as we ended, a truly fine building might have been produced..'[120] Lord Shrewsbury expressed himself more prosaically. When Pugin's earlier approval of St Giles' was quoted to him, he smiled and said, 'He won't say that now, though; he abuses it as much as everything else that he has done.'[121] In August 1851 Pugin visited the church for what proved to be the last time, and, not having seen it for three years, changed his opinion once again. 'It looks magnificent', he wrote to his wife, 'it is a very glorious building & stands capitally I assure you it quite astonished me.'[121]

Lord Shrewsbury had predicted that St Giles' would be a 'text-book for all good people', and Pugin had promised that it would be 'a Model in every respect'. The reality, had either of them lived long enough to see it, would have exceeded their expectations. Yet as early as 1846 Pugin was well aware of the dangers of plagiarism when he wrote,

> there are so many catholic architects now that there is not a chance of any new buildings. I believe I design for all of them for I see actually my own Casts & figures used – and then they abuse me afterwards. These men can afford to Sell cheap for they <u>steal</u> their <u>brooms ready made</u>. However the movement progresses and the right sort of thing becomes general & that is the great point.[122]

Foreign visitors in particular were amazed that such a comprehensive range of applied arts could have emanated from a single mind. Though Didron regretted Pugin's constant love of the floriated style, he could see that Pugin had revived the whole medieval period, body and soul. 'Everything comes to life in this building.'[123] Reichensperger compared Pugin to the rising sun whose rays had revived the dormant medieval roots, making them spring into living architecture again, and he looked for a comparable architectural revival in Germany.[124] At St Giles' Pugin demonstrated a principle that was to surface again in the later nineteenth century with Norman Shaw and the Arts and Crafts Movement, namely that an architect should take responsibility not just for the design of the fabric of a church, but also for its furnishings, fittings and decoration. Pugin drew together not just a variety of art forms, but also a multiplicity of sources. The breadth and depth of his knowledge of medieval antiquities were astonishing, and this nourished his great talent as a designer who could draw deeply upon the details of Gothic art and architecture which he had observed and accurately sketched. Diverse though his sources may have been, Pugin drew them together into a coherent whole, and the key unifying factors are his deep understanding of Catholic doctrine and liturgy, and his overwhelming desire to express them through the media of 'Christian'

6.31 The Convent of St Joseph (Michael Fisher).

(i.e. Gothic) art and design. It is with these factors in mind that we can understand his passionate resolve that for Cheadle nothing less than perfection would do, and his intermittent arguments with the earl to ensure that it would be in every respect a 'True Principles' church. St Giles' is therefore as much a theological text-book as an artistic one, and whatever might, with the aid of hindsight, be said about the proportions of the building or the density of its colouring, it is a brilliant realisation in every respect of Pugin's vision of what a parish church should be, and of how it should instruct the faithful. 'It is, in fact, by parish churches', he had written in 1841, 'that the faith of a nation is to be sustained and nourished.'[125] Pugin, whose busy schedule allowed time for daily Mass as well as morning and evening prayers in his private chapel at home, regarded himself first and foremost as a servant of the Church, as 'a builder up of men's minds and ideas as well as material edifices.'[126] It is this which singles out Pugin among the architects of the Gothic Revival, and St Giles' as the perfect expression of what he believed an English parish church should be.

The social and educational dimensions of the Catholic Faith, stressed by Bishop Gillis at the opening of St Giles', found its expression in the nearby school and the convent of St Joseph, both designed by Pugin. The school was finished in the Spring of 1846. In February he wrote to Lord Shrewsbury, who was away in Sicily, and commented on how quickly the building work had progressed over the winter, without interruption by frosty weather. 'The school is roofed & looks exceedingly well. In fact I think it improves the church & forms a grand mass of building ... the schools will be light & spacious & the upper room looks really grand.'[127] It is of brick with stone trim, L-shaped in plan, with a tower and pyramid-capped belfry at the angle. The main building is similar in design to the Guildhall at Alton, which also accommodated a school. It has large brick buttresses and the upper floor runs the length of the building. From the end of April 1846 Mass was celebrated there, pending the completion of the church. The convent was begun a little later, and finished in 1848. It is also brick-built, with a tall tower with a saddleback roof and belfry (restored 2000) **(6.31).** It was furnished with its own chapel, and it has a cloister, constructed largely of timber, enclosing a small garden and with a direct access into the churchyard. There is a window set with Hardman glass in the north-west corner. The convent was occupied from 1848 to 1875 by a community of the Sisters of Mercy who came over from Carlow, Ireland, and who worked in the schools and in the parish at large. A third domestic building, the presbytery, was built in Chapel Street, opposite the church on the site of the former Adjutant's house. It has high gables with stone crosses, large chimneys, and mullioned windows. Both the presbytery and the convent are now in private ownership, and some excellent restoration work has been carried out on both buildings.

The year after the consecration of St Giles' its first priest, Francis Fairfax, left the parish, having served the Cheadle mission since 1833. It had been the intention of Lord Shrewsbury to place the church in the hands of a religious order, and Fr Frederick Faber, of the Wilfridian order recently set up at Cotton, had consented to take it over once the Wilfridian community was more strongly established. The land adjoining the south side of St Giles' churchyard, on which the convent was built, had originally been bought by Lord Shrewsbury as an intended site for the Wilfridians in addition to, or as an alternative to, Cotton Hall. The amalgamation of the Wilfridians with the Oratorians frustrated the earl's plans, because Fr Newman put a strict interpretation on the Oratorians' brief that they were to work only in the larger towns, and Cheadle was only a small one. In the meantime the earl nominated an Irish priest, Fr William Gubbins, who, it was said, had more love for horses than he had for his parishioners, and the spiritual life of the congregation suffered as a consequence. When Bishop Ullathorne intervened, having received complaints from the parish, Gubbins told him that his allegiance was to the earl as his patron, but, as he must have known, that did not absolve him from canonical obedience to his bishop, and he had now antagonised the earl too. Ullathorne finally put St Giles' under interdict so that no services could be held there, and those Catholics who could manage it went over to the Cresswell Mission for Mass. Gubbins responded by conducting devotions in the Catholic Guild Hall, attended mainly by Irish immigrants, and by threatening a lawsuit. He was dismissed from Cheadle in 1855.

Earl John died in November 1852 and was succeeded by his cousin Bertram as the seventeenth earl. In 1854 Bertram revived the idea of placing Cheadle in the care of a religious order, and expressed a preference for the Redemptorists. Bishop Ullathorne agreed, but the Gubbins affair was still unresolved, and when he finally left St Giles' he was succeeded by another secular priest, Canon Jones, who came from Brewood.[128]

The death of Bertram, the last Catholic earl of Shrewsbury, in 1856, and the failure of his executors to keep the titles and estates in Catholic hands, deprived the church, school and convent of the financial and moral support they had hitherto enjoyed from the Talbot family. 'Pugin's Gem' was therefore something of a mixed blessing to the local Catholic community, which was not wealthy. From 1856 it was left to the parish priest to arrange for the upkeep of the church. Canon Jones sold his books and his piano to raise funds, while Fr Stuart Bathurst (1861-71), though a man of independent means, gave away most of what he had to the poor. It may have been through Bathurst's influence that in 1866 the Anglican eigtheenth earl of Shrewsbury contributed £1500 towards the fabric of St Giles', thus acknowledging its wider architectural importance. It was widely known that the late Earl John had intended to endow St Giles', but had died before the requisite deeds could be drawn up.

It is doubtful if the ritual arrangements of the Sarum Rite were ever as fully observed at St Giles' as Pugin had hoped. Significantly, perhaps, the altar missal, finely bound and embellished though it is, contains the Tridentine text which appears to have been used from the outset. The provision of six candlesticks on the high altar, rather than Pugin's preferred two, has already been noted, and among the other brassware items ordered from Hardman's was a communion rail – common enough in nineteenth-century Catholic churches, but definitely not *ad usum Sarum,* and according to Pugin a seventeenth-century Anglican invention. It has since been removed. There is no doubt, however, that churches such as St Giles' did much to raise the standards of Catholic worship, and inculcate a better sense of reverence. Old photographs show that the tabernacle was for a time removed from the Blessed Sacrament Chapel to the high altar, and the superb brass screen likewise disappeared. Both have since been restored to their proper places. The removal of the *coronae* from the nave has already been noted. Otherwise, St Giles' has suffered to a far lesser degree than most of Pugin's other churches from the excessive zeal of those who, particularly in the wake of the Second Vatican Council, were given to large-scale 're-ordering' as the Tridentine Rite was itself superseded. The rood screen at St Chad's Cathedral in Birmingham, controversial even in Pugin's own time, was notoriously removed, along with much else, by Archbishop Dwyer, in 1967. The screen at St Giles' has survived intact, and although Mass is generally said facing the people, the

6.32 'Perfect Cheadle ... my consolation in all afflictions' (Pugin to Lord Shrewsbury, 9 March 1842). St Giles' viewed from the south-east (Mark Titterton).

present working altar (a finely-carved alabaster one brought from St Wilfrid's, Cotton) stands east of the screen, thus preserving something of Pugin's concept of the essential separation between 'the faithful, and the sacrifice, the nave and the chancel'. A Latin High Mass is still occasionally celebrated, and on such occasions it is tempting to imagine that at any moment Pugin himself might emerge from the sacristy, vested in his cassock and full English surplice, ready to assist at the altar: 'I assure you', he once wrote, 'you would hardly know me when issuing from the sacristy door in full canonicals.'[129]

7

Community and controversy: St Wilfrid's, Cotton

'Pugin says it will have the only perfect chancel in England, with an east window he could die for'
F.W. Faber to Michael Watts-Russell, 5 October 1846[1]

Cotton lies about two miles north of Alton Towers; a community of scattered houses and farms set in a wooded valley, with the spire of St Wilfrid's church and the now-derelict college buildings visible above the trees **(7.1)**. Its remoteness and the small number of inhabitants belie the significant place which Cotton holds in the history of the Catholic Revival. It is important for three reasons. Different in style and function from the churches at Alton and Cheadle, St Wilfrid's was the last church of the Pugin-Shrewsbury partnership; it brought Pugin and Lord Shrewsbury into close contact with Frederick Faber, Bl. John Henry Newman, and others who embraced Roman Catholicism as a result of the ferment caused by the Oxford Movement, and it plunged them into bitter controversy with the people who were to be Pugin's greatest opponents on matters of architectural and liturgical style – the Oratorians.

By the early 1840s the impact of the Oxford Movement was being felt in the parishes of England through the activities of young clergymen who had fallen under the spell of its leaders – Keble, Pusey and Newman – during their time at the University. Among them were Michael Watts-Russell (1815-75), and Frederick William Faber (1814-63). Michael Watts-Russell was the second son of Jesse Watts-Russell of Ilam Hall near Ashbourne, and was therefore a near-neighbour of Lord Shrewsbury. He went up to Oxford in 1833 – the year of Keble's Assize Sermon which triggered the Oxford Movement – and subsequently became Rector of Benefield in Northamptonshire. Faber was a contemporary of Watts-Russell at Oxford, where he remained after graduation as a Fellow of University College before, eventually, becoming Rector of Elton, Huntingdonshire. Pugin had close contacts with Oxford through his friend John Rouse Bloxam of Magdalen College, with whom he corresponded regularly. He met Faber for the first time in March 1843 and took him to Birmingham to meet John Hardman. He told Bloxam afterwards of an Emmaus-like experience when the three of them had walked together and conversed deeply about matters of faith. 'I never saw a man more deeply imbued with the spirit of the

7.1 'A wild and beautiful solitude among the hills of Staffordshire' (F.W. Faber): south-east view of Cotton dell. Cheadle and the spire of St Giles' can also be seen in the far distance. (Mark Titterton).

ages of faith … We may say without prophanity did not our hearts burn within us – at his wonderful description of Catholic devotions.'[2] Pugin corresponded also with Newman, over the Tractarian publication, *Lives of the English Saints,* for which he provided eleven illustrations.[3]

The Oxford Movement, and its publications, *Tracts for the Times,* emphasised the continuity of the Church of England with its medieval, Catholic, past, and it fostered in the minds of some the hope that the Church of England might be 'catholicised' to the extent that re-union with Rome might become a real possibility. Ambrose Phillipps – himself a convert – certainly believed it, and Dr Wiseman was broadly sympathetic. As early as March 1841 Pugin wrote enthusiastically to Lord Shrewsbury, 'These Oxford men do more good in one week than we do in a whole year towards Catholicising England. … Some great result must shortly attend their labours for it is impossible the church of England can go long in its present position.'[4] Lord Shrewsbury was not entirely convinced. He was one of the 'Old Catholic' school who were mystified at the sight of Anglicans embracing Catholic doctrines which their forebears had rejected and condemned, and for which so many English Catholics had suffered torture and martyrdom. Yet they did not take what to Catholics seemed the logical step – submission to Rome – and therefore they could be seen as a hindrance. Thus Lord Shrewsbury was suspicious of Newman, and he denounced Pusey as both deluded and insincere.[5] 'It is extraordinary we cannot catch a few Puseyites', he complained to Dr Rock, 'Has even one of them come over?'[6]

Soon, however, a number of individual conversions took place, including, famously, that of Newman himself on 9 October 1845, when he was received into the Church by Fr Dominic Barberi of the Passionist community at Aston-by-Stone. It was this which precipitated the conversion of Watts-Russell and Faber, and a stream of others followed them, both clerical and lay. Pugin was 'rejoiced beyond measure' on receiving the news about Newman,[7] and he was equally delighted to hear of Faber's conversion on 17 November. 'It is really glorious,' he wrote to Lord Shrewsbury who had gone abroad for the winter. 'Newman will be a wonderful instrument in the hand of God.'[8]

For many who 'crossed the Tiber' there was a heavy price to pay. Having resigned their livings, clerical converts such as Faber suddenly found themselves without an income, and some had wives and children to support. Michael Watts-Russell was married, so for him and for others in his situation there was then no prospect of ordination into the Roman priesthood. Such men found themselves vilified by former friends and colleagues whom they had left behind, and suspected and mistrusted by many in their new Church. At this time the principal centre for converts was Birmingham. It was not far from Oxford, Wiseman was there to give support and encouragement, and there was the pro-cathedral of St Chad's and the new Oscott College. At Wiseman's instigation, Newman and five of his friends set up an informal community at Old Oscott which he renamed Maryvale. Meanwhile, in May 1846, Faber and his companions took over Michael Watts-Russell's house in Colmore Terrace where they adopted the name of the Brothers of the Will of God under the patronage of the Anglo-Saxon St Wilfrid (d. 709) to whom Faber had a particular devotion, Faber himself adopting the name of Brother Wilfrid **(7.2)**. One of the rooms was furnished as a chapel, decorated in Gothic style with red walls, a blue ceiling, and an altar by Pugin.[9] Hardman supplied a tabernacle for which 'Brother Wilfrid' was charged £19.10s.[10] They also adopted some exuberant Italian devotions as a consequence of Faber's visit to Italy in the Spring of 1846

7.2 'Brother Wilfrid' – F. W. Faber.

in the company of another young convert, William Antony Hutchison, the wealthy son of a former head cashier of the Bank of England. They returned laden with devotional books and ornaments, and Hutchison commented on the consequences for the new community: 'I think we succeeded to a great extent in doing what Brother Wilfrid proposed, ignoring the existence of Protestantism, and living as if we were in Italy'.[11] Faber's conversion from Gothic to Classical was seen by Pugin as 'perversion' destined to frustrate his hopes that the former 'Oxford men' would be in the vanguard of propagating the 'true principles' amongst their fellow Catholics.

In spite of his earlier misgivings about the 'Puseyites', once Newman, Faber and others had made their submissions and been received into the Catholic Church, Lord Shrewsbury extended to them his warm friendship and financial support. In July 1846 he suggested that the Wilfridians should move from Birmingham to Cheadle. He had bought a piece of land adjoining St Giles' on which a monastery could be built for them. He had also, in 1843, bought Cotton Hall, intending it perhaps as a possible residence for his cousin and heir Bertram, but he now offered it to the Wilfridians as a rural retreat. Faber was given the choice of accepting either or both. He was present with Newman at the consecration of St Giles' on 1 September and it seems that the question of the move was discussed during the subsequent celebrations at Alton Towers. Faber decided to accept Cotton Hall rather than build anew at Cheadle, and the community moved almost immediately from what Faber called the 'hot choking *allezo* of Birmingham' to 'a wild and beautiful solitude among the hills of Staffordshire'.[12] A temporary chapel was provided within the house pending the building of a new church which was to be designed by Pugin. Unbeknown, perhaps, to Brother Wilfrid, his was not the first religious community to inhabit Cotton dell. In 1178 a group of French Cistercians from Aunay had made a temporary settlement at 'Chotes', as it was then called, pending the construction of permanent buildings in a neighbouring valley at Croxden. The founder, Bertram de Verdun, was an ancestor of Lord Shrewsbury. Pugin had made a study of the ruins of Croxden in preparing his design for St Barnabas', Nottingham, and so this touch of historicism would have appealed to him too.

Ambrose Phillipps, a friend of both Pugin and Lord Shrewsbury, had achieved remarkable success in winning converts in the Leicestershire villages around Garendon, and in addition to the monastery at Mount Saint Bernard he was able to provide missions in the area. Among these was his own chapel at Grace Dieu which Pugin enlarged and re-furnished; and a new church at Shepshed, also by Pugin, to which Lord Shrewsbury made a generous contribution. Phillipps staffed these missions by bringing over from Italy members of the Order of Charity like Fr Gentili, and of the Passionists such as Fr Dominic Barberi who, in 1842, settled at Aston Hall, near Stone, and for whom Pugin built the small church of St Anne in the town of Stone itself. Lord Shrewsbury was not entirely convinced of the wisdom of using Italian missionary priests whose English was not good, and who might only serve to reinforce popular notions that Catholicism was foreign. 'We must have a new race of zealous English Missionaries, such as we are now bringing up at Oscott, under the good Bishop (Wiseman) and Pugin.'[13] The Oxford converts arriving at Birmingham in the mid-1840s were ideally suited – Englishmen who from their personal experience and conviction could argue the case for Catholicism amongst their fellow-countrymen. Those who had held livings as Anglican clergy brought with them the practical experience of pastoral work. This was especially true of Frederick Faber who had transformed his Huntingdonshire parish of Elton by his enthusiastic leadership, teaching and visiting. Such experience could prove valuable in furthering the Catholic cause in the rural communities around Cotton, and in the neighbouring villages of Oakamoor, Kingsley and Whiston which as yet had no Catholic mission.

Within a few weeks of the opening of St Giles', the community of three choir brothers and nine lay brothers moved into Cotton Hall which had to be adapted to suit their needs. A temporary chapel was fitted up in some adjacent farm buildings, and a boys' school was opened in a loft over the stables. Meanwhile the ground was prepared for the foundations of the new church. At the beginning of October Faber described the scene to Michael Watts Russell:

> You can scarcely form an idea of the confusion, hurry, work, I may actually say, ubiquity, which have been required of me during the past weeks. From Alton Towers to Cotton, at Cotton from the house to the garden, from the new church to the new school, from the quarry to the wood, from bricklayers and carpenters to painters and glaziers, from Dr Winter the Dominican to Mr Winter the steward, from Lord Shrewsbury to Brother Chad, trees, walls, windows seemed to echo Brother Wilfrid, Brother Wilfrid.[14]

On 12 October, on the same day that the foundations of the church were blessed, Bishop Walsh admitted Faber and two other Wilfridian brothers to minor orders in the Towers Chapel. Meanwhile, the Wilfridians undertook a systematic programme of missionary work, which may well have been in Lord Shrewsbury's mind when he first invited them to Cotton, despite the controversies that similar activities had aroused in Alton.

Faber had originally intended that Cotton should be a retreat at which the brothers would prepare for missionary work in the large towns; but there was a change of direction as it was realised that there was much to be achieved locally. Faber found that some preparatory work had already been done by Fr Kennedy, himself a convert from Anglicanism, who from 1845 had been chaplain to the previous tenant of Cotton Hall, John Campbell-Smith, and who remained for a time because Faber was not yet in priest's orders. The Wilfridians soon organised things on a systematic basis. Districts of the locality were assigned to individual brothers who spent a good part of the day making house calls. Instruction of converts was undertaken by a First Confession Brother, a First Communion Brother and a Further Instruction Brother; there was a Confraternity of the Precious Blood, and a brass band. During the summer of 1847 Faber preached outdoors because the chapel in the Hall was too cramped, and Pugin's new church was still under construction. The Abbé Vandrival who visited in May 1847 wrote that the outdoor sermons took place each Sunday when 300 people would fill the courtyard, and 150 came on Thursdays.[15] Stations of the Cross were set up in the garden, and large wooden crosses on the hills either side of the valley. Lady Shrewsbury paid for the building of a school to which the earl made an endowment of £65 in addition to the £2,300 he had already contributed to the church and the extensions at the hall. Pugin sent an image of Our Lady which, in line with his generosity to other churches he built, may have been a gift. Faber told him that it had 'worked something like a miracle, which has bred a great devotion among our poor.'[16] It is thought by some that this was the image set up in the terrace in front of the hall, under a stone canopy, also by Pugin, surmounted by a floriated cross, whereas others assert that the *virgo praedicanda* statue, as it came to be called, was set up by the Oratorians in 1848.[17] To the disquiet, no doubt, of the more conventionally devout, Faber affectionately referred to Our Lady as 'Mamma'.

Among the other converts of Faber's acquaintance was Edward Caswall, who, like Michael Watts Russell, was married and therefore could not join the community. Nevertheless he was befriended by Lord Shrewsbury and he visited Alton Towers and St Wilfrid's where he made his own contribution in the form of the crucifix which he carved on a rock between Cotton and the Towers. His wife, Louise, seems to have had a particular fondness for St Wilfrid's, for she was buried there in 1849. Her memorial is under the trees on the north side of the church: a ledger-stone with a cross on the top, and unmistakably Puginian in style. Following her death, Caswall joined the Oratory, but he is best remembered as a translator of Latin and German hymns, including *Bethlehem, of noblest cities,* and *When morning gilds the skies.* Faber was a hymn-writer too, and some of his best-known hymns, like *Faith of our fathers,* may have been sung for the first time to accompany one of his outdoor processions through Cotton dell; while *Pilgrims of the night* – better known as *Hark, hark, my soul* – includes

7.3 St John's Anglican church, Cotton (Michael Fisher).

as verse said to have been inspired by the sound of bells from the distant tower of Kingsley church:

> Far, far away, like bells at evening pealing,
> The voice of Jesus sounds o'er land and sea

The result of the Wilfridians' systematic missionary activity in their first six months at Cotton was an impressive number of converts from the immediate neighbourhood and from the nearby village of Oakamoor. Faber's description of the welcome he received on returning from his ordination at Oscott on Holy Saturday 1847 shows that work at St Wilfrid's had a momentum all of its own:

> We arrived from Oscott about 9 at night; about three-quarters of a mile from St Wilfrid's two guns were fired to our no little astonishment, and then the carriage was stopped by a huge crowd of peasants and labourers. ... This crowd, composed almost all of <u>Protestants</u>, took the horses from the carriage and dragged us home amid volleys of guns and fireworks and a brass band; a series of really most tasteful triumphal arches were reared along the road with illuminations and crosses on them; under each of these we stopped, for cheering and music. ... The poor Protestant minister had to pass to his chapel under the triumphal arches; he had only seven to preach to.[18]

The 'poor Protestant minister' was the Revd Mr Hendrickson, whose curious Regency Gothic church of St John **(7.3)** stood almost within the grounds of Cotton Hall, and who viewed with dismay the erosion of his congregation. A verbal battle ensued, not unlike the one between Dr Winter and the Revd John Pike Jones at Alton. There were also brushes with the Primitive

7.4 Cotton Hall and St Wilfrid's: postcard, *c.*1900.

Methodists, as for example when one of their ministers pushed his way into a house demanding to hear what a dying man said to Faber in confession. Such activities only proved to be counter-productive according to Faber who wrote an open letter to his adversaries, concluding that

> You and yours are far more effective Catholic missionaries than we are; and I assure you, hardly a week passes without some one or more stragglers being driven into the bosom of the Holy Roman Church, declaring themselves fairly wearied out by the incessant curses fulminated against them from the pulpits of the State Church, and humbly echoed back with fury even wilder still, from the Dissenters' chapel and camp meeting, and desirous to seek refuge where they hear only of Almighty God, of the love of Jesus, and of duty, charity, peace, and kindly affection towards all, whether Catholic or Protestant.[19]

It might seem strange that the flamboyant devotions which Faber established at Cotton – such as outdoor processions of the Blessed Sacrament, and veneration of Our Lady which far exceeded anything that English Catholics had hitherto known – should have had such a profound effect upon non-Catholic farm-labourers, mineworkers and blacksmiths in a remote area of the Staffordshire Moorlands where outsiders – let alone monkish ones dressed in strange costume – were regarded with some suspicion. Yet the Wilfridians of Cotton Hall offered a style of religion with a fresh appeal that was very different from the bigoted tirades issuing from the pulpit of the 'government preaching-house' next door, or from that of the dissenting chapel. It was, moreover, undergirded with sound teaching given in the boys' and girls' schools, in evening lectures for adults, in the tireless visiting of the poor in their cottages, and Christian charity shown to those whom both Establishment and Dissent had woefully neglected. It needs to be said also that not all of the Wilfridians were Oxford men. Some, like Tom Godwin (Brother Frederick of the Will of God), and John Strickson (Brother Chad of the Sacred Heart), were village lads who had been among Faber's household staff in his Anglican days at Elton Rectory, and who even then had become a kind of spiritual brotherhood. Such men would have established an instant rapport with north Staffordshire countryfolk. Writing to Lord Shrewsbury in January 1847, Faber confessed that he was

> worked to death by young men from Oakamore and all parts: from 25 to 30, several grown up, one of 40 to 50 years, come to the night school to hear the *fervorini* I give every night. … They hardly know there is a God and even in this retired spot we are all overworked. I catechize publicly twice a day except Saturdays, then there is Sundays' *conversazione,* and hours of private talk to these young men … the mother of two of my converts has been brought by them, and was received yesterday. Thus we received 10 into our flock last week, God be praised![20]

This was all before the new church of St Wilfrid had taken shape, although the sight of this new building rising before their eyes with its tall tower and spire must have been an attraction in itself.

Preparatory work for the new church began almost as soon as the Brothers took possession of Cotton Hall, and the foundations were blessed on 12 October – St Wilfrid's Day – by Bishop Walsh. The architect was, of course, Pugin, and the project excited him. He vowed that it would have 'the only perfect chancel in England' and 'an east window he could die for.'[21] Considerable alterations and additions had to be made to the house, which was basically Georgian but with some seventeenth-century survivals **(7.4)**. Pugin added two new ranges, one of stone, and a more utilitarian brick one. The builder was George Myers of Lambeth who had been responsible for many of Pugin's buildings in other parts of the country, and for much of his wood-carving.[22] That Myers, rather than the 'indefatigable' John Denny of Alton, should have been given the work might seem strange in view of Denny's prominent role as clerk of works at Cheadle, but Cotton needed to be built quickly, and Denny and his men were now fully committed to completing Lord Shrewsbury's other projects at Alton Castle, St John's Hospital, and Alton Towers. The Abbé Vandrival, who was staying at Alton Towers as a guest of the Shrewsburys in May 1847, went down to Cotton with the earl to see the work in progress, and recorded his impressions of what was going on at this time:

> The stonemasons work under a hangar, the carpenters under another. It is extremely interesting to see in separate places all the elements which comprise this edifice: a half-carved capital, a cross of which only the sketch is traced on the stone etc. The Wilfridians wear their cassocks everywhere, fifteen miles around; everywhere they receive marks of respect. They carry the Blessed Sacrament – publicly – in surplice and stole under a kind of large silk umbrella … the current pulpit of these holy men is the top step of their yard. It is there that they preach twice a week. On Sundays 300 people fill the yard.[23]

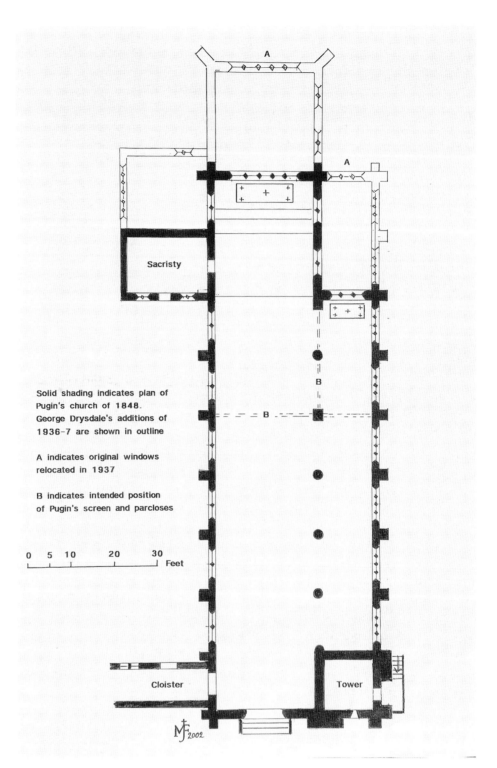

Solid shading indicates plan of
Pugin's church of 1848.
George Drysdale's additions of
1936-7 are shown in outline

A indicates original windows
relocated in 1937

B indicates intended position
of Pugin's screen and parcloses

0 5 10   20   30
⊢⊢⊢⊢——⊢ Feet

7.5 Plan of St Wilfrid's (Michael Fisher).

Writing to Pugin in November 1847, Faber said that the most straightforward
way of working would be for Pugin to deal directly with the community as
paymasters, leaving the community to deal with Lord Shrewsbury.[24] Building
work had progressed surprisingly quickly during the autumn. The gables were

7.6 An asymmetrical composition: St Wilfrid's from the east (Michael Fisher).

up, the roof was on, and the weatherings were being applied to the top of the tower. Faber asked Pugin if he had spoken to John Hardman about the organ (Hardman may have been the donor, as his father previously had been at Oscott) and if Myers had spoken to him about the screen. The reference to

7.7 South aisle: postcard, *c*.1900.

the screen is interesting, in the light of the later controversies on this subject. The rapid progress led Faber to hope that it might be possible to say Mass in the new church on the Feast of St Joseph (19 March 1847), ahead of the formal consecration, since St Joseph was the Superior of the Wilfridian Order.[25]

Built of local sandstone, St Wilfrid's is asymmetrical in plan **(7.5)**, consisting of a six-bay nave, south aisle, chancel, sacristy, and at the south-west corner a tower with a broach spire **(7.6)**. The aisle has a pitched roof rather than the lean-to variety which Pugin had used at Cheadle and Brewood **(7.7)**. The tower is entered by an external staircase and door on the north side, and the church is attached to the hall by a cloister on the south side **(7.8)**. All of these features contribute to the asymmetrical nature of St Wilfrid's. Pugin had lauded the Ecclesiologists for their astute observation that symmetry and uniformity were not among the 'true principles of ecclesiastical architecture', and that this applied particularly to the position of the tower.[26] St Wilfrid's is therefore typical of Pugin's later churches where, in contrast to Cheadle (begun in 1841) and Brewood (1842), the tower is not placed in the centre of the west front, but to one side. The tower contains two bells cast by Mears of Whitechapel, and their inscriptions reflect the changes which took place at Cotton at that time. The smaller one, cast in 1847, is dedicated to St Wilfrid, whereas the larger one, cast a year later, invokes the patron saint of the Oratory, St Philip Neri.

Internally St Wilfrid's presents a somewhat confusing picture on account of

7.8 Cloister linking the church to Cotton Hall (Michael Fisher).

7.9 Detail of nave capital. (Michael Fisher)

the alterations carried out at various times after 1848. The nave arcade is now of eight bays, but the piers are of two different types. The first six bays have round columns with rich leaf carving on the capitals **(7.9)**, the one exception being the pier where the rood screen was intended to be. It is square in section and the arch mouldings are carried down to floor-level without a break. This was the only demarcation between the nave and chancel until George Drysdale's alterations of 1936, and such an arrangement was unusual for Pugin who normally liked the nave and chancel to be delineated by different roof-levels.[27] Drysdale extended the chancel and Lady Chapel by creating two new bays, introducing a chancel arch, and enlarging two side windows to continue the arcade eastwards. The additional piers, like the one at the intended position of the screen, are rectangular in section, and the arch mouldings continue down to floor level.

The stained glass and metalwork came, naturally, from Hardman's, and originally there was more of it than now survives. The east window, which had excited Pugin from the very beginning, contained figures of the English saints Etheldreda, Wilfrid, Chad and Hilda, and it was completed, along with the other glass, only after the opening of the church in April 1848: 'of course they do not expect any glass for their opening,' Pugin told Hardman, 'unless indeed you could send them the <u>tracery</u> of the windows.'[28] In 1936 the stonework of the five-light east window was re-used in the new chancel, but with new glass, the figures from the original being re-set in the west window **(7.10)**. The four original side windows of the chancel disappeared altogether, but the east window of the Lady Chapel was re-set as a side window in the south aisle **(7.11)**. The centre light depicts the Virgin and Child under a canopy, flanked by St Andrew and St Peter, with the small kneeling figures of St Wilfrid and Fr Faber.[29]

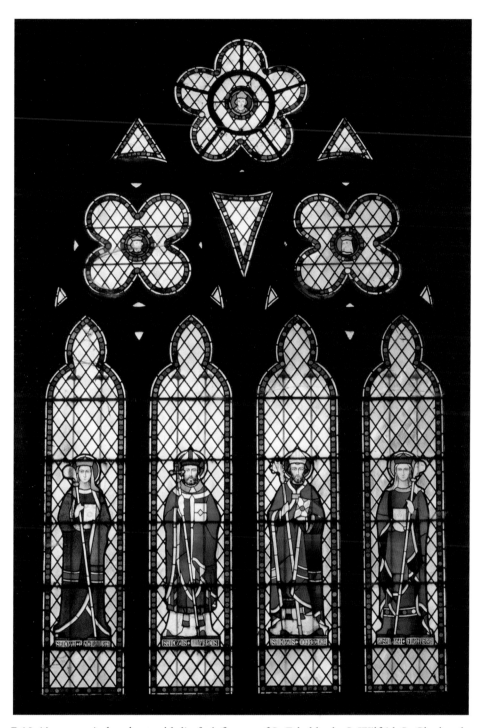

7.10 'An east window he could die for': figures of St Etheldreda, St Wilfrid, St Chad and St Hilda, now re-set in the west window (Mark Titterton).

The Hardman daybooks list the metalwork and other requisites supplied to St Wilfrid's between November 1847 and April 1848. These included a set of six brass lanterns for the outdoor processions, a set of six tall candlesticks for the high altar, and a tabernacle with a gilt door and surmounted by a gilded

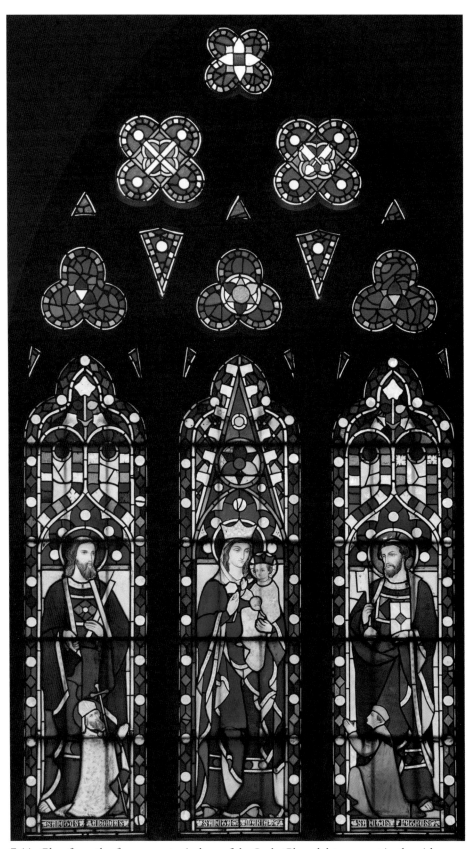

7.11 Glass from the former east window of the Lady Chapel, later re-set in the aisle (Mark Titterton).

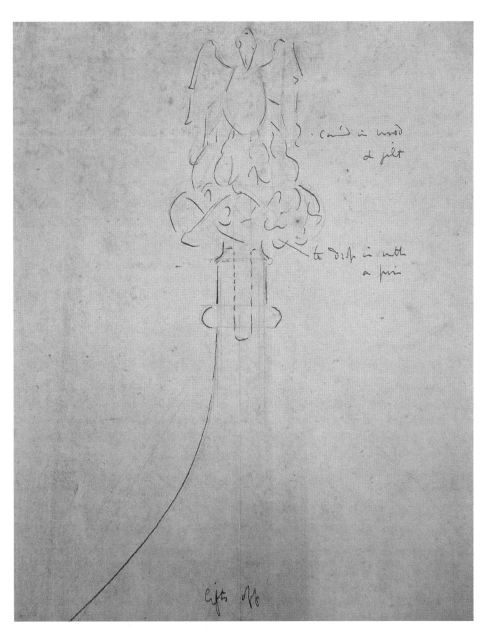

7.12 Detail of Pugin's drawing of the pelican for the tabernacle (Hardman Archive Loans Collection: Birmingham Museum & Art Gallery).

pelican, a symbol of Christ's self-sacrifice **(7.12)**.[30] The most expensive item was 'a large gilt monstrance of fine form, with rays, set with enamels & stones, the whole richly engraved', and set on a stand supported by angels. Entered to Faber at £81 4s.6d., it was more than twice the price of the splendid 'sunburst' monstrance given by Lord Shrewsbury to St Giles', Cheadle, and it reflects the great devotion of the Wilfridians and the Oratorians to the Blessed Sacrament.[31] Pre-1936 photographs show coloured wall decorations in the sanctuary, and stencilled patterns around the windows, but St Wilfrid's was never as intensely coloured as Cheadle, and such colouring as there was disappeared a long time ago. Minton tiles in the nave bear the expected Talbot iconography.

Though the zeal and the achievements of the Wilfridians were impressive, their relationship to the wider Church was undefined, and Wiseman thought that they should be more regularised. Meanwhile Newman had been in Rome seeking guidance on what form of religious association would be best for him and his colleagues, and the result was the Congregation of the Oratory, set up initially at Maryvale under the auspices of Bishop Wiseman. Faber was induced to join forces with it, and so in February 1848 he and his companions were received into the Oratorian Order, after Faber had been to Maryvale to learn how to be an Oratorian under Newman's guidance. This had immediate and serious consequences for St Wilfrid's, even before it was fully furnished and ready for use. Pugin sensed trouble ahead. In January 1848 he told Hardman that an architect – unnamed – had been to see Lord Shrewsbury and had persuaded him that the tower of St Wilfrid's would collapse. The tower stood firm, but Pugin's assessment of his own role at Cotton was not far wide of the mark: 'I believe my reign is rapidly drawing to a close there.'[32] The Oratorians were no lovers of Gothic.

St Wilfrid's was opened as an Oratorian church on 25 April 1848, the Tuesday in Easter week, amid uncertainties about its future. Wiseman sang the Mass, and Newman preached. Pugin was not present, being in a state of extreme emotional turmoil over another failed love-affair, this time with 24-year-old Helen Lumsdaine whose parents objected to Pugin much as Mary Amherst's mother had done, and for the added reason that he was a Catholic.[33] He almost got Helen to the altar: a wedding-ring had been made in readiness, and with it a most expensive *parure* of gold jewellery specially designed by Pugin and crafted by Hardman at a cost of over £250. Though he had told Lord Shrewsbury that he would arrive at Alton Towers early in Easter week, presumably to attend the opening of St Wilfrid's, Helen's final refusal, coming at precisely this time, resulted in his spending Easter alone at Ramsgate in a 'deplorable state of mind & body – from which there is little prospect of recovering for the present.'[34]

In the first week of May Pugin found some consolation by visiting his friends Ambrose and Laura Phillipps at their Leicestershire home, Grace Dieu, where he was making alterations to their domestic chapel. A few days later they all went over to Alton Towers to spend a few days as guests of Lord and Lady Shrewsbury. The Towers and its peaceful surroundings had always been something of a haven for Pugin, while his home at Ramsgate, now thrice denied the prospect of a lady of the house, had for the time being lost some of its wonted charm. On Sunday, 7 May, Phillipps and Pugin walked from the Towers to Cotton hoping there would be a High Mass, but because Fr Faber was indisposed they had to make do with Benediction and English prayers.[35] Benediction would no doubt have been given in the Oratorians' ostentatious fashion, and Pugin would also have noticed that the screens he had designed were not in place. He and Phillipps therefore decided to return to Cotton a day or so later and confront Faber face to face. So began the great rood screen controversy which was to reverberate for the remainder of Pugin's life. Faber later sent a detailed report of the confrontation to Newman in the form of a script which might have come from the pen of a playwright, with its mixture of diatribe and dark comedy.[36] When Phillipps asked why there was yet no screen at St Wilfrid's, Faber explained that it would interfere with the modern rites of Exposition of the Blessed Sacrament. He denounced the screen at Cheadle, and said that if he had his way all the surviving sixteenth-century screens would be pulled down and burnt. Furthermore, he told Pugin, 'You might as well treat the Blessed Sacrament as Henry VIII's people did, as do what you do at Benediction at Cheadle.'[37] It was a clear conflict between the Italianate 'all-seeing principle', and Pugin's belief that the Blessed Sacrament should be protected from 'irreverent gaze' behind screens and that, preferably, Benediction should be given with the Sacrament enclosed within a pyx rather than exposed in a monstrance. Pugin and Ambrose Phillipps saw something far more sinister at work, namely the subversion of their cherished belief that Gothic was the only truly Christian style of architecture. If Italian devotions were to be adopted, then why not Italian architecture; and if 'pagan' styles of architecture were to prevail, then where would it all end?

The issue of screens became a major one, with heated public debate on either side including, famously, Pugin's last major publication, the *Treatise on Chancel Screens and Rood Lofts* (1851). That such controversy should have raged over this single item of church furniture might seem absurd, but the real point at issue was whether Renaissance Italian or Medieval English ideas were to prevail in the Catholic Church in England, and Pugin believed that in fighting for screens he was fighting for the whole Gothic principle. He was further incensed by the fact that among the leading Oratorians were former 'Oxford Men' who had been admirers of the revived Gothic and who therefore ought to have known better. Faber complained bitterly to Newman, accusing Phillipps of having 'cursed' the Oratorians, while Phillipps complained about Faber's 'violent and excessive' ideas. Thus Newman found himself having to rein in Faber's devotional excesses which were in any case upsetting the 'old Catholics', while at the same time attempting to cool the 'Gothic passion' of Pugin and Phillipps. Newman was by no means anti-Gothic and he readily acknowledged Pugin's genius. 'His zeal, his innate diligence, his resources, his invention, his imagination, his sagacity in research are, all of the highest order'.[38] Could not Gothic then be adapted to suit the needs, for example, of the Oratorians who were, after all, a post-medieval Order? Had Pugin been prepared to compromise over what Newman regarded as 'details' – and these would almost certainly have included screens – the outcome might have been different. Newman was not overly hopeful. 'If Mr. Pugin persists,' he wrote to Phillipps, 'as I cannot hope he will not, in loading with bad names the admirers of Italian architecture, he is going the very way to increase their number.'[39]

A few weeks after the row with Faber, Pugin was at Alton again for a few days. His diary records another visit to Cotton on 25 June, but the purpose of the visit is not known, and Faber was in any case in London. Pugin did not see Cotton again until late October, by which time he had courted and married Jane Knill, the 'first-rate Gothic woman' for whom the costly jewellery originally intended for Helen Lumsdaine was rapidly altered. The purpose of his going to Cotton this time was to see the full complement of stained glass which was now in place. This time he was well-pleased, and he wrote to Hardman, 'The windows at St Wilfrid's are splendid.'[40]

Problems at Cotton did not merely consist of arguments over screens and florid Italian devotions before the statue of 'Mamma'. Within a few months of the opening of St Wilfrid's the whole future of the enterprise was thrown into doubt. Since the Oratorians were committed to working in the large towns, Cotton was out of the question as the principal house. Faber and the former Wilfridians left in April 1849 to establish the London Oratory, leaving Newman and the remainder to find an alternative use for Cotton before transferring themselves to the Birmingham Oratory established in Alcester Street. It was a grave disappointment to Lord Shrewsbury. Not only had he provided the premises and considerable funds; he had also seen the spiritual and social benefits of having a regular order like the Wilfridians at work in the area. The earl was most annoyed by the Oratorians' suggestion that the parish should be served by two secular priests, and he wrote a strong letter to Bishop Ullathorne who had now succeeded Thomas Walsh as Vicar Apostolic:

> It would be perfect sacrilege to divert it from monastic purposes. I gave it to them *because* they were a community, because I felt that a religious community alone could convert that neighbourhood. This Father Faber knew from the beginning. … I approved of their joining the Oratory, because I considered it would strengthen their community, not dissolve it. …Least of all did I think it would induce them to act as they have done since and wholly frustrate my views in giving them the property. … The very prospect of St Wilfrid's being abandoned appears to me so shocking that I can only attribute Father Faber's letter to a certain aberration of mind; indeed we have often suspected him of being hardly sound.[41]

Pugin was not at all sorry to see the Oratorians leave Cotton for good, taking the stone statue of 'Mamma' with them; but a way had to be found of maintaining the parish. Eventually, in December 1850, the Passionists took over St Wilfrid's as a House of Studies for their English Province. This at least fulfilled the earl's intention that it should be in the hands of a religious community, and he gave an annual subsidy of £155 for the upkeep of the church and the school which still retains Faber's name.[42] While at Alton in August 1851 Pugin wrote triumphantly to Jane, 'I am to turn out of St Wilfrid's all the trash the Oratorians set up which is delightful, & the Passionists will have the screens up. Things have taken a wonderful turn in a few days.'[43] Pugin's design for the rood screen survives[44] but there is no evidence of its ever having been installed. The later screenwork which now runs across the east end of the chancel behind the modern working altar formerly enclosed the Lady Chapel and was placed there as late as 1987.

In spite of Pugin's high hopes for St Wilfrid's, it may be said that what actually happened there indicates the limits of his influence, given the changes that were taking place within the Catholic Church in England at this time. The growth and the ultimate triumph of Ultramontanism meant that his concept of an English Catholic Church *ad usum Sarum* could never be fully realised. Though in principle the Sarum Rite could have been revived at the time of the restoration of the Hierarchy in 1850, it did not happen; partly

7.13 Interior, *c*.1900 (Michael Fisher Collection).

because the Tridentine Rite was firmly entrenched, and also because Cardinal Wiseman, who had once been sympathetic to Pugin, was now firmly allied to the Oratorians and their love of all things Roman. Yet there are indications that towards the end of his life Pugin, though still disparaging the 'Italian abortions which can only excite disgust', came to a view not far removed from that of Newman when he wrote, 'Our churches should now combine all the beauty and symbolism of antiquity with every convenience that modern discovery has suggested, or altered ecclesiastical discipline requires. … Above all, we must remember that everything old is not the object of imitation – everything new is not to be rejected.'[45]

Pre-1936 photographs indicate some of the changes made to St Wilfrid's at the end of the nineteenth century **(7.13)**. By this time the church had an alabaster altar with a reredos of carved and painted wood. The tabernacle was now crowned by an exceedingly tall openwork spire of the kind that Pugin installed in some of his later churches such as St George's, Southwark, St Cuthbert's, Ushaw, and even in his own church at Ramsgate – an indication perhaps that towards the end of his life Pugin was in fact making concessions to modern liturgical practice. The Benediction altar at St Wilfrid's is not, however, by Pugin, but an addition made as late in 1900 by Joseph Aloysius Pippett (d. 1904), one of the chief designers for Hardmans. Some fragments are preserved in the aisle: painted figures of saints under wooden Gothic canopies. The alabaster altar survives, in a reduced form, at St Giles', Cheadle. The original Lady Chapel altar and reredos have also been replaced. The interior of

7.14 The Faber school, Cotton (Michael Fisher).

St Wilfrid's has thus changed more radically than those of Cheadle and Alton, but it never did receive its full complement of Pugin furnishings.

The Passionists left Cotton in 1856 following the deaths of the sixteenth and seventeenth earls of Shrewsbury whose financial support had been crucial. The mission was then handed over to the Alton priests, and St Wilfrid's was virtually closed until 1868 when it was re-opened at the inauguration of what became known as Cotton College, the preparatory school for Sedgley Park, an historic Catholic boys' school near Wolverhampton. Additions were made to the College buildings in 1874-5 to designs by E.W. Pugin, pirated, so Pugin claimed, by the builder George Heveningham, from drawings he had made in 1866 for a buildings to house 200 boys.[46] Further extensions were made in 1886-7 and 1931-2, but sadly all of these buildings are currently (2011) derelict following the closure of the College in 1987, and the church itself faces an uncertain future. On the road from St Wilfrid's to Cotton crossroads, the Faber School **(7.14)**, with its distinctive bell-cote and other Pugin features, retains its Catholic ethos and head teacher.[47]

Cardinal Newman is not the only Cottonian to be numbered among the Blessed. Joannes Andreas Houban (1821-93), a Dutch Passionist who became Vice-Master of Novices at St Wilfrid's and then parish priest in the mid-1850s, was beatified in 1988 and canonised in 2007 as St Charles of Mount Argus. When in 1850 the Passionists moved from Aston Hall to Cotton, they brought with them the body of Fr Dominic Barberi who had received Newman into the Church, and there it rested for several months prior to final burial at St Anne's Church at St Helen's (Lancashire). In 1963 he was beatified as Bl. Dominic Barberi of the Mother of God.

8.1 'We said the *de profundis* in
the middle of the old ruined
church': the ruins of White Ladies
Priory (Geoff Brandwood).

8

Faith in the countryside:
St Mary's, Brewood

'if this little church can be raised it will be the means of saving the remnant
of the old faith that remains, and of laying the foundations of better things'
A.W.N. Pugin to Lord Shrewsbury

While still heavily committed financially to the building works at Alton
and Cheadle, to say nothing of his major contributions to St Barnabas'
Cathedral, Nottingham, Lord Shrewsbury found himself drawn, largely through
Pugin's entreaties, into to the scheme to provide a new Catholic church for the
south-west Staffordshire town of Brewood. Though the earl's contribution was
comparatively small, the fact that he became involved with it in the first place is
testimony both to Pugin's powers of persuasion, and also to Lord Shrewsbury's
own dedication to the Catholic cause in the Midland District where Bishop
Walsh – not always sensible in the management of finances – frequently needed
his support in leading the Catholic community 'from the shadows of recusancy
into the light of the Second Spring.'[1] The building of new parochial churches
to replace the private chapels in gentlemen's houses which had sufficed during
the Penal years, was a part of Walsh's vision, and it is also the background to the
building of St Mary's Church at Brewood.

The market town of Brewood (pronounced 'Brood') stands about seven
miles north-west of Wolverhampton, close to the Shropshire border. Though less
thickly wooded than in former days (it once formed part of a Royal Forest) the
area retains the essentially rural character which charmed Pugin in the 1840s.
It is particularly rich in Catholic history. A return made in 1767 to the House
of Lords giving the numbers of Catholics in England and Wales showed that of
just under 3,000 in Staffordshire, no less than 389 lived in and around Brewood,
second only to Wolverhampton with its 491.[2] A number of landed Catholic
families resided in the area. The most important of these were the Giffards,
whose ancestors had come to England with the Conqueror and held high
positions of state in medieval England. Following the Reformation the Giffards
remained firm Catholics, yet continued to be buried in the parish church at
Brewood where fine alabaster tombs of Elizabethan and Jacobean date stand
prominently in the chancel. Naturally, most of their tenants were Catholics too,
and when in 1688 Pope Innocent XI divided England into four districts each
with a bishop styled 'Vicar Apostolic', he appointed Bonaventure Giffard, a

member of the Wolverhampton branch of the family, as first Vicar Apostolic of the Midland District. The Giffards lived at Chillington Hall, two miles south-west of Brewood. A Tudor house had replaced its medieval predecessor, and this in turn was superseded by a Georgian mansion begun in 1724 and completed in the 1780s by John Soane. Other Catholic landowners in the area included the Fitzherberts of White Ladies and Boscobel, the Whitgreaves of Moseley, and the Talbot earls of Shrewsbury. There are Talbot tombs in the parish church at Albrighton,[3] five miles south-west of Brewood, and Peperhill, near Albrighton, was for much of the seventeenth century a favourite residence of the Talbots, until George, the fourteenth earl (1743-87) developed Heythrop (Oxfordshire) as the family's principal seat. The Albrighton estate was, of course, retained by the Shrewsburys, along with the title of High Steward. Bishop Thomas Talbot, a brother of the fourteenth earl, was Vicar Apostolic of the Midland District from 1778 to 1795, and lived at Brewood.

The area is rich too in historic sites evocative of its Catholic past. Close to Brewood are the remains of two religious houses: Black Ladies, a Benedictine nunnery founded around 1140, and the slightly later White Ladies, properly the Priory of St Leonard at Brewood. A house built on the Black Ladies site was in Giffard hands, and for a short period in the eighteenth century the relics of St Chad of Lichfield were kept there. Thomas Joseph Giffard (1764-1823) refurbished the Catholic chapel at Black Ladies as a place of public worship in about 1786 to replace the one demolished during the alterations to Chillington Hall, and he presented it with an impressive set of altar plate which had been in the chapel at the old hall: a gold chalice, eight silver candlesticks, a silver ciborium and a silver crucifix.[4] Described in 1834 as a low, half-timbered building with an oak ceiling, the chapel was denoted externally by a cross on the gable and, until it was removed in 1789, a bell-turret.[5] Communicants in 1834 numbered upwards of 160.

Four miles from Brewood is Boscobel House, built by the Giffards in about 1630, possibly as a place of concealment for priests. It is well-equipped with secret hiding-places or priest-holes, and in the grounds is the celebrated 'royal oak' where Charles II hid after the Battle of Worcester in 1651.[6] Charles had in fact been sheltered at nearby White Ladies, a substantial timber-framed house attached to the ruins of the Priory, yet another Giffard property. White Ladies and Boscobel subsequently passed into the hands of the Catholic Fitzherberts[7] who held them until 1812. The ruins of the priory church were used as a Catholic burial-ground until 1844.

In addition to the chapel at Black Ladies there was a centre for Catholic worship at Longbirch House, another Giffard property. The chapel there was used for public worship from at least 1779 and it had its own priest-in-charge. Among those who served in this capacity was Thomas Walsh who became Vicar Apostolic of the Midland District in 1825. Longbirch was used as the residence of the Vicars Apostolic until 1804 when the residence was removed to Giffard House, Wolverhampton. The chapel was then enlarged by extending it into what had been the bishop's sitting room. The number of communicants at Easter 1834 was 96.

Given all these circumstances, to say nothing of an influx of Irish immigrants, and the 1829 Catholic Emancipation Act, the Catholic cause in Brewood appeared to be in a flourishing state in the early nineteenth century. By 1837 west and south galleries had been built in the chapel at Black Ladies, and the chapel at Longbirch had been enlarged. It would seem that the provision of a new Catholic church in Brewood itself to replace these chapels was only a matter of time, but there were clouds on the horizon too. The Fitzherberts had already parted with the bulk of the White Ladies estate including Boscobel (though not the site of the priory itself), and the incoming Evans family were not Catholic. Meanwhile the Giffards, who had so staunchly upheld the Catholic cause during the years of persecution, were gradually becoming distanced from it. Thomas Joseph Giffard, who held Chillington at the beginning of the nineteenth century, had married an Anglican, the Hon. Charlotte Courtenay, in 1788, and it may be significant that when he rebuilt Chillington in the 1790s no provision was made for a chapel within the house. Of their children only the eldest, Thomas William, continued in the faith of his fathers until his death in 1861. Waiting in the wings as heir and successor was his brother Walter who, along with all the female members of the family, was a member of the Church of England.[8] Sooner or later, therefore, the estates would pass out of Catholic hands, and the future of the chapels at Longbirch and Black Ladies was to say the least uncertain. By the early 1840s this prospect was causing considerable anxiety to both priest and people, and it further highlighted the need for a parish church in its own right.

The leading figure in the scheme for a new church was the Revd Robert Richmond (1781-1844), who had served at Longbirch from 1808 to 1811 when he became spiritual director to the nuns at Caverswall where he also established a mission and two schools. Pugin would have seen the fruits of Richmond's labours when he visited Caverswall with Dr Weedall in 1837. After another spell at Long Birch from 1819 to 1821, Richmond became chaplain to the Constable family at Tixall and oversaw the building of the new Gothic chapel attached to the hall. Having been Professor of Divinity and Vice-Principal of Oscott, Richmond returned to Longbirch in 1838, hoping for a quiet life of semi-retirement, but instead he found himself in the forefront of yet another church-building scheme. His nephew, Henry Richmond (1802-67), became chaplain at Black Ladies at the same time, while another nephew, William (1798-1848) was chaplain to the Fitzherberts at Swynnerton, near Stone, and was the effective founder of the Swynnerton mission and their associated Catholic schools[9].

Robert Richmond had been at Oscott when Pugin burst upon the scene there in 1837, aged only 25, a convert of barely two years' standing, yet brimful of ideas for a revived Gothic England. Richmond would have witnessed at first hand the beginnings of Pugin's meteoric rise as architect, designer, and Professor of Ecclesiastical Antiquities, and he was there when Pugin delivered the first of his definitive lectures on art and architecture. Pugin had a high regard for Richmond, with whom he appears to have remained in contact after he left Oscott, and the location of Brewood in an 'Old Catholic' area which

8.2 St Mary's from the south-east (Geoff Brandwood).

appeared to be under threat appealed to him too. A statement needed to be made, and Pugin approached the task with a mixture of delight and passion. His design for St Mary's appeared in the frontispiece of *An Apology for the Revival of Christian Architecture in England* (1843) where it is shown as a modest-sized building consisting of nave, chancel, aisles, and a west tower with a broach spire, which are very much as actually built. Unfortunately Pugin's diary for 1843 is missing, and there are no references to Brewood in his earlier diaries. However, a particularly important letter written by Pugin to Lord Shrewsbury about the proposed new church has survived.[10] It contains a detailed account of what appears to have been Pugin's first visit to Brewood in April 1843 – almost certainly at Robert Richmond's invitation – and he was clearly impressed with the area and the visible reminders of its Catholic past. He visited the church at Albrighton, where he saw the alabaster tomb of Lord Shrewsbury's ancestor, Sir John Talbot. He thought it would be worth making a cast of it, probably to add to the two replica tombs of Talbot ancestors he had already installed in the Octagon Gallery at Alton Towers. Pugin also visited the ruins of White Ladies Priory **(8.1)** where he was thrilled to see the Catholic cemetery with tombs ranging from the sixteenth to the eighteenth centuries and inscribed 'pray for the soul of …'. 'No protestant has ever polluted the consecrated ground', he wrote, 'and this in England. Delightful. We said the *De Profundis* in the middle of the old ruined church. How could Fitzherbert sell such a property?'

'We' indicates that Pugin was not alone on this occasion, and there is little doubt that his companion was Robert Richmond of whom he wrote warmly: 'Mr Richmond is a most holy man, a real old parish Priest of venerable aspect, and if you saw his grief and anxiety for the Catholic population over which he is pastor, your Lordship would feel as I do. I will serve him from my heart for the love of God and blessed S. Chad.'

Fr Richmond's main problem was raising sufficient funds to build the church, as well as the continuing anxiety over what would eventually happen to the Catholic population once the Giffards had parted company with them. In March 1843 he wrote to Thomas Giffard that only £340 had been raised through subscriptions. Bishop Walsh had viewed the plans, but had told Richmond that he was unable to donate any money.[11] The scheme was clearly in jeopardy, and Pugin's letter to Lord Shrewsbury reflects a desire to enlist the earl as a benefactor:

> this seems to me a cause of the greatest importance, it is one of which the loss of souls is involved. I mean to do everything in my power for it, and I implore of your Lordship not altogether to turn away from this matter for it is urgent beyond any I know. This is the only means of keeping up religion among your Lordship's tenants in the Albrighton estate, and if you would only build enough of an aile (*sic*) to hold these poor people it would be a right good service. … It is heartrending to think of three fine estates thus lost to the church and cause, but if this little church can be raised it will be the means of saving the remnant of the old faith that remains, and of laying the foundations of better things.

In view of Lord Shrewbury's involvement in church-building schemes elsewhere, and his ownership of tenanted properties in the Brewood area, Pugin may even have considered him to be the eventual successor to the Giffards in the seigneurial role, and the one to secure the future of the church at Brewood. The earl promised to donate £100 – enough to secure the choice of Pugin as architect, if indeed that had ever been in doubt. So that the work could start promptly, Pugin advanced the money himself 'as they were hard up', and in November he had to remind Lord Shrewsbury that he had not yet been reimbursed.[12] The contract with George Myers as builder was signed at the end of April, and building began soon afterwards.[13] The total cost of the church was £1,345. Thomas Giffard had been prevailed upon to pay for the land, which cost him the not inconsiderable sum of £486 and it probably represents the Giffard family's last benefaction to the Catholic Church.[14] The site was at the west end of the village, close to the Shropshire Union Canal. Among the other benefactors were Bishop Wiseman and the Revd George Spencer who made donations in the name of the clergy, and Henry Whitgreave of Moseley Hall. It appears that Bishop Walsh may have had a change of heart, for in a letter of 4 June 1843, Pugin thanks the bishop for his 'kind note' and says that the chancel at Brewood, about which there had apparently been some doubt, could now proceed. 'It will now make a perfect church', he added.[15]

Pugin pointed out in his earlier letter to Lord Shrewsbury that there was sand (for mortar) on the site, and plenty of freestone and rubble close by, so St Mary's was built largely of local materials, chiefly red sandstone. The rural setting of the church amid trees on the edge of the village also pleased him greatly: 'The church can stand due East and West with the south porch to the road, and a church in such a situation for an old Catholic population is most interesting.'[16]

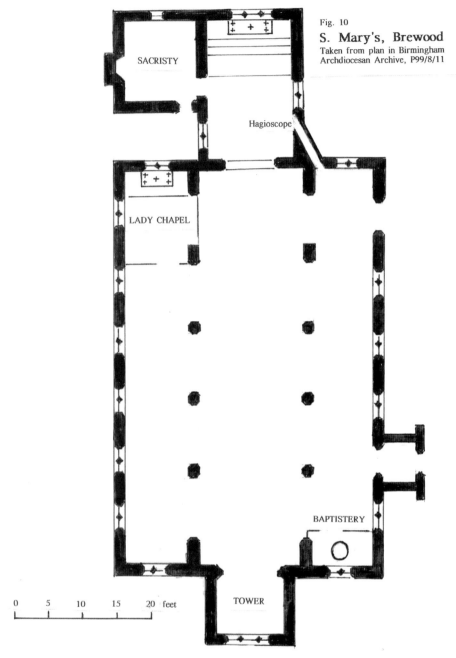

Fig. 10

S. Mary's, Brewood
Taken from plan in Birmingham
Archdiocesan Archive, P99/8/11

SACRISTY

Hagioscope

LADY CHAPEL

BAPTISTERY

0   5   10   15   20 feet

TOWER

8.3 Plan of St Mary's.

Pevsner observed that St Mary's is 'not as starved as most of Pugin's churches',[17] a reminder that financial constraints often resulted in Pugin's buildings being rather less grand in reality than they appeared in his drawings. Brewood was an exception, remarkably so given all the circumstances **(8.2, 8.3)**. It was therefore possible to complete it in one build, just as Pugin had planned it, and it has been described as 'one of the finest surviving examples of Pugin's English parish churches.'[18] As at Alton and Cheadle, the building of a school would have been considered especially important in providing for the future of Catholic families in the area, and the school was completed in 1849. The building of the school and presbytery brought the total bill for Brewood to £2,010.

Pugin's diary records a visit to Brewood on 1 March 1844 – his 32nd birthday – by which time the church was virtually complete. It was brought into use rather sooner than had been anticipated. By the beginning of March Thomas Giffard had let Black Ladies, so the chapel was to be evacuated by Lady Day, and the chaplain, Henry Richmond, was obliged to leave. Therefore Robert Richmond carried out a private blessing of the new church on the Feast of the Annunciation (25 March). 'The consecration and grand opening will be later – perhaps in May' Fr Richmond told John Hardman Jnr., 'Mr Pugin tells me you are getting the Altar furniture ready for Lady day.'[19] He sent Hardman the head of an antique processional cross – 'a real catholic one' – that had come from Black Ladies, to have a staff fitted 'in as cheap a manner as will be decent'. There was little money left for the provision of altar furnishings and other requisites. Pugin had hoped that, with the permission of Bishop Walsh, the eight silver candlesticks from Black Ladies could be sold, and the proceeds used 'so as to have a really good & useful set of altar furniture & a stained window for the chancel which would produce a glorious effect.'[20] Thomas Giffard had other ideas. He insisted on taking the candlesticks back to Chillington, promising Bishop Wiseman that he would not use them, but keep them for Black Ladies if ever that chapel should be restored.[21] In the end, Pugin himself paid for the east window, which was made by Wailes of Newcastle upon Tyne, and had the figures of the Virgin and Child in the centre light with geometrical patterns in the side-lights (8.4). A note in the back of his diary for 1844 gives the cost as £30. The elder John Hardman donated the tabernacle. This reduced Hardman's bill for the altar furnishings to just under £38, which included a set of six candlesticks and a cross for the high altar, elevation candlesticks, holy water vat and sprinkler, and wine and water cruets.[22] This stands in sharp contrast to the huge amount of metalwork supplied to St Giles', Cheadle, and it underlines the problems faced by a parish such as Brewood which had a much larger Catholic population than Cheadle, but lacked an enthusiastically committed and wealthy lay patron. Pugin made an additional gift in the shape of a statue of the Virgin and Child from his own collection of fifteenth-century wooden sculptures acquired on his visits to the continent (8.5). The figure, which is almost certainly of Flemish origin, was painted and gilded at Hardmans, and equipped with a metal lily and crown.[23] Robert Richmond was delighted: 'The image of our B. Lady is just come, & put up in its place', he wrote to Hardman . 'It is beautiful indeed. It is come safe, except that the lily in the hand is loosened, but it remains well in its position, & part of the Crown is lost, but it is on the left side, & not seen.[24] Intended originally for the Lady Chapel in the north aisle, the statue now stands in the south-east corner of the south aisle, close to the font (8.5). A rood screen of simple form was set up at the chancel arch. Pugin records its cost, together with its crucifix and figures of Our Lady and St John, at £40.[25]

The consecration on 13 June was carried out by the Bishop Wiseman, at that time President of Oscott, with twelve or more priests of the district assisting. Pugin was not present, since he was at Nottingham that day with Lord Shrewsbury, doubtless involved with discussions about the progress of St Barnabas' Church (later the Cathedral) which was to be opened in August. He would, however, have been pleased to know that the consecration of St Mary's was properly done within the context of a High Mass *Coram Episcopo* sung to a setting by Palestrina. Robert Richmond had wanted the choir of St Chad's Cathedral to be present, and had written to John Hardman, a cantor and founder member of the choir, to that effect. Bishop Wiseman objected on the grounds of expense, preferring instead either the Sedgley Park School choir,

8.4 Detail of former east window: glass now reset in north aisle (Geoff Brandwood).

8.5 Fifteenth-entury statue of the Virgin and Child, restored by Hardman (Geoff Brandwood).

or the choir of Oscott College: 'and of course his word is law', Richmond explained, hoping that Hardman would nevertheless still attend the opening.[26] According to the account of the opening in *The Tablet*, however, St Chad's choir was in attendance after all.[27] Sadly, Robert Richmond died just a week after the opening of the church which, without his devotion and tenacity, might never have been built. The inscription on his monument rightly describes him as the founder, as well as the first rector, of St Mary's. He was succeeded by his nephew, William Richmond, who died in 1848.

Built largely of coursed sandstone rubble, St Mary's has a centrally placed west tower, and a broach spire with two tiers of lucarnes. There is a south porch with stone benches and a stoup. Outside the porch is a medieval pillar-stoup reputed to have come from White Ladies. The nave has north and south aisles,

8.6 Interior showing the rood-screen: postcard *c*.1900.

but no clerestory. The aisles have two-light windows with ogee tracery. The chancel has a three-light east window with Geometrical tracery, and there is a sacristy on the north side. All the elements of the building are thus clearly defined externally as Pugin believed they should be.

Inside there is an impressively tall tower arch, with double-chamfered mouldings which continue down the jambs without capitals. The nave is of five bays, low octagonal piers carrying tall double-chamfered arches. The easternmost piers are elongated, and the mouldings of the eastern arches are continued downwards without capitals as in the tower arch. This may have been done to demarcate the east ends of the aisles as side chapels. The south aisle has an interesting piece of historicism, namely a hagioscope giving a view of the high altar. It is demarcated in the exterior stonework where the south aisle joins the chancel. The nave has an open timber roof with purlins and collar-beams; and the chancel roof has closely set scissor-trusses. Minton floor tiles adorn both the chancel and the north aisle.

As in many of Pugin's other churches, the interior fittings and decorations have undergone considerable changes, although old photographs record what there once was **(8.6)**. The original seating ran right across the nave, leaving passageways only down the aisles, an arrangement which Pugin would have abhorred, but which was necessary in order to seat 400 people.[28] Gone too is the rood screen from under the chancel arch: it had three single-light divisions either side of the door. The hanging crucifix is the only survival from it.

The original stone altar survives **(8.7)**. It has three deep quatrefoils in the front, containing the *Agnus Dei* flanked by censing angels, and there is a simple stone reredos flanked by angels kneeling on brackets. In the south wall is a single stone sedilium with an adjacent piscina. Set in the floor of the chancel are two fine memorial brasses designed by Pugin and made by Hardman commemorating the priests Robert and William Richmond as full figures in

8.7 The sanctuary and high altar (Geoff Brandwood).

8.8 Memorial brass to Robert Richmond (Geoff Brandwood).

vestments under Gothic canopies **(8.8)**. Pugin also designed the memorial for Robert's grave in the churchyard.

The south aisle contains a plain tub-shaped font with a folding hinged lid and padlock. It was originally sited at the west end, close to the door, which

Pugin believed was the only proper location for a font, and enclosed within a low screen. Nearby is a large seventeenth-century crucifix which came from Black Ladies, and also the statue, already described, of the Virgin and Child.

The north aisle/Lady Chapel was refurbished in the 1880s. At this time a stone altar was placed at the east end. In the north wall a fine Hardman brass to members of the Whitgreave family suggests that it was they who became the principal benefactors of the church following the secession of the Giffards. Kneeling on one side of a large floriated crucifix is Henry Whitgreave (1816-81) and his two sons, George (1842-71) and Thomas (1849-76); while on the other side are his two wives, Henrietta Clifford and Mary Selby, along with the children of his second marriage, Walter who died in infancy, and Alice who survived him.

Over the Lady Chapel altar, and set in an alabaster shrine of twentieth-century date, is one of the most interesting – and controversial – items in the church, namely the statue of the Virgin and Child known as 'Our Lady of Brewood'. It is made of wood, and partly painted. Tradition has it that this statue was kept at White Ladies until the ransacking of the building in 1651 by

8.9 Part of the wall decoration which did not please Pugin (Geoff Brandwood).

Parliamentary troops during their search for Charles II. The gash in the lower part of the statue, which still 'weeps', was allegedly made by a soldier's sword. It would appear that from White Ladies the statue was taken to Chillington Hall, and eventually to the chapel at Black Ladies. It remained there for some time after the opening of St Mary's, for in his account of Black Ladies (1867) James Hicks Smith makes mention of 'a ponderous little statue of the Blessed Virgin, carved in wood', continuing to occupy the place of the altarpiece.[29] It was moved to St Mary's, one assumes, when the Black Ladies chapel was finally demolished in 1872.

The walls of the nave and chancel were enriched with coloured painting, but this has been whitewashed over, with the exception of a very small section in the south wall of the chancel which has been exposed again to give an idea of the nature of the decoration (**8.9**). It was not of the same quality as Pugin's decorative patterns at St Giles', Cheadle, and it would appear to be the work, not of Pugin himself, but of the same local Catholic painter whom Robert Richmond had used to paint the consecration crosses prior to the opening of the church.[30] When, in 1849, *The Rambler* made disparaging remarks about his church decoration, Pugin felt obliged to make specific mention of Brewood in his published response, lest anyone should think that he was responsible for it:

> Several churches that I have built have been miserably bedaubed by journeymen painters, who have been employed on the cheap principle of saving designs, but whose miserable performances are, no doubt, generally attributed to me. The chancel of Brewood church presents a most lamentable and almost ludicrous example of private judgment in colour. This was the work of a devout amateur, whom some demon whispered that he had a taste, and having provided himself with plenty of blue, red and green, he proceeded to enliven the building by their application, giving the most prominent mouldings the greatest proportion of positive colour. As for the pattern of the walls, I know not what it resembled, but it might have been produced by a troop of beetles crawling through a paint pot and then up the plaster. Indeed I have seen the slime tracks of snails describe much better figures. This eccentric production is still, I believe, in existence, unless some friendly whitewasher has delivered the chancel from the disgrace.[31]

The 'demon' was, of course, either Robert Richmond himself, or his nephew and successor, William. However warmly Pugin may have felt towards the Richmonds and their stalwart ministry at Brewood, he knew that they, like many clergy at the time, were priests and not artists, and that they had much to learn about what he considered to be appropriate in terms of church decoration. Conversely, Robert Richmond's opinion of Pugin's buildings was by no means unequivocal. In a letter to his brother written in January 1844 he expressed the view that Pugin's churches were generally too dark, and he thought the lych-gate at Brewood was ugly.[32]

The alterations made to the church in the 1920s included the provision of more stained-glass windows, all by Hardman & Co. The west window was done in 1920, and the south aisle east window, and baptistery window, in 1924. At the same time, Pugin's east window was replaced. The figure of the Virgin and

Child was re-set in the east window of the Lady Chapel. The glass from the side lights is still in storage at the church. Finally, the two side windows of the chancel were made in 1926.

The presbytery and school lie immediately to the north-west of the church. As with the ones at Cheadle, they are built of brick with stone trim. Like the church, the school was intended to promote not just the survival of the Catholic Faith in Brewood, but its growth; as Pugin had put it to Lord Shrewsbury, 'laying the foundation of better things'. Fr Richmond was well-pleased with the early success of the project. In June 1845 he wrote to his brother, George, that in the previous two weeks 156 people had been confirmed, and there had been twenty conditional baptisms.[33]

The story of the building of St Mary's highlights one of the weaknesses of the 'seigneurial system' of church patronage which had been so significant in upholding the Catholic cause during the times of persecution: there was no guarantee that a landed family would remain Catholic. The case of Brewood is especially ironic in that the Giffards, who had remained loyal to the Faith – and at some considerable personal cost – throughout the days of the Penal Laws should have seceded just as Catholicism was entering its 'Second Spring'. The Shrewsburys' patronage of the Catholic Church was set to suffer a similar fate, and with devastating consequences, when their titles and estates passed into Protestant hands in 1858.[34]

9.1 Edward Pugin (private collection).

9

After Pugin: new brooms and 'broom-stealers'

'These men can afford to Sell cheap for they <u>steal their brooms ready made</u>. however the movement progresses and the right sort of thing becomes general & that is the great point'
A.W.N. Pugin to Lord Shrewsbury, 15 February 1846

The demise of Pugin and Lord Shrewsbury within a few weeks of each other in the autumn of 1852 left a considerable amount of unfinished business in 'Pugin-land' and elsewhere to be taken up by their teenage heirs and successors, along with projects that might have been envisaged but not actually begun. The new earl, Bertram, was nineteen, and Pugin's eldest son, Edward **(9.1)**, only eighteen. One of Edward's first major tasks was to oversee the arrangements for the late earl's funeral,[1] only seven weeks after his own father's obsequies at Ramsgate, in collaboration with Pugin's son-in-law, John Hardman Powell who succeeded Pugin as chief designer at Hardman's, and who, at the age of 25 was now the senior figure. Edward took a house in Birmingham's Jewellery Quarter, no. 44 Frederick Street, and shortly afterwards Jane Pugin and the rest of the family joined him, not returning to The Grange until 1858. For a time Powell divided his time between Ramsgate and Birmingham, before taking up residence near to John Hardman's house in Hunter's Road. Thus Edward Pugin and John Powell stepped into the shoes of 'the Governor', and quickly achieved what had not been possible in his lifetime, namely the bringing together of the different aspects of the Pugin-Hardman operation into one place.

Bertram Arthur, seventeenth earl of Shrewsbury, had been educated almost entirely by private tutors at Alton Towers, and he had also accompanied the late earl and countess on their travels abroad. He was described as 'a person of singularly mild and gentle disposition and of refined and elegant tastes; and an accomplished scholar, especially in modern languages.'[2] Edward Pugin was more than willing to continue his family's association with the Shrewsburys, and to complete any outstanding work. For his part, the new earl wrote to Edward assuring him that the Shrewsbury patronage would continue, but reminding him also that until he came of age in December 1853, the estate and all other assets inherited from his uncle were held in trust.[3] One particular concern was the cathedral which A.W.N. Pugin and Earl John had planned at Shrewsbury following the establishment of the new diocese. They had corresponded about it

9.2 Serjeant Edward Bellasis (E. Bellasis, *Memorials of Mr Serjeant Bellasis,* London, 1893, facing p. 18).

early in 1852,[4] and Pugin had done a sketch on the back of one of his drawings for the Palace of Westminster.[5] It shows an ambitious building with a south-west tower and spire, and other features which E.W. Pugin developed into the watercolour which he produced later that year.[6] The cathedral was subsequently built, between 1853 and 1856, though in a reduced form. Meanwhile, at Alton Towers, Edward Pugin inherited the unfinished Great Dining Room which awaited its large oriel window, sideboard and panelling, and the 'New Rooms' above the Drawing Room. The estate accounts show that masons, joiners and painters were still working in these areas of the house in 1855.[7] At least one new panelled ceiling was emblazoned with Bertram's initials.[8] Work was also continuing at Alton Castle, although there was doubt as to its ultimate purpose.

There was indeed a degree of provisionality about all of it. Bertram, the last of the senior line of Catholic Talbots, was unmarried and not in the best of health. Waiting in the wings, and ready to lay claim to the Shrewsbury titles and estates if Bertram should die without issue, as seemed more than likely, was Henry John Chetwynd Talbot (1803-68), third Earl Talbot of Ingestre Hall. Like earls John and Bertram, Henry could claim descent from the first Earl of Shrewsbury, but the line of succession was tortuous, and Earl John had told his chaplain, Dr Winter, in the presence of witnesses that the Talbots of Ingestre had no more title to the Shrewsbury estate than the pen he then held in his hand.'[8] Moreover, Earl Talbot's line was solidly Protestant and an eighteenth-century Bishop of Durham was among his ancestors. At the time of the restoration of

9.3 James Hope-Scott (E. Bellasis, *Memorials of Mr Serjeant Bellasis*, London, 1893, facing p. 72).

the Catholic Hierarchy in 1851, Earl Talbot lent his support to local protests against so-called 'papal aggression' and was elected chairman of one of the meetings held to form a branch of the 'Protestant Alliance' in Stafford. Thus the sixteenth earl had good reason to fear the consequences of a Protestant succession to the earldom, and so he made an extraordinary will to the effect that if Bertram were to die leaving no son, the Shrewsbury estates were to be divided between Charles Robert Scott Murray and Ambrose Phillipps. Scott Murray (1818-82) was among the generation of 'Young England' MPs elected to Parliament in 1841, the first sitting member to become a Catholic, and among those befriended by Lord Shrewsbury and Bishop Wiseman. Under the terms of Lord Shrewsbury's will, Phillipps and Scott Murray were to receive unconditional legacies of £40,000 each. The will effectively disinherited the earl's daughter, the Princess Doria Pamphili, and her family in Rome.

The trustees appointed to administer the Shrewsbury estates until Earl Bertram came of age were two convert lawyers, Edward Bellasis (1800-73) and James Hope-Scott, Q.C. (1812-73). Both were former Tractarians. Bellasis **(9.2)**, a parliamentary lawyer, had been a serjeant-at-law since 1844. His conversion to Catholicism in 1850 had come about as a result of reading Newman's works, and through a developing personal friendship with him. He was present at Littlemore when Newman preached his last sermon as an Anglican in June 1843, and Newman dedicated one of his influential books, *The Grammar of Assent,* 'To Edward Bellasis, Serjeant-at-Law in memory of a long, equable, sunny friendship.'[9] Bellasis had Staffordshire connections too, having married Frances, daughter of William Lycett of Stafford. His sister, Anna Marie, was married to the Stafford surgeon and one-time mayor of the borough, John Masfen. The other trustee, James Hope **(9.3)** as he was born, took the additional name of Scott following his marriage to the grand-daughter of Sir Walter Scott. They lived at Abbotsford, the romantic Scottish Baronial house which Scott had built for himself in Roxburghshire. Like Bellasis, he was a friend of Newman, and an even closer friend of W.E. Gladstone. Hope-Scott's conversion took place in April 1851, and Edward Bellasis stood godfather at his confirmation in Cardinal Wiseman's private chapel. Though their role as trustees of the Shrewsbury estate came to an end in December 1853, they continued to support Bertram both as friends and legal advisers in his efforts to ensure that the Shrewsbury titles, as well as the estates, would remain in Catholic hands. In gratitude, Bertram made them his residuary legatees, and also willed them parts of his landed estates in the Midlands, but they declined to take any material benefit. A new will was therefore drawn up in March 1856 whereby Bertram left the whole of his estate to Lord Edmund Howard (1855-1947), the infant second son of the Catholic Duke of Norfolk.

A few weeks after Bertram had amended his will, the shadow of death fell swiftly and suddenly across 'Pugin-land', and with serious consequences for the Catholic buildings and institutions which the sixteenth and seventeenth earls had created and maintained. On 4 June Maria Teresa, Dowager Countess of Shrewsbury, died while on a visit to Paris, aged 61. Her funeral took place a week later in the Towers Chapel which was draped and furnished much as it had been for her late husband, and she was buried in Earl John's grave on the north side of the altar in St John's, Alton. The Latin inscription on the simple brass memorial plate tells its own story. In translation it reads, 'So united were their hearts whilst living that it seemed fitting that their bodies should be placed in the same tomb where they await the mercy of the same Redeemer'. Only a few weeks later, on 10 August, Earl Bertram died in Lisbon. In accordance with his request for a simple funeral without any outdoor pomp, everything took place within St John's, where his grave had been prepared on the south side of the altar. A memorial brass, in similar style to that of the sixteenth earl on the north side, was later supplied by Hardmans. Edward Pugin was present at the funeral and it was noted that 'the management of the entire proceedings was ably effected by Mr J.B. Denny, formerly master of the works at Alton.'[10] Though now the agent for the family's Oxfordshire estates, the 'indefatigable' Denny, as A.W.N. Pugin had called him, was called back to perform this last service for his master. Work on the various buildings at Alton Towers and in the village abruptly ceased pending the settlement of Bertram's will, and one of the last entries in the estate accounts is, poignantly, a payment to masons William and James Burton for 'making the Earl's grave.'[11]

As expected, Earl Talbot of Ingestre laid claim to the Shrewsbury titles and challenged the terms of the will. A lengthy and widely reported lawsuit ensued, involving detailed investigations into the genealogy of the Talbot family and the legal status of the landed properties which were spread over several English counties and also included the Irish earldoms of Waterford and Wexford. The claim advanced on behalf of Lord Edmund Howard was based on his descent from the first line of the Talbot family, through Alathea, sole heiress of Gilbert, the seventh and last earl in the senior line who died in 1616. She had married Thomas Howard, Earl of Arundel and Surrey. Lord Edmund's trustees, and the executors of Earl Bertram's will, took immediate action to secure the properties and to contest Earl Talbot's claims. The Alton estate was administered on their behalf by a resident agent, assisted by loyal servants such as John Denny and head gardener, James Whittaker. In January 1857 the Duke of Norfolk himself visited the Towers along with trustees Serjeant Bellasis and James Hope-Scott to address the principal tenants, and to entertain them to dinner in the new Banqueting Hall, when a toast was drunk to Lord Edmund as heir to the estate, and the trustees appealed for the cooperation of the tenants in carrying out the late earl's wishes.[12]

Though the succession to the earldom and the estates was in dispute, there was nothing to prevent the moveable properties being disposed of in accordance with Earl Bertram's will. Some important items were therefore removed from Alton Towers by the Duke of Norfolk and taken to Arundel Castle. These included a quantity of maps, plans, and other papers relating to the Alton estate, and some articles from the cabinets in the chapel corridor. Amongst these were a silver bell and other relics from the former nunnery at Syon House, and a collection of crucifixes and other devotional items.[13] Significantly, the contents of the chapel, and family portraits, do not appear in the catalogue of the great sale which took place at the Towers in July 1857. The rest of 'the magnificent contents of Alton Towers', as the catalogue describes them, were auctioned in some 4,000 lots over period of 30 days, and the sale attracted a good deal of attention in the local and national press.[14]

The reason for the sale, so it was said, was to defray considerable costs incurred by Lord Edmund's trustees in contesting Henry Chetwynd Talbot's claim to the earldom. The Peerage Case was finally settled in June 1858 when the House of Lords ruled in favour of Earl Talbot who thereafter took his seat as the eighteenth earl of Shrewsbury. The recovery of the title did not necessarily involve that of the estates, so another legal battle ensued, with the new earl fighting now to establish that they were inalienable from the titles and that the provisions of the late earl's will regarding them were therefore invalid. The Alton estate continued for the time being to be administered by Bellasis and Hope-Scott on behalf of Lord Edmund Howard. Although the house was now virtually empty, a few staff were retained, and Mass was said in the Towers Chapel. There was however an atmosphere of provisionality and uncertainty which was noted and brilliantly recorded by Mary Howitt of Uttoxeter, who visited the Towers in June 1859: 'Passing into a vast court, we noticed on a lofty tower the tattered hatchment flapping in the wind. We entered, through an arched doorway, the gorgeous Catholic chapel, and were led onward by a pale-faced young man, with an anxious, depressed countenance, and who could not speak without sighs.'

The un-named young man turned out to be an organist, and he took Mary Howitt and her companion up into the gallery, lamenting the fact that the fine three-manual organ was very rarely played. When asked if Mass was still celebrated in the chapel, he replied that it was: 'Only Low Mass,' he said, with a mournful cadence, 'and therefore no music.' He then agreed to play if Mary and her friend would pump the bellows.

> The next moment after commencing, the lofty chapel, from the highest centre of its roof to the lowest level of its floor, seemed throbbing and heaving with tempestuous swell of the most wonderful melody. ... No longer dim-eyed, dreaming, and melancholy, he sat there an inspired musician, with flushed and upturned eye ... I wished from my heart that the Catholic heirs might come into possession, the old faith and worship be maintained, and he be chosen organist.[15]

It was a forlorn hope. On the very day of Mary Howitt's visit the news broke that Earl Talbot's action in the Court of Common Pleas for the recovery of Alton Towers had succeeded. Bellasis and Hope-Scott then appealed to the Exchequer Chamber where, in February 1860, the matter was decided in favour of the earl. On 13 April 1860 he took formal possession of the Towers after lavish celebrations in Stafford and a triumphal procession from Uttoxeter to Alton. By this time the late earl's trustees had removed the most significant items from the chapel, including the altar and reredos which were relocated in St Peter's Church at Bromsgrove, close to Grafton Manor, one of the Shrewsbury properties not entailed to the titles and which had served as a Catholic mission. The ivory-clad reliquary which had stood at the centre of the altar was given by James Hope-Scott to the Church of Our Lady and St Andrew which he built at Galashiels, and it later came into the care of the Bridgettine nuns at Syon Abbey, South Brent (Devon). This was not the end of the affair. Although the greater part of the unsettled estate passed to Lord Edmund Howard, whose name then changed to Lord Edmund Talbot, the legal battle continued until 1867. Hope-Scott and Serjeant Bellasis made a further appeal, and they recovered, on Edmund Talbot's behalf, parts of the unentailed estate, including Grafton Manor, which had previously been awarded to Earl Talbot.

The prolonged nature of the Shrewsbury Peerage Case, and its eventual outcome, had serious consequences for the Catholic Church locally, and for the whole Diocese of Birmingham. Enthusiastic though he had been about church-building, and supporting the schemes of Lord Shrewsbury and Pugin, Bishop Walsh had not managed his finances well, and his successor, William Bernard Ullathorne (1806-89), had some serious problems to address. Earl John had promised the diocese a legacy of £25,000, but this had not been written into the will, and Ambrose Phillipps, as executor, insisted that nothing could be done retrospectively. Earl Bertram made an annual donation of £500 to the diocese, but this ceased on his death, and the liabilities on the Shrewsbury estate cancelled out an anticipated legacy of £10,000, so Ullathorne had good reason to complain that 'in addition to other difficulties all the Shrewsbury missions are now thrown on my hands without one penny of endowment.'[16] All of this illustrates the dangers inherent in the 'seigneurial system' of ecclesiastical patronage, especially when the Church became excessively dependent upon a single source. The character of the Catholic Church in England was in any case beginning to change following the restoration of the Hierarchy as the clergy sought to free themselves from the kind of lay domination which Lord Shrewsbury had represented, and which was a relic of the days of persecution. In 1857 George Montgomery, a convert priest in the Midlands, well expressed the changing climate: 'I am not one who would join in any cry to any earthly patron *oculi omnium in te sperant Domine,* as we seemed lately to cry to Lord Shrewsbury: but I do not despise the aid of the worldly great, and would do what I could without flunkeyism to secure it.'[17]

Some help for St Giles', Cheadle, came from an unexpected source, namely the Protestant eighteenth earl who, recognising the architectural and artistic importance of the church, contributed £1,500 to the maintenance of the fabric. He also tried to complete the unfinished work at Alton Towers under the guidance, one must assume, of Edward Pugin. Pugin's great 42- light chandelier for the Great Dining Room was not put in place until 1869, and the Hardman metalwork daybook for that year also records the supply of brass tender guards for the fireplaces in that room, and for the suites of rooms on the upper floor including the 'Pugin Room', at a total cost of £715.[18]

Outside the immediate environs of 'Pugin-land' and the sylvan valley of the River Churnet, and without Talbot patronage, Edward Pugin built one of his very first churches: the Abbey of Our Lady of the Immaculate Conception at Oulton, near Stone (1853-4), and also what is undoubtedly his earliest secular building, Burton Manor, Stafford, which was begun at almost the same time. Both projects had at least been planned by his father, whose illness in the closing months of his life had halted their further progress. Both buildings show Edward following his father's established principles of architecture and design, but they also show that even at this early stage in his career, Edward was developing some innovative ideas of his own.

In the 1840s A.W.N. Pugin had carried out alterations and additions to the chapel at Caverswall Castle for the community of Benedictine nuns, and he had maintained contact with them, particularly when his daughter, Agnes, was at school there from 1848 onwards. It seems that a move to a new, purpose-built, convent at Oulton, near Stone, was already envisaged, but it was Edward Pugin who, in 1853-4, built their new abbey church (**9.4**). It is an impressively large building in a mixture of Decorated and Perpendicular styles. Pugin gave it a well-defined chancel after the fashion of his father; it is crisply executed in local sandstone, and it shows none of the fussiness of some of his later churches. There are, however, some original features, for example in the tracery of the west window, and in the internal treatment of the roofs. Whereas A.W.N. Pugin would have insisted on open roofs, exposing all the structures, his son hid them with a coved ceiling. There is Hardman glass, including representations of six English abbesses in the west window. Oulton Abbey has suffered less than many of E.W. Pugin's through subsequent 're-ordering' and the removal of original furnishings and decorations. John Hardman Powell designed the metal screen, lighter and more open than the carved timber variety such as A.W.N. Pugin had insisted upon, and Edward's richly carved altar and reredos are still in place, as are the later decorations by J.A. Pippett on the chancel arch. Some domestic buildings connected to the east end of the chapel are also by Pugin.

While Oulton Abbey was in progress, Edward Pugin undertook the building of Burton Manor, close to Stafford. At the time it was set amidst open fields and woodland within a mile or so of Stafford Castle; but today the M6 motorway passes within a hundred yards of it, so that those who travel along the motorway between junctions 13 and 14 may well catch sight of the high gables, tall chimney-stacks, and castellated turret of this important but little-known house which now forms a part of Stafford Grammar School.

Burton Manor was built on a medieval ancestral site for Francis Whitgreave (1819-96), a former friend of A.W.N. Pugin, and second son of George Whitgreave (1787-1863), of Moseley Court, near to Wolverhampton. A barrister by profession, Francis had the distinction of being the last lay student to have been admitted to the Venerable English College in Rome, where priests had been trained for the English mission throughout the penal years. He later expressed his gratitude by donating a two-light window with the figures of his parents' patron saints, St George and St Amelia. Made by Hardman, it was, naturally, designed by A.W.N. Pugin who told John Hardman that he had 'kept it in the Italian style of medieval glass.'[19] By the late 1840s Francis was living with his elder brother, Joseph, at Talbot House, Rugeley, and they were leading benefactors of the new Catholic church built in 1849 to designs by Charles Hansom, and dedicated to St Joseph and St Etheldreda – Etheldreda being

9.4 Oulton Abbey, *c.*1900 (Hardman Private Collection).

the name of Joseph Whitgreave's sister. Shortly afterwards, Joseph built a new house, Heron Court, opposite the church, and Francis moved to Radford Bank, Stafford, on the Wolverhampton Road and not far from the site of Burton Manor. The Whitgreaves were well-integrated into Staffordshire society, not surprisingly since they had remained solidly Catholic throughout the Penal years. As early as 1837, only eight years after the Catholic Emancipation Act, George Whitgreave became High Sheriff of Staffordshire, and Francis in his turn became Deputy Lieutenant of the county and a Justice of the Peace. Their Royalist past may have worked in their favour. Moseley was not far from Boscobel where, after his defeat in the Battle of Worcester in 1651, King Charles II famously hid in the oak-tree, and Charles was given refuge at the hall before being spirited away to the Continent. Francis was a direct descendant of Thomas Whitgreave 'the preserver' (1618-1702) who had played such a leading role in the king's escape, so there was a very powerful Romantic element upon which to build. The family's roots, however, lay in the village of Whitgreave, just north of Stafford, and amongst their former properties was the site of a moated manor house, Burton Manor, on the south-west side of the borough. The house itself had been demolished in 1606-7[20] and the land sold off, but in about 1850 Francis bought the site with the intention of building a new home there in preparation for his marriage to Teresa Mostyn, sister of the wealthy Catholic landowner, Sir Pyers Mostyn of Talacre Hall, Denbighshire. Burton Manor had been home to another ancestor, Robert Whitgreave (d. 1449) who had represented Stafford borough in Parliament, and had also been teller of the Exchequer and treasurer to Henry V during the French wars. Francis Whitgreave was a scholar and an antiquary with a keen interest in his family's history. Like Ambrose Phillipps, Francis was a 'Young Englander', enthused by the romantic Catholic ideal, and he most certainly enthralled by Pugin's Gothic passion. By re-purchasing the Burton estate, he was returning to his medieval roots, and, like the Talbots of Alton and the Phillippses of Grace Dieu, he was set to recreate his family's glorious past. Who better, then, to build his new house than the greatest 'medieval Victorian' of all, A.W.N. Pugin?

The Whitgreaves were friendly with Lord and Lady Shrewsbury, and it is likely that Pugin first encountered them as members of the wealthy Catholic coterie who supported the building of his new churches in the Midlands, and who frequented Alton Towers. Francis, with his antiquarian interests and Royalist background, soon entered Pugin's circle of friends, along with Francis Kerril Amherst (1819-83), an exact contemporary of Whitgreave, and a future bishop of Northampton. It was his sister, Mary Amherst, whom Pugin later hoped to marry. In June 1844 the two 'Franks' and Pugin took ship across the Channel, and Whitgreave remembered that Pugin was 'as usual most interesting and amusing during the voyage, full of life and spirit', as well he might have been if, as has plausibly been suggested, the real reason for Pugin's journey was a rendezvous with Mary Amherst in the Rhineland.[21] Francis Whitgreave's spirit of adventure also appealed to Pugin. In January 1847 he and Amherst went on a pilgrimage to the Holy Land, first taking ship to Cairo, then travelling overland by camel.[22] Pugin followed this expedition with some interest, and in a letter to Lord Shrewsbury he expressed grave concern for his friend's safety:

> I am very uneasy indeed about Francis Whitgreave. He sailed from Marseilles some weeks ago & the vessel has not since been heard of. It was just at that time the tremendous hurricane swept the mediterranean – he was at my house 2 weeks before Xmass & I expressed surprise he should go at this time of year.[23]

9.5 St Augustine's Grange, Ramsgate (Landmark Trust).

Two years later Francis' father, George Whitgreave, embarked on an adventure of another kind when he took as his third wife an Irish girl called Anne Sandford. He was more than old enough to be her grandfather. 'Old Mr Whitgreave (age 70) has married a 19 year old girl in Ireland', Pugin told his wife, Jane, in the autumn of 1849.[24]

Francis Whitgreave's visit to Pugin's home in December 1847 was not the first, and it was probably not the last. In the summer of 1845 he spent several weeks at Ramsgate, where he saw much of Pugin and other members of the family. He was particularly delighted with John Hardman Powell, who was living at The Grange as Pugin's pupil.[25] Powell remembered Whitgreave's visits to Ramsgate 'among those who were specially interested in Medieval Revival'.[26] St Augustine's Grange **(9.5)**, as he called it, was designed by Pugin to serve as his family home and his work-place, constructed entirely on Christian principles, 'a most substantial catholic house not very Large but convenient & solid', combining 'the delight of the sea with catholic architecture & a Library.'[27] Shockingly Gothic and asymmetrical in contrast to the regular Regency terraces of Ramsgate, and embodying Pugin's 'true principles' of fitness for purpose, truth to materials, and honesty to design, it rapidly became 'a durable model, its sense of familiarity to us today a measure of its imitation by thousands of later Victorian vicarages and substantial family homes.'[28] Burton Manor was one of the very first of these, and it was based upon Francis Whitgreave's own perceptions of St Augustine's Grange **(9.6)**.

The prospect of building a 'true principles' house on a medieval moated site would have excited Pugin, and it may well have been discussed at the time Whitgreave brought the Burton estate back into his family's ownership. Pugin's final illness, and death, intervened, leaving it amongst the commissions to be picked up by eighteen-year-old Edward, who for a time moved to a house in Frederick Street, Birmingham, so as to be close to his father's friends and

9.6 Burton Manor, Stafford (Michael Fisher).

business associates, the Hardmans. The building of Burton Manor began in 1854.

No original plans or drawings for Burton Manor appear to have survived, but the attribution to Edward Pugin is confirmed by a number of entries in the Hardman metalwork daybooks in respect of this house, and noted 'E. W. Pugin'. They include vanes and finials for the turrets and gables, a large wrought-iron cross for the tower, and internal metalwork such as door furniture, grates and kitchen ranges.[29] The entries also give the name of the builder as W. T. Woollams of Stafford.

The plan and the size of the new house were governed by the extent of the land available inside the dry moat, but in its layout, elevations and fixed furnishings it followed the Ramsgate model very closely. The house is built of red brick with stone dressings, and there are bands of polychrome brickwork including crosses, geometrical patterns, and the monograms of Francis and Theresa Whitgreave **(9.7)**. The fenestration is irregular: stone-framed windows of two, three and four lights with trefoiled heads, and transoms **(9.8)**. There are canted bays, just as there are at Ramsgate, to the library, drawing room and principal bedroom. There was, of course no 'prospect of the sea' to be had from the library, as at The Grange; only fields and hedges, and the wooded hills of Cannock Chase beyond. Plate glass, rather than diamond quarries, filled the windows: this was modern, domestic Gothic, not a wholesale return to the fifteenth century. The Middle Ages were a source of inspiration, not a blueprint, and The Grange and Burton Manor were in many ways innovative and visionary. Much as he feared civil disorder and anti-Catholic unrest, A.W.N. Pugin did not furnish The Grange with an anachronistic drawbridge, and although Burton Manor's authentically medieval moat might have given his son the excuse to build one there, he did no such thing. Instead a practical double-arched bridge carries a practical glazed walkway giving access to the front door. As was the case at Ramsgate, security was provided by means of stout doors and massive sliding window shutters which, when pushed back into the wall cavities are concealed behind narrow doors. Set into the gable of the outer doorway is a proud piece of genuine historicism: a stone plaque carved with the Whitgreave coat of arms

9.7 The Whitgreave coat of arms: bookplate designed by Hardmans for Francis Whitgreave (Hardman private collection).

9.8 Burton Manor: photograph *c.*1900 (Stafford Grammar School).

and the motto *regem defendere victum* (to defend the vanquished king), a direct reference to the family's role in the escape of Charles II. The walkway was the prototype for the one which Edward Pugin built at The Grange a decade later.

At Ramsgate the kitchen wing was set at right angles to the north front of the house. This allowed Pugin's private chapel to be built immediately to the east of the principal rooms, separated from them by a large square staircase tower. Not needing to make the same provision at Burton Manor, E.W. Pugin placed the service rooms in the equivalent position to the chapel at The Grange. They are defined by lower roof levels and plainer windows. As at Ramsgate there is a tower at the junction, but it is an octagonal one rising from a square base. It contains a staircase giving access to the first-floor rooms and to the servants' quarters in the attics. The tower was originally crowned by an elaborate timber spirelet. Twentieth-century extensions to the house have obscured the central part of the north-east front, but old photographs show how strikingly similar it originally was to the south elevation of The Grange. The south-eastern exteriors, comprising the library, drawing room remain as near-replicas in both plan and elevation.

Internally, the layout of Burton Manor and the treatment of the rooms matches The Grange **(9.9)**. This undoubtedly reflects the mind of Edward Pugin who knew his own home better than any other domestic building, and the conscious intention of Francis Whitgreave to model his new home on a house that he knew well and greatly admired. First of all there is the entrance hall, rising through both storeys, with big windows on the north side, and a panelled dado. It is the pivotal point of the house; all the principal rooms are accessed from it, so that the traditionally 'alien communities' of family, servants,

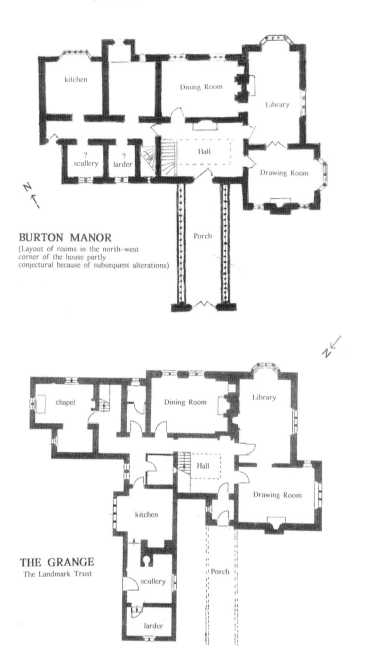

COMPARATIVE PLANS OF
BURTON MANOR AND THE GRANGE
(Not to scale)

9.9 Comparative plans: The Grange and Burton Manor (Landmark Trust and Michael Fisher).

children and guests would constantly pass through it. Everything consciously mirrors The Grange, not only the structures, but also its practical function as 'a modest and practical adaptation of the mediaeval great hall.'[30] The staircase with its intriguing openwork balustrade is clearly adapted from the one at The Grange, though the hall itself is somewhat larger in area. The most original

9.10 Burton Manor, dining room fireplace, copied almost exactly from that at The Grange (Michael Fisher).

feature of the entrance hall is the stone chimneypiece. It has a gabled mantel carried forward on slender detached columns, much more elaborate than the quite plain one at Ramsgate. Like all the others in the house, it has richly patterned tiles in the reveals and in the hearth. They are, naturally, by Minton of Stoke-on-Trent. Edward Pugin continued to use the same team that his father had gathered around him: Minton for ceramics, Hardman for metalwork, and Crace for wallpapers and fabrics. There was once much patterned wallpaper in the principal rooms, but only the ceiling of the stairwell now retains its original, though recently restored, stencilling.[31] It was all very different from the Regency house which Francis' father, George, had built for himself and his first wife at Moseley Court some 40 years earlier.

The disposition of the principal ground floor rooms – dining room, drawing room and adjacent library – is copied from Ramsgate, and there is a close similarity in details. Chief of these is the dining room chimneypiece, simple and massive, with outward curving stone brackets and a bressumer just like the one in Pugin's own dining room (9.10). The difference lies in the decoration which, instead of the carved panel of St Augustine at The Grange, consists of painted red roses and a white swan with outstretched wings. Both of these are Lancastrian motifs, the latter featuring on Henry V's tomb and the celebrated Dunstable Swan Jewel, and there are clear references here to Francis Whitgreave's fifteenth-century ancestor, Robert.

The woodwork of the drawing room and library is richer than that of the dining room, with linenfold panelling, and a pair of Gothic connecting doors embellished with fine brass furniture by Hardman. The chimneypieces are typically E.W. Pugin, with intricate carving. That in the library carries a text cut in a florid Gothic style: 'Kindle in our hearts, O Lord, the fire of thy charity'. The ceilings are wood-panelled, and the panels have shields blazoned with various religious emblems and coats of arms of the Whitgreaves and other prominent Catholic families – much as A.W.N. Pugin had embellished the ceiling and cornices of his library at Ramsgate.

On the first floor is Francis Whitgreave's master bedroom, connecting with that of his wife, an identical arrangement to those of Augustus Pugin and his wife Jane. In the attic above is the former chapel which has closely set scissor trusses. The glass and Gothic tracery of its pointed window are no longer in place, although it is visible in photographs of around 1890 which show other features now lost, such as the polygonal spirelet and wrought-iron cross on the tower, bargeboards and ridge-crests.[32]

It was almost certainly through the Pugins that Francis Whitgreave became acquainted with Belgium's most noted Gothic revivalist, Jean-Baptiste Bethune (1821-92) who established stained-glass and metalworking studios in Bruges and Ghent, and was a friend of both Augustus and Edward.[33] It was Bethune who produced the stained glass for the chapel window at Burton Manor in 1872, and he also designed a sideboard, writing desk and clock for the house.[34] Thus Burton Manor became the family home that Francis Whitgreave intended it to be, but only for a short time, and herein lies another parallel with The Grange. Theresa Whitgreave died in 1873, and Francis in 1896, leaving two sons and two daughters through whom the house remained in the family's hands until the 1920s when it was sold and then adapted for non-residential purposes.[35]

That E.W. Pugin should have built a second house, roughly contemporary with Burton Manor, on another medieval moated site only six miles away, and likewise modelled on The Grange, is quite extraordinary, but such is Aston Hall at Aston-by-Stone. The connecting links are the Whitgreaves of Burton Manor, and the Revd Edward Huddlestone, priest at St Austin's, Stafford, who left in 1856 to take charge of St Michael's, Aston. Apart from the ruinous old hall, finally vacated by the Passionists in 1855, there was nowhere for him to live, and so, being a man of substantial private means, Huddlestone was able to prepare for his move by building a new presbytery which also came to be known as Aston Hall **(9.11)**. Work began in 1855. The Whitgreaves worshipped at St Austin's, and Francis Whitgreave commissioned a silver-gilt chalice and paten to present to Fr Huddlestone as a farewell gift.[36] It seems likely that Huddlestone, who had previous connections with the Pugins, knew and admired the Whitgreaves' new house even before it was finished, and so he engaged Edward Pugin to build his new presbytery in similar style. The Grange was clearly the model, adapted, of course, to the needs of its unmarried clerical occupant. Though contemporary documentation is slight, it is sufficient,[37] and the stylistic evidence for an attribution to Edward Pugin is compelling enough. Built of brick with stone dressings, Aston Hall has bands of polychrome brickwork – identical to those at Burton Manor – incorporating Edward Huddlestone's monogram and the date 1855. William Bernard Ullathorne, first bishop of Birmingham following the restoration of the Hierarchy, is also encoded in the brickwork by the initials W and B set under mitres. The stone-framed windows have pointed trefoiled

9.11 Aston Hall, Stone, by Edward Pugin 1855 (MF).

lights, the drawing room and library are set transversely to the main block, the domestic offices are defined by a lower roof level and plainer windows, and there is an octagonal stair-turret – all of these features being common to Burton Manor. Internally, the entrance hall rises through both storeys, and there are some finely executed stone chimneypieces. The most elaborate of these is in the hall. It is set with a carved panel in which the initials EH are encircled with roses and rich foliage. Fr Huddlestone lived at Aston Hall until his death in 1871, when he was succeeded by the Revd Stuart Bathurst who came from St Giles', Cheadle. The chapel attached to the hall incorporates the remains of a church built for the Passionists by Charles Hansom in 1847 and the Lady Chapel added by Edward Pugin in 1856. The remainder was demolished in 1882.[38]

The Whitgreaves were noted benefactors of the Catholic churches in their area, including A.W.N. Pugin's church at Brewood, and St Austin's at Forebridge, Stafford, on the main Wolverhampton Road. Established in 1791, St Austin's was rebuilt in Gothic style in 1817-18 to designs by the amateur architect Edward Jerningham, who was also rebuilding Stafford Castle at the time. This is the St Austin's that Pugin visited in August 1837 when he met Edward Huddlestone who had been priest at the mission since 1831 and was to spend a further nineteen years there. Pugin supplied him with some new furnishings for St Austin's, including a font with a pinnacled canopy – one of three which Pugin instanced in *The Present State* (1843) as examples of the medieval-style font which he was seeking to reintroduce.[39] By the mid-1850s the Catholic population of Stafford had grown considerably, and a larger church was needed. Fr Huddlestone was succeded in 1856 by Francis Whitgreave's friend, Francis Kerril Amherst, who found St Austin's to be 'one of the best missions in the diocese and well endowed', and noted that on the first Sunday of May 1857 the church was 'crammed morning and evening.'[40] The thwarting of Pugin's plans to marry Mary Amherst had done nothing to spoil his friendship with her brother Francis who had been in favour of the marriage, and, given the established links between the Amhersts, the Pugins and the Whitgreaves, it is hardly surprising that Edward Pugin was chosen as the architect for the third St Austin's, but although some initial steps were taken by Fr Amherst – notably the purchase of the site – it was not until after he left to become Bishop of Northampton in 1858 that detailed plans were drawn up.

Edward Pugin's original design for St Austin's was quite ambitious, [41] including a tall tower and spire at the north-east angle, but, as at Shrewsbury Cathedral, the scheme had to be modified on grounds of cost **(9.12)**. The base of the tower was built, but at the north-west angle, above the entrance. For a time it had only a framework turret to contain the bell given by Mrs Anna Marie Masfen in thanksgiving for the conversion of herself and her four sons in 1861. She was the sister of Edward Bellasis who also a benefactor of St Austin's. As an Anglican, Mrs Masfen had earlier commissioned A.W.N. Pugin to design a memorial window to her deceased son, John, in St Mary's Church, Stafford.[42]

The nave of St Austin's is of six bays, with polished marble columns, and it has a short, open chancel with a polygonal apse, and aisles terminating in side

9.12 St Austin's, Stafford: drawing by E.W. Pugin (Birmingham Archdiocesan Archive).

chapels. The battle for rood screens had ended abruptly with the death of their
champion in 1852, and St Austin's, like most of Edward Pugin's churches, was
built on the 'all-seeing' principle which his father had hotly contested. Some
furnishings from the old church were reinstated. Pre-1950s photographs show
two Pugin/Hardman *coronae* hanging in the sanctuary, remarkably similar in
style to one commissioned in 1849 by Marianne Jerningham after the death of

her husband, Edward, architect of the second St Austin's. The inscription makes it clear that it was an *in memoriam* gift, and designed to hang before the Blessed Sacrament.[43]

The new church was opened on 16 July 1862, with Bishop Ullathorne presiding, and with Edward Pugin in attendance. Ullathorne's speech at the

9.13 Interior of St Austin's showing the reredos by P.P. Pugin (photograph at St Austin's Church).

luncheon which followed was reported in the *Staffordshire Advertiser,* along with an account of the ceremony and an account of the church. Having described the churches designed by the Pugins as 'speaking symbols of the faith', the bishop said that

> for this they had to thank a man whose name was illustrious through the world (Hear, hear). It had been said that it was rare to find a man of genius who had bequeathed that genius to his son, but they had a distinguished exception to that proverb in the architect of this church. ... Mr Pugin, young as he was, had already given to the world many beautiful fruits of the genius – it was wonderful how he had produced a church so beautiful out of means so limited.[44]

In his response, Pugin said that the church as it stood represented 'about the fifth edition of what the building was to have been', and paid warm tribute to the builder, Mr Jeffreys of Stone, for having achieved so much on so limited a budget.

The projected 110-foot tower and spire remained for the future, and additions were gradually made to the interior **(9.13)**. Some old Flemish glass with figures of saints, preserved from the former church, was re-set in the five-light west window, and six remaining panels, having been restored by Hardman's, was sold for £60 to the Edinburgh Museum of Science and Art.[45] The three windows in the apse were designed by John Hardman Powell whose figure-painting was more expressive and mobile than that of his mentor, A.W.N. Pugin. In 1884 Edward Pugin's brother, Peter Paul (1851-1904), designed a new high altar and a carved stone reredos, and he was also responsible for the altars in the Lady Chapel (1887) and the Sacred Heart Chapel (1894). The reredos of the high altar was demolished in 1958, although the flanking statues of St Thomas More and St John Fisher, given by Francis Whitgreave to mark their beatification in 1886, were retained. Some other original features, including wall-decorations and the nave roof, were either obscured or removed at the same time, the work being carried out, ironically, by the firm which had created so much of it in the first place – Hardman of Birmingham – under the direction of its latter-day proprietor, Patrick Feeny. Extensive restorations carried out in 1998 did much to restore the Puginian character of the interior, and the truncated tower was given a lead-covered spirelet.

In spite of Ullathorne's fulsome tribute at the opening of St Austin's, Edward Pugin found that in other parts of north Staffordshire, and indeed elsewhere in the Diocese of Birmingham, his opportunities were somewhat restricted because of the bishop's favouring of another Catholic architect, Charles Hansom (1817-88), whom he had encountered during his time in Coventry in the early 1840s. Hansom had already made inroads into the area with his churches at Aston-by-Stone (1847-9), and Rugeley (1849-50), and he continued with the Dominican church and convent at Stone (1852-4), and the convent of the Holy Angels in Stoke (1857). Ullathorne's apparent reluctance to use Pugin was the cause of verbal battles over additions to Oscott College and the proposed new church of the Sacred Heart at Hanley, Stoke-on-Trent. Pugin accused

Ullathorne of showing undue favour not only to Charles Hansom, but also his son, Edward, who was Ullathorne's godson, and a partner in the firm.[46] Surprising as it might seem, Hansom's elder brother, Joseph Aloysius (1803-82) formed a brief partnership with Edward Pugin in 1862. It lasted barely a year, and the ending of it was accompanied by a battle of words in the press. Edward Pugin, it would seem, was as easily provoked as his father had been. Another Catholic architect, Gilbert Blount (1819-76), was responsible for the new Catholic churches at Caverswall (1863-4) and Swynnerton (1868-9), and he also made additions to St Dominic's, Stone. Like Hansom, he used Hardmans for stained glass and metalwork. Between 1854 and 1882 fourteen Hardman windows were commissioned for St Dominic's, and amongst the considerable amount of metalwork was a rood screen for Blount at the substantial sum of £450.[47]

The 'broom-stealers', as A. W. N. Pugin had called them, did not get things entirely their own way, and Edward Pugin scored a notable success when he won the contract for a new church for the Lane End Mission in Longton. Lane End Mission was an offshoot of the Caverswall Mission, established in 1819. Its church was extended in 1835 and again in 1850: Pugin's replacement, dedicated to St Gregory, was built in 1868-9 adjacent to the existing building which thereafter served as a parish hall. It is somewhat ironic that Longton, which the Dominican Margaret Hallahan had described as 'the fag-end of the world' should have been the location of one of Edward Pugin's grandest churches. The new St Gregory's, built of red brick with bands of blue brick, and stone dressings, consisted of a tall aisled nave with clerestories, a vestibule at the west end, and a high, vaulted chancel (9.14). The east end terminated in a polygonal apse, roofed in a series of small gables with statues in between. Internally the two-bay chancel (and apse beyond) were marked off from the rest by a very low marble screen: the only other internal structural division was a high arch at the entrance to the apse. Edward Pugin was willing to dispense with the full rood screens which his father had regarded almost as an article of faith, and to have short, open chancels which his father had opposed. The focal point was the high altar, one of Edward's most impressive designs. It was of the Benediction type with a tall spire soaring high above the tabernacle. When the church was opened in the summer of 1869 it merited special praise in the *Staffordshire Advertiser*:

> The high altar is raised on nine steps, and with the reredos may be pronounced one of the most successful efforts of the architect, the effect being unusually dignified and refined. In the centre stands the Tabernacle of carved stone with metal gilt doors, and above it rises a lofty canopied niche, five and twenty feet high for benediction – not a cramped diminutive recess, but a noble throne-like baldachino resting on marble columns.[48]

The location of so grand a church in such a dismal neighbourhood was remarked upon by Bishop Ullathorne at the opening. 'It should prove a great boon,' he said, 'to the poor Catholics in this dreary town of sin and mud.' Some work remained unfinished, doubtless for financial reasons. The carved

9.14★ St Gregory's, Longton, *c.*1905: altar by E.W. Pugin, stained glass by Hardman, and wall decoration by Elphege Pippett (Hardman private collection).

panels intended for the recesses either side of the tabernacle were added later, likewise the stained glass for the tall windows of the apse. The central window was installed in 1870 to a design by John Hardman Powell, and the remainder in 1903, along with the windows of the Lady Chapel and Sacred Heart Chapel, all, of course, made by Hardman. A complete redecoration of the sanctuary was undertaken by Hardmans in 1903 to designs by Elphege Pippet who had joined his father, Joseph Aloyius as a senior artist-draughtsman in the firm. The completed scheme, well-documented in the Hardman collection of watercolours and photographs, and in their written archive, illustrates the continuity of the Pugin style within the firm of John Hardman & Co. well into the twentieth century. St Gregory's is considered by some to have been the best of Edward Pugin's churches in the diocese,[49] and therefore its demolition in 1970, on account of mining subsidence (so it was said), is all the more to be regretted.

Although the buildings at St Wilfrid's, Cotton, were to all intents and purposes finished by the time the Oratorians left in 1849, the adaptation of the hall for other purposes required additional buildings. One of Edward Pugin's last works in north Staffordshire, carried out shortly before his death in 1875, was an extension to Cotton Hall for the Sedgley Park Preparatory School which had moved in from Wolverhampton in 1868 under the name of St Wilfrid's College. His principal addition was a wing set at right-angles to old Cotton Hall and in the shadow of his father's church of St Wilfrid which was now serving the needs of both school and parish. Known as the Souter Wing after Canon Souter, the President of Sedgley Park, it is of stone, two storeys tall, and with two-light traceried windows. There are some similarities with A.W.N. Pugin's Guildhall range at St John's, Alton, built in the 1840s. Pugin claimed that he had drawn up the plans as early as 1866.[50] The steep roof has dormers, and at the south-east angle there is a polygonal tower with a truncated spire-cap.

There are two interesting tailpieces to this story of Catholic Revival emanating from the heart of Staffordshire's Pugin-land. John Bunn Denny, the clerk of works who supervised so much of Pugin's building, and who was thoroughly schooled in 'true principles' Gothic, was among those who quit the Alton estate after the demise of the Catholic earls. He became acquainted with one of Pugin's 'broom-stealers', namely William Wilkinson Wardell (1823-99). Described as 'the ablest of the Roman Catholic architects working in the tradition of Pugin,'[51] Wardell considered Denny's practical experience of superintending Pugin's buildings to be an asset that he could readily use, and so following his emigration to Australia in 1858 he invited Denny to join him, and to superintend the building of his churches in Melbourne. Denny eventually became an architect in his own right, responsible for some fine Gothic churches which in their form and detail express his indebtedness to Pugin.[52] Thus the Australian 'Gothic paradise' which, under Pugin's influence, was begun by Bishop Willson of Hobart a decade earlier,[53] was further extended by migrant architects who had caught the Pugin flame. None, however, could claim to have worked directly under Pugin as both foreman and friend, and handled his plans and drawings, in the way that Denny had done. Given that no working drawings for the buildings at Alton and Cheadle appear to have survived in the United Kingdom, it is not unlikely that Denny retained many of them and put them to good use in Australia, where he continued in practice almost to the end of his life. He died in 1892.

In the summer of 1927, three years after the departure of the Chetwynd Talbots, Alton Towers was the scene of a gathering of many thousands of Catholics at which Dr Barrett, Bishop Auxiliary of Birmingham, and his assistant clergy, officiated in the famous Shrewsbury cloth-of-gold vestments, borrowed for the occasion from Oscott College.[54] Though emptied, for the second time, of furnishings and paintings, the house and chapel retained their fine woodwork, sumptuous wall-coverings, and radiant stained glass windows. Amongst the thousands of people present on this occasion there may well have been a few score octogenarians for whom it evoked powerful childhood memories of Catholic celebrations of yesteryear, and of the Alton they had known and loved in the days of 'Good Earl John'.

10

Prayer-Book Catholics: the Anglican connection

'even in its present position, by its own existing canons and rubrics, the Anglican Church is bound, consistently, to work exclusively on the principles of Christian architecture, and to renounce all pagan adaptations whatsoever'
A.W.N. Pugin, Apology

In October 1847 Pugin wrote to John Hardman, 'I have just got a positive order for £4020.0.0. of stained glass ... all for one church – an anglican job of course.'[1] This fairly reflects the position in which Pugin found himself in the late 1840s. Apart from St George's, Southwark, there were no big Catholic churches after Cheadle, and, thanks partly to the 'broom-stealers', Pugin became more and more a decorator and furnisher of other architects' buildings. As the Gothic Revival enveloped the Anglican Church, its architects also looked to Pugin and Hardman to furnish and decorate their buildings in accordance with long-forgotten Ornaments Rubric of the *Book of Common Prayer.* Although Pugin designed only one complete Anglican church – St Lawrence's, Tubney (Berkshire) – he made significant additions to others, and north Staffordshire has two important examples. The area also has some outstanding buildings by other Victorian architects who were greatly influenced by Pugin: George Gilbert Scott at St Mary's, Stafford, George Edmund Street at All Saints', Denstone, George Frederick Bodley at the Holy Angels', Hoar Cross, and Richard Norman Shaw at All Saints', Leek. All of these are Anglican churches, and they all reflect the impact of the Catholic Revival within the Church of England from the 1840s.

Pugin had a number of Anglican friends with whom he corresponded at some length. Chief of these was John Rouse Bloxam (1809-81), a Fellow of Magdalen College and a founder member of the Oxford Architectural Society. Following Pugin's visit to Oxford in February 1841, Bloxam wrote excitedly to their mutual friend, Ambrose Phillipps,

> Mr Pugin has gratified me, more than I can express, by his three days' sojourning within our College walls. His conciliating manners and extensive knowledge of ecclesiastical and architectural antiquities have gained him the respect and commendation of all who have had the pleasure of meeting him. ... I cannot resist acknowledging with grateful delight the instruction imparted by his drawings, lectures and conversation. To know such a person is a privilege.[2]

It was men like Bloxam who convinced Pugin that, despite the upheavals of the sixteenth century and the surrender of the English Church to the secular power of the State, there remained within Anglicanism a dormant Catholic element that was now being stirred into life. He was, for example, impressed by the 'Oxford men', as he called them, who visited Alton to experience his revivals not just of medieval architecture and furnishing, but of liturgy too: 'they bow reverently to the altar in the chapel at Alton. Speak in Wispers & Mrs Winter has been asked by them before entering if the blessed Sacrament was in the chapel that they might pay their proper devotions.'[3] Pugin knew also that for every catholic-minded Anglican like Bloxam there were dozens of dyed-in-the-wool Protestants for whom a simple cross placed on the communion table was a badge of 'popery' and who showed absolutely no reverence towards the Blessed Sacrament. In the summer of 1842 he was scandalised by an incident at Leeds parish church – newly-opened and supposedly in the vanguard of better standards of worship – when consecrated bread and wine left over from the Communion service were allegedly stuffed down a drain-pipe instead of being 'reverently consumed' as the Prayer Book directed.[4] When his ideas on church architecture and furnishings were being eagerly adopted by Anglicans, Pugin praised them for their Catholic spirit and drew sharp contrasts with the lukewarm and even hostile attitude of some fellow Catholics towards his Gothic vision; yet when he delved deeply into Anglican history he was forced to conclude that 'the present Church of England is 10 times more protestant than I thought it.'[5]

Pugin's writings were keenly studied by members of the Oxford and Cambridge architectural societies. These were the Anglican Ecclesiologists who in the 1840s were attempting to restore the beauty of holiness through the restoration and re-furnishing of old churches and the building of new ones in a Gothic style, based on proper understanding of architectural principles, and thorough research. Impressed by the Catholic spirit of the pamphlets which the Cambridge Camden Society were publishing for the benefit of Anglican churchwardens and church-builders, Pugin commented on them in some detail and recommended that they should be studied also by English Catholics who, 'owing to their long exclusion from the sacred buildings raised by their ancestors in the faith, have woefully departed from the principles which influenced them in the erection of their religious buildings.'[6]

Praise from a Catholic propagandist such as Pugin could, however, be embarrassing. John Ruskin tried to rid Gothic of its Catholic associations in order to make it more widely acceptable, and in the process was most unkind to Pugin. The Cambridge Camden Society broke with him when in 1846 it published a derogatory article entitled 'The Artistic Merit of Mr Pugin'. The author of this attack was Alexander Beresford Hope, a wealthy Staffordshire landowner and an ardent Ecclesiologist, who concluded that 'Mr. Pugin, clever and enthusiastic as he is, has not answered the expectations that were formed of him.'[7] Yet nothing speaks more clearly or more succinctly of the local impact of Pugin's ideas outside the Roman Catholic Church than Holy Trinity, Hartshill Road, Stoke-on-Trent (1842), with its tall spire and Geometrical tracery owing much to St Giles', Cheadle, which was then under construction. Designed by G.G. Scott and financed by Pugin's potter-friend, Herbert Minton, Holy Trinity is copiously decorated with coloured tiles, and is as 'Puginesque' as it was then possible for an Anglican church to be. Two Hardman windows, designed by Pugin, were added in 1849.[8] Whatever *The Ecclesiologist* might have said about Pugin, individual members of the Cambridge Camden Society continued to use him. In Staffordshire, Ecclesiology found early sympathisers and active supporters among a number of wealthy families who were prepared to direct their wealth towards the restoration and rebuilding of decaying churches, and the county was also a meeting ground for Puginians and Ecclesiologists who mingled freely as visitors to Alton Towers chapel and St Giles', Cheadle.

When Pugin first visited Staffordshire in 1834 he saw Lichfield Cathedral as restored some 30 years previously by James Wyatt (1746-1813) and local architect Joseph Potter (1756-1842) who was still working there. Wyatt had re-ordered the east end of the Cathedral by demolishing the altar screen so as to join together the choir and Lady Chapel, a favourite device of his. Pews had been introduced into the choir, the choir aisles had been walled off, and a glazed screen erected to separate the whole of east end from the nave. Pugin's reaction to Wyatt's treatment was fairly predictable:

> Yes – this monster of architectural depravity, this pest of Cathedral architecture, has been here. need I say more. … The man I am sorry to say – who executes the repairs of the building was a pupil of the Wretch himself and has imbibed all the vicious propensities of his accursed tutor without one spark of even practical ability to atone for his misdeeds..[9]

Had Pugin lived long enough to have returned to Lichfield some 40 years later he would have seen the results of the restoration work carried out from 1857 by Scott, and he would have been delighted to see the undoing of the misdeeds committed by 'the Wretch' – the restoration of the Lady Chapel to its proper function, the high altar replaced and correctly furnished, and the stonework and statuary of the building restored in true Gothic style. Yet none of this could have happened without Pugin, for it was the 'thunder' of Pugin's writings which enlightened and excited the young Scott almost to frenzy, to the extent of wishing that all his previous work could be burnt down. 'I suddenly found myself like a person awakened from a long feverish dream. … I was in fact a new man.'[10]

St Mary's Church in Stafford was the first to be restored by Scott following his awakening **(10.1)**. He began in 1842, the year of Pugin's *Dublin Review* article which had so excited him, and the year in which he built Minton's church in Stoke-on-Trent. St Mary's is a commodious building, with a vast chancel and transepts which, until 1548, had housed a prebendal college. By 1840 it was in a dilapidated condition; the chancel and transepts were rarely used, and the nave was filled with an assortment of box-pews which faced westwards towards a huge gallery containing the pulpit and organ. Jesse Watts Russell of Ilam Hall contributed £5,000 for the restoration of the interior along the lines advocated by the Cambridge Camden Society.[11] It was an impressive amount of money,

10.1 St Mary's, Stafford: Scott & Moffatt's drawing of the exterior (St Mary's parish records, Staffordshire Record Office, D834).

enough to finance a whole new church, and it excited Ambrose Phillipps to comment on the likely benefits to church-building within the Catholic Church consequent upon the reunion of Rome and Canterbury for which he hoped. 'This as a specimen when they are still in schism, may serve to show what the Anglicans will do when the *reunion* shall once be fairly accomplished.'[12] The scale of the restoration, and the controversies over the rebuilding of the south transept,[13] established Scott's reputation, and when recalling his visit to St Giles', Cheadle, Lord Shrewsbury referred to him as 'the Stafford church architect.'[13]

Jesse Watts Russell's generosity made it possible for St Mary's to be furnished in grand style. The nave was equipped with fine 'poppy-head' benches, and the chancel **(10.2)** with cathedral-style choir-stalls so that the choir, now robed in surplices, could sing the offices of Morning and Evening Prayer in the properly appointed place instead of the now-demolished west gallery. Richly carved oak sedilia were set on the south side of the altar which was raised on three steps and furnished with tall candlesticks and a coloured altar-frontal worked by Jesse Watts Russell's daughters, standing beneath an east window glowing with

10.2 St Mary's, Stafford: John Masfen's drawing of the chancel for *Views of the Church of St Mary at Stafford*, 1852.

10.3 Pugin, frontispiece to Masfen's *Views of St Mary's*, showing proposed memorial window.

stained glass. The entire east end of the church was paved with encaustic tiles by Minton, those of the sanctuary being the gift of Herbert Minton himself. They comprise an exceedingly rich pavement of differing patterns on each of the four rising levels, and a dado with sacred emblems for the east wall, two years before those at St Giles', Cheadle. Thus the internal appearance of the building was transformed almost beyond recognition, yet at the time none of these 'advanced' ritual arrangements seems to have provoked the kind of adverse reaction that was experienced elsewhere. It was after all completed a year before the furore raised by Newman's conversion to Rome, and the consequent growth in suspicion of all things savouring of 'popery'. However, during the wave of Protestant agitation that swept across the country following the restoration of the Catholic Hierarchy in 1850, a speaker at one of the local meetings made the point that the threat was less from the pope and the cardinals than from the 'romanising clergy within the Church of England' who were turning St Mary's into a 'popish chapel'. It was further noted that the rector of St Mary's, the Revd W. Coldwell, who had initiated the restoration, was not present at the meeting, and people were left to draw their own conclusions.[15]

It was restorations along these lines which impressed Pugin, and persuaded him that all was not yet lost within the Church of England. When travelling to Cheadle and Alton from the south, he would usually alight at Stafford and board a coach at the Swan Hotel. The short walk from the station would have taken him through St Mary's churchyard, and so he would have seen the church at the various stages of its restoration. The account of the re-opening contains the statement that Pugin had visited it on more than one occasion, and that he had pronounced it to be 'the best restoration which has been effected in modern times.'[16] Nor was that all. When John Masfen, a brilliant young artist who had drawn a set of very fine illustrations of the restoration, died in 1846 at the age of nineteen, his mother commissioned Pugin to design a memorial window for the north aisle of St Mary's. It shows the figure of St John the Evangelist under a Gothic canopy. Mrs Anna Marie Masfen, a sister of Serjeant Bellasis, later arranged for the publication of her son's drawings, with a detailed account of the restoration written by Scott himself[17] and for which Pugin designed a magnificent frontispiece showing the memorial window flanked by angels, and views of St Mary's and Stafford Castle **(10.3)**.

Among the leading Anglican families of north Staffordshire were the Bagots

10.4 All Saints', Leigh (Michael Fisher).

10.5 Bishop Richard Bagot (photograph in Leigh Church).

of Blithfield Hall, who, in the early nineteenth century, boasted a number of clerics amongst their younger sons. In 1829 Richard (1782-1854), a younger son of the first Baron Bagot, became Bishop of Oxford, a position which he held through the upheavals caused by the Tractarian Movement, before being translated to Bath and Wells in 1845. Pugin wrote in praise of Bishop Bagot for his refusal to condemn the *Tracts for the Times* in general, or the infamous Tract 90 in particular.[18] The Bishop's younger son, Lewis, was at Christ Church along with his cousin Hervey, second son of the second Baron. Both graduated in 1834, were subsequently ordained, and eventually returned to home ground; Hervey to be rector of Blithfield, and Lewis to be rector of the neighbouring parish of Leigh. These churches underwent extensive alterations between 1844 and 1851, and Pugin was involved with both of them.

All Saints', Leigh, is one of the most remarkable of north Staffordshire's Victorian churches, yet its importance has gone largely unrecognised, possibly on account of its location in a small village approached through country lanes. The medieval church was described in 1834 as 'a handsome Gothic structure', with a central tower supported by arches 20 feet high. There was an impressive collection of old glass, painted with figures of apostles, martyrs and bishops.[19] The tower and crossing arches appear to have been retained within the new building, along with much of the medieval glass, but the rest is 'the outstanding masterpiece'[20] of an otherwise little-known architect, Thomas Johnson (1794-

1865) of Lichfield. Just as Gilbert Scott was awoken by Pugin's writings, so Johnson had a similar conversion experience, and became a founder member of the Lichfield Society for the Encouragement of Ecclesiastical Architecture, one of several diocesan bodies which modelled themselves on the Cambridge Camden Society. Johnson's church at Leigh **(10.4)** is impressively large, with a five-bay nave, three-bay chancel, and transepts, all in the Decorated style, and with fine rib-vaulting in the crossing and in the chancel. It shows an extraordinary degree of archaeological accuracy for its date (1844-6), reflecting the architect's knowledge and understanding of Ecclesiology.

How Pugin became involved at Leigh is not entirely clear, although it is likely that he came to know the Bagots through Lord and Lady Shrewsbury who attended archery parties and other social gatherings at Blithfield Hall.[21] By reputation if not in person, Pugin would have been known to Bishop Bagot who had been rector of Leigh since 1807 and had continued to hold the living in plurality with his bishopric from 1829 to 1846 **(10.5)**. As Bishop of Oxford, Bagot initiated the provision of the church which Pugin designed at Tubney, and it was Bagot who paid for the restoration and furnishing of the chancel at Leigh. Pugin visited Leigh at least once, for a drawing he did of the chancel in March 1846 survives.[22] George Myers carried out Pugin's designs for the chancel screen and the choir-stalls which have returns at the west ends **(10.6)**. This woodwork is almost identical to the chancel furnishings which Pugin and Myers installed at St Mary's, Wymeswold (Leicestershire) at exactly the same time for the Ecclesiologist, the Revd Henry Alford.[23] The chancel has a very

10.6 All Saints', Leigh: chancel furnishings designed by Pugin (Michael Fisher).

10.7 Leigh: chancel tiles by Minton to Pugin's design (Mark Titterton).

rich pavement of richly coloured Minton tiles specially designed by Pugin and incorporating the arms of Bishop Bagot **(10.7)** who later expressed the view that these were the only modern tiles which pleased him entirely.[24] By Pugin also is the superb five-light east window **(10.8)**. Made by Wailes – who was making Pugin's Cheadle windows at this time – it takes up the theme of the church's dedication to All Saints, with the figure of Christ surrounded by groups of saints in a series of fourteen panels.[25] Leigh church is therefore of considerable importance as the design of a recent convert to Ecclesiology working in collaboration with Pugin on an Anglican project.

In 1851 Pugin was working at St Leonard's church, adjacent to Blithfield Hall – a church which retained an almost complete set of medieval bench-ends, a rood screen, and some fine grisaille glass **(10.9)**. Pugin designed altogether seven windows for the aisles and clerestories containing figures of Apostles, Evangelists, and archangels.[26] Much of the glass on the north side of the church sustained damage from bombs during the Second World War, but four complete windows survive in the south aisle and clerestory **(10.10)**. Pugin's work at

Blithfield also included the restoration of the dilapidated chancel. The tradition is that he reproduced faithfully what was already there, but a watercolour from just before the restoration tells a different story. Though Pugin retained significant items such as the sedilia and piscina, and a fine array of Bagot memorials, he replaced the Perpendicular flat roof with a pitched one. The three-light east window was replaced with one of five lights and intersecting tracery.[27] The Hardman glass was not added until 1856, as a memorial to Bishop Bagot, and

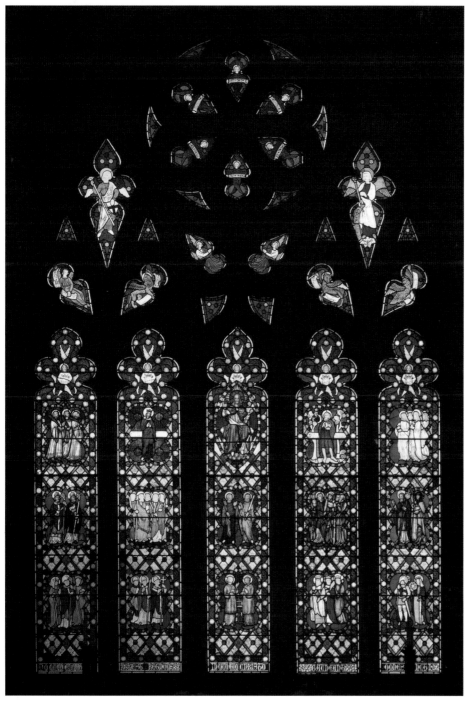

10.8 Leigh: east window by Wailes (Mark Titterton).

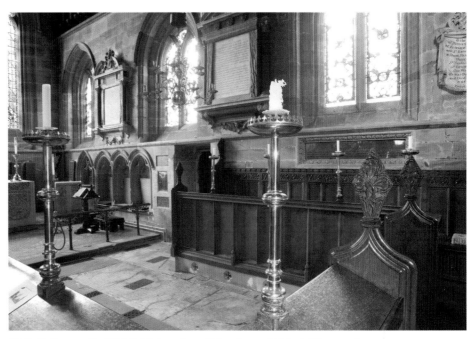

10.9 St Leonard's, Blithfield: interior of the chancel (Mark Titterton).

it was, regrettably, removed in 1965, an unfortunate period for Gothic Revival art in general.

John Ruskin is credited with having 'discovered' the Italian Gothic forms which became popular during the High Victorian period, following the publication of *The Stones of Venice* (1851-3), but Pugin was already well aware of them when, in 1847, he visited Florence and wrote back enthusiastically to Lord Shrewsbury that it was a perfect mine of Gothic art. 'I have seen 3 of the finest altars in Christendom, and one of silver about 12 feet long … the sacristies are full of Gothic shrines, reliquaries, chalices etc. … Rome is certainly a miserable place, but Italy is yet the richest country for true Christian art & I do not despair of S. Peter's being rebuilt in a better style.'[28] Had Pugin lived longer there is little doubt that he would have used Italian Gothic forms, including structural polychromy. In the decade following his death other continental sources came into fashion, particularly the Romanesque and robust early Gothic forms which, combined with polychromy and the use of coloured marble, produced the 'muscular' churches of the High Victorian period. The leading exponents included G.E. Street who in 1862 built one of his very best churches of this type within a few hundred yards of what was then the principal entrance to Alton Towers – All Saints' Church, Denstone.[29]

Pugin's 'country church' model, which became popular with builders both in Britain and overseas, is typified by the churches at Uttoxeter and Alton: a nave, chancel, bellcote, and perhaps a porch. In the interests of economy, aisles could be dispensed with. All Saints', Denstone is of this variety **(10.11)**. It has a nave without aisles, a south porch, a chancel, and a bell-turret, each element delineated by a different roof level as Pugin said it ought to be done. It is how Street handles these features that makes Denstone such an interesting building,

10.10 Blithfield: detail of the memorial window to Louisa Bagot (Mark Titterton).

and takes us beyond Pugin. The polygonal chancel is taller than the nave, and the importance of the chancel is emphasised by the downward slope of the ground at the east end. It is deliberately asymmetrical, as many of Pugin's later churches were. The treatment of the churchyard is not unlike that at Alton: a large churchyard cross, and, in the older part of the burial ground, small memorials of local stone with crosses instead of the 'pagan' urns, inverted torches, cherubs, broken pillars and obelisks which Pugin believed should have no place in a Christian cemetery. There is also a lych-gate, timber-framed with a tiled roof.

10.11 All Saints', Denstone: watercolour by G.E. Street of the chancel (All Saints' PCC).

Unlike Pugin's churches, in which internal space is compartmentalised, and where the view of the sanctuary is filtered through a fretted screen, Denstone is open from end to end, in accordance with the Tractarian belief that the altar should be visible from all parts of the building. The font, pulpit and reredos are all made of alabaster and coloured marble, with rich sculpture and inlaid work. Street's patron at Denstone was Thomas Percival Heywood, a member of a Manchester banking family, who lived in the village. He was an Anglo-Catholic like Street who, it should be remembered, was for a time churchwarden at the Ecclesiologists' model church, All Saints', Margaret Street in London.

Denstone typifies the radical and widespread changes that, influenced strongly by Pugin, the Ecclesiologists had wrought on the setting of Anglican worship in little more than two decades. Gone is the 'preaching house' style of box-shaped buildings overlaid with a veneer of Gothic ornament. In their place are solid, well-defined churches like Denstone, with well-ordered interiors in which the focus is unmistakably the altar. There was a strong philanthropic side too. All Saints' was very much a church for the rural poor. The inscription, 'Every seat in this church is free' is cut into the stonework just inside the door, a reference to the odious system of pew-rents by which those who could afford it could reserve their own seats.

Twelve miles south of Denstone, between Uttoxeter and Burton-on-Trent, is the tiny village of Hoar Cross, the scene of one of the most spectacular achievements of the Gothic Revival anywhere in England: the Church of the Holy Angels. When, in 1872, Emily Charlotte Meynell-Ingram commissioned G.F. Bodley to build this church, neither could have foreseen the long-term consequences of what they were doing. Emily's immediate concern was to build a memorial to her husband Hugo who had died tragically in 1870; but it became a project which absorbed her energies well beyond the opening of the church in 1876 as alterations and additions continued until her own death in 1904.

Just as Lord Shrewsbury's generosity allowed Pugin to build his 'perfect Cheadle', here Mrs Meynell-Ingram's wealth and generosity enabled Bodley to show what heights of perfection and refinement could be reached within the rubrics of that fourteenth-century English style which had so captivated Pugin and which was chosen for Hoar Cross. This church exemplifies the reaction against the muscularity of the High Victorian, and the move towards the elegance and refinement of the late Victorian age, and thus it is very different from Denstone. Bodley's own career reflects this change of taste. Many of his earlier churches, such as St Michael's, Brighton (1858-63) and St Martin, Scarborough (1861-3), were similar to those of Street and Butterfield, robust and with polychrome decoration showing the influence of thirteenth-century Burgundian and Italian Gothic. As Pugin had reverted from the intense colouration of Cheadle to the more refined three-dimensional stonework of his own church at Ramsgate, so Bodley moved away from polychromy and muscularity in his churches at Cambridge (All Saints', 1863-70) and Liverpool (St John's, Tue Brook, 1868-70), and *The Ecclesiologist* noted with some satisfaction that 'Mr Bodley has restricted himself to pure English forms. …

10.12 Church of the Holy Angels, Hoar Cross (Michael Fisher).

The time for reaction from exclusively French or Italian types has at length arrived.'[30]

Hoar Cross could not be more English. The decoration is lavish, but it is of the three-dimensional moulded and sculpted type. No expense was spared, either on the fabric, executed principally in sandstones from Alton and Runcorn, or on the furnishings. How Pugin would have loved this church, with its dimly lit nave, soaring font cover, and glorious rood screen; the rich sanctuary with its legions of stone angels and saints; the founder's tomb and the chantries – just about everything that, as he had said back in the 1840s, there ought to be in an English Catholic church, and all of the most exquisite workmanship **(10.13)**. There is much about the interior of the nave especially that is reminiscent of St Augustine's, Ramsgate, which is also cruciform in plan, with a central tower **(10.12, 10.13)**. Latin texts and inscriptions executed in impeccable black-letter make visitors ask, 'Can this really be an *Anglican* church?' It is altogether 'more Pugin than Pugin', and thus it demonstrates a strange paradox, namely that those who paid most attention to Pugin's visions of a Catholic country filled once more with soaring towers and spires, stained glass, twinkling candles, gorgeous vestments and incense-laden ritual were members not of the Church of Rome but of the Church of England.

Emily Meynell-Ingram's brother was the second Viscount Halifax, President of the most influential of the Anglo-Catholic societies, the English Church Union; and like Pugin and Ambrose Phillipps before him, he looked towards the eventual reconciliation of the Church of England with Rome.[31] The reunion never came, for although Anglo-Catholicism emerged as a powerful force, it failed to convert sufficient of the Anglican hierarchy, while at grass-roots level the majority remained stubbornly Protestant, and churches like Hoar Cross were the exception rather than the rule.

Among those present at Ramsgate on 21 September 1852 for Pugin's funeral was Richard Norman Shaw, a pupil of G.E. Street, and representative of a new generation of British architects who built on Pugin's achievements. Better known as the architect of domestic and public buildings such as the great Northumbrian mansion, Cragside (1869-83) and New Scotland Yard (1887-90), Shaw designed sixteen churches, the largest and grandest of which was All Saints', Leek (1885-7). He described it as 'the best and most satisfactory piece of work I have ever had done',[32] and it represents the full flowering of Shaw's ideas, developed over several years, of what he believed a church should be.[33] As one might expect from a pupil of Street, All Saints' **(10.14)** is open and spacious with an uninterrupted west-east view towards the altar, and Shaw treats the crossing under the tower in a novel and daring fashion, with broad arches pitched high so as not to impair the view into the chancel, and flying buttresses cleverly incorporated into the aisle walls and roofs. Many of the details are, however, clearly derivative in style, the motifs of the window tracery being generally Decorated/Perpendicular in character. Thus Norman Shaw produced a remarkable synthesis. To visit Bodley's church at Hoar Cross is almost like entering a fourteenth-century time-warp; one cannot do that at All Saints'. Built on the 'all-seeing' principle, it is exactly the kind of church that would have answered the needs of the Oratorians had Pugin then been willing to do as Newman suggested and broaden his vision of Gothic as a style capable of adaptation and development.

All Saints' is remarkable for other reasons too. The internal decor and furnishings make it a significant landmark in the early history of the Arts and Crafts Movement of the late nineteenth century, for two of Shaw's pupils and assistants, William Richard Lethaby and Gerald Horsley, became leading members of that movement, and both had a significant role at All Saints'. Horsley decorated the walls and ceiling of the chancel which are as intensely coloured as St Giles', Cheadle, and Lethaby designed the frame for the huge triptych altarpiece, along with the pulpit and font. All of these show highly original interpretations of traditional forms. The re-integration of the visual arts with architecture was something in which Shaw ardently believed, and it echoes

10.13 St Augustine's, Ramsgate: watercolour of *c.*1847 by A.W.N. Pugin (St Augustine's Abbey, Ramsgate).

Pugin's conviction that an architect should be responsible for both. All Saints' is also very much a north Staffordshire church in that it has a rugged, gritty, rock-faced exterior which accord with its natural surroundings, and which also belies the refinements within. The materials chosen were the sandstones and gritstones from nearby quarries, and Shaw was fortunate in having as builder and local clerk of works a man who knew his quarries and materials.[34] Here is another parallel with Pugin, who likewise preferred local materials and was concerned that architecture should harmonise with its natural surroundings:

so well did the ancient builders adapt their edifices to localities, that they seemed as if they formed a portion of nature itself, grappling and growing from the sites in which they are placed. ...The rubble stones and flinty beach furnish stones as rich for the natural architect, as the limestone quarry or granite rock.[35]

Pugin had demonstrated this principle at Cheadle, with the infinite care he had shown over the Counslow quarry, while his own church at Ramsgate – St Augustine's – is very much a Kentish church, built largely of stones from the nearby 'flinty beach'. Norman Shaw visited Ramsgate again in 1892, by then a mature architect, and arguably the dominant figure in English architecture. After the visit he wrote:

> There is a charming little church here (Roman Catholic), built by the great Pugin, some forty-five years ago, for himself. He designed and paid for the whole thing, and it is full of interest all through … a most delightful and interesting work, and done *so* long ago. I am afraid we have not advanced much. Such work makes one feel small, <u>very</u> small.[36]

All Saints' is not the only noteworthy Gothic building in Leek. On the southern approach to the town from Cheadle Road the skyline is broken by no fewer than six towers and spires. The spires are those of the cemetery chapels (by W. Sugden), the Congregational church (also by Sugden, 1863), and the Roman Catholic Church of St Mary (by Albert Vicars, 1886) which is more prominent than the others on account of its size and the fact that it is built of Bath stone rather than the darker local stones. Pugin would have done it very differently had Lord Shrewsbury's intention to give Leek a new Catholic church been fulfilled in his lifetime. In addition to the squat tower of All Saints' there is the remarkably tall one of St Luke's (by F. & H. Francis, 1848) with its stair-turret and pierced parapet, and finally the pinnacled tower of Leek's medieval parish church of St Edward Confessor, which also has a High Victorian chancel by Street, with much fine carving in marble and alabaster.

Next to All Saints' the most interesting of these buildings is the Congregational church in Derby Street, with its 130-foot high tower and spire, and lush Decorated window tracery – a successful adaptation of Gothic to the requirements of Nonconformist worship. Though by no means unique in this respect, Leek exhibits well the diverse applications of Gothic Revival architecture: Roman Catholic, Anglican, Nonconformist, and, in the case of the cemetery chapels, municipal. It is all serious too: gone are the plaster shams, false ceilings, flimsy pillars and wiry tracery of the early years of the nineteenth century, and the credit for that lies with the pioneering work of A.W.N. Pugin.

The revival of Gothic architecture and furnishings necessarily involved textiles; the production, for example, of vestments and altar frontals. In the Middle Ages the manufacture of ecclesiastical textiles had given England an international reputation, with the name *opus anglicanum* (English work) being universally applied to the superb embroideries done in silk and in silver and gold thread, mainly in London workshops, and by men. Then came the Reformation, which witnessed the wholesale confiscation and destruction of ecclesiastical art in all its forms. Such examples of *opus anglicanum* as survived were safeguarded in English Catholic families for occasional clandestine use, or in Catholic Europe where some items were held in sufficiently high esteem to ensure their preservation. It was to these surviving examples, and to illustrations in medieval illuminated manuscripts and on old memorial brasses, that leaders of the Gothic Revival turned when seeking to recover a long-lost art. Lord Shrewsbury's role as a collector of medieval textiles has already been noted, and in particular his ownership of the Syon Cope, one of the most magnificent pieces of *opus anglicanum* to have survived; and it was to examples such as these that Pugin directed those who, he hoped, might revive this important art form.

In *The Present State of Ecclesiastical Architecture* (1843) Pugin made a direct appeal for the revival of ecclesiastical textile-manufacture in England:

> why should not many of the looms which have so long laboured to supply the changing demand of worldly fashion, be again employed in clothing the spouse of Christ – the Church – in her ancient glorious garb. … York and Canterbury will furnish far better patterns than either Paris or Protestant Berlin.[37]

Generally speaking, and in the interests of economy and speed of production, Pugin used machine-produced braids and appliqués in the manufacture of vestments. The production of suitable threads and dyestuffs, and the working of designs by hand, were in any case highly specialised skills which had to be re-learned, and Pugin readily admitted that this would take time: 'We cannot yet hope to revive the expression and finish of the old work. … We may have made great improvements in steam-engines, but not in frontals and orphreys.'[38] By the 1870s, however, the silk mills and embroiderers of Leek were set to take this particular art-form beyond anything that Pugin had been able to

10.14 The spacious interior of All Saints', Leek (Roger Bennett).

10.15 *Opus Anglicanum* revived: the festal altar frontal at All Saints', Leek (Roger Bennett).

achieve, and even to match the original *opus anglicanum* of the Middle Ages. The key figures were silk manufacturer Thomas Wardle[39] whose mills produced and dyed the fine silk threads and fabrics, and his wife Elizabeth who formed the Leek School of Needlework. They did exactly as Pugin had urged back in the 1840s, studying the ancient authorities such as illuminated manuscripts, stained glass, memorial brasses and surviving examples of original work. At the same time they joined forces with contemporary architects and designers such as Shaw, Horsley, and William Morris, to produce new work primarily for the Leek churches. The success of their venture meant that by the 1890s 'Leek Embroidery' was making a great impact in exhibitions at home and abroad.[40] All of the Leek churches have splendid collections of this work, the most extensive being at All Saints' and St Edward's which have full sets of altar frontals in all the liturgical colours, vestments, and many smaller items **(10.15)**. Along with the ceramic products of Herbert Minton's factory, and the revival of alabaster carving, the work of the Leek Embroidery Society highlights the very special role of north Staffordshire in the history of the Gothic Revival. The key influence at work in this Anglican dimension, even with those who were reluctant to admit it, was undoubtedly Pugin. Newman may have well have been right in saying that Gothic was not the only setting appropriate for Christian worship, and that Gothic itself was like an old coat that needed to be adapted to changing circumstances. It was nevertheless Pugin who fixed in the minds of English people – Catholic, Anglican, Nonconformist – a certain picture of what an English church should be, and that vision was unmistakably a Gothic one.

11.1 Alton Towers chapel ceiling under restoration, 1993 (Alton Towers Resort Ltd).

11

'Gothic For Ever'

In 1952 – as in 1837 – the accession of a young Queen was hailed as the dawn of a new age. 1952 was also the 100th anniversary of the death of A.W.N. Pugin, but that was barely marked in the changed climate of post-war Britain. Whereas the Young Englanders of the 1840s had drawn inspiration from an idealised view of the Middle Ages, the New Elizabethans rated the Abercrombie Plan for the regeneration of London on modernist lines more highly than any Puginian vision of a revived Catholic town such as had appeared in the 1841 edition of *Contrasts*. In the previous year, the Festival of Britain, though consciously recalling the Great Exhibition of 1851, had no place within it for a 'Medieval Court', and when Queen Elizabeth II opened her first parliament, few would have given much thought to the fact that every square inch of the grandeur that surrounded her – down to the very throne upon which she sat – was the product of Pugin's 'Gothic passion'. On the other side of the Central Lobby, the House of Commons – rebuilt after devastation in the Second World War – had been reopened only in 1950. That it should have been done in the style of Pugin and Barry was no foregone conclusion. Among the 'anti-Goths' who wanted a modern building that would be symbolic and expressive of the post-war world were MPs Nancy Astor, Aneurin Bevan, and Arthur Duckworth who argued for something more imaginative than a 'prim, anaemic edition of the old Chamber.'

Locally and nationally, the immediate post-war period was a time when the legacy of Pugin and the Victorian Gothic Revival was severely underrated and even despised. The absence of any major commemoration or exhibition to mark the Pugin centenary in 1952 speaks for itself. These were also years of economic stringency. In 1948 a scheme advanced by Fr J. McDonald, parish priest of St Giles', Cheadle, for the re-leading of the windows and a thorough cleaning of the stencilled decorations was vetoed by Archbishop Masterson, probably on grounds of cost. Furthermore, the centenary of the deaths of A.W.N. Pugin and his patron the sixteenth Earl of Shrewsbury was marked, coincidentally, by the gutting of the once-magnificent interiors of Alton Towers in a ruthless asset-stripping exercise carried out by the Towers' post-war owners at a time when the building had no legal protection. Thus perished what, outside the Palace of Westminster, were arguably Pugin's greatest achievements in the field of domestic interior design, along with the work of several other noted architects and designers. When Pevsner surveyed the building some 20 years later for the Staffordshire volume of The Buildings of England, he found Pugin's great banqueting hall to be 'in a sad state, totally given up and only reached along a tunnel and across rubble'. The loss was felt particularly keenly amongst the villagers of Alton and Farley for whom the Towers had, since 1839, been as much a part of their lives as it had been for 'Good Earl John' who had first encouraged them to look upon the house and gardens almost as a common heritage.

The liturgical revolution which followed the Second Vatican Council radically affected the internal appearance of many of Pugin's churches, likewise the whims and fancies of individual clergy whose enthusiasm for modernity ran beyond the mere shifting of altars and the removal of rood screens to obliterating stencilled wall decorations, demolishing reredoses, and disposing of tiles, statuary and metalwork. Not even the church which Pugin paid for himself and where he lies buried – St Augustine's, Ramsgate – was safe from the hands of those who pulled down his rood screen and removed his altar fittings. The removal of the rood screen from St John's, Alton, and the destruction of P.P. Pugin's altarpiece at St Austin's, Stafford, are but two local examples. None of this, it has to be said, was actually required by the *Constitution on the Sacred Liturgy* of Vatican II. A tall reredos fixed to the east wall is no obstacle to the celebration of Mass facing the people. The Anglican Church was not slow to advance its own revolution in liturgical stagecraft. Although faculty jurisdiction and diocesan advisory committees offer protection against ill-considered and precipitate action, 're-ordering' left some churches looking, as Pugin would have it, 'like an aisle sacked by the Calvinists'.

Pugin scholarship also lay dormant after the publication in 1932 of Michael Trappes-Lomax, *Pugin: A Mediaeval Victorian*. When, just after the Second World War, Phoebe Stanton (1914-2003) proposed a doctoral thesis on Pugin, she was told by none other than Nikolaus Pevsner that everything that needed to be said about Pugin had already been written. Miss Stanton wrote a million words, Pevsner apologised for his scepticism, and in the preface to Stanton's published work, *Pugin* (1971), he said that 'what we have here is an essay of which every paragraph is worthwhile'. Thus began the post-war re-assessment of Pugin as the key figure of the Gothic Revival. It continued with Alexandra Wedgwood's meticulous cataloguing and annotation of the Pugin papers and drawings at the Royal Institute of British Architects and the Victoria and Albert Museum. Then in 1994 there occurred that memorable watershed, *Pugin: A Gothic Passion*, a major exhibition at the V&A (followed by another at the Bard Institute in New York) which drew together as never before in one place the many strands of his prolifically creative genius. Pugin at last received the public recognition which he had long deserved, and which in the opinion of many he had been unjustly denied. More than that, the exhibition encouraged those who visited it to look again, or even for the first time, at Pugin buildings in their own localities, to help make them better known, and where appropriate to press the case for conservation. The Pugin Society, founded as a direct result of the V&A Exhibition, is an international organisation which seeks to promote public interest in the life and work of A.W.N. Pugin and other members of the Pugin family. It publishes two excellently produced journals each year, and also acts as a watch-dog with respect to buildings at risk. As a consequence of all this, Gothic Revival architecture and art in general, and the work of A.W.N. Pugin

11.2 Awaiting restoration, 2011: the banqueting hall window, Alton Towers (Pugin,
Hardman & Powell).

11.3 Her Ladyship's Oratory, restored in 2011 (Michael Fisher).

in particular, are better understood than was the case a generation ago, and the legacy of his buildings is better appreciated and cared for.

This is especially true of Staffordshire's 'Pugin-land'. After the wanton destruction of the interiors, subsequent owners of Alton Towers began to take an interest in the conservation of what remained, and the house received grade II★ listed status. Pearson PLC, who sponsored the Pugin Exhibition in 1994, were at that time the parent company of the Tussauds Group which then owned the Towers, and to coincide with the exhibition they undertook the restoration of Pugin's ceiling decorations in the Chapel **(11.1)**. Other parts of the building have since been stabilised and restored, and the current owners have put in place a systematic restoration programme overseen by a heritage committee which includes representation from various conservation bodies. The bicentenary of Pugin's birth is marked by the restoration of the 27-light oriel window in the banqueting hall: one of his last additions to the house, and arguably one of the most important of Pugin's heraldic windows outside the Palace of Westminster **(11.2)**. Nor is that all. Close to the house, and situated in what was Lady Shrewsbury's private garden, is the little Oratory designed

11.4 Cast of Pugin's tomb-effigy at Ramsgate, made for the V&A Exhibition in 1994 and currently at Alton Towers (Michael Fisher).

for her by Pugin, complete with a star-shaped window and a floriated cross on the gable. Having fallen into disrepair, and further damaged by the fall of a large tree in the winter of 2010-11, this delightful little building **(11.3)** has now been fully restored by Alton Towers Resort Ltd, with a new window designed and made by Pugin, Hardman & Powell Ltd, the successor to the firm of John Hardman & Co. which worked so closely with Pugin and who kept his standards of craftsmanship alive for decades after his death. Thomas Hopper's house conservatory which Pugin repaired and paved with Minton tiles in the 1840s, has been rescued from dereliction and it once again fulfils its original function as the link between the Octagon and the Great Drawing Room. A replica of the life-like effigy of Pugin cast from his tomb at St Augustine's, Ramsgate, for the exhibition at the V&A in 1994 and taken thereafter to Alton Towers, has been carefully cleaned and refurbished in the Towers workshops in readiness for the 2012 celebration of Pugin in 'the House of Talbot' **(11.4)**. Meanwhile the future of Alton Castle has been secured, and extensive restoration work has been carried out there and in the other Pugin buildings associated with St John's. This included complete repointing and repair of the exterior stonework of the castle, and renovation of the roofs, notably the renewal of the unique coloured tiles on the roof of the Chapel. Sensitively adapted for use by the Catholic Youth Association as a residential centre for young people, the buildings were officially reopened in June 2002. The Pugin churches of the area, notably St Giles', Cheadle, show that modern liturgical needs can be met without destroying the whole character of a building as originally conceived by its architect. Thus the Pugin bicentenary is the occasion for some rejoicing as Staffordshire's special place in the career of this extraordinary man is now more fully understood. The words 'Gothic For Ever!' were to Pugin a kind of battle-cry which he appended to some of his passionate letters on the subject of architecture and design, and at the Pugin Exhibition in 1994 they were set in large letters over the exit as if to remind the visitor that Gothic is not all in the past. This book came to be written because a ten-year-old schoolboy was enthralled by what he saw on his first visit to Pugin-land many years ago. Now more young people than ever before are being brought into contact with this unique heritage, and thus with the minds of Pugin and Lord Shrewsbury. Who can deny that these buildings are capable of speaking powerfully to present and future generations of a spirit which believes that beauty is preferable to ugliness, that order is better than chaos, that worship should be uplifting, and that art and architecture have a spiritual as well as an aesthetic role? 'The mere inspection of them is nothing,' said Pugin. 'It is when they become associated with the life of divine worship that they produce the full power and lift the soul in ecstasy' (*Treatise on Chancel Screens*, 1851).

Notes & abbreviations

Abbreviations

Apology	Pugin, *An Apology for the Revival of Christian Architecture in England,* London, 1843
BAA	Birmingham Archdiocesan Archives, St Chad's Cathedral, Birmingham.
Diary	Diaries of A.W.N. Pugin, V&A MS L.5156–L.5170-1969, printed in Wedgwood 1985
Glossary	Pugin, *Glossary of Ecclesiastical Ornament and Costume,* London, 1844
HLRO	House of Lords Records Office
JHA	John Hardman Archive, Birmingham Central Library
JHA ML	Metalwork letters in JHA
JHA MWDB	Metalwork Day Book in JHA
Letters, I, II, III	*See* Bibliography: Belcher (ed.), *The Collected Letters of A.W.N. Pugin*
LDOJ	*London & Dublin Orthodox Journal*
Present State	Pugin, *The Present State of Ecclesiastical Architecture in England*, London, 1843
SA	*Staffordshire Advertiser*
SCRO	Staffordshire County Record Office
True Principles	Pugin, *The True Principles of Pointed or Christian Architecture,* London, 1843.
V&A	Victoria & Albert Museum.
Vandrival	Abbé Vandrival, 'Pèlerinages en Angleterre', unpublished MS in the possession of the Squire de Lisle.
VCH	The Victoria History of the Counties of England

Chapter 1 Pugin-land

1   Pevsner, 1974, 97.

2   Hill (*see* bibliography) skillfully weaves Pugin's private life into the rich tapestry of his career as an architect and designer.

3   *See* below, pp. 56-7.

4   *Present State,* 90.

5   Pugin to Lord Shrewsbury, 31 Mar. 1841, Letters, I, 221.

6   Denny to Pugin, 21 Nov. 1848, Letters, III, 656; and *see* pp. 132-3, 153-5.

7   Letters, I, 7.

8   Pevsner, 121.

9   Pugin to Ambrose Phillipps, 18 Dec. 1840, Letters, I, 175.

10   Pugin to Daniel Rock, 2 Jan. 1841, Letters, I, 201.

11   Pugin to J.R. Bloxam, 30 Mar. 1842, Letters, I, 338.

12   *Present State,* 31.

13   For a history of Oscott, *see*, for example, Champ 1988.

14   A return of Catholics in England and Wales made to the House of Lords in 1767 showed just under 3,000 in Staffordshire, 491 of whom lived in Wolverhampton.

15   *Catholic Magazine,* n.s. 2, 1838, 37; Belcher 1987, 38.

16   This tour is described in detail in two letters sent by Pugin to his friends William Osmond of Salisbury, one dated 27 Oct. 1833, the other 30 Jan. 1834, both in private collections; printed in Ferrey, 76-89.

17   Ferrey saw fit to omit this incident from his transcript of the letter. The full text is given in Letters, I, 22-3.

18   *See* below, p. 287.

19   Pugin to Ambrose Phillipps, 18 Dec. 1840, Letters, I, 175.

20   *See* Rosemary Hill, 'Reformation to Millennium; Pugin's *Contrasts* in the History of English Thought', *Journal of the Society of Architectural Historians*, 58, 1999, 26-41.

21   For discussion of the date and circumstances of Pugin's introduction to Lord Shrewsbury, *see* below pp. 61-2.

22   For the significance of Oscott in Pugin's career, *see* R. O'Donnell, 'Pugin at Oscott' in Champ, 45-66.

23 William Howard was one of the 136 English and Welsh martyrs beatified in 1929.

24 Greenslade 2006, 153 & *passim*.

25 *See* below, p. 287.

26 St Chad was bishop of the Mercians from 669 to 672, and he established his see at Lichfield where his remains were enshrined in the Cathedral. At the Reformation the shrine was destroyed, but some of Chad's bones were secreted away by Canon Arthur Dudley, and they came eventually into the custody of the Fitzherberts, a noted Catholic family who lived variously at Norbury (Derbyshire) and Swynnerton (Staffordshire). They were taken to Aston Hall in 1797 when the widow of Basil Fitzherbert moved there. At the time of their rediscovery in 1839 they were contained in a silk-lined box covered in velvet, of mid-seventeenth-century date. Radiocarbon tests in 1995 revealed that five of the six bones are indeed of 7th-century date. *See* M.W. Greenslade, *Saint Chad of Lichfield and Birmingham*, Birmingham, 1996.

27 Letters, I, 243.

28 Pugin to Lord Shrewsbury, 4 July 1843, Letters, II, 88.

29 J.H. Powell, 'Notes for a Preface to "Photographs from Sketches by A.W. Pugin", 1865', unpublished MS in a private collection.

30 The letter, from Pugin to Minton, turned up at a collectors' fair in Australia, and is now in a private collection at Chatswood, New South Wales. It is postmarked Birmingham, 19 Sep. 1841, and in it Pugin requests Minton to send the tiles to Birmingham. I am most grateful to Mr Willem Irik, a friend of the owner, for informing me of this, and for supplying a photocopy.

31 *See*, for example, the articles on Pugin's textiles in Atterbury & Wainwright, 207-16.

32 VCH, *Staffordshire*, 8, 1963, 140.

33 Letters, I, 294.

34 Pugin to Lord Shrewsbury, 28 Nov. 1841, Letters, I, 290: Pugin mis-spelt Croxden as Croxton, which is the name of a Premonstratensian abbey in Leicestershire, of which nothing survives.

35 Fisher 1999, 115; Fisher 2009, 111-12; and *see* below p. 88.

36 In 1815 Michael Bick, Lord Shrewsbury's agent at Alton, submitted claims for expenses for 'going to Prayers at Cresswell 12 Sundays there being no priest at the Abbey', Shrewsbury Papers, SCRO, D240/E/F/2/19.

37 Ferrey, 262.

38 A gazetteer of the Catholic chapels in Staffordshire appeared in the *Catholic Magazine*, 5, 1834, 301-

641, and 6, 1835, 100-3. It appears to have been compiled by Dr John Kirk, the mission priest at Lichfield, and is reprinted in *Staffordshire Catholic History*, 14, 1974.

39 Letters, III, 348. Edward Vavasour was known to Pugin, having been among guests at Alton Towers.

40 *See* P. Bailey, *Painsley: A History of Cresswell's Roman Catholic Community*, Market Rasen, 2005. The embroidered orphreys are now mounted on new fabric.

41 Greenslade 2006, 223. Pugin had estimated £471 10s. including all the furnishings, and the builder George Myers was 'ready to start at a days notice'; Pugin to Bishop Walsh, 4 June 1843, Letters, II, 71.

42 Pevsner, 268.

43 Champ, 2006, 197.

44 Brian Doolan, *The Pugins and the Hardmans*, Birmingham, 2004, 11.

45 Pugin to Lord Shrewsbury, 15 Feb. 1846, Letters, III, 29.

46 Quoted in *The Tablet*, 15 Sep. 1852; Trappes-Lomax, 260.

47 JHA MWDB, 18, 23 Mar., 12 May, 9 Sep. 1864.

48 Pugin to J.J. Hornby, 10 Aug. 1848, Letters, III, 568.

49 Greenslade 2006, 227.

50 Pugin to John Hardman, 13 Oct. 1848, Letters, III, 603.

51 Jane Pugin to Pugin, 30 Aug. 1849, HLRO PUG/3/293.

52 St Gregory's was, regrettably, demolished in 1970. *See* below p. 282.

53 Pugin, *Some Remarks on the Articles which have recently appeared in the 'Rambler'*, 1850, quoted by Trappes-Lomax, 321-2.

54 Lord Shrewsbury to Pugin, 1846, HLRO PUG/3/110.

55 Ferrey, 115-16.

57 *Apology*, 39-40.

58 Pugin to David Charles Read, 14 Jan. 1841, Letters, I, 193.

59 'A Medieval Victorian' is the subtitle of Michael Trappes-Lomax's biography of Pugin.

Chapter 2 *Prest d'Accomplir* : The earl and the architect

1 Extract from a verse based on the family motto, and painted over a doorway in the Octagon at Alton Towers. The verse was, apparently, written in the reign of Elizabeth I (Adam, 252).

2 In the mid-1850s both Daniel Rock and Henry Winter were helping to gather information an intended life of Lord Shrewsbury to be written, so it would seem, by Henry Wilberforce to whom

Rock sent a collection of eighteen letters, and other information about the earl; BAA R825 (Revd H. Campbell to Winter, 5 Jan. 1854), and R833 (Rock to Wilberforce, 27 Feb. 1856).

3 This particular fantasy may have its roots in the fact that the estranged wife of the 20th earl (of the Chetwynd-Talbot line) lived alone at Alton Towers between 1896 and 1923.

4 The reredos at Grafton was of embroidered tapestry. It is no longer extant, but the drawings are in the V&A Drawings Collection, D.1065-1908; D.1134-1908; Wedgwood 1977, nos 307-8.

5 St Edmund's College, Ware, Hertfordshire, also known as Old Hall, was established in 1793, and traces its ancestry back to the English College at Douai.

6 Printed by J.B.G. Vogel, London, 1809.

7 J. Chetwode Eustace, *A Tour through Italy, exhibiting a View of its Scenery, Antiquities, and Monuments* … , 2 vols., London, 1813. Several revisions and enlargements between 1815 and 1841 earned him a sudden and extended reputation: 'His acquaintance was sought by almost all persons in this country, distinguished by rank and talents', Gillow, II, 185. Eustace was criticised by Bishop Milner for associating with Protestant clergy, and for the liberal tone of the book on his tour.

8 Revd Edward Price, 'Memoir of the late Earl of Shrewsbury, *Catholic Directory,* 1854, 141-61, from which much of the information about the early life of the earl has been taken. *See* also Gillow, V, 503.

9 *See* below p. 100..

10 *Annual Register,* 1827, 241.

11 Fisher 1999, 15-48.

12 LDOJ, 11, 1840, 110-12; *see* also Fisher 1999, 77-8.

13 Gustav Friedrich Waagen catalogued and commented on the collection in 1838 as *Kunstwerke und Kunstler in England und Paris,* vol. 3, Berlin (Waagen's work was translated by Elizabeth Eastlake and appeared as the four-volume *Treasures of Art in Great Britain,* London, 1854-7 [at vol. 3]); Alton Towers sale catalogue, 1857; Adam, 246-51.

14 In 1857 the *Communion of St Jerome* was removed to All Saints', Glossop (Derbyshire), and the *Transfiguration* to the new church of St Charles Borromeo at Hadfield, a few miles away. Both churches were endowed/built by the Howard family, and the paintings were among the properties willed to Lord Edmund Howard by Bertram, 17th earl of Shrewsbury. The paintings were removed/destroyed in the early 1960s, but two smaller paintings from the Towers Chapel survive at All Saints'; information from Mr C. Sharples.

15 Both Lord Shrewsbury and Ambrose Phillipps had a particular devotion to St Elizabeth of Hungary (d. 1231), and Phillipps wrote a *Life of S. Elizabeth* which he intended to be presented to Queen Victoria.

16 Adam, 257.

17 The album was recently offered for sale by Hugh Pagan (*Catalogue 38*) at £11,500.

18 Fisher 1999, 74; Fisher 2009, 70. The 1857 sale catalogue lists over 300 items of arms and armour.

19 Adam, 258.

20 *The Times,* 8 July 1857, has a lengthy description of Alton Towers on the eve of the great sale.

21 Ibid.

22 Shrewsbury Papers, SCRO, D240/E/F/2/24.

23 Zeloni, 51.

24 Gwynn, xxx-xxxv.

25 'Memoir of the late Earl of Shrewsbury', *Catholic Directory,* 1854, 146.

26 Central to the Catholic understanding of the Mass, the doctrine of Transubstantiation teaches that Eucharistic bread and wine become the Body and Blood of Christ. Though the outward appearance remains the same, the inner substance is changed.

27 Ward, II, 34-5.

28 Letter from Lord Shrewsbury to Ambrose Phillipps, 1 July 1834; Purcell, I, 64-5

29 The *Almamach de Gotha* shows that Prince Frederick was still alive, and it seems unmarried, in 1857. One difficulty is hinted at in Lord Shrewsbury's letter to Phillipps: 'We are perfectly satisfied on the score of religion'. The House of Saxony was generally Lutheran, and there may have been a subsequent breakdown over this issue.

30 *Catholic Magazine,* n.s. 3, 1839, 353.

31 Mark Bence-Jones, 135, 138.

32 LDOJ, 2, 1839, 76.

33 Several letters from Pugin to Lord Shrewsbury contain references to the building of the Doria Rooms, HLRO 339/8, /60, /83.

34 *See* n. 24.

35 Zeloni, 231.

36 Bertram was son of Charles T. Talbot (d. 1838), a nephew of the 14th earl, and his wife Julia (*née* Tichbourne). In 1839 Julia married Captain John Washington Hibbert of Bilton Grange, Warwickshire.

37 Lord Shrewsbury writes to Pugin in Jan. 1851: 'Bertram is going on extremely well ... all he wants is warmth to put his blood into good circulation', HLRO PUG/3/100.

38 Vandrival, 121-5.

39 A former Anglican priest, George Spencer (1799-

1864), was a major benefactor of Oscott College, and became better known as Father Ignatius. Pugin built the church of Our Lady and St Thomas of Canterbury for him at Dudley.

40   Gwynn, 147, and Purcell, II, 103-14.

41   The *stigmata* are the marks of the Crucifixion which have manifested themselves enigmatically, on the living bodies of several holy men and women. The *Letter Descriptive of the Estatica ...* has an Appendix on the doctrine of the Mass and the Anglican position. So extensive was the earl's historical and theological knowledge that doubts were expressed as to whether he was in fact the real author. In the Preface to the second edition of *Estatica,* he takes pains to refute these allegations.

42   For a description of Pugin's first visit to Ambrose Phillipps' chapel at Grace Dieu in 1837, *see* Purcell, II, 288.

43   Lord Shrewsbury to Pugin, undated, but since it refers to the start of the scheme for St Mary's, Ducie Street, Manchester, it must be no later than 1837 (*see* V&A catalogue 573 for correspondence and drawings for this eventually abandoned project).

44   Ferrey, 117.

45   Fisher 1999, 103-4; Fisher 2009, 96-100.

46   Winifrede M. Wyse, 'Personal Recollections of Augustus Welby Pugin', MS HLRO 339/348. She quotes a letter written by her uncle 'about 1832' telling her of the incident, and of his own introduction to Pugin.

47   Rock to Pugin, 19 Aug. 1836, Ferrey, 122-4.

48   *See* J.A. Hilton, *Daniel Rock: Goth and Cisalpine,* Wigan, 1999, and J.A. Hilton (ed.), *Daniel Rock: The Church of Our Fathers: A Selection,* Preston, 1992.

49   *True Principles,* 55.

50   Lord Shrewsbury to Pugin, Mar. 1840, HLRO PUG/3/101.

51   Lord Shrewsbury to Rock, 1 Nov. 1841, 25 Sep. 1852, BAA R801, R824.

52   As n. 50.

53   E.g. Gillow, V, 304, states that the earl's gifts to the Church and to charitable causes is 'said to have considerably exceeded to sum of half a million pounds'. This statement appears to have been based on the estimate given by the Revd. Edward Price in his 'Memoir of the late Lord Shrewsbury', *Catholic Directory,* 1854, 141-61. Trappes-Lomax attributed the entire half million to church-building projects, to the tune of £20,000 per year, and wrote that 'the list can be prolonged almost indefinitely of ecclesiastical buildings which were

largely or entirely erected at Lord Shrewsbury's expense', Trappes-Lomax, 100-1. So the legend grew.

54   Quoted in VCH, *Cheshire,* 2, 1980, 93.

55   Lord Shrewsbury to John Hall, priest at Macclesfield, 14 Sep. 1838, quoted in Hill, 201.

56   The lectern was removed to Oscott, and then sold in 1967 to the Metropolitan Museum in New York: Atterbury & Wainwright, 101.

57   For the altar cross, *see* below pp. 139-40.

58   The Bridgettine Convent at Syon was one of the monastic restorations carried out during the reign of Mary I (1553-8). Lord Shrewsbury also had the silver bell given by Mary to the nuns, the Deed of Restoration, a variety of crosses and seals, and a large crucifix which he gave to Ambrose Phillipps and which is still in the possession of the de Lisles. *See* Adam, 261; also J.R. Fletcher, *The Story of the English Brigettines of Syon Abbey,* Syon Abbey, 1933.

59   The Antiphonal described in an account of the sale of Lord Shrewsbury's books, SA, 11 July 1857: 'A very large and fine MS on vellum, written about the middle of the 15th century, with richly illuminated borders and initial letters ... knocked down to Mr Toovey for £40'. The report also says that as a whole, the library 'was scarcely worthy of so princely a residence'. It needs to be remembered, however, that the 16th earl had to create a library almost from scratch, following the fire at Heythrop in 1831, based around what his uncle had taken to Alton between about 1810 and 1827. There were just over 4,000 individual volumes and sets. *See* Fisher 1999, 75-6

60   *See* R. O'Donnell, 'The Pugins in Ireland', in P. Atterbury & C. Wainwright (eds), *A.W.N. Pugin: Master of Gothic Revival,* New Haven & London, 1995, 137-60.

61   Pugin to Lord Shrewsbury, 15 Apr. 1846; Letters, III, 48. Mary Amherst was sister to Francis Kerril Amherst, later Bishop of Northampton, and their mother was a cousin of Lord Shrewsbury.

62   Lord Shrewsbury to Pugin, 14 Aug. 1848, Letters, III, 567.

63   Jane wrote back to Lady Shrewsbury on 28 Oct. 1848, 'I take an early opportunity of thanking your Ladyship for the truly kind and beautiful Rosary Mr Pugin brought me from Alton. I shall value it most highly, not only on account of the benediction it has received from the Holy Father, but as a gift from so distinguished a member of the noble and antient House of Talbot, so intimately connected with Catholicity in this Country', Letters, III, 604.

64 Pugin to Lord Shrewsbury, 17 Aug. 1841, Letters, I, 261-2.

65 Pugin to Lord Shrewsbury, 23 June 1847, Letters, III, 246. Pugin included details of train times from London Bridge Station to Ramsgate. This time, however, the earl was unable to accept.

66 Letters, I, 309, note to letter from Pugin in which he congratulates the earl on his appointment to the Commission, 24 Dec. 1841.

67 Pugin to Lord Shrewsbury, 26 Oct. 1845, Letters, II, 465.

68 Pugin to James Chadwick, 1 May 1847, Letters, III, 239.

69 Letter from G.J. Caley to the Revd Dr Charles Newsham, 30 Nov. 1847, Letters, III, 240.

70 He was later horrified to find that someone had bought the 'horrid figures' and cast-iron brackets he had removed from the Towers Chapel and given them to the new church he had built in Manchester (St Wilfrid's, Hulme). 'They pursue me like the flying Dutchman': Pugin to Lord Shrewsbury, 26 Sep. 1846, Letters, III, 128.

71 Pugin to Ambrose Phillipps, 1 Dec. 1839, Purcell, II, 222; 'For this he has been censured!!!' adds the outraged Pugin, reacting to a letter from Propaganda denouncing Gothic vestments.

72 Lord Shrewsbury to Ambrose Phillipps, 16 Apr. 1839, Purcell, I, 106

73 Pugin's second lecture at Oscott, Catholic Magazine, n.s. 2, 1838, 332.

74 Pugin to William Dunn, 9 Jan. 1844, Letters, II, 154.

75 Pugin to J.R. Bloxam, 16 July 1843, Letters, I, 92.

76 Pugin to Lord Shrewsbury, 6 Nov. 1842, Letters, I, 390.

77 Lord Shrewsbury's Library contained some key works on Anglican theology and ecclesiology, including Richard Hooker (c.1554-1600), The Laws of Ecclesiastical Polity, the classic defence of the Elizabethan Settlement of 1559, works by Pusey, and issues of The Ecclesiologist.

78 Appendix to Letter to Ambrose Phillipps ... descriptive of the Ecstatica, etc ..., 1842, 143.

79 Anon., The Life of Cornelia Connelly, 1809-1879, London, 1924, from which much of the ensuing information is taken. There is also a large collection of letters and other material relating to Pierce and Cornelia Connelly in BAA R246-332.

80 Enquiries from Robert Berkeley Snr to Lord Shrewsbury about Connelly's suitability are in BAA 328-30; also notes by the boy himself about his journeys with Connelly.

81 The headstone is no longer extant, but in 1847 an identical one was sent, unlettered, to Australia, as an exemplar for Bishop Willson's memorial. This is now in Cornelian Bay cemetery, Hobart. Brian Andrews, Creating a Gothic Paradise: Pugin at the Antipodes, Hobart, 2002, 103-4.

82 Vandrival, 154-6.

83 Wiseman to Lord Shrewsbury, 8 Jan. 1849, Anon., Connelly (n. 79), 95.

84 Dessain, XIII, 460.

85 The demonstrations reached their peak on Guy Fawkes' Night, 1850. In Exeter there was a move to burn an effigy of the Tractarian Bishop Philpotts along with those of Pope Pius IV and Cardinal Wiseman.

86 Lord Shrewsbury to Pugin, 28 Nov. 1850, PUG/3/106.

87 Lord Shrewsbury to Pugin, 13 Sep. 1841, Purcell, I, 80.

88 Gwynn, 41.

89 As above, n. 86.

90 It was based on the French Oeuvre pour la Propagation de la Foi established in 1822.

91 Pugin to Lord Shrewsbury, 30 Jan. 1851, HLRO PUG/3/100.

92 Lord Shrewsbury to Jane Pugin, 3 Mar. 1852, HLRO PUG/3/111.

93 Pugin to Lord Shrewsbury, 15 Nov. 1845, Letters, II, 478.

94 Lord Shrewsbury to Pugin, 1 Mar. 1852, HLRO PUG/3/112. Shrewsbury Cathedral was eventually built by Pugin's son, Edward; see below pp. 259-60.

95 The nature of Pugin's illness, and the exact cause of his death, have been the subject of a good deal of discussion; see David Meara, 'The Death of A.W.N. Pugin', True Principles: The Newsletter of the Pugin Society, 3, 1997, 12-16; see also Hill, 481-91.

96 BAA R824.

97 Letters, II, 231 gives details of Louisa Pugin's funeral, including the chapelle ardente, and Pugin's gift of it to the Cathedral. It was set up again in St Chad's for the solemn requiem celebrated for Pugin. His funeral and burial took place, of course, at St Augustine's, Ramsgate.

98 JHA MWDB, 9 Dec. 1852.

99 For Lord Shrewsbury's funeral, see Illustrated London News, 25 Dec. 1852, 564; Catholic Magazine, 1854, 141-61; Fisher 1999, 154; Fisher 2009, 149-50; and R. O'Donnell, 'No maimed rites – the funeral obsequies of the 16th earl of Shrewsbury', True Principles: The Voice of the Pugin Society, 2, 2002, 17-24.

100 A Funeral Discourse, delivered in the Domestic Chapel

of Alton Towers, after the Solemn Requiem Mass, celebrated for John, Earl of Shrewsbury …, London, 1852.

101 Ward, I, 198-9.

102 Gwynn, xxxvi, part of the Introduction written by Fr S.J. Gosling, parish priest at Alton 1923-50 who would have doubtless have heard of this from elderly parishioners who had taken part in the earl's funeral procession.

Chapter 3 Living the medieval dream: Pugin at Alton Towers

1 *See,* for example, Rosemary Hill, 'Scarisbrick Hall', *Country Life,* 8 Aug. 2002, 44-9, 15 Aug. 2002, 44-7; Alexandra Wedgwood on Pugin's domestic architecture in Atterbury & Wainwright, 43-59.

2 For the full history of Alton Towers, *see* Fisher 1999 and Fisher 2009.

3 In 1997 this author was commissioned by the then owners, Tussauds Ltd, to undertake detailed structural and historical survey of the Towers buildings, and to submit a report and recommendations for future conservation/restoration. This survey formed the basis of the published history of the building as in Fisher 1999 and Fisher 2009.

4 Pugin to Phillipps, 6 June 1851, HLRO 339/119.

5 For the life and work of George Myers, *see* Spencer-Silver.

6 For details of Pugin's association with Denny, *see* pp. 20-1, 153-5.

7 Adam, 267.

8 Ibid., 266.

9 Pugin to Lord Shrewsbury, 31 Mar. 1841, Letters, I, 227.

10 Pugin to J.R. Bloxam, 19 Mar. 1843, Letters, II, 29.

11 E.g. Pugin to Lord Shrewsbury, 1 July 1842, contains much detail about this project, Letters, I, 360.

12 JHA MWDB, 30 June 1842. The sword was charged to Lord Shrewsbury at £14 and was engraved, *Ego sum Talboti pro vincere inimicos meos* (I am the [sword of] Talbot for the vanquishing of my foes). The coronet is entered at £6.

13 The celebrated Eglinton Tournament took place in Aug. 1839 at the Ayrshire home of the Earl of Eglinton. It was a medieval-style jousting tournament reputedly attended by 80,000 people, many of whom turned up in medieval costume. Much of the armour was supplied by Edward Hull, the London antiques dealer whom Pugin approached about the armour for the Grand Talbot. The Eglinton Tournament, the Octagon at Alton Towers with its replica sarcophagi, and the re-creation of the Grand Talbot, are examples of what Rosemary Hill terms 'the Romance of Facts', reflecting a phase in the Gothic Revival in which 'the sublime and the ridiculous frequently rubbed shoulders' (*Caledonia Gothica: Pugin and the Gothic Revival in Scotland,* Edinburgh, 1997, 17).

14 Pugin, *True Principles,* 49.

15 Pugin to John Hardman, 8 Mar. 1848, Letters, III, 474.

16 Pugin to Lord Shrewsbury, 26 July 1842, Letters, I, 368

17 E.g. A. Zeloni, *Vie de la princesse Borghese,* 1843, 32.

18 *Catholic Magazine,* 5, 1834, 662; *see* also LDOJ, 11, 1840, 110-12.

19 JHA MWDB, 25 July 1840. 'A rich altar lamp' is also entered at £68/10/-. The ivories for the reliquary are charged separately in the sales ledger at £14. They could well have been supplied by Pugin who was a collector of ivory carvings; *see* Atterbury & Wainwright, 47. Lord Shrewsbury and Ambrose Phillipps had a collection of religious items formerly belonging to Syon Abbey. At the Reformation the nuns emigrated to Lisbon, returning to England in the 19th century. The reliquary in question is currently kept at Syon Abbey, South Brent, Devon.

20 LDOJ, 11, 1840, 112, states, 'Around the sanctuary are arranged the panels formerly belonging to Magdalen College, Oxford'. Magdalen Chapel was restored in 1829-34 by L.N. Cottingham, so the panels were probably removed then.

21 Pugin to his artist friend, Clarkson Stansfield, 13 Oct. 1841 (Feast of St Edward Confessor), Letters, I, 384.

22 Pugin to Lord Shrewsbury, 22 June 1840, 'I will proceed to Alton & get the figures fixed on Screen &c in chapel' (Letters, I, 137).

23 Pugin to Lord Shrewsbury, 5 Dec. 1841, Letters, I, 297.

24 Pugin to Jane Pugin, 1 May 1850, Wedgwood 1985, no. 83.

25 Adam, 259-61.

26 Letters, I, 141 n. 3.

27 Pugin to Rock, 3 Apr. 1839, Letters, I, 113.

28 LDOJ, 8, 8 June 1839, 364-5, stated to be taken from the *Staffordshire Examiner,* and copied in the *Catholic Magazine,* n.s. 3, 1839, 498-9.

29 Pugin to Rock, 9 May 1839, Letters, I, 115.

30 Lord Shrewsbury to Pugin, 13 Sep. 1841, Purcell, I, 80.

31 *See* Fisher 1999, 94, Fisher 2009, 123-7, Letters, I, 123-7.

32 The Walsh family were of Irish origin but settled in France in the 18th century and acquired noble status. The late Prof. Clive Wainwright kindly drew my attention to the vicomte's account of the visit of the Duke of Bordeaux which provides the key to some otherwise enigmatic statement in Pugin's correspondence and offers a rare first-hand glimpse of one of the grand functions at Alton. It was published in Paris in 1844.

33 Pugin to Bloxam, 5 Nov. 1843, Letters, I, 129.

34 Pugin to R.W. Fitzpatrick, 2 Aug. 1844, Letters, II, 223.

35 Pugin to Lord Shrewsbury, 16 Sep. 1846, Letters, III, 128.

36 Pugin to Lord Shrewsbury, 26 Nov. 1844, Letters, II, 286.

37 Pugin to Hardman, 25 Apr. 1846, Letters, III, 56.

38 Pugin to Jane Pugin, HLRO PUG/3/274.

39 *True Principles*, 50-1.

40 Pugin to Lord Shrewsbury, 30 July 1847, Letters, III, 260.

41 Pugin to Lord Shrewsbury, 3, 11 Aug. 1847, Letters, III, 263-4.

42 Pugin to Lord Shrewsbury, 16 Aug. 1847, Letters, III, 268.

43 Pugin to Hardman, 15 October 1848, Letters, III, 603.

44 Pugin to Lord Shrewsbury, 28 February 1849, Stanton, 1950, Appendix 8, 27.

45 The drawing is referred to in a letter from Pugin to Lord Shrewsbury, HLRO PUG/3/50, undated but clearly of 1849, cf. Pugin to Lord Shrewsbury, 16 Dec. 1848: 'I am preparing an interior view of the new Dining Hall at Alton for next year's exhibition at the Royal Academy', Wedgwood 1977, no. 63.

46 As n. 43.

47 Pugin to Lord Shrewsbury, 23 Oct. 1849, Letters, III, 613. Belcher tentatively dates it 1848, but the railway to which Pugin refers was not open until July 1849.

48 Ibid.

49 Fisher 1999, 141, 149-51; Fisher 2009, 136, 145-7.

50 The drawing, which measures 45½ inches by 24¼ is signed by John Wilson Carmichael (1799-1868) who appears to have been the colourist of what is so obviously an architect's perspective, rather than a view. I am most grateful to Mr Henry Potts, the current (2011) owner for giving permission to reproduce this picture and for supplying me with a digital image.

51 These drawings are in the loans collection in Birmingham Museum & Art Gallery.

52 The sideboard dishes are entered into MWDB on 31 Dec. 1853 at a cost of £260 10s. 0d. The collection of plate is also described in the 1857 Alton Towers sale catalogue which lists fourteen sideboard dishes by Hardman. The sideboard itself is not listed in the sale catalogue, nor in the inventory of contents made in 1860, but it appears on an illustration of the Medieval Court at the Great Exhibition along with a detailed description (*Illustrated London News,* 20 Sep. 1851). There is an identical sideboard, complete with brass candle sconces, at Abney Hall, Cheshire, for which Pugin designed furnishings and interior decorations. It is possible that this is one and the same sideboard which – because of the dynastic upheavals and the halting of building work at Alton – was never delivered to the Towers but was later purchased from Crace by James Watt of Abney Hall. *See* M.J. Fisher, 'Abney Hall and the Great Sideboard Mystery', *True Principles: The Journal of the Pugin Society,* 3, 2005, 18-25.

53 Pugin's manuscript account of estimates and expenses, 1845-52, 109; V&A MS L.50/3-1982; Wedgwood 1985, no. 96.

54 Pugin to Jane Pugin, 13 Oct. 1848, Letters, III, 601.

54 *Report from the Select Committee on Fine Arts,* House of Commons, 18 June 1841.

55 E.g. Alexandra Wedgwood in a review of Fisher 1999 in the Society of Architectural Historians of Great Britain, *Newsletter,* 69, 2000, 20.

56 Pugin to Lord Shrewsbury, 26 Nov. 1844, Letters, II, 286.

Chapter 4 St Mary's, Uttoxeter: the first 'True Principles' church

1 LDOJ, 11, 1839, 33

2 P.F. Wilson, *S. Mary's R.C. Church, Balance Street, Uttoxeter, 1839-1989*, Uttoxeter, 7: BAA holds very little documentation on Uttoxeter for the early years.

3 *Present State,* 95.

4 Ibid., 5-6.

5 Published in the *Catholic Magazine,* n.s. 2, 1838, 324-6, Belcher 1987, 37.

6 Pugin to Ambrose Phillipps, 1 Dec. 1839, Purcell, II, 224.

7 According to the census returns, Denny came originally from Swainsthorpe, Norfolk, and his wife, Jane, was born in Croydon. The 1841 census gives his age as 30; i.e. he was just a year or so

older than Pugin, and only 28 when he undertook the work at Uttoxeter. Payments to Denny from the Alton Estate accounts begin in July 1839 (SCRO, D240/E/F/9/2). For his subsequent career in Australia, *see* Brian Andrews, 'Pugin in Australia', Atterbury & Wainwright, 257. Denny's Australian churches were greatly influenced by those he had worked in Staffordshire. *See* also below pp. 132-5, 153-5.

8   Mr E. Bailey of Alton informs me that in 1987 an aunt living in Alton sold through Sotheby's a quantity of 19th-century drawings that had been held in the family. Sotheby's sale catalogue, *Early English and Victorian Watercolours, Architectural Drawings and Watercolours,* 30 Apr. 1987, show that these were sold in several lots. Lots 514-18 consisted of pre-Pugin drawings for Alton Towers, and lot 521 comprised eight drawings for Uttoxeter, four signed by Pugin with his initials in monogram, and dated 1838 and 1839. Most of the Alton drawings were bought by Alton Towers where they are currently displayed, and the Uttoxeter drawings were bought by the Getty Center for the History of Art and Humanities, Santa Monica, California. *See* note in Letters, I, 108-9.

9   Pugin generally preferred the medieval spelling 'Marie' for dedications to the Bl. Virgin Mary, but this does not affect the pronunciation.

10   LDOJ, 9, 1839, 36.

11   Ibid., 34.

12   Ibid., 35, and *see* below pp. 195-6 for an explanation of these features which Pugin believed were absolutely essential for the correct performance of the Sarum Rite.

13   The tower tabernacle is no longer in use, but is stored at St Mary's.

14   Later reprinted in *Present State,* 1843, pl. XV.

15   JHA MWDB, 16 Aug. 1839.

16   Ambrose Phillipps wrote an address on the subject of Gregorian Chant (Purcell, II, 186-98) and in 1850 Pugin published *An Earnest Appeal for the Revival of the Ancient Plain Song.*

17   E.g. the 13th-century Clare Chasuble, now in the V&A Museum, was severely cut down from a very full vestment to one which barely covered the shoulders. The Syon Cope, also at the V&A and once owned by Lord Shrewsbury, is an example of a chasuble which has been converted into a cope: an indication of the voluminous nature of a 14th-century chasuble.

18   Pugin to Rock, 9 May 1839, Southwark Archdiocesan Archives; Letters, I, 115. The 'Pugin'

chasubles had been in use at Oscott since 1838, but Uttoxeter was probably the first occasion in which they were used in a parish church. Surviving examples of these vestments show that they were generally rather less full than the medieval type. It has been suggested that Pugin may have misinterpreted their shape from his studies of figures on medieval brasses and manuscripts. This is very unlikely given what he actually writes about the chasuble in the *Glossary* and elsewhere. A more convincing explanation is that he modified the design somewhat on the grounds of practicality and to forestall criticism that the full medieval chasuble was so radically different as to be tantamount to an innovation. Bishop Wiseman appears to have suggested such a compromise: 'As a coat may have different dimensions and form, yet still remain indisputably a coat, so may a chasuble; but if the change is so great as to make the coat look like some other garment, e.g. a cloak, or that of a chasuble like a cope or other garment, the change of the latter is not justifiable' (quoted by Bishop Baines in a letter to Dr Walsh, 26 May 1841, Ward, II, 14). In the discussions in Rome in 1839 a width of 3' 6" was talked about, which both Pugin and Baines knew was considerably less than the full width.

19   Trappes-Lomax states that Baines refused to attend the opening of Uttoxeter, but the report of the proceedings in *Staffordshire Examiner* includes him in the list of those present.

20   Bishop Briggs to Dr Griffiths, 10 Oct. 1839, Letters, I, 129.

21   Pugin to Lord Shrewsbury, 1 Dec. 1839, Letters, I, II, 127-8.

22   Purcell, II, 222-5.

23   *Staffordshire Examiner,* Aug. 1839, printed in P.F. Wilson, op. cit.

24   LDOJ, 9, 1839, 336

25   Ibid., 36

26   Pugin to the editor of LDOJ, 11, 1839, 150-4.

27   Letter signed 'A looker-on', LDOJ, 9, 1839, 198-9.

28   Gwynn, 133.

29   Pugin to Walsh, 25 Dec. 1841; Birmingham Archdiocesan Archives R870b; Letters, I, 311.

30   Pugin to J.R. Bloxam, 24 Oct. 1840; MS Magdalen College, Oxford 528/12, Letters, I, 53.

31   Information on later additions to St Mary's taken from P.F. Wilson, op. cit.

32   Stanton, 1970, 41.

33   Pugin's first Oscott lecture, given in 1837, published in the *Catholic Magazine,* n.s. 2, 1838, 193-213; Trappes-Lomax, 153.

Chapter 5 To heaven by Gothic: St John's, Alton, and Alton Castle

1   Pugin to Lord Shrewsbury, 24 Dec. 1841, Letters, I, 306-7.

2   Pugin to Lord Shrewsbury, 5 Jan. 1841, Letters, I, 88.

3   Purcell, I, 69.

4   *Present State*, 95.

5   Ibid.

6   Pugin remarked in 1843: 'The ruins of this castle, as engraved in Buck's work, appear to have been very considerable in his time, but they have been sadly demolished during the last century, huge masses being frequently hurled down for the purpose of mending the roads. The ravages were stopped by the late earl; and these interesting remains are now preserved with the greatest care', *Present State*, 95.

7   E.g. the Alton Abbey accounts record payments to stonemason Thomas Bailey for 'underbuilding the ruins at the old castle to prevent their falling', Shrewsbury Papers, SCRO, D240/E/F/2/22, 9 (1824).

8   *Present State*, 95. The text originally appeared in the *Dublin Review* in Feb. 1842.

9   *True Principles*, 51.

10 He describes them in a letter to Lord Shrewsbury, 24 Dec. 1841, Letters, I, 307.

11 Pugin to Lord Shrewsbury, 13 Feb. 1842, Letters, I, 320.

12 As n. 10, 306.

13 Ibid., 307.

14 For the significance of the *Bauhütten, see* Chris Brooks, *The Gothic Revival,* London, 1999, 262-6.

15 *Present State*, 93, contains a brief excursus on the use of alabaster, and Pugin's hopes for its revival.

16 Pugin to Lord Shrewsbury, 24 Dec. 1841, *see* n. 9.

17 For details of Samuel Firth's plasterwork, *see* p. 83.

18 Lord Shrewsbury to Pugin, 5 Dec. 1841: 'Roddis is working the Altar screen for the hospital in alabaster. It is a series of niches to hold the beautiful small images of apostles that I purchased for your Lordship some time ago', Letters, I, 298.

19 Pugin to Lord Shrewsbury, 23 Feb. 1842, Letters, I, 325.

20 Pugin to Lord Shrewsbury, 29 Sep. 1841, Letters, I, 276.

21 The building itself was not consecrated as a parish church until 1930, nor was it licensed for Catholic marriages which, until 1854, took place in the Towers Chapel.

22 *Present State,* 93.

23 'A Chronological List of the Principal works in Stained Glass etc., designed and executed by Thomas Willement of London F.S.A. from the year 1812 to 1865', British Library Add. MSS 54413 & 34871, nos 142-3. *See also* Shepherd, 328-30.

24 As n. 11.

25 As n. 18.

26 For the significance of the Easter sepulchre, and the ceremonies connected with it, *see* St Giles' Cheadle, below p. 195.

27 As n. 18.

28 *See* ch. 1 n. 27. In Mar. 1840 Pugin told Daniel Rock, 'I have at Length Succeeded in re-establishing the manufacture of church paving tiles & shall have a capital specimen to shew you when I come down', Letters, I, 135.

29 Pugin to Lord Shrewsbury, 21 July 1843, Letters, II, 94. The 1851 census returns for Alton describe Kearns as a 'Master painter employing 7 men' including his eldest son, also named Thomas, serving a painter's apprenticeship.

30 Pugin to Lord Shrewsbury, 1 Aug. 1843, Letters, II, 97.

31 *See Present State,* 94, and letter from Pugin to Lord Shrewsbury, 6 Nov. 1840, Letters, I, 161. JHA MWDB, 24 June 1842 enters the cross at £15 and the candlesticks at £35.

32 In a private collection of drawings done by Pugin for Hardman, deposited in the Birmingham Museum & Art Gallery.

33 Pugin to Lord Shrewsbury, 5 Dec. 1841, Letters, I, 298-9. Pugin had difficulty in finding a sacristan for St John's, but an excellent one was found for St Giles', Cheadle. Pugin told him to go occasionally to St John's to look after the candlesticks and cross.

34 *Present State,* 19.

35 *Apology,* 37.

36 Vandrival, 217.

37 Pugin to Lord Shrewsbury, 24 Dec. 1841, Letters, I, 306-7.

38 Pugin to Lord Shrewsbury, 29 Mar. 1846, Letters, III, 44.

39 As above n. 37.

40 Pugin to Lord Shrewsbury, 13 Dec. 1841, Letters, I, 298.

41 This was the time when Alton Towers was fortified against possible attacks by the Chartists, *see* above pp. 89-90.

42 According to Sister Mary Rose, one of the Sisters of Mercy at Alton, in Higham & Carson, 16. There is an interesting detail in the altarpiece, once in the Towers chapel, and now at St. Peter's church, Bromsgrove (*see* above p. 296-7). On one of the side panels the countess is shown kneeling in prayer, and the window behind has a view across

the Churnet Valley exactly as it would be seen from the Castle.

43 Pugin to Lord Shrewsbury, 24 June 1843, Letters, II, 83

44 Pugin's *Apology* was dedicated to Lord Shrewsbury, but his most severe criticisms of 'mock' castles are in *True Principles*.

45 Pugin to Lord Shrewsbury, 25 June 1843, Letters, II, 84-5.

46 *See* below p.172.

47 *Present State,* 101, contains a detailed description of the bishop's house and its function.

48 Hill, 376.

49 Lord Shrewsbury to Wiseman, 30 July 1847, Wiseman Papers, Ushaw College (reference kindly supplied by Rosemary Hill).

50 Shrewsbury Papers, SCRO, D/240/E/F/2/24, 139; William Bick's cash account with the Earl of Shrewsbury.

51 As n. 37.

52 Lord Shrewsbury had an interest in Mary, Queen of Scots, who had been held prisoner in several Shrewsbury properties.

53 Pugin to Lord Shrewsbury, 30 July 1847, Letters, III, 261.

54 For an examination of the influence of the buildings on Normandy on the young Pugin, *see* T. Brittain-Catlin, 'A.W.N. Pugin and Nodier's Normandy' *True Principles: The Voice of the Pugin Society,* 23, 2001, 3-6.

55 Pugin to Lord Shrewsbury, 28 Sep. 1848, Letters, III, 90. Externally the east end of the chapel is strikingly similar to that of the Convent of Our Lady, Bermondsey, designed by Pugin in 1838. It is illustrated in the *Catholic Directory,* 1839; *see* also LDOJ, 9, 1839,100

56 Pugin to Lord Shrewsbury, 17 Nov. 1848, 'I think the look out turret will look very picturesque. The arrangement of the caps on the jambs are from Brown's hospital and are very knowing', Letters, III, 652.

57 Pugin's father had produced illustrations for John Britton (1771-1857), the compiler of very detailed illustrated books on English architecture, including a fourteen-volume series on English cathedrals. Pugin's diary records his visit to Southwell in Sep. 1842, but he had also been there in Mar. 1840 on his way to visit the East Anglian churches which he used as sources for St Giles', Cheadle. Drawings of the Minster are included in his sketchbook of this tour, V&A L.5192-1969, 1000, Wedgwood 1985, no. 1000.

58 Pugin to Lord Shrewsbury 8 Oct. 1848, Letters, III, 598.

59 Pugin to Lord Shrewsbury, 26 Dec. 1848, Letters, III, 686.

60 Pugin to Lord Shrewsbury, 19 Nov. 1848, Letters, III, 655.

61 Denny to Pugin, 21 Nov. 1848, given as a note to 57 above.

62 Ibid.

63 Pugin to Lord Shrewsbury, 23 Nov. 1848, Letters, III, 662.

64 Lord Shrewsbury to Pugin, 1 Mar. 1852, HLRO PUG/3/112.

65 It was suggested in the letter of 1 Mar.; then two days later the earl wrote to Jane Pugin urging her to arrange for her husband to go to Palermo immediately and to stay through the Spring and Summer; details of trains and steamers are included. HLRO PUG/3/111.

66 Drawings in the Pugin collection at the V&A Museum, Wedgwood 1985, no. 176.

67 Pugin to Lord Shrewsbury, 24 Dec. 1841, Letters, I, 307.

68 This was the view expressed in Pevsner, 60.

69 Pugin to Lord Shrewsbury, 2 Nov. 1845, Letters, II, 471.

70 Brunel's father, Marc Isambard Brunel, like Pugin's, had come to England from France during the Revolution. They became friends, and worked together on designs for Kensal Green Cemetery. Brunel, like A.W.N. Pugin, was a visionary who believed passionately in what he was doing, and they were both enthusiastic for the Great Exhibition, but, tantalisingly, there is no record of their having met.

71 Pugin to Lord Shrewsbury, Oct. 1844 (day unspecified), Letters, II, 270.

72 Pugin to Lord Shrewsbury, 17 Oct. 1847, Letters, II, 258.

73 Pugin to Lord Shrewsbury, 2 Oct. 1849, Wedgwood 1985, no. 66.

74 Pugin to Lord Shrewsbury, 10 June 1849, Wedgwood 1985, no. 65.

75 From the point of view of style, Alton Station has much in common with the Italianate estate lodges on the Farley Road ('Pink Lodge') and Red Road ('Ramblers' Retreat'). These were by Thomas Fradgley (1801-83) whom Pugin displaced as architect at the Towers.

76 Pugin to Lord Shrewsbury, 24 Oct. 1848, Letters, III, 613: 'Lodge is a modern word savouring of the Regent's Park, and Jackson is a plebeian name. All the entrances should be called gate, and gate houses, after the manner of the ancients'.

77 Pugin to Lord Shrewsbury, 30 June 1841, Letters, I, 250.

78 Pugin to Lord Shrewsbury, 24 Dec. 1841, Letters, I, 306.

79 Pugin to Jane Pugin, 12 Oct. 1849, HLRO PUG/3/274.

80 According to his obituary in SA, 7 Feb. 1857.

81 Vandrival, 36, 125.

82 Speake, 184.

Chapter 6 'Pugin's Gem': St Giles', Cheadle

1 Hill, 360.

2 Pugin to Lord Shrewsbury 23 Feb. 1842, Letters, I, 325.

3 'Commissioners' Gothic' is the derogatory term applied to the unscholarly Gothic style used (along with Classical designs) by the Commissioners for Building New Churches under an Act of Parliament of 1818, and it was imitated by other architects. Since the object was to provide as many 'sittings' as possible, as cheaply as possible, many churches in this style were utilitarian preaching-houses with a thin layer of ornament. There were, nevertheless, some serious buildings by competent architects. *See* M.H. Port, *Six Hundred New Churches: The Church Building Commission, 1818-1856,* Reading, 2006.

4 For an analysis of the Sarum Rite, *see* Philip Baxter, *Sarum Use: The Ancient Customs of Salisbury,* Reading, 2008.

5 Pugin to Lord Shrewsbury, mid-Jan. 1841, Letters, I, 194.

6 *Catholic Magazine & Review*, 5, 1834, 664.

7 Pugin to Lord Shrewsbury, 24 Dec. 1840, Letters, I, 178.

8 Pugin to Bloxam, 10 Jan. 1841, MS Magdalen College Oxford, Belcher 2001, 191.

9 Pugin to Lord Shrewsbury, 5 Jan. 1841, Wedgwood 1985, no. 22.

10 Pugin to Lord Shrewsbury, 23 Feb. 1842, Letters, I, 325.

11 For details of the Counslow quarry and masons' works, *see* above pp. 130-1.

12 Pugin to Lord Shrewsbury, 30 June (?)1841, Letters, I, 250.

13 Pugin to Lord Shrewsbury, 28 Aug. 1841, Letters, I, 269.

14 Pugin to Lord Shrewsbury, 31 Mar. 1841, Letters, I, 226.

15 Pugin to Lord Shrewsbury, 28 Nov. 1841, Letters, I, 293.

16 As n. 13. Pugin later abandoned Wailes and set up his own stained-glass manufactory with Hardman. In Feb. 1846 he wrote to Lord Shrewsbury, 'I have quite succeeded in establishing my new manufactory for stained glass at Birmingham. I shall be able to make very fine windows with old thick glass etc.' (HLRO PUG3/15).

17 V&A Drawings Collection, D.1064/1067/1068-1908, Wedgwood 1985, nos 248-50.

18 Lord Shrewsbury to Pugin, undated but appears to be winter of 1845-46, HLRO PUG 3/110.

19 Pugin to Lord Shrewsbury, 17 Mar. 1841, Letters, I, 219.

20 Pugin to Lord Shrewsbury, 9 Mar. 1842, Letters, I, 328.

21 Pugin to Lord Shrewsbury, 15 Apr. 1846, Letters, III, 48.

22 Pugin to Mary Amherst, 21 Apr. 1846, Letters, III, 53. For details of the Mary Amherst affair see above p. 66.

23 Pugin to Lord Shrewsbury, 26 Apr. 1846, Letters, III, 61.

24 *True Principles ,*17-18.

25 Pugin to Ingram, 25 May 1843, Letters, II, 57-63.

26 Pugin to Lord Shrewsbury, 28 Nov. 1843, Letters, II, 139.

27 Pugin to Bloxam, 26 Mar. 1844, Letters, II, 182.

28 Pugin to Rock, 26 Mar. 1844, Letters, II, 183-4.

29 Pugin to Lord Shrewsbury, 30 May 1844, Letters, II, 200.

30 Pugin to Lord Shrewsbury, 24 Oct. 1844, Letters, II, 263.

31 Pevsner, 27.

32 As n. 25.

33 Pugin to Lord Shrewsbury, 15 Feb. 1846, Letters, III, 29.

34 Reported in SA, 5 July 1846.

35 As n. 20.

36 'Dr. Rock was mistaken about it, for the church will be seen by thousands', Pugin to Lord Shrewsbury, 30 June 1841, Letters, I, 250.

37 Pugin to Lord Shrewsbury, 28 Aug. 1841, Letters, I, 270.

38 Pugin to Thomas Doyle, 25 Jan. 1839, Letters, I, 116.

39 As n. 20.

40 Pugin to Lord Shrewsbury, 28 Aug. 1841, Letters, I, 269.

41 Pugin to Ambrose Phillipps, 18 Dec. 1840, Letters, I, 175. Pugin here refers to the opening of St Anne's, Keighley, which he describes as 'a most horrible scene … a regular Row took place between the musicians, who quarrelled about their parts in the church … and a Miss Whitwell – whose name appeared in the bills in gigantic letters – quavered away in most extraordinary style'.

42 As n. 40.

43 As n. 20. Jonathan Martin was a notorious arsonist who, on the night of 1-2 Feb. 1842, set fire to York Minster, causing extensive damage.

44 Pugin to Lord Shrewsbury, 17 Nov. 1843, Letters, II, 132-3

45 Pugin to Lord Shrewsbury, 17 Nov. 1845, Letters, III, 479

46 As n. 40

47 Pugin to Lord Shrewsbury, 22 or 23 Feb. 1844, HLRO 339/78

48 So Pugin told Lord Shrewsbury in 1841, letter in MS University of Notre Dame, Indiana, 28 Nov. 1841, Letters, I, 290.

49 Pugin's third lecture on ecclesiastical architecture to students at Oscott, *Catholic Magazine*, n.s. 3, 1839, 93.

50 For a detailed analysis of the Cheadle glass, *see* Shepherd.

51 *Present State,* 27. Letter from Pugin to Ambrose Phillipps, Purcell I, 223.

52 Pugin to Lord Shrewsbury, 17 Aug. 1841, Letters, I, 261-2.

53 Pugin to Lord Shrewsbury, 9 Mar. 1842, Letters, I, 328.

54 *Present State,* 75.

55 Pugin to Lord Shrewsbury, 25 Apr. 1844; Letters, II, 191; cf Diary, 22-27 Apr. 1844.

56 Diary 3-6 July 1845; V&A MS L.5190-1969; Wedgwood 1985, 1007.

57 Pugin to Lord Shrewsbury, Mar. (?)1845, Letters, II, 362-3.

58 Castle Acre, Norfolk, which Pugin visited on his East Anglian tours. In *Present State* he says that the lower parts of the Cheadle screen will have 'images of the apostles and martyrs, painted in the severe style of Christian art' (p. 79).

59 Pugin to Lord Shrewsbury, Apr. 1846 Letters, III, 47.

60 Pugin, *Apology,* 44.

61 Pugin, *Contrasts,* 1841, 18.

62 Pugin to Lord Shrewsbury, 9 Mar. 1842, Letters, I, 328.

63 Pugin to Lord Shrewsbury 26 Mar. 1842, Letters, I, 335.

64 *Glossary,* 84.

65 Pugin to Hardman, 28 Dec. 1844, cf. JHA MWDB, 17 July 1847, 'An Iron Hexagon Corona, with Gilt Inscription, richly pierces & chains &c & Brass Pans with Pierced Borders'.

66 SA, 5 Sep. 1846; *Illustrated London News,* 9 Jan. 1847.

67 The genealogy of Jesus was a favourite subject for medieval artists in stained glass, sculpture and embroidery. It was usually in the form of the winding trunk of a vine springing from the recumbent body of the patriarch Jesse. The various stems carried representations of his descendants, and at the top were the Virgin and Child. Pugin includes a description of such windows in the *Glossary.* Lord Shrewsbury paid for a similar window for St George's, Southwark. Cheadle was one of five Jesse windows designed by Pugin. *See* Shepherd, 161-3, 334-5.

68 So he told Lord Shrewsbury; letter of 28 July 1843, Letters, II, 140. Minton was also producing large quantities of tiles of various patterns for the chancel of S. Mary's, Stafford, and which were in place by Dec. 1844.

69 Lord Shrewsbury to Pugin, undated, but internal evidence suggests late autumn 1845 before Lord Shrewsbury went off to Palermo for the winter. The letter includes the remark, 'no snow yet'; HLRO PUG 3/110.

70 The Blessed Sacrament was still reserved from the Maundy Thursday Mass, but only for the Mass of the Presanctified on Good Friday.

71 Purcell, II, 187-8.

72 Pugin's letter to the editor of *The Tablet,* published 2 Sep. 1848, Letters, III, 551.

73 The addition of the Blessed Sacrament Chapel had been agreed by the middle of Aug. 1841; Pugin to Lord Shrewsbury, 17 Aug. 1841, Letters, I, 262.

74 Dessain, XI, 210.

75 'Powell is modeling the chalices for the screens', Pugin wrote to Hardman, 5 Jan. 1845, Letters, II, 316.

76 Pugin to Hardman, 28 Dec. 1844, Letters, II, 310. Hardman was John Powell's uncle. He has begged Pugin to take Powell on as a pupil, and Pugin had agreed somewhat reluctantly. Powell went to live with the Pugin family in Ramsgate.

77 Pugin to Hardman, 26 Sep. 1845, Letters, II, 442. 1845 had, for various reasons, been a bad year for Lord Shrewsbury.

78 JHA MWDB, 6 June 1846.

79 Pugin to Lord Shrewsbury, 24 May 1846, Letters, III, 72.

80 For details of the showroom and of Hardman metalwork, *see* Fisher, 2008.

81 Pugin to Lord Midleton, 14 Dec. 1844, Letters, II, 295.

82 Pugin to Hardman, 22 Dec. 1844, Letters, II, 301.

83 Pugin to Hardman, 2 Feb. 1845, Letters, II, 334.

84 Pugin to Hardman, 27 Dec. 1844, Letters, II, 308.

85 Pugin to Lord Shrewsbury, 16 Mar. 1845, Letters, II, 365.

86 Pugin to Lord Shrewsbury 26 Oct. 1845, Letters, II, 465.

87 Pugin to Lord Shrewsbury 29 Mar. 1846 Letters, III, 43.

88 Pugin to Lord Shrewsbury 21 May 1846, Letters, III, 71.

89 The author of the article was almost certainly A.J. Beresford-Hope, successively chairman and president of the Cambridge Camden Society (renamed the Ecclesiological Society in 1845). Following the reception of Newman and other Oxford Tractarians into the Roman Catholic Church in 1845, the Society and its journal felt is necessary to distance itself from all things which savoured of 'Romanism', including Pugin.

90 Pugin to the editor of *The Ecclesiologist,* 24 Jan. 1846, Letters, III, 11-15. The editor refused to accept Pugin's letter, and so it was published in *The Tablet,* 24 Jan. 1846.

91 Pugin to Lord Shrewsbury, 29 Mar. 1846, Letters, III, 44.

92 Pugin to Lord Shrewsbury 24 May 1846, Letters, III, 72.

93 Pugin, 1850, 9

94 Pugin to Lord Shrewsbury, 17 Mar. 1841, Letters, III, 219.

95 Pugin, 3rd Lecture at Oscott, *Catholic Magazine,* n.s. 3, 1839, 17-34, 89-98.

96 Pugin to Lord Shrewsbury 25 Apr. 1844, Letters, II, 191.

97 Pugin to Lord Shrewsbury, 1 Aug. 1843, Letters, II, 97.

98 Lord Shrewsbury to Pugin, undated, but internal evidence suggests the winter of 1845-6, Letters, III, 113.

99 The numerous entries for Cheadle in the Hardman metalwork daybooks are most usefully collated by Margaret Belcher in Letters, II, 311-13.

100 For example, Shepshed (Leicestershire) built a small aisled church with screens, stained glass, and even a crypt, for £700, and at Southport he built St Mary's-on-the-Sands for £1,500 'with every requisite for a parish church', Gwynn, xii.

101 Pugin to Hardman, 16, 18 Mar. 1845, Letters, II, 365-6.

102 Pugin to Hardman, 18 Mar. 1845, Letters, II, 366.

103 Pugin to Hardman, 27 Dec. 1844, Letters, II, 308.

104 Pugin to Lord Shrewsbury, 5 Dec. 1841, Letters, I, 298-9.

105 Pugin to Lord Shrewsbury, 25 Apr. 1846, Letters, III, 61, and 21 May 1846, Letters, III, 71. Pugin suggested that Mr Wheelwright could also go up to St John's, Alton, from time to time and look after the metalwork there.

106 Pugin to Lord Shrewsbury, 26 Aug. 1843, Letters, III, 113.

107 Ibid.

108 Pugin includes these details in a letter to John Knill, 30 Aug. 1846, Letters III 115.

109 Powell to Hardman, undated, Letters, III, 114.

110 It should be remembered that before the unification of Italy the kingdom of Sardinia comprised the Italian mainland state of Piedmont as well as the island of Sardinia. It was the ruling House of Piedmont which held the crown of the united Italy, established between 1861 and 1870.

111 Brian Andrews, 'Pugin in Australia' in Atterbury & Wainwright, 246-57.

112 Dessain, II, 241.

113 Quoted in Hill, 311, 360.

114 R. O'Donnell, *The Pugins and the Catholic Midlands,* Leominster, 22.

115 Pugin to William Leigh, 8 Sep. 1846, Letters, III, 119.

116 *The Tablet,* 5 Sep. 1846, 589.

117 Pugin to Hardman, 8 Sep. 1846, Letters, III, 118. Pugin was referring to his early days as an acolyte at the Catholic church in Salisbury, but it could well apply to other occasions.

118 For an analysis of some of these criticisms, particularly of the decoration, *see* Stephen Kowal, *True Principles: The Journal of the Pugin Society,* Winter 2010-11, 163-74. The quotation is from Pugin's description of St Giles in the *Gentleman's Magazine,* Nov. 1846.

119 Pugin to Lord Shrewsbury, 15 Mar. 1846, Letters, III, 36.

120 *Some Remarks which have recently appeared in the 'Rambler',* 1851, 9.

121 Pugin to Jane Pugin, (?)26 Aug. 1851, HLRO PUG/3/247.

122 Pugin to Lord Shrewsbury, 15 Feb. 1846, *Letters, III, 29.*

123 A.-N. Didron, 'Promenade en Angleterre', *Annales Archéologiques,* 5, Dec. 1846, quoted by S. Kowal, *see* n. 113.

124 Belcher 1987, 359-60.

125 *Present State,* 1.

126 Trappes-Lomax, 259.

127 As n. 122.

128 For information about the later clergy at St Giles', *see* J.S. Connelly, 'St Giles', Cheadle: its priests 1827-1874', *Staffordshire Catholic History,* 16, 1976, from which the information about the Gubbins

affair has been taken.

129 Pugin to Edward James Willson, 16 Aug. 1835, Letters, I, 50.

Chapter 7 Community and controversy: St Wilfrid's, Cotton

1   J.E. Bowden, *Life and Letters of Frederick William Faber, D.D.*, London, 1869, 315.

2   Pugin to J.R. Bloxam, (?)15-18 Mar. 1843, Letters, II, 27. 'Did not our hearts burn within us' is a quotation from Luke 2 v.32, the story of the risen Christ walking with the two disciples on the road to Emmaus. That Faber, as an Anglican, had travelled to Birmingham with the Catholic Pugin was noted disapprovingly in the anti-Tractarian *Oxford Chronicle*. 'It is most disgusting', Pugin wrote to Bloxam, '& a compleat system of espionage that is carry on by the protestant party', Letters, II, 33.

3   The story of this ill-fated series of publications is told in Letters, II, 157-60. Six of the eleven authors whose work Pugin illustrated joined the Roman Catholic Church in 1845-6, reinforcing the suspicion that Tractarians were covert Catholics.

4   Pugin to Lord Shrewsbury, 17 Mar. 1841, Letters, I, 219.

5   Purcell, 1, 275-6.

6   Quoted in Hill, 203.

7   So he wrote to Bloxam on 13 Oct., Letters, III, 454.

8   Pugin to Lord Shrewsbury 17 Nov. 1845, Letters, II, 479.

9   Ronald Chapman, *Father Faber,* London, 1961, 147.

10 JHA MWDB, 22 July 1846.

11 Chapman, *op. cit.,* 146.

12 Ibid., 153. What Faber meant by *allezo* is unclear.

13 Lord Shrewsbury to Ambrose Phillipps, 16 Apr. 1839, Purcell, I, 106.

14 Faber to Michael Watts Russell, 5 Oct. 1846, Chapman, *op. cit.,* 154; original in vol. 21 of the Faber letters at the London Oratory. Dr Winter was the priest at St John's, Alton, George Winter was the steward at Alton Towers, and Brother Chad (formerly John Strickson) was one of the young men who had come from Elton with Faber.

15 Vandrival, 152.

16 Faber to Pugin, dated 'St Edmund', i.e. 20 Nov. 1847, Letters, III, 316.

17 According to F.G. Roberts, *The Church and Parish of St Wilfrid's, Cotton*, Birmingham, 2007 (reprint of n.d. edition), the statue was erected by the Oratorians who took it with them when they left

Cotton. It was returned in 1868. Having become badly weathered, it was replaced by a replica in 1949. When Cotton College closed in 1987 the statue was moved to the church of St Thomas More, Coventry.

18 Faber to F.S. Gabriel, 1847, Chapman *op. cit.,* 166-7.

19 Chapman, *op. cit.,* 168-9, citing J.E. Bowden, *op. cit.,* 278.

20 Faber to Lord Shrewsbury, 24 Jan. 1847, Chapman, *op. cit.,* 163-4.

21 Faber to Michael Watts Russell, 5 Oct. 1846, Chapman, *op. cit.,* 156.

22 Patricia Spencer-Silver, *Pugin's Builder: The Life and Work of George Myers,* Leominster, 2010, 264.

23 Vandrival, 151-2.

24 As n. 15.

25 Ibid.

26 *Present State,* 65-6.

27 St Marie's, Newcastle (opened in 1844) has nave and chancel under one roof. It needs to be remembered that Cotton was both a parish church and a conventual one. Provision would have had to be made for the Brethren to sing their offices in choir, which would account for the intended position of the screen between the fourth and fifth bays, i.e. to create sufficient space for choir stalls to the east of it.

28 Pugin to John Hardman, 10 Mar. 1848, Letters, III, 340.

29 Shepherd, 338-9 gives details of all the Pugin glass at Cotton.

30 JHA MWDB, 24 Nov. 1847, 15 Apr. 1848.

31 JHA MWDB, 20 Apr. 1848; drawing in Birmingham Museum & Art Gallery, L.187.84.

32 Pugin to Lord Shrewsbury, 18 Jan. 1848, Letters, III, 403.

33 For details of the Helen Lumsdaine affair, *see* Hill, 378-96, and Letters, III, 291-3.

34 Pugin to Nicholas Wiseman, 14 May 1848, Letters, III, 499.

35 Diary of Laura Phillipps, MS in collection of the Squire de Lisle. Prayers in the vernacular was another unusual feature of the Oratorians' style of devotion.

36 Faber to Newman, 28 May 1848, Chapman, *op. cit.,* 183-4.

37 Ibid.

38 Newman to Ambrose Phillipps, 15 June 1848, Purcell, II, 205-6.

39 Newman to Ambrose Phillipps, 3 June 1848, Purcell, II, 204.

40 Pugin to John Hardman, 17 Oct. 1848, Letters, III, 604.

41 Lord Shrewsbury to Bishop Ullathorne, quoted in Ward, II, 254

42 Gwynn, 111.

43 Pugin to Jane Pugin, 24 Aug. 1851, V&A cat. 92.

44 V&A Museum, Drawings Collection, E77(23) – 1970, Wedgwood 1985, no. 280.

45 R. O'Donnell, *The Pugins and the Catholic Midlands,* Leominster, 83.

46 Because of a procedural fault, the Faber School was mistakenly taken under local authority control in 1944, but it retained, uniquely, its Catholic ethos and head teachers. In 1999 it reverted to voluntary-aided status within the Birmingham Archdiocese (Tim Cockin, *The Staffordshire Encyclopaedia,* Stoke-on-Trent, 2000, 160).

Chapter 8 Faith in the countryside: St Mary's, Brewood

1 Brian Doolan, *The Catholic Bishops of Birmingham,* Birmingham, 4.

2 M.W. Greenslade & D.G. Stuart, *A History of Staffordshire,* Chichester, 64.

3 Among the tombs at Albrighton is that of Sir John Talbot of Albrighton (d. 1555) from whom the Second Line of the Talbot Earls of Shrewsbury (1630-1856) was descended. Not only that; through his second marriage he was also the forebear of the Third Line, the Chetwynd Talbots, who succeeded to the titles after the Peerage Case following the death of the seventeenth earl, Bertram, in 1856.

4 VCH, *Staffordshire,* 5, 1985, 44; Greenslade, 2006, 189.

5 *Staffordshire Catholic History,* 14, 1974, 303; Greenslade, 2006, 192, shows a view of the chapel in 1837.

6 Boscobel was at this time tenanted by the Catholic Penderel family. The present 'royal oak' is said to have been grown from an acorn from the original tree which appears to have perished in the eighteenth century. *See* O.J. Weaver, *Boscobel House and White Ladies Priory,* London, 1987.

7 The Fitzherberts' principal residence was at Swynnerton, Staffordshire. They inherited the barony of Stafford on the extinction of the Jerningham family in 1913.

8 James Hicks Smith, *Brewood – A Resumé Historical and Topographical,* Wolverhampton, 1867, 28: 'Since the marriage of Thomas, nineteenth Lord of Chillington, the Giffard family have ceased to be all Roman Catholics, but the late Mr [Thomas] Giffard on his death-bed received the rites of the Church according to the Roman formula, and the same were celebrated over his body before it left Chillington'.

9 F.C. Husenbeth's contemporary monographs on Robert, William and Henry Richmond are printed in *Staffordshire Catholic History,* 1980, 12-27.

10 Pugin to Lord Shrewsbury, 20 Apr. 1843, Letters, II, 43-4. In another letter to Lord Shrewsbury 26 June 1843 (Letters, II, 85), Pugin states his intention of going to Brewood.

11 Robert Richmond to George Richmond, 20 Jan. 1844, BAA P99/8/45.

12 Pugin to Lord Shrewsbury, 28 Nov. 1843, Letters, II, 139.

13 Pugin to Robert Richmond, 24 Apr. 1843, Letters, II, 46. Although Pugin addressed the letter to 'Revd. W. Richmond, Breewood', it is clear that it was intended for Robert, who commissioned the church, rather than for his nephew, William, who had moved to Swynnerton in Mar. 1843.

14 P.J. Doyle, 'The Giffards of Chillington: a Catholic landed family, 1642-1861', unpublished University of Durham M.A. thesis, 1968, 244 (copy in William Salt Library, Stafford).

15 Pugin to Bishop Thomas Walsh, 4 June 1843, Letters, II, 70-1.

16 As n. 10.

17 Pevsner, 79.

18 Stanton 1971, 97.

19 Robert Richmond to John Hardman, JHA ML, 10 Mar. 1844.

20 Pugin to Robert Richmond, as n. 13.

21 Robert Richmond to John Hardman, JHA ML, 29 Mar. 1844.

22 JHA MWDB, 25 Mar. 1844; Letters, II, 45.

23 JHA MWDB, 19 Apr. 1844. Pugin was charged £8 10s. for the painting of the statue, and 17s. 6d. for the lily and crown.

24 JHA ML, 26 Apr. 1844.

25 'Expenses for Breewood' (*sic*) entered in Pugin's account book include the screen and images at £40, side-screens at £20, and the font at £10. MS V&A L.50-1982/3; Letters, II, 44.

26 JHA ML, 22 May 1844.

27 *The Tablet,* 22 June 1844.

28 Pugin had to fight Lord Shrewsbury's proposal to introduce a similar seating arrangement at St Giles', Cheadle (*see* above pp. 176-7). The religious census of 1851 records that St Mary's was always filled to its capacity with around 400 at the 10 a.m. Mass, and usually about two-thirds full at the afternoon service.

29 J.S. Smith, *op. cit.,* 21. A collection of documents

in BAA (P99/14-20) concerns investigations
into the age of the statue, and sampling of the
substance exuding from it. Fr Grady, parish priest
of Brewood, sought permission from Archbishop
Dwyer to re-establish devotions to Our Lady of
Brewood, but was advised against it.

30 'there is a good Catholic painter here in the town
who could paint them from a pattern', Robert
Richmond to John Hardman, JHA ML, 22 May
1844.

31 A.W.N. Pugin, *Some Remarks…*, 11.

32 Robert Richmond to George Richmond, 20 Jan.
1844, BAA P99/8/45.

33 W.Richmond to G.Richmond, 18 June 1845,
BAA P99/8/51.

34 SEE BELOW, PP. 263-5.

Chapter 9 After Pugin: new brooms and 'broom-stealers'

1 An account of the funeral was published in
Illustrated London News, 25 Dec. 1852. *See* above
pP. 176-7, and also Fisher 1999, 154-5.

2 SA, 23 Aug. 1856.

3 Earl Bertram to E.W. Pugin, 28 Nov. 1852, HLRO
339/114.

4 Lord Shrewsbury to Pugin, 1 Mar. 1852, HLRO
339/112.

5 Birmingham Museum, private collection, L25.83.

6 The painting is currently at Shrewsbury Cathedral.
It is shown in Atterbury & Wainwright 1994, 264.

7 Shrewsbury papers, SCRO, D/240/E/F/9/25.

8 SA, 18 July 1857.

9 Edward Bellasis, *Memorials of Mr Serjeant Bellasis,*
London, 176-7.

10 SA, 30 Aug. 1856.

11 Shrewsbury papers, SCRO, D240/E/F/9126.

12 SA, 10 Jan. 1857.

13 A list of articles from Alton Towers is annexed to
the will dated 10 Dec. 1873 of Minna, Duchess of
Norfolk, and mother of Lord Edmund Howard.
There were some 40 items in all, and many of
these can be identified as having been in the
chapel corridor at Alton from William Adam's
detailed description of what was there in 1851 in
Adam, 261. A few of the items are still at Arundel
Castle. I am grateful to Miss A.P. Taylor, Archivist
at Arundel, for supplying me with a copy of the
list, and for other useful information. Over 50
maps, plans and surveys of the Alton estate in the
17th to 19th century are currently in the Arundel
Archives.

14 E.g. *The Times,* 8 July 1857; SA, 11 July, 18 July, 1
Aug. 1857. *See* also Fisher 1999, 159. The sale was
conducted by Christie & Manson. The contents of

the libraries were auctioned separately in London
by Sotheby's, 22 June-3 July 1857.

15 *Mary Howitt – An Autobiography,* 1889, 127-9.

16 Champ, 2006, 211.

17 'The eyes of all wait upon thee, O Lord': Psalm
144.

18 JHA, Copy Bill Book, 15 Apr. 1869; JHA MWDB,
16 Nov. 1869.

19 Pugin to John Hardman, 17 Mar. 1850, HLRO
PUG/1/844.

20 SCRO, D(W)1734/3/1/109. The Whitgreave
papers at SCRO do not unfortunately contain
anything relating to the building of Burton
Manor.

21 Hill, 305-6.

22 Mary Francis Roskell, *Memoirs of Francis Kerril
Amherst, D.D.,* London, 1903, 157. The month is
given as July, but Pugin's Diary makes it clear that
they sailed on 21 June The contract, in Arabic,
for the hire of five camels and dromedaries for
the journey from Cairo to Ramlet is amongst the
Whitgreave papers, SCRO, D/718/5/4-5. There
was a third member of the expedition, François
Baudry.

23 Pugin to Lord Shrewsbury, 24 Jan. 184, Letters, III,
215.

24 Pugin to Jane Pugin, Oct. 1849, HLRO: George
Whitgreave was actually 63 at the time, but the
point is academic.

25 So Whitgreave wrote to John Hardman, 20 Oct.
1845, JHA ML 1845.

26 A. Wedgwood, *Pugin in his Home: Two Memoirs by
John Hardman Powell,* Ramsgate, 2006, 35.

27 Pugin to J.R. Bloxam, 26 Sep. 1843, Letters, III,
110.

28 Caroline Stanford, *The Grange, Ramsgate,*
Shottesbrooke, 2006, 13.

29 There are ten such entries in JHA MWDB between
Feb. 1855 and Aug. 1856.

30 H.-R. Hitchcock, *Early Victorian Architecture in
Britain,* New Haven, 1954, vol. 1, 232.

31 Mr R.E.L. Button, of Stafford, who knew the
house before it became a school, remembers that
in the early 1980s much of the original wallpaper
was still in place.

32 In 2007, during the excavation of foundations
for a new building in the grounds, a quantity of
old ironwork was unearthed. The most significant
item was the large floriated cross which had once
surmounted the spirelet on top of the tower. The
cross was fully restored at the Hardman studio, and
it is now kept inside the school.

33 For details of Bethune's relationship with
Hardman and the Pugins, *see* M.J. Fisher, *Hardman*

of Birmingham, Ashbourne, 139-40.

34 I am grateful to Peter Howell for providing me with these references from Jules Helbij, *Le Baron Bethune,* Lille & Bruges, 1906.

35 In the 1920s Burton Manor was sold to the British Reinforced Concrete Co. who used it as a sports and social club. It now forms part of Stafford Grammar School, and some careful conservation work has recently been carried out. The building it not presently listed.

36 JHA MWDB, 3 Oct. 1856 enters to Francis Whitgreave a silver-gilt chalice and paten at £30 10s. 'for presentation to Fr. Huddlestone'.

37 *The Builder,* 27 Sep. 1856, 528-9, notes Edward Huddlestone's acquisition of the hall, and Edward Pugin as the architect of the presbytery and the Lady Chapel of St Michael's Church.

38 I am grateful to Dr Gerard Hyland for his assistance in teasing out the complicated story of the churches and chapels which were built/ demolished on the Aston Hall site.

39 The others were at St Mary's, Nottingham, and St Chad's, Birmingham; *Dublin Review,* May 1841, reprinted in *Present State* (p. 27). The font no longer exists.

40 Greenslade, 1962, 22.

41 A set of six large drawings for St Austin's, signed by E. W. Pugin, are in the Birmingham Archdiocesan archives (BAA APD/P255/1-6). They include elevations, sections, and alternative schemes for the west front. A south-east prospect of the proposed church was produced for a Mission Book (BAA P255/5/1) which is the one shown here.

42 *See* below p.P. 291-2.

43 James Joll, 'A Pugin Commission', *The Decorative Arts Society Journal,* 24, 2000, 6-18.

44 SA, 19 July 1862.

45 JHA, Rough Glass Day Book, 6 May 1874.

46 As n.16, 403-4.

47 JHA MWDB, 1 June 1863.

48 SA, 24 July 1869.

49 This is the opinion of Dr R. O'Donnell who has also kindly supplied me with references to St Gregory's. Pugin appears to have incorporated some of his unexecuted ideas for St Austin's, Stafford, notably the high chancel and gabled apse.

50 *See* above pP. 240-1.

51 As n. 30, vol. 1, 94.

52 Denny's career in Australia, along with those of other migrant architects, is examined by Brian Andrews, *Australian Gothic,* Melbourne, 2001.

53 Pugin did not visit Australia in person, but his designs were taken there by Bishop Willson, first Catholic Bishop of Hobart, in 1844, through whom Puginian Gothic was firmly planted in Tasmania. *See* Brian Andrews, *Creating a Gothic Paradise: Pugin at the Antipodes,* Hobart, 2002.

54 C. Calvert, *History of Stafford,* Stafford, 1886, 44. A lozenge-shaped stone plaque with a floriated cross was built into the foundations on the north side of the house where it was photographed before being obscured by the extensions built in 1930. According to some, this was the Greyfriars' cross (information from Mr B. Astbury, Bursar, Stafford Grammar School).

Chapter 10 Prayer-Book Catholics: the Anglican connection

1 Pugin to John Hardman, 1 Oct. 1847, Letters, III, 283.

2 Purcell, l I, 227-8.

3 Pugin to Lord Shrewsbury 28 Aug. 1841, Letters, I, 270. Sophia Winter was one of the domestic staff at Alton Towers.

4 Pugin to J.R. Bloxam, 2 July 1842, Letters, I, 361.

5 Pugin to Ambrose Phillipps, 9 Jan. 1842, Letters, I, 317.

6 *Present State,* 56.

7 *The Ecclesiologist,* 5, 1846, 10-16.

8 Shepherd, 342.

9 Pugin to William Osmond, 3 Jan. 1834, Letters, I, 23. The pupil of 'the wretch' was Joseph Potter who preceded Pugin as architect at Oscott.

10 G.G. Scott, *Personal and Professional Recollections,* London, 1879, 97.

11 Jesse Watts Russell had already rebuilt Ilam Hall, near Ashbourne, in Gothic style, and added an octagonal chapel to Ilam church. He had obviously come under the influence of the Ecclesiological Movement, and his second son, Michael, was one of the 'Oxford Men' who followed Newman into the Roman Catholic Church.

12 Phillipps to Lord Shrewsbury, undated but probably 1841, Purcell, I, 79-80.

13 For a full account of Scott's restoration of St Mary's, *see* Fisher 2006, 44-62.

14 Lord Shrewsbury to Pugin, undated, HLRO PUG/3/15.

15 Quoted by Greenslade, 2006, 21.

16 SA, 21 Dec. 1844: 'The Church is now one of which not only the Town but the County of Stafford may well be proud – the highest authority, perhaps, on such a subject, Mr Pugin, the celebrated Ecclesiastical Architect and Author (who has, we believe, seen it more than once), having pronounced it the best restoration wich

has been effected in modern times.'

17 John Masfen, *Views of the Church of St. Mary at Stafford,* London, 1852.

18 Pugin to J.R. Bloxam, 13 Apr. 1841, MS, University of St Andrew's, Ward Papers V, 15; Letters, I, 231-2. It was the *Tracts for the Times,* written by Newman and others, which gave the name Tractarian to the Movement which sought to emphasise the continuity of the Church of England with the medieval Church. *Tract XC* caused a great furore by maintaining that even the most protestant of the 39 Articles of Religion (1562) could be interpreted in a wholly Catholic manner. For Bagot's role in this controversy, *see* Owen Chadwick, *The Victorian Church,* vol. 1, London 1971, 186-7, 194-5.

19 William White, *Directory of Staffordshire,* Sheffield, 1834, 754.

20 So described in Pevsner, 173.

21 Information kindly supplied by Lady Bagot from the 19th-century diaries of Mary and Ann Bagot.

22 Private collection, Myers Family Trust.

23 For an account of Pugin's extensive work at Wymeswold, *see* M.J. Fisher, 'A.W.N. Pugin and the restoration of St Mary's Church, Wymeswold, Leicestershire', *Ecclesiology Today,* 34, 2005, 3-15.

24 So Pugin told the Revd J.J. Hornby in a letter of 24 Nov. 1846, Letters, III, 172

25 Letters, II, 206 notes a letter from Pugin requesting a payment to Wailes of £100 in respect of the east window (1844), also references to a letter of 1846 in which Pugin mentions that he designed the tiles. Pugin's account book (V&A, MS L.50/31982) has an entry for the stalls at Leigh.

26 Pugin's Diary records visits to Blithfield on 17 Jan. and 6-7 June 1851. Payments in respect of 'windows Blithfield' and 'Bagot' are noted in the front end-papers. Stanton 1971, credits Pugin with the glass of the east window, but she must have meant the east window of the clerestory. The chancel east window was reglazed in 1856 as a memorial to Bishop Bagot who died in 1854. It was replaced in 1965.

27 The watercolour by Charlotte Sneyd is dated 1852, but clearly shows the interior of the church prior to the restoration of the chancel. There is heraldic glass in the east window (SCRO, D4752/3). *See* also Pevsner, 72, and Stanton 1971,

205. The stone pulpit has been attributed to Pugin, but, as Pevsner says, 'It does not look it'.

28 Pugin to Lord Shrewsbury, 13 May 1847, Letters, III, 241-2.

29 The principal entrance to Alton Towers in those days was not the present visitor entrance on the Alton-Farley road, but the Quixhill Gate at Denstone. The Classical gateway remains, but it no longer belongs to Alton Towers.

30 Quoted by David Verey, 'George Frederick Bodley' in J. Fawcett (ed.), *Seven Victorian Architects,* London, 1976, 89.

31 Halifax was one of the leading figures in the attempt to secure formal recognition by Rome of the validity of Anglican Orders upon which no pronouncement had been made since the Reformation. Notwithstanding the eventual condemnation of Anglican Orders by Pope Leo XIII in 1896, Lord Halifax continued discussions, notably with Cardinal Mercier in the Malines Conversations of the 1920s; *see* J.G. Lockhart, *Charles Lindley Wood, Viscount Halifax,* London, 1935.

32 Shaw made this comment in a conversation with the builder, James Heath, 21 Sep. 1887, and it is recorded in Heath's very detailed diaries for 1885-7 which contain a day-by-day account of how All Saints' was built (private collection).

33 Andrew Saint, *Richard Norman Shaw,* New Haven & London, 1976, 308.

34 James Heath of Endon and Leek. He used pink sandstones from Ladderedge, and gritstones from nearby Kniveden and the Roaches.

35 *Apology,* 21,

36 Shaw writing to Mrs Foster, the patron of the church he was building at Richard's Castle (Shropshire), quoted in Atterbury & Wainwright, 21.

37 *Present State,* 83.

38 Ibid.

39 Thomas Wardle (1831-1909) was churchwarden of St Edward's, Cheddleton, near Leek, and a friend of William Morris. In 1863 he brought in G.G. Scott Jun. to restore the chancel at Cheddleton, which was furnished with a screen and a reredos made from a 15th-century Flemish carving of the Deposition to which Morris added side panels to make a triptych. These, together with some fine Morris glass and items of Leek embroidery, make this an important building in the context of the Gothic Revival.

40 The history of the Leek Embroidery Society and the Wardle family is told in detail by Ann Jacques, *The Wardle Story,* Leek, 1996.

Glossary of ecclesiastical terms

AGNUS DEI. Literally 'Lamb of God', it is an artistic representation of Christ shown as a Lamb bearing a flag with a Cross upon it. *Agnus Dei* is also a devotion said during Mass.

ALTAR. The most important item of furnishing in a church. Made of stone or wood, it is the place where the Holy Sacrifice of the Eucharist is offered. On the surface of the altar (the *mensa*) five crosses are normally incised, representing the Five Wounds of Christ. The principal altar is known as the high altar.

AUMBRY. A small cupboard set in the wall close to the altar, used for the keeping of sacred vessels. In medieval times, and currently in many Anglican churches, an aumbry is used for the Reservation of the Blessed Sacrament (q.v.)

BAPTISTERY. The area of the church, normally at the west end, where the font is situated, and sometimes defined by structural screenwork.

BENEDICTION. A service of devotion to the Presence of Christ in the Blessed Sacrament. A blessing is given by the priest, using the Sacrament enclosed in a vessel known as a monstrance (q.v.).

BENEDICTION ALTAR. An altar and reredos (q.v.) with a large central niche above the tabernacle (q.v.) on which the monstrance (q.v.) is placed for Benediction (q.v.).

CHALICE. The cup used to contain the wine at Mass. The bowl of the chalice, if not the entire vessel, is usually made of precious metal such as silver gilt, because it holds the Precious Blood of Christ.

CIBORIUM A vessel similar in shape to a chalice, but with a lid. It is used to contain a quantity of the small Sacred Hosts for the communion of the people at Mass.

CHASUBLE. The principal priestly vestment worn at Mass. It is found in two main styles; 'Gothic' which is very full, and 'Latin' which has the sides cut away for ease of movement.

COPE. A semi-circular full-length cloak, often elaborately embroidered, worn in processions and at Benediction. It is fastened across the chest with a clasp known as a morse.

CRUETS. Jug-shaped vessels used to contain the unconsecrated wine and water used in the Mass.

DE PROFUNDIS. 'Out of the deep', the opening words of Psalm 130 which is often used in prayer for the Departed.

DOOM. A representation of the Last Judgement showing Christ in Glory surrounded by angels and saints, welcoming the Blessed and condemning the wicked. In medieval times the Doom was often painted over the chancel arch.

HOST. A large wafer of unleavened bread which is consecrated in the Mass. The word derives from the Latin *hostia* (victim), signifying the Body of Christ.

MASS. The name given to the Church's principal act of worship. At the heart of the celebration of the Mass are the bread and the wine which, by the words of Christ and the invocation of the Holy Spirit, become Christ's Body and Blood. Christ is thus really and mysteriously made present in the Mass *(Catechism of the Catholic Church,*1994, pp.299 & 305). It is also known at the Eucharist ('Thanksgiving') and Holy Communion. The word 'Mass' (*Missa*) is derived from the concluding words of dismissal in the Latin Rite, *Ite, missa est*. 'High' Mass is celebrated with music, incense, and elaborate ceremonial; 'Low' Mass is said rather than sung, and the priest is usually attended by only one server (assistant).

Glossary

MISSAL. The book containing the texts of the Mass, used by the priest at the altar.

MONSTRANCE. An ornate vessel, often of precious metal, for the exposition of the Host (q.v.) for veneration and the rite of Benediction.

ORPHREY. A band of embroidery or braid applied to a vestment, originally to cover seams, but later as embellishment.

PATEN. The plate, usually of precious metal, on which the Host (q.v.) is placed.

PISCINA. A small recess in the sanctuary wall near to the altar (usually on the south side) containing a basin for washing the sacred vessels after Mass

PYX. A metal container for the reservation of the Host, and for carrying the Reserved Sacrament (q.v.) to the sick and dying.

REREDOS. A picture, sculpture, or hanging placed behind the altar.

RESERVATION OF THE BLESSED SACRAMENT. The setting aside of the consecrated Elements (generally the Host (q.v.) in a special vessel which is kept in a tabernacle set at the centre of the high altar, or in a separate chapel of the Blessed Sacrament, as a focus of Eucharistic devotion and for the communion of the sick and housebound

ROOD. A large crucifix, often flanked by figures of Our Lady and St John, and carried on a beam or rood screen spanning the chancel arch.

SACRAMENT. An outward sign of an inward and spiritual grace. A sacrament is efficacious in that it actually conveys the grace which is signified. The two sacraments recognised by most Christian bodies are the Holy Baptism and Holy Eucharist. Churches of the Catholic tradition recognize seven sacraments, the other five being Confirmation, Penance, Holy Orders, Holy Matrimony and Holy Anointing. The expression 'Blessed Sacrament' generally refers to the Holy Eucharist.

SACRARIUM. A recess in the wall close to an altar, with a shelf for the cruets (q.v.), and a stone basin (piscina) for washing the vessels ad the priest's hands.

SACRISTY. The place in a church where the sacred vessels and vestments are kept.

SANCTUARY LAMP. A hanging lamp suspended before an altar. A lamp showing a clear white light signifies that the Blessed Sacrament is reserved (q.v.) nearby. Blue is used at altars dedicated to Our Lady, and red elsewhere.

SEDILIUM(A). The seat or seats of the Sacred Ministers (priest, deacon, subdeacon) at Mass; normally on the south side of the sanctuary.

STOLE. A priestly vestment resembling a narrow scarf, often embroidered.

STOUP. A vessel placed near the door of church, containing holy water used to make the sign of the cross by those entering, as a reminder of their baptism.

TABERNACLE. A small safe fixed centrally at the altar, and used for the Reservation of the Blessed Sacrament (q.v.).

THURIBLE Also referred to as a censer; the bowl-shaped vessel in which incensed is burned, usually suspended on chains and carried by a liturgical assistant known as a thurifer.

TRIPTYCH. A carved or painted panel, often a reredos (q.v.) which has two folding panels enabling it to be closed up.

VESTMENT. The collective name used of any garments worn by the priest at Mass, and including also those proper to bishop, deacon and subdeacon

Select bibliography

Archival Material
House of Lords Record Office: papers of A.W.N. Pugin, PUG/3. The microfilm versions of these collections used for this publication are Historical Collections 304 (Pugin-Hardman) and 339 (Pugin-Lord Shrewsbury)
Staffordshire County Record Office: the Shrewsbury Papers, D240
Victoria & Albert Museum, London: Pugin diaries, letters, correspondence between Pugin and Lord Shrewsbury; some drawings of items for Alton Towers chapel etc., Crace Archive

Unpublished research
Doyle, P.J., 'The Giffards of Chillington: A Catholic Landed Family 1642-1861', University of Durham, M.A. thesis, 1968
Stanton, Phoebe, 'Welby Pugin and the Gothic Revival', University of London, PhD. thesis, 1950

Printed Sources
Adam, William, *The Gem of the Peak,* London and Derby, various editions, 1838-1857. The 5th edition (1851) is the one most frequently referred to in this book
Anon., *The Life of Cornelia Connelly, 1809-1879,* London, 1924
Andrews, Brian, *Australian Gothic,* Melbourne, 2001
Atterbury, Paul, & Clive Wainwright (eds.), *Pugin: A Gothic Passion,* New Haven & London, 1994
-------- *A.W.N. Pugin, Master of Gothic Revival,* New Haven & London, 1995
Belcher, Margaret., *A.W.N. Pugin: An Annotated Critical Biography,* London, 1987
-------- (ed.), *The Collected Letters of A.W.N. Pugin,* Oxford, vol. 1, 1830 to 1842, 2001; vol. 2, 1843 to 1845, 2003; vol.3, 1846 to 1848, 2009
Bence-Jones, Mark, *The Catholic Families,* London, 1992
Brooks, Chris, *The Gothic Revival,* London, 1999
Champ, Judith F., (ed.), *Oscott College, 1838-1988,* Oscott, 1988
-------- *William Bernard Ullathorne,* Leominster, 2006
Chapman, Ronald, *Father Faber,* London, 1961
Cockin, Tim, *The Staffordshire Encyclopaedia,* Barlaston, 2000
Dessain, Charles S., (ed.), *The Letters and Diaries of John Henry Newman,* 31 vols, London, 1961-72, and Oxford, 1973–84
Doolan, Brian, *The Catholic Bishops of Birmingham,* Birmingham, 2003.
-------- *The Pugins and the Hardmans,* Birmingham, 2004
Ferrey, Benjamin, *Recollections of A.N. Welby Pugin and his father Augustus Pugin,* 1861; reprinted with an introduction and index by Clive & Jane Wainwright, London, 1978
Fisher, Michael J., *Alton Towers: A Gothic Wonderland,* Stafford, 1999 (revised and reprinted as Fisher, 2009)
-------- 'Perfect Cheadle': St. Giles' Catholic Church, Cheadle, Staffordshire, a History and Guide, 2004

-------- *Staffordshire and the Gothic Revival*, Ashbourne, 2006

-------- *Hardman of Birmingham: Goldsmith and Glasspainter*, Ashbourne, 2008

-------- *Alton Towers, Past & Present*, Ashbourne, 2009 (reprint and revision of Fisher 1999)

Gillow, Joseph, *A Literary and Biographical History, or Bibliographical Dictionary, of the English Catholics; from the Breach with Rome in 1534 to the Present Time*, 5 vols, London & New York, 1885-1903

Greenslade, Michael W., *St Austin's, Stafford*, Birmingham, 1962 & 1998

-------- *Catholic Staffordshire*, Leominster, 2006

Gwynn, Denis, *The Second Spring, 1818-1852*, London, 1944

-------- *Lord Shrewsbury, Pugin, and the Catholic Revival*, London, 1946

Higham D., & P. Carson, *Pugin's Churches of the Second Spring*, Cheadle, 1997

Hill, Rosemary, *God's Architect: Pugin & the Building of Romantic Britain*, London, 2007

Ker, Ian, *John Henry Newman*, Oxford, 1988.

Pevsner, Nikolaus, *The Buildings of England: Staffordshire*, Harmondsworth, 1974

Pugin, A.W.N., *Gothic Furniture in the Style of the 15th Century*, London, 1835

--------- *Contrasts, or a Parallel between the Noble Edifices of the Middle Ages and Corresponding Buildings Showing the Present Decay of Taste*, 2nd ed., London, 1841

-------- *The True Principles of Pointed or Christian Architecture*, 1841

-------- *An Apology for the Revival of Christian Architecture in England*, London, 1843

-------- *The Present State of Ecclesiastical Architecture in England*, London, 1843

-------- *Glossary of Ecclesiastical Ornament and Costume*, London, 1844

-------- *Some Remarks on the Articles which have recently appeared in the 'Rambler', relative to Ecclesiastical Architecture and Decoration*, London, 1850

Purcell, Edmund S., *Life and Letters of Ambrose Phillipps de Lisle*, 2 vols, London, 1900

Redfern, Francis, *History and Antiquities of the Town and Neighbourhood of Uttoxeter*, 2nd edn, 1886

Rock, Daniel, *Hierurgia; or, The Holy Sacrifice of the Mass*, 2 vols., London, 1833 (vol. I dedicated to John, 16th earl of Shrewsbury)

-------- *The Church of Our Fathers*, 8 vols, London, 1849-54

Shepherd, Stanley, *The Stained Glass of A.W.N. Pugin*, Reading, 2009

Speake, Robert, (ed.), *A History of Alton and Farley*, Keele, 1996

Spencer-Silver, Patricia, *Pugin's Builder: The Life and Work of George Myers*, Hull, 1993

Stanton, Phoebe, 'Some Comments on the Life and Work of A.W.N. Pugin', *RIBA Journal*, 3rd ser., 60, 1952, 47-54

-------- *Pugin*, London, 1971

Trappes-Lomax, Michael, *Pugin: A Medieval Victorian*, London, 1932

Ward, Bernard, *The Sequel to Catholic Emancipation*, 2 vols, London & New York, 1915

Webster, Christopher, & John Elliott (eds.), 'A Church as it should be': The Cambridge Camden Society and Its Influence, Donington, 2000

Wedgwood, Alexandra, *Catalogue of the Drawings Collection of the Royal Institute of British Architects, The Pugin Family*, Farnborough, 1977

-------- *Catalogue of the Architectural Drawings in the Victoria & Albert Museum: A.W.N. Pugin and the Pugin Family*, London, 1985.

Zeloni, Alexandre, *Vie de la princesse Borghese*, Paris, 1843

Periodicals

    Annual Register
    Catholic Directory
    Catholic Magazine
    Illustrated London News
    London & Dublin Orthodox Journal
    Staffordshire Advertiser
    Staffordshire Catholic History

Index

Numbers in **bold** indicate pages with illustrations
Places are in Staffordshire unless otherwise stated or are well-known towns and cities.

Domine dilexi decorem domus tuae et
locum habitationis gloriae tuae

North front of Alton Towers. 1840s aquatint, possibly
by J.B. Denny, showing the actual and proposed
alterations (Henry Potts).